THE WIDOW WASHINGTON

The

WIDOW
WASHINGTON

THE LIFE OF MARY WASHINGTON

Martha Saxton

FARRAR, STRAUS AND GIROUX

New York

Farrar, Straus and Giroux
120 Broadway, New York 10271

Library of Congress Cataloging-in-Publication Data
Names: Saxton, Martha, author.
Title: The widow Washington : the life of Mary Washington / Martha Saxton.
Description: First edition. | New York : Farrar, Straus and Giroux, 2019. |
   Includes bibliographical references and index.
Identifiers: LCCN 2018056295 | ISBN 9780809097012 (hardcover)
Subjects: LCSH: Washington, Mary Ball, 1708–1789. | Washington, George,
   1732–1799—Family. | Mothers of presidents—United States—Biography. |
   Widows—United States—Biography. | Slaveholders—Virginia—Biography. |
   Virginia—History—Colonial period, ca. 1600–1775. | United States—History—
   Colonial period, ca. 1600–1775. | United States—History—Revolution, 1775–1783.
Classification: LCC E312.19.W35 S38 2019 | DDC 973.4/1092 [B] —dc23
LC record available at https://lccn.loc.gov/2018056295

Designed by Richard Oriolo

Our books may be purchased in bulk for promotional, educational, or
business use. Please contact your local bookseller or the Macmillan Corporate
and Premium Sales Department at 1-800-221-7945, extension 5442,
or by e-mail at MacmillanSpecialMarkets@macmillan.com.

www.fsgbooks.com
www.twitter.com/fsgbooks • www.facebook.com/fsgbooks

1   3   5   7   9   10   8   6   4   2

To Frances Greene,
my beloved but unsung mother

CONTENTS

MARY BALL WASHINGTON:
LIKE MOTHER, LIKE SON

||||||||||||||||||||||||||||||||||||||||||||||||||||||||||||||||||||||||||||||||||||||||||||||||||||||||||||||||||

A contemporary Russian saying claims that the past has become much more unpredictable than the future.

—SVETLANA BOYM, *THE FUTURE OF NOSTALGIA*

MARY BALL WASHINGTON WAS ORPHANED early, grew up poor, and was later widowed with five children under the age of twelve to support. She did the best she knew how for her family in the harsh world of the eighteenth-century Chesapeake. She poured her exceptional vitality, deep religious convictions, and unflagging persistence into her first son, George. We still admire him for the honorable way he used those qualities to create a country and a government. Why has she not received historians' respect for her years of lonely and challenging work?

Since her death in 1789, the Founder's mother has endured a tumultuous half-life. George Washington's first chroniclers extolled her as the pious and self-sacrificing mother of the sainted president. President Andrew Jackson praised her richly at a ceremony to lay the cornerstone for a monument planned for her. But after the Civil War, she started a steep descent in the esteem of her son's scholars. By the mid-twentieth century, she had become unloving, jealous, whiny, and greedy. That monument was never erected.

The caricature of an incompetent, crude, imperious, selfish, and unloving woman flowered fully in the 1940s and '50s with Douglas Southall Freeman's massively detailed six-volume work. In James Flexner's Pulitzer Prize–winning *Indispensable Man*, the author called her a "termagant." Most recently, Ron Chernow described Mary as "crude," "illiterate," "self-centered," and "slovenly." In the index to his biography of Washington, subcategories for Mary include "critical nature of," "stubborn and difficult personality of," and "thwarting of GW's career attempted by." (Martha, by contrast, merits the entries "kindness and generosity of," "strength and practical nature of," "support and devotion of.")

As I read George Washington's biographers' shape-shifting accounts of his mother, my confusion gave way to anger. I have spent my life studying and writing North American women's history to try to retrieve some of what has been lost, to try to replace incomprehension or criticism with historical context, and to substitute evidence for stereotypes and sentiment. I research and write to try to be fair to women whom historians have ignored or misjudged. Mary had clearly suffered from egregiously unfair treatment.

I am normally not drawn to write about women whose fame derives from men or about slaveholding women. But the double standards many historians used in judging mother and son and more than a century of gratuitous hostility toward Mary called out to me for a response. Trying to be fair to a slave-owning woman was a complicated challenge, as complicated as our nation's history. It was a challenge analogous to those historians in the past had faced in writing about her, at which I felt they had largely failed. They did not like her style of mothering and of womanliness. I had to try to see what kind of a mother she really was, and what kind of a woman. I didn't like her ownership of slaves. I had to try to understand it: what it meant for her slaves, for her, and for her children.

Mary Washington had the singular destiny to have a son whose potential for being idealized seems to have been even greater than that for motherhood. Maternal stereotypes into which historians slotted Mary in the absence of evidence have become darker and more complex over the centuries. Maintaining George Washington's elevated reputation has come at the cost of his mother's, because it has seemed to his scholars to be a zero-sum game. She has been the object of both meaningless praise and, more often, antagonism from writers who dreamed of a different mother for their hero George.

Since her death, politicians and historians have used their idea of her to make a wild assortment of arguments. Of course, she was instrumental in early hagiography about George. Then, when stereotypes about mothers became less rosy and evidence of George's intermittent irritation with Mary emerged, a now-nasty mother served to show how George bravely managed to escape her (with his heterosexuality intact) to fight the British and found the nation. Implicit in this view was that the Founding Father (and the nation) didn't really need a mother, but a bad one would serve, too. Along the way, she has also served for white supremacists as a reminder of the good white stock from which good Americans must come. And she has served, erroneously, as an example of a loving mistress of slaves. Mary's memory (the one where she is a prop in George's hagiography) served as a rallying cause for women in the late nineteenth century to try to soften North-South animosity.

The ways in which Mary Washington's life had been used with little or no attention to her actual experiences and choices distressed me as a historian and a feminist. They motivated me to try to find out as much as I could about who she was. Perhaps she could finally tell us something about the world in which she lived and how she raised her children, including her famous son.

Understanding Mary Washington's life requires disassembling old assumptions and constructing a new story about her that will have some stability. Most scholars have used only the handful of readily available but ambiguous sources about her. They consist of evidence of her unwillingness to let her son George enter the British navy at fourteen; letters from George telling her that he was called to military service by his colony and criticizing her reluctance to see him serve; and letters in which he complained about her asking him for money.

I first stumbled over mother and son when I was doing research on eighteenth-century widows in the Chesapeake. In that society, white widowed mothers and their firstborns were often at odds over land, money, slaves, timber, and other valuables. Husbands typically left their widows use of their property—or some portion of it—but only during their lifetimes, or in the case of Mary Washington for a limited number of years. Her husband's will also threatened her with losing custody of the children if she remarried and was found to be not fulfilling her duties as proper guardian of their property. Legally, a widow's role was to be transmitter of property from man to man.

As a consequence, the inheritance laws of early Virginia built ill will between inheriting widows and their oldest sons. Laws reinforced the belief that women should not own land or run farms and plantations. Adult sons were likely to see their mothers' possession of family land as illegitimate and often acted on that perception.

The annoyance George expressed about his mother's requests for money seemed to me to be connected to the inherent widow's dilemma in Virginia. I was willing to believe, as her critics said, that she might not have run her farm profitably, but that was hardly unusual for a man or woman in mid-eighteenth-century Virginia. I could imagine that she was a brusque person, distracted by the labor of raising both crops and five children, but the antagonism scholars directed at her continued to surprise me.

Reading through biographies of George, I saw that few historians took into consideration that Mary was born into a culture where mothering was extensive rather than intensive. Mothers looked out for their flock's health and safety and trained them to Christian virtue and for their adult roles. But with the cares of running a farm, early eighteenth-century mothers had little time to attend to the drawing out and loving nurturing of each child's individuality. And no historians seem to have noted with any sympathy that Mary was born in a rougher time and came from a rougher social background than that of her children, or that it was largely through her work that they ascended to a higher status than hers.[1]

With these thoughts in mind, I started looking at primary sources. She was hard to find. She left no diary, and only a few of her letters have survived. Mary married the widower Augustine Washington, who himself left few traces. Her children and grandchildren mentioned her in letters, usually briefly.

Her family of origin litigated tirelessly, their disputes flickering across her childhood and lighting up aspects of it. Her mother, although apparently illiterate, learned to use the courts herself.

Archaeological work at Ferry Farm in Fredericksburg has produced much valuable material evidence about her life and efforts to keep her family together after she was widowed. Mount Vernon has a few of her lists of expenditures and two small gold rings. Her few letters are scattered. I have learned a considerable amount about Mary Ball Washington as a widow directly or indirectly from her son's lengthy and expertly edited papers. Michelle Hamilton at Mary Washington House also has collected useful materials on its onetime owner, as they have at the Mary Ball Washington Museum in Lancaster County, Virginia.

It is oddly fitting that George, with his lifelong preternatural attention to the cost of things, mentions Mary first in his teenage account book. He was in touch with all the family members, and through their notes about gatherings, gifts, illnesses, loans, debts, real estate dealings, and purchases, glimpses of Mary's busy later years emerged.

George, of course, is a problematic source because their relationship was complex and at times taut with his aggravation and defensiveness. Also, as the years went by, he wrote with increasing attention to protecting his reputation. The gaps in his correspondence with Mary show that he or someone else did not keep all her letters. After his death, his widow, Martha, made a first edit of his letters, destroying those between Mary and George. There is circumstantial evidence that she did not like her mother-in-law. Perhaps she found Mary's letters superfluous.

Another source of information about Mary comes from the books she owned and read and reread. Her first book, John Scott's *Christian Life from Its Beginning to Its Consummation in Glory*, came to her several years before her marriage and introduced her to meditative and devotional reading. Arguably, the most important book in her small collection was Matthew Hale's *Contemplations Moral and Divine*, which had belonged to her husband Augustine's first wife and which he gave to Mary. Mary made it her own learning and teaching manual. Her children and grandchildren recalled her quoting from it and retelling its stories and wisdom.

The records do not produce a picture of a crude, selfish, poor manager from whom George had to escape to make his mark on the world. The admittedly incomplete brushstrokes of the portrait suggest a determined, energetic, anxious woman who loved her children and tried to do her utmost for them. Her love came with worry and conditions. She raised her children with the hopes of securing their prosperity in this world and salvation in the next. She persisted in her lessons and demands with a thoroughness that no doubt could be wearying. George, her firstborn, probably received the strongest charge of her intense piety, drive, and high standards. She read devotional literature and introduced the habit to George. Neither illiterate nor slovenly, she practiced frugality to a fault. She was not trained in genteel drawing rooms, but she gained access to them for her children.

Death haunted Mary's life, like those of so many Virginians of her generation. Her father died when she was three, her stepfather when she was six. Her mother and brother died when Mary was about twelve. Her culture taught her to resign herself as quickly as possible to loss and carry on. A scarred girl working to make herself useful, she grew to adulthood in the family of her half sister Elizabeth. Her early experiences, like those of so many of her contemporaries, left her emotionally battered, with fierce survival instincts, blunted empathy, and the firm belief that bettering her circumstances by holding on to what she had—including the labor of other people—was her duty. Also like her fellow white Virginians, the fragility, mutability, and transatlantic dimension of her family kept her attention focused relentlessly on sustaining and bettering her family.

Mary became a slave owner at three years old, in a period when Virginia was importing large numbers of Africans and working out the brutalities of exploiting their labor. She never doubted the necessity of slavery and seems to have given no regard to the family ties of slaves or their preferences of any kind. Owning slaves distorted and limited the sensibility of white Virginians. Mary was no exception. Raised on a small family farm, she had hands-on experience in forcing men and women to do her will. She had to prove herself extra strong because she was a girl and, by twelve years old, parentless. Unlike wealthier slave owners, she did not have overseers to shield her from the coercion and "foul means," as the planter William Byrd put it, required to force people to toil for her.

Mary lived surrounded by slaves her entire life. The slave owner Lizzie Bain Partin wrote later that it "requires force" to get slaves to *be* slaves.[2] One surviving anecdote has Mary enraged by a young slave boy's disobedient handling of her carriage. She is reputed to have grabbed the whip out of his hands and lashed him with it, cursing him.[3] If the story is true, it is in no way remarkable or hard to believe. In a similar incident, the eighteenth-century slave owner Lucy Byrd beat her slaves brutally, shocking even her callous husband, William, not because she beat the slaves, but because she did it before the guests went home.[4] Evidently, like Lucy Byrd, Mary did not care that there were witnesses.

Mary's detractors include this as evidence of her crude, overbearing character. But if George or Mary's husband, Augustine, had done it, and there is no doubt that they did similar things, it would have gone unnoted. Patriarchs beat their slaves. The myth is that women slave owners largely did not.

Mary's small inheritance of land and slaves allowed her to marry up, like her mother and like each of her five children. She lost her husband when she was in her mid-thirties. She raised her four boys and one girl, struggling with little cash, worn-out acreage, and often indifferent or dishonest overseers. She never remarried, preferring independence and the secure guardianship of her children to the chance of acquiring a delinquent spouse.

Apart from Mary's displays of aggression and independence that have put off George's biographers, her wrangling with her son over money has been central to their antagonism. As Mary's sons and stepsons married, taking with them lands and slaves that had previously been under her control, her circumstances became more and more straitened. In the interval between the Seven Years' War and the Revolution, George was living with his new wife, the enormously wealthy Martha Dandridge Custis. He himself was going deeply in debt, beautifying Mount Vernon, buying elegant clothes for his children, wife, and himself, acquiring luxuries like a green coach and lacy livery for his slaves, adding land and slaves to his holdings. George started complaining about his mother's relatively modest demands as he grew more anxious about his own and Martha's expenditures. He was skeptical of her need and found her requests irritating and burdensome, although he lent his brothers Samuel and Charles, who would prove to be utterly profligate, much larger sums.

Almost none of George's biographers have questioned his disbelief about Mary's claims that she was suffering financially. Nor have his biographers put in the balance George's remarkable wealth with his mother's reduced circumstances.

Mary and her son's quarrels over money brought up questions about changing dependency and shifting ideas of reciprocal responsibilities, while underneath lay their mutual tightfistedness. George also felt defensive about his reputation as a good son. Mother and son stubbornly argued from a sense of right, and in Mary's case from economic want. But they remained tied to each other throughout their lives in a relationship that blended love, resentment, respect, and conflict. It is hard to conclude that these battles were entirely about Mary's greed.

George and his historians have criticized Mary particularly strongly for complaining about her hard life as the Revolution drew to a close and she had to flee with family members to the mountains. Mary, her daughter, Betty, Betty's husband, Fielding Lewis, and Mary's younger sons had all suffered from the Revolution, in which they were so intimately caught up. They endured shortages of essentials, rapid, devastating inflation, and social turbulence. At the end of the Revolution, Mary had to trek one hundred miles across the Shenandoah and up into the Alleghenies to avoid an anticipated British attack. Within three weeks, she lost her son Samuel, and Betty lost her husband, Fielding, on whom Mary, too, had depended for financial support and comfort. And Betty became alarmingly ill. Mary was frightened. She had lost those she relied on; she was in her seventies and uprooted by the Revolution, and she had not seen George in five years. She complained about her difficult life and circumstances to those around her. No doubt she repeated herself.

Historians have incorrectly accused her of starting a petition for a pension from the state legislature of Virginia. There is no evidence that she did that. Someone brought up the idea of a possible pension, and the governor of Virginia, a friend of George's, notified him. George had it squelched. There is evidence to suggest that an enemy of his initiated the idea to embarrass him.

Mary Washington was hardworking and surrounded by fears to the end. She loved her children and, for better and worse, seems to have loved George above all. The death of his father left him more open to his mother's training and emotional patterns than a child with both parents would have been. Her experience of having to be her own parent at twelve or thirteen also no doubt affected the high degree of family collaboration that she expected from her older offspring.

Mother and son were very similar, but their paths diverged dramatically. Mary and the rest of the family made it possible for George to learn and to grow. Mary had only a smattering of education before taking on her increasingly exhausting family responsibilities. She used her books to grow spiritually, but they could not take her beyond the limits of the hierarchical and violent society in which she spent her life.

Both mother and son loved the outdoors and gardens. They shared the joyous confidence that comes from physical strength and well-being. Both of them enjoyed exercise, particularly horseback riding, and were good dancers. (George, who from childhood had had a number of health crises and whose public life put him under years and years of strain, was not as strong as his mother. She outlived two of her children, dying at about eighty; he at about sixty-seven.)

They had similar religious views. George started quoting the philosophy of Matthew Hale and the other divines that Mary gave him to read at a very early age. Their thinking influenced him profoundly throughout his life. Mary worked hard to live up to her and George's shared ideals of stoicism and the calm acceptance of life's evils, but sometimes she failed. During the Revolution and in the turbulent years afterward, the strength to pacify her spirit often eluded her.

Mary pinched pennies, having come from very little. George, even when he became wealthy, drove a very hard bargain and paid remarkable attention to the cost of things. His calculations of labor efficiency among enslaved people after his retirement and his obsessively detailed letters to his overseers and managers attest to this trait. Part of his ultimate decision to free his slaves came from his knowledge that they were unprofitable to him; he would have done better with a smaller labor force. I do not dispute, indeed I admire, his humane reluctance to separate families and his inclination to go along with his dear friend Lafayette and the others who urged him to liberate his workers. But it is impossible to read his papers and not conclude that his calculations about the costs of slavery to himself were significant in his decision.

That as a mature man George began to refuse to sell slaves who were unwilling to be sold and, famously, freed his own slaves in his will reveals his wide experience and habit of reflection, which helped distinguish him from both his mother and his wife. Mary lived her life, as did most other white Virginians, limited by a society with exploitation and cruelty at its core.

Mary had a "high temper." She was easily displeased and exacting. No doubt George suffered from this. He was endlessly defensive throughout his life, particularly with her, but also with superiors or critics. But like her, he had a strong temper, and the critic in him seldom rested.

Mary's hard early life prepared her to struggle, and perhaps she found enjoyment elusive. She was, I suspect, at her best with her daughter, who understood the constraints Mary lived under as a woman in a male-dominated world. Betty comes down to us as a capable businesswoman and an intelligent and loving mother, sibling, and daughter.

While they cannot be completely separated, I have tried to disentangle the biographical fates of mother and son. George, after all, did not dominate the North American public stage until his mother was in her sixties, with much of her tough, active life behind her. There are many things we will probably never know about Mary Ball Washington, but I know she could be prickly, opinionated, and stern. (So could her son.) I have tried in what follows to give her the dignity of her independent existence. She deserves better than what she has had at the hands of scholars.

THE WIDOW WASHINGTON

A CHILD IN THE
CHESAPEAKE

||||||||||||||||||||||||||||||||||||||||||||||||||||||||||||||||||||||||||||||||||||||||||||||||||||||||||||||||||||||||||

*M*ARY BALL WAS THE ONLY CHILD of Mary Johnson Ball and Colonel Joseph Ball of Lancaster County, Virginia. She was born around 1708 or 1709. Lancaster is the southernmost county in Virginia's Northern Neck, which runs along the northern bank of the Rappahannock River, south of the Potomac. Surrounded and penetrated by rivers, its southeastern tip reaches out into the Chesapeake Bay.

Of Mary's mother's family, nothing is known for certain, although tenacious local historians now believe with strong evidence that she was born Mary Bennett and was brought over to Maryland from England as an indentured servant and made her way to Virginia.[1] Eighty percent of the immigrant women to Virginia came over as indentured workers. That percentage was a very small portion of the immigrants altogether—the great majority of whom were male. By and large, women did not choose to come to Virginia; some were kidnapped, or "trapanned." An eighteenth-century indentured servant woman in Maryland described life to her father as "toiling almost Day and Night, and very often in the Horses druggery, with only this comfort that you Bitch you do not halfe enough, and then tied up and whipp'd to that degree that you'd not serve an animal . . . nay many Negroes are better used."[2] There is no way of knowing how Mary fared in her years of service in Maryland, but it was a very hard life, and she was a strong and resourceful young woman.

The Mary who gave birth to Mary Ball first married a man named Johnson. She had two children with him, Elizabeth and John, and after his death met and married the wealthy planter and widower Joseph Ball. Joseph Ball's father, William Ball, had immigrated to the New World from England during the English Civil War. Like the Washingtons, the family little Mary would marry into, the Balls became prosperous tobacco planters. They aggressively acquired land, slaves, and church, military, and government offices, securing themselves places in the coalescing ruling class shaping Virginia life in the late seventeenth century. Mary's father, Joseph, William's youngest child, owned, at various times, between nine and fourteen slaves.[3] This made him among the wealthiest men in their community, although he was not among the colony's grandees, like his neighbor on the Corotoman Creek, Robert "King" Carter, who was tithed on over a hundred slaves in these same years.[4]

Joseph was probably born in England in 1649, and his family brought him to Virginia by the mid-1650s. Like his father and his brother, his son and his nephews, Joseph became an officer in the militia, a churchwarden, a vestryman, and at times a member of the House of Burgesses, a high sheriff, and a justice of the court. Joseph and his nephew William frequently presided together at the Lancaster Court House, and Joseph's younger nephew, Richard, joined them on the bench in the early eighteenth century, giving the county three Balls weighing in out of a shifting group of more or less eight magistrates.[5]

The governor appointed magistrates from among the communities' wealthiest and best-educated men. They served for life and, as the Balls did, usually petitioned to pass on their positions to their sons, relatives, or friends.[6] The magistrates, including the Ball contingent, made an impressive-looking group, wearing wigs, elegant jackets, knee breeches, and buckled shoes to court, where they sat on a bench raised a foot or more off the floor, under the royal arms. In cold weather, Joseph Ball cut an imposing figure in his broadcloth suit and his "fine broadcloth cloak with gold edging and silver clasps," with his "old sword and belt" and his "new woolen stockings" with his wood-heeled shoes.[7] The Balls had the satisfaction of knowing that the 1701 brick courthouse they served in, across the Corotoman Creek from Joseph Ball's house, was built on land they had sold to the community. The court building was the centerpiece of the waterside village of Queenstown, which the Balls had founded on a brook then known as Madam Ball's Creek. (Queenstown, like many other towns established in this period to centralize the place for ships to pick up and deliver tobacco, failed when residents preferred to ship from their own docks, shifting the inconvenience to the shipmasters.) When the court building was finished, William Ball the elder had built a pillory, stocks, and a whipping post.[8]

Virginia in the late seventeenth and early eighteenth centuries was building a slave society. Men like William and Joseph Ball, John and Lawrence Washington, William Byrd I, George Eskridge (who would become Mary's mother's friend and oversee young Mary's inheritance), and the Balls' neighbor on the Corotoman Creek, Robert Carter, to name only few, were amassing as much land as they could. Together, these settlers dispossessed the Indians of their territory in northeastern Virginia through arms and through "fraud, petition . . . and unceasing encroachment upon reserves."

By 1700, English planters had patented and paid taxes on about two million acres of Virginia. In the next seventy years, they would occupy another seven million.[9] With the rapid concentration of land in private hands coupled with the emergence of tobacco as a highly salable export crop in the early seventeenth century, these colonizers developed a voracious appetite for laborers to clear and work their lands. Indentured servants from England and to a lesser extent orphaned children had supplied this need until the middle of the seventeenth century.

Wealthy men who were also officeholders, like the men of the Ball family, began accumulating slaves as soon as they could. Mid-seventeenth-century Virginians wanted more slaves than the Royal African Company, which had a monopoly on the trade to the colonies, was providing. The hunger of white planters for slaves eventually ended the Royal African Company's monopoly on the trade, and smaller merchant shippers from Great Britain and the colonies began capturing and filling their ships with West Africans, bringing more and more to the coasts of Virginia.[10]

Slaves cost more than indentured servants, who would serve from five to seven years, but African workers were enslaved for life. Planters could work them from daylight to nightfall, six days a week, unlike English subjects, who had customary and legal protections and could negotiate, within limits, over food and shelter.[11] The "middling sort" of English people prized industriousness, but in the colonies the coercive conditions of indenture and the much more coercive conditions of slavery stigmatized labor and accelerated the market in laborers.

Anglicanism in the Chesapeake gave settlers a moral patina to the emerging class structure and the development of slavery. The Virginia Anglican church had no colonial bishop or ecclesiastical courts to direct it and adjudicate for it, so prominent laymen like William and Joseph Ball became vestrymen and occupied this office for life. They provided the strong local, secular leadership that characterized the southern colonial Church of England and that made Virginia the "most thoroughgoing religious establishment in colonial British America."[12] They had significant

power over the church and the community, especially because the Anglican church tithed every settler regardless of his or her religious affiliation.
Among other things, vestrymen appointed the tobacco inspectors who
checked to see that farmers weren't growing too much so as not to flood
the market and lower prices.[13] Vestrymen also "processioned" or went
around all parish dwellers' property every four years to check on boundaries and update landmarks. After three such visits, if the property lines
were uncontested, the settler became rightful owner of the land so bounded.
They probated wills and granted marriage licenses.[14] As slave owners, vestrymen were important in preventing the church from advocating strongly
for conversion and religious education for slaves. (In the late seventeenth
and early eighteenth centuries, most slave owners resisted the church's
efforts even when several pieces of legislation assured them that conversion
would not affect slaves' status.)[15] The vestrymen selected and hired ministers; they distributed alms and controlled the charity work of the church,
the source of help for the white poor in the colony. They established regulations like setting minimum standards for church attendance.[16]

Vestrymen also assigned the pews in their churches, creating a seat-
ing pattern that reproduced the parishioners' social standing. The prominent families sat in the great pews on the ground floor in Christ Church in
Lancaster County. Damask curtains on brass rods hung about Robert
Carter's pew. (A cedar-lined road extended over the three miles between
his plantation, Corotoman, and Christ Church.) He, his tenants, and his
servants filled the whole northern end of the church. The less affluent sat
in the more cramped single and double pews on the ground floor, and the
poorest whites and sometimes a few blacks occupied the least comfortable benches upstairs in the gallery.[17] The grandee William Byrd II, in
December 1710, crowed in his diary that his vestryman gave him "the best
pew in church."[18]

Before Mary Johnson married Joseph Ball, he and his first wife, Elizabeth Romney, had four daughters—Elizabeth, Hannah, Ann, and Easter
(or Esther)—and one son, Joseph junior. Elizabeth Romney Ball probably

died in 1703.[19] As early as 1702, Mary Johnson was witnessing legal transactions at the Lancaster Court House. In 1703/1704, she witnessed a transfer of land that Joseph Ball made to his son-in-law Rawleigh Chinn, married approximately three years to Ball's daughter Easter.

It is a sign of their times that the couple's first appearance to historians is on a legal document about property. It was a bit unusual but hardly unheard of for women to witness legal transactions in Virginia, where the high death rate made adults scarce. It would become less common as the white settler population stabilized and grew. Both gender and class would proliferate behavioral definitions and requirements that would limit women's activities. Over the eighteenth century, colonial rulers excluded most women from legal and economic life.[20]

Mary Johnson made her mark with an *X*. While she could not write, writing and reading were taught separately, so it is possible that she could read. Anglicans valued Bible reading, and Anglican indentured children sometimes learned to read without learning to write.[21]

In June 1706 and February 1708, Ball deeded slaves to his four daughters and land to his son, Joseph junior. Young Joseph received 450 acres and another land grant as well as a "negroe man going by the name of Dukey," two "negroe" boys, and a Negro woman "going by the name of Lucy." In a subsequent deed, young Joseph received three more male slaves and a woman named Murrcah and her children. He also received a silver chalice and important items of furniture including a feather bed and bed furniture, Russian leather chairs, and a costly looking glass. To his daughter Hannah Travers, wife of Raleigh Travers, the elder Joseph gave "a Negro woman named Bab, a Negroe lad named Jacob," a silver tankard, and half a dozen cane chairs. He left his daughter Ann Conway an enslaved boy named Jack, a son of Murrcah,[22] a "negroe woman named Kate," and a silver salt cellar. To Easter Chinn, his daughter, he left a man named "Sam (or in lieu of him a new Negroe man)" and "my biggest to-eared silver cup."[23] (A "new Negroe" meant a new arrival from Africa.) It later turned out that Easter received a boy, James, another of Murrcah's children.

"Boys" and "lads" like Murrcah's sons went in all directions. Joseph Ball took no note of the relations among the men, women, and young. Ball's gifts sundered Murrcah's little family. Joseph Ball's children might have paid more attention to the fact that the overwhelming bulk of his estate went to his son, the daughters each getting two enslaved workers, a piece of silver, inferior in value to Joseph's chalice, and some furniture. But it was customary, so perhaps it went unremarked upon.

Ball deeded the 720-acre plantation on the Corotoman Creek where he was living to his son but reserved it to himself during his lifetime. He also reserved dower rights to a small part of the land, carefully spelled out for processioning, in case he should marry. In a second deed, in February 1707/1708, he repeated the lifetime stipulation clause, with the phrase "if the said Colonel Joseph Ball shall take a wife that then it shall be lawfull for him to assigne for her dowre the tract of land whereon . . . Ball now dwells," adding that the land should be "peaceably enjoyed during her natural life," then to return to Joseph Ball Jr. and his "issue." In a subsequent deed at the same time, he delivered to his son plots for 300 acres, 200 acres, and 80 acres, beyond the 720 acres he'd already deeded over.[24]

As he hinted he would, the colonel did take a wife: his onetime witness Mary Johnson.[25] He was a seasoned litigator trying to provide his wife with a little security from the anticipated predations of his grown son. Maybe it was no coincidence that Joseph Ball the younger was in London at the time the couple married. He, too, married in 1709, shortly after his father's wedding. His wife, Frances Ravenscroft, was born in England and would die there.[26]

Mary Johnson was marrying a litigious man, member of a litigious family, living in a quarrelsome, grasping society. The young cousins William Ball and Richard Ball and their uncle Joseph Ball would all sue one another as well as Joseph's sister Hannah. Joseph Ball's son, Joseph junior, had sued his mother's estate and would sue his uncle as his father's executor as well as his stepmother. All of them, including Mary, would sue their neighbors. The status of the Balls and other white Virginians rested on their ownership of property, land, people, and human futures. The legal system structured their material lives and provided the tools for protecting their possessions and acquiring more. It also shaped their emotional lives by legitimating and making desirable relationships of domination and subordination. The Ball family men wielded the court system enthusiastically, and Mary Johnson Ball, with some help and encouragement, would follow their example.

Mary Johnson married just as the planter elite was tightening up its restrictions on widows' ability to dispose of any property their husbands might have left them. After 1680, it became more common for courts to side with fathers, to invalidate the activities of married women, and to rein in widows' prerogatives. Between 1705 and 1748, the colony reclassified slaves—normally the most valuable bequests made to women, as "realty" not "personalty"—to encourage their owners to tie them to the land on which they worked. Widows could retain use of land and slaves, but if they tried to give them or will them away, the colony might challenge them.[27] Joseph Ball was acutely aware of the popular legal moves denying widows their right to dispose of property inherited from their husbands because he had used them.

Ball's father, William, had died in 1680, leaving his daughter, Hannah (Joseph Ball's sister), only five shillings, writing that these represented an "overpayment both of her portion and deserts." William's widow (Joseph's mother), Hannah Ball, loved her daughter, Hannah, better than her husband had. When she was dying ten years later, she wished to bequeath furniture and two slaves to the child shut out of her husband's legacy. According to testimony in a lengthy lawsuit, Joseph (Hannah's son) and Joseph's nephew William, Hannah's grandson, harassed her in her final illness about leaving their sister, Hannah, an enslaved mulatto girl, Bess, and a boy named James. (As a mixed-race woman, Bess might have been the child of an enslaved woman and an indentured servant, or possibly of William Ball Sr. or one of his sons.) As one witness remembered Hannah Ball's deathbed, Joseph and William wearied the old woman so much that she permitted them to write a codicil to her will renouncing her gift of Bess and James to her daughter. George Eskridge, the lawyer for Hannah Ball Fox (Hannah was married to the Reverend David Fox) against her brother and nephew, lost the case. He appealed to the General Court at Williamsburg, where the ruling went against Eskridge and Hannah Ball Fox again.

Having lost this suit, Hannah, her husband, David Fox, and the lawyer Eskridge sued Joseph and William for some red serge bed hangings and a cabinet. The court ordered Joseph Ball and William Ball to deliver the items to the Foxes.[28]

Back in court again in 1712, a year after Joseph Ball Sr., little Mary's father, had died, Richard Ball took up battle against his cousin William for the slaves, who by now had become three, because Bess had had a child. The magistrates of the court, however, continued to support their fellow magistrates and confirmed William and Joseph's ownership of James, Bess, and her "encrease, a girl named Hannah."

In the inventory of Joseph Ball's estate, taken a few months after his death in the summer of 1711, a list of his slaves included a "boy named James." Before dying, Joseph Ball had gone and taken young James from Hannah's family, removing him also from whatever family he might have had.

The case affirmed—more than once—the right of the wishes of living and dead patriarchs to overrule the wishes of living widows. Ball, when he was thinking about marrying Mary Johnson, was well aware of the ways widows could be separated from their property. He maneuvered to protect Mary's dower claims on a small piece of his land from the challenges he could imagine his son launching.[29]

While the suit demonstrated William Ball's patriarchal privilege to overrule—from the grave—his widow's wishes in disposing of property, it also illuminates the value and vulnerability of slave women. William, the grandson, insisted that his grandmother had specifically drawn up a codicil giving Bess "with all her future Encrease forever" to him. He parried the renewed charges that he and Joseph had wearied Hannah Ball when she was tired and sick and said that so far was he from being avaricious that sixteen years went by before he felt he had to defend his right to the slaves and their "encrease." It took precisely those sixteen years for Bess to demonstrate that she was capable of having children, and her fertility re-excited William's and his cousin Richard's interest in Bess and her little Hannah.[30]

Since 1662, Virginia had reversed the legality of normal patriarchal lineage that structured English families and made the slave mother's status determine the condition of her children. An enslaved mother could only have enslaved children, whether the father was a slave of African origin or a free white Englishman.[31] Thus, the children Bess and Hannah bore would not belong to them in any legal sense. This distinguished them from other women living under English law. Normally, the offspring in a marriage were the father's, but if fathers died, as they did so often in the Chesapeake, mothers usually had custody, unless they were too poor to raise them. The absence of divorce meant that mothers were usually assured of raising their children.[32] Of course, there was no legal marriage for slave men and women.

Joseph Ball willed his land to his son, Joseph, and his "issue"—used interchangeably with "heirs" in wills of the period—which meant as a verb "to give birth to" and as a noun "offspring." The first meaning of "increase," used for the children of slaves, on the other hand, is profit, and its other meanings of growth apply equally to plants, cattle, crops, and people in the sense of becoming more numerous and multiplying.[33]

The Ball men and other southern whites created legal capital of the children who might come out of the wombs of the women and girls like Hannah and Bess whom they enslaved.[34] This all but destroyed the possibilities for enslaved families to protect themselves and expanded extraordinarily the reach and muscle of these burgeoning Virginia dynasties.

Litigation, inventories, and wills testify to the desires of white Virginians to shape the future as they tried to buck the high mortality rate—their own and that of their human property—and stabilize the transitory nature of wealth. By harnessing the "encrease" of Hannah and Bess for themselves and their sons, the Balls fought for precedence, nourishing prodigious ambitions to be realized through the anticipated babies of enslaved women.

‖‖‖‖‖‖‖‖‖

JOSEPH BALL and Mary Johnson Ball's child, Mary, was born a year or so after their marriage, sometime between late 1708 and 1709, when Ball was about fifty-nine years old.[35] In the absence of church records of Mary's baptism or a family Bible entry, we do not know her year of birth. (Birth dates were often a casualty of the high mortality rate, illiteracy, and slavery. One of the jobs of magistrates in this period was to estimate the ages of slaves for tax purposes. They estimated the ages of indentured children so that their employers would know how many years of service they were getting. Slaves became taxable property at sixteen years old, when they were thought capable of work in the tobacco fields. A typical indenture might run from eighteen to twenty-five unless the young person had a black parent, in which case he or she would work until thirty-five.)[36]

Mary had her daughter in one of Joseph Ball's two substantial two-story homes, one at the mouth of the Morattico Creek and the other a bit farther north on the Corotoman Creek, both tributaries of the Rappahannock.[37] Because Ball lived at the Corotoman residence in 1704 when he deeded land to Chinn and when he died in 1711, this was likely Mary's birthplace.[38] (The Corotoman "Creek" was oddly named in that it was two miles wide at its mouth, where it poured into the Rappahannock.) The spot was very convenient to the courthouse and directly across the water from Robert "King" Carter.[39]

Mary Johnson Ball was pregnant and gave birth to her daughter in a spacious, comfortable house with rooms set off for sleeping, cooking, and socializing. One of the houses had a cellar as well as separate sleeping quarters for slaves, a tobacco-drying house, and a dairy shed. Both doubtless had separate kitchens behind the main house, a feature of large homes, designed to prevent kitchen fires from igniting the main house. Both of Ball's houses were considerably more roomy and far more well appointed than the average Virginia dwelling: a small, unpainted, wooden abode of one or two rooms sometimes mounted on blocks to keep it off the ground, whose floor might be of planks or earth. In the majority of houses, there would be a large fireplace at one end of the main room, which also functioned as the kitchen and bedroom. There was little of the privacy or separation of activities that Mary was able, albeit briefly, to enjoy.[40]

By the time of Mary and Joseph's marriage, Ball had already—defensively—distributed among his older children a variety of luxury items.[41] He retained enough to furnish in comfort the house of his new family. The house both Marys inhabited had a kitchen well supplied with iron pots, kettles, glass and ceramic bottles, ewers, and earthenware jars of all sizes, spits for cooking meat, pewter objects, forks and knives, punch bowls and ladles, cups and plates, tables and leather chairs, numerous tablecloths and dozens of napkins. These kinds of accoutrements were still very rare in the early eighteenth century and only began to become widespread at mid-century, when the British industrial revolution started producing commodities at relatively low cost.[42] Even at mid-century forks were rare.[43] The Balls had brought these items with them or imported them. Most white families ate out of communal dishes, few had utensils, and even fewer had napery or, as important, the means or the labor to launder it. Mirrors were beginning to be popular among the very wealthy and would soon become an item of necessity for the majority. Ball had given away his costly one and was left with a small one valued at only a shilling and six pence.

The Balls apparently lived without much interior illumination, given that Ball's inventory does not mention equipment for making candles or a supply of candles. Without these, which were just beginning to emerge as an important consumer item, the Balls lived by the light of the sun by day and by the fires in their home in the early evening.

Joseph Ball also possessed a strikingly wide array of fabrics—among the most costly and sought after of imported items. He had different qualities of linen, flannel, cotton, wool, silk, mohair, and dimity, as well as buttons, threads, and numerous cloaks including his "fine" one edged in gold with silver clasps. Mary Johnson Ball was in charge of repairing and making clothes out of this rich supply. Ball also had wool cards and combs for processing the wool of his sheep and spinning wheels. The Balls' slaves grew flax for linen. Processing it was a complex and skilled process. Rough linen, or "osnaburg," clothed slaves and was scratchy and uncomfortable. The coarse linen originally made in Germany was the bestselling item (after rum) in one Virginia shop, so being able to make it was a great advantage.[44] In this early period, it was rare for families to have the capability of making cloth, and the wool cards, combs, spinning wheels, and flax crop indicated that the Balls could engage in considerable local exchange. In a period in which tobacco prices had been low for almost three decades, the Balls, unlike the majority of settlers who grew only tobacco, had numerous other items for their own consumption as well as barter or sale, like wool and dairy products.[45]

Other possessions marked the Balls as very prosperous: matched leather chairs, a wide selection of oval tables, and many chests with locks and keys as well as supplies of beds and bedclothes: quilts, sheets, blankets, and "bed rugs" (heavy, warm, handworked bedcoverings and hangings that protected the sleepers from cold). The Balls' big bed downstairs dominated a room that, like most early modern bedrooms, served as a room for socializing as well as sleeping. Ball owned an "elbow chair" with cushions that probably sat in the bedroom and was intended for old or sick people who planned to sit for a spell. He might well have used it himself in his last illness. They had a large table and a "Turky workt [Oriental] carpet." Dining rooms were common among those who had a house with more than a room or two, and these items probably belonged there, not in a heavily trafficked room like the bedroom. The Balls had reading matter, including a "Large" Bible and the Anglican Book of Common Prayer, as well as an assortment of "old books."[46] Without candles, what reading they did would have been in daylight.

Ball's ownership of land and slaves, of course, underlie the family's social position. Joseph's particular possessions illustrate his broad array

of privileges. Ample supplies of corn, beans, and salt (essential for raising cattle and preserving meat) were stored in his outbuildings, which,
with numerous cows, steers, heifers, sheep, and hogs, meant that he and
his family, if not his slaves, were never hungry. Enslaved blacks (and a
total of eight broad hoes and twelve narrow ones) meant that he and his
immediate family were not exhausted by the demands of work. His houses
and furniture meant that Joseph, Mary, and little Mary Ball slept on soft
beds (filled with the feathers of their ducks and geese), not on straw. Bed-
steads meant they did not sleep on the floor. They had enough wood to
stoke their fireplaces, bed curtains so they could sleep in warmth, and a
large cooking hearth to heat several dishes at a time and eat and converse
in comfort. Ball's abundant collection of fabrics not only meant that they
could cover themselves against inclement weather but also illustrates their
wealth and the power it gave them. So, too, their pewter and silver, their
leather chairs and "elbow chair," rugs, and mirrors told visitors in this society, so alert to rank, where they stood in relation to the owners. Many of
similar rank did not live nearly so well. The floor coverings, curtains, silver, and matched chairs were unusual even among the elite in this period.[47]

Few visitors to the house would have ranked higher, and most would
have been deferential in the presence of the Balls.

WHEN MARY JOHNSON BALL felt her labor pains coming on, her women
friends and neighbors gathered to help and support her through labor and
birth. Her daughter, Elizabeth Johnson, would have been there to learn
and to help. It is doubtful that her new sisters-in-law would have shown up
because they would likely have regarded her as a lower-class opportunist.
One experienced midwife would have attended her. Typically, a group
could be large and would include several women who had had children.
But Mary's history as an indentured servant might not have won her friends
among Ball's gentry acquaintances. Ball had an experienced slave named

Dinah who seemed to tend the several children on his plantation, and she would likely have helped.

This all-female gathering could last anywhere from a few hours to several days, depending on the length of labor and the health of the mother. Mary and Joseph's slaves would have provided food and drink for the visitors. Midwifery books suggested that the light be kept low so as not to irritate the mother and that the group be kept to six or seven.

Mary was probably in her late thirties, not young for her era. If she suffered from the "intermittent fever" or malaria as so many did in Tidewater Virginia, that would have heightened the danger associated with her daughter's birth.[48]

The law required (white) children to be baptized quickly, and because the Balls had wealth and influence, a minister would have come to their home to baptize the infant Mary, somewhere between one and three months after her birth. As a girl, she would have acquired a godfather and two godmothers to make sure her parents gave her a Christian education. Joseph's son-in-law (the baby's uncle) the Reverend John Carnegie, minister of not one but two churches in Lancaster County, probably performed her baptism. (Carnegie, the husband of Ball's daughter—Mary's half sister—Elizabeth Ball Carnegie, who had died by the time of little Mary's birth, was a Scot who had graduated from Oxford and been ordained by the bishop of London on October 26, 1700.) He became minister of St. Mary's in White Chapel Parish in 1702 as well as Christ Church, both in Lancaster County.

Anglicans believed in swift baptism to ward off the possibility of damnation for their tiny children and to confer church membership upon them. Although Anglicans believed that original sin stained infants, they were considerably less worried than Puritans and other Dissenters about their children's going to hell once they had been baptized. They believed not that baptism saved their children but that having been placed on the right ritual road, they were advantaged.[49]

Mary's mother and/or Dinah likely swaddled the tiny child as was the long-standing custom among Europeans and colonial parents in the seventeenth and early eighteenth centuries. Mothers or nurses tightly wrapped their babies with cotton or linen bands that kept the child immobile, head fixed, arms and legs straight and warm. Advice givers recommended changing them every twelve hours, but every twenty-four seems more likely for busy adults. The infant, stiff and unable to look around freely, was also frequently wet and chafed. After some months of swaddling, parents put children of both sexes into petticoats, which inhibited their mobility—but less so than swaddling—and marked their status as toddlers and small children. Girls would never outgrow these cumbersome, restrictive garments and would have stays added to them not long after. Boys at about six years would exchange the skirts of childhood for the freedom of breeches.

European parents swaddled to keep their infants' limbs straight, to help them learn the erect posture that distinguished humans from animals, and to hasten babies to assimilate quickly into adult society. In the early modern world, infants risked death from many diseases and infections. Parents did not set infancy or childhood apart as a period deserving special treatment or concern as they would by the middle to end of the eighteenth century. On the contrary, parents trained the young to produce adult behavior early rather than prolong what later parents would consider the charms of childhood.[50]

Mary's mother would have nursed her new daughter. As a prosperous woman with servants to command, she could have had a slave woman wetnurse the child. But it seems unlikely, given that Ball's adult enslaved workers were not so numerous that he could have spared a potential field or household worker. And Mary had no doubt nursed her earlier children; as an indentured servant and not to the manor born, she would not have considered a wet nurse an indispensable privilege. Colonial white women usually nursed for ten to sixteen months—slave mothers for less (and their schedules were restricted, sacrificing infant feeding time to their masters' demands).[51]

As a tiny girl, Mary might have had a rattle (usually made of coral) for entertainment and teething. Early eighteenth-century colonial parents usually did not buy children toys. She might have had a rag doll of some kind, but toys do not appear in portraits of children until around 1750. Southern white families were more tolerant of children's play than their Puritan neighbors to the north, but both believed that children's central charge was to imitate adult behavior and grow up as soon as possible. They regarded idleness as a particular danger to children.[52]

By June 15, 1709, Carnegie, little Mary's uncle, had died, and Joseph Ball became the administrator of his son-in-law's estate. He and a certain captain Richard Hughes, who often served on juries and in other judicial capacities, appraised the estate on that date. Throughout the next year, judgments rolled in against Carnegie's estate, requiring Ball to pay his numerous outstanding debts. Even the trustees of the estate were litigating; on May 1711, Rebecca Pew, who was an administratrix of Carnegie's estate, claimed 1,669 pounds of tobacco from Ball, her fellow administrator. This claim was later dismissed. (It is easy to see the utility of having three members of the Ball family on the court.) In May 1711, Captain Richard Hughes was appointed to recover a debt to Carnegie of five hundred pounds of tobacco for Ball, but Ball was already mortally ill. Lying in the large downstairs "lodging chamber," Ball died before July 25, 1711, when his will was proved. He was about sixty-two and, by local standards, had lived to a ripe old age in a place where most men began surviving into their fifties only in the mid-eighteenth century.[53]

Little Mary would have witnessed the large gathering that collected around her father's sickbed as he, his family, and his friends all helped to prepare themselves for this death. Dinah and Tony, an older slave belonging to Ball, would have been present, and Dinah, Mary, Mary's older daughter, Elizabeth, and perhaps Ball's adult daughter the abused Easter Chinn[54] tended the dying man. When Ball's death was near, the Reverend John Bell, who took over St. Mary's and St. Stephen's after Carnegie, began coming by, talking with Ball about death. He would learn that Ball had fully repented of his sins and expected to be forgiven them, as well as what Ball's last wishes about his property and burial were. His death, like much of his life, played out with prescribed rituals, which confirmed his significance in this world, although this ritual directed attention to preparing for the next.[55]

When Ball died, the family had three days to notify acquaintances about the "decent interment" he desired. Mary and Dinah probably washed and prepared the corpse for burial. Families put on black clothing, or first mourning. In the heat of a Virginia summer, Bell probably read a prayer for the dying that concluded, "And teach us who survive, in this and other like daily spectacles of mortality, to see how frail and uncertain our own condition is" that we may live in a holy way and achieve eternal life through Christ.[56]

It is chilling that Virginians had passed a law against private burials to prevent masters from beating their servants to death and burying the evidence. But as a member of the master class, Ball would have been permitted to choose a private burial for himself—to be buried near his home or in the church graveyard. His son, who was executor but in England at the time his father died, believed he had been buried on his property. When Joseph Ball the younger was in Great Britain, many years later, he asked his nephew to locate the spot. The nephew seems to have succeeded, but failed to find bones.[57] (This was a colonial departure from the long-established and rather rigid English custom of churchyard burials, bodies with their heads pointing east. It might have had to do with the size of Virginia parishes, the power of the vestry, and the scarcity of ministers. It might have been solidified because English law provided that absolutely everyone—Dissenters as well as Anglicans—had a right to a burial in the parish where he or she died. Virginians did not extend this age-old law to Africans, free or enslaved, so they quickly diverged from the ancient English codes for treatment of the dead.)[58] The family would have taken Ball's body in a coffin (black walnut for the wealthy) to the spot Ball had designated, where the parson would have met them. The family paid him to preach a funeral sermon before the interment. Afterward, bereaved families served refreshments. If Mary Johnson Ball were initiated into the customs of the elite, she would have served wine and molasses cookies seasoned with ginger and caraway stamped with hearts and cherubim.[59]

By August 1711, Joseph Ball Jr., little Mary's half brother, had returned to administer his father's estate. He also petitioned successfully to take over the administration of his brother-in-law Carnegie's estate, pledging forty thousand pounds of tobacco security to Captain Richard Hughes, who had been appointed by the Northumberland County court, along with another local landowner, to oversee Ball's administration. Hughes would become very familiar to little Mary and her mother over the next few months.[60]

Mary Ball at three years old would not have understood the meaning of much of what she witnessed. But she would have felt the serious and sad nature of her father's illness and death, and she would have noticed that a few months after her father disappeared, after the crops came in, most of the grown-up enslaved people with whom she was familiar, some of whom might have taken care of her, disappeared.

The culture in which the Balls lived militated against the display of grief. Death was still regarded in Western culture as banal rather than the terrible rupture with the past that it would represent in the nineteenth century. Although Ball himself had lived a relatively long life, he died in a place where the frightening regularity of early fatalities had habituated settlers to an outward attitude of resignation and stoicism toward death. Anglican rituals stressed living piously as preparation for dying, and local custom stressed keeping a stiff upper lip. Virginians strove for equanimity before the finality of death because its omnipresence kept them so fearful. They circulated among themselves the idea that grief was of no use. "The most excessive grief cannot raise . . . the dead," as William Lambert wrote to a bereaved woman.[61]

Mary's mother had already survived the death of two husbands and had been on her own with two children. Now she had three children, two of an age to give emotional support in her bereavement. But little Mary was more isolated. Although Ball's age and gender probably meant that he had had little to do with Mary's day-to-day life, his death would have saddened and frightened her. Mary's first loss, however, was probably marked by little recognition of her fear or sadness. Nor would the adults and her two older siblings, preoccupied as they were with their own worries about the future, have done much to allay the anxiety that Ball's death caused her. She began early to be trained through the ritual language of Anglicanism and through the adults around her in the habits of self-control rather than expressivity, lessons of a piece with swaddling.[62]

2.

A GENERATION
OF ORPHANS

|||||||||||||||||||||||||||||||||||||||||||||||||||||||||||||||||||||||||||||||||||||||||||||||||||||||||||||||||||||||||||||||||||||||||||||||||||

ITH BALL'S DEATH, MARY LEGALLY became an orphan. Orphans were defined by the loss of their fathers, who had legal rights over them and were expected to support them.[1] While Mary would not have registered the full meaning of her father's death, she would have understood that she had lost an affectionate father who had cared for her and her mother. His legal protectiveness, his expression of gratitude toward his wife in his will, and his generosity to Mary all indicate that Ball felt warmly toward his last family. Mary's mother, however, and the culture in which she lived would have encouraged her not to grieve for her father but to accept the loss as God's will and to soldier on.

The expressivity, however formulaic, of Ball's will suggests that he was part of a growing population among the English and Virginians of individuals increasingly given to articulating feeling, rather than the more muted emotional style of the authoritarian family. The family in this era was undergoing a slow and uneven transition from a group that was organized around work, under the direction of a patriarch, to one characterized more by ties of affection and directed toward the individual development and well-being of the children. By the mid-eighteenth century, many southern planter families adopted a consciously affectionate tone in family life and encouraged in young people some freedom, particularly in the choice of marriage partners.[2] This transformation corresponds to the moment when the falling death rate gave parents the time and the confidence to sweeten and enrich the biological ties that bound them to their children.[3]

The Ball family might have been affectionate, although court records document how the scramble for property interfered with sentiment. An eighteenth-century Anglo-colonial family could display warmth for its members and express itself in the growing vocabulary of sensibility and sympathy,[4] which focused attention on empathy, but its members would have been most unlikely to subscribe to or even to understand the notion that each child should pursue individual goals or realize him- or herself. God's purposes were still more important in the early eighteenth century than man's, and infinitely more important than woman's. Patriarchy tightly hedged about the unique development of individual family members, especially females. Indeed, both sex roles and class distinctions in Virginia grew more rigid in the eighteenth century even as individualism for males increased. Mary was born into a family that was concerned with obtaining and transmitting property, not with the personal realization of the talents and desires of its (female) members.[5]

Contemporary middle-class mothering that idealizes the special, empathic bond between mother and child has its roots in the nineteenth century. Unlike the premodern mother, the early nineteenth-century mother was to devote her attentions fully to her children, who were likely to be fewer in number than those of a premodern mother. The ties between mother and child were to vibrate with mutual feeling.[6]

Premodern mothers' care, like that of Mary Johnson Ball, was intended not to develop and sensitize a cord between mother and child (although it could) but to preserve the child from early death and to train her rapidly to be a prudent housewife and mother. Early eighteenth-century parents did not view their children as innately innocent or possessed of a unique individuality that needed to be coaxed forth. Parents saw their job as instilling in their children the values and skills they would need to fulfill their place in life and getting them to adulthood as quickly as possible. The mother was to accomplish these things while vigilantly overseeing her household and feeding and clothing its members. A mother protected her daughter and taught her womanly duties and correct behavior; she attempted to mold and curb rather than imagine, cultivate, and share her child's feelings. Girls were trained more rigorously than boys to give up their own desires in the interests of their birth families and, eventually, their husbands and children.[7] To the extent that a family goal was harmony, women had significantly greater responsibility for achieving it than men did. On the other hand, Mary Johnson Ball's particular mothering would demonstrate that harmony was not necessarily the main responsibility for women and that they could also accumulate and pass on land, objects, and people.

Harmony ranked low in relative importance for the greater Ball clan. And in Joseph Ball's second family, he could not have run his extended family without coercion. His second wife's indenture would not have trained her in the ethos of sensibility and refined feelings. She had come up the hard way, where feelings were incidental to the fight for survival, not ends in themselves to be nurtured and expressed artfully.

The Ball family had a sometimes-affectionate patriarch, but a patriarch, nevertheless, whose authority and decisions would have trumped the free expression of emotions among family members and prevented some from ever surfacing. In Virginia, where labor was increasingly captive, land plentiful, and institutions at a minimum, patriarchs exercised more authority than their English counterparts.[8]

Unlike the great majority of Virginia children losing a parent, Mary benefited from Ball's generous will. In addition to the three slaves he left his daughter, Joseph Ball left her four hundred acres north on the Rappahannock, near Fredericksburg, and the feathers collected in "the kitchen loft" to make her own down bed, and fifteen head of cattle. To his wife, he left dower rights to a well-specified parcel of land on the Corotoman farm—meaning she could use it during her lifetime, or until she remarried, but not sell it—as well as numerous bequests including, as we saw, two slaves and the use of a third "girl," as well as the remaining years of labor that Ball's indentured servant, Ellen Grafton, owed him. He left his "beloved wife" a feather bed, chests, a third of the household linen, the pewter, the iron, and the brass of the kitchen, as well as a third of the earthenware and woodenware. He also left her the entire crop of flax, half of the corn and the wheat, eleven sheep including one ram, half of his hogs, and a number of cattle. He left her half of the crop that the overseer was supervising, that is, the tobacco.[9] That was the equivalent of a bit of cash because they were interchangeable—and tobacco more common. In addition, he willed her daughter Elizabeth Johnson one hundred acres of land.[10] As a special, personal gift, he left his wife a white horse named Dragon, with "her" bridle, sidesaddle, and other "furniture," and a bay named Rush. Mary Johnson Ball would share her skill and love of riding with little Mary.[11]

In death, Ball behaved liberally with his wife and daughter. It was unusual to leave a daughter land and more unusual to leave a stepdaughter land. He made sure to leave young Mary cattle and slaves to go with her land. Ball had already left his only son, Joseph, land, a house, and slaves, so he tried to furnish his youngest daughter with the land and laborers for her independence. In addition, both mother and daughter received the typical woman's legacy, the feather bed—or at least the feathers to make one.[12]

Members of the community's wealthiest families including the Carters and the Tayloes witnessed Ball's inventory. The list of Ball's stock, which includes four "old bulls," fifty-two sheep, seven cows and calves including six yearlings, is interrupted by a list of slaves that includes three who were six years old, three of three years old, and three of two years old. Below them on the list is Tony, and, further on, the "Negro Boy Called James," who had once belonged to Hannah Fox, Joseph Ball's sister, but whom Joseph had successfully possessed.[13]

Dinah no doubt helped care for Mary. Mary's most constant companions when she was very small had likely been nine enslaved children. At her father's death, Mary came to own one of these companions, a boy named Tom. James would probably have been working in the fields, and the six-year-olds, among whom Tom probably numbered, would have begun to do simple jobs in the milk house, in the kitchen, and in the garden under the supervision of Mary's mother. Children sometimes helped to pick the hornworms off tobacco leaves and crush them. They also might feed the poultry.[14]

When Mary lost a parent, she became one of a very large number of children, white and black, in the Chesapeake who were similarly afflicted. Mary was born toward the end of a period in which most children would probably not grow up with both biological parents caring for them and who were even less likely to know their grandparents. In 1699, Lancaster County had 243 households, 865 tithables (that is, white and black men and black women considered capable of doing field work and whose labor was therefore taxable after the age of sixteen), and 1,224 nontithables, totaling 2,089 persons.[15] Water, insects, and settler conflict with the Indians had kept the English population down in Virginia, and only migration from the British Isles and slave imports accounted for its early population growth. Malaria, commonly called "ague," did not usually kill directly but weakened its victims so that they were vulnerable to the many other illnesses that circulated in the humid warmth. White Virginians had only started to reproduce themselves in substantial numbers with the turn of the eighteenth century. And African Americans would not do so until the mid-eighteenth century.

For white children, orphaned by the loss of one or both parents, what came next depended upon the wealth and connections of the child's remaining relatives. Mary's widowed mother could afford to keep her family intact, but the relatives of other orphans often had to turn to the Virginia Orphans' Court to find legal solutions to the problems that attended losing a parent.[16] When a child lost a father or mother, a vestryman would probably bind him or her out to a family, where there was little time for grief or opportunity for comfort. The child had to prove his or her value through work. These families received the child's labor in exchange for lodging, food, clothing, linen, and "washing," or seeing that the child's few items of clothing and linen were laundered.

If the indenture was for a boy, he would learn a trade and be taught to read and write and do arithmetic. A girl would learn to do household work, to sew, and to read the Bible. If a child had powerful connections, the indenture would specify that he not be put to work in the ground, that is, to work in the ubiquitous tobacco fields. (People who labored at raising tobacco were, theoretically, poor white and black men and black women. Wealthy white men supervised tobacco cultivators, or their overseers, but did not labor themselves. Rapidly developing colonial racial ideas about the special delicacy and privilege of white women specified that they did not work in the fields. In fact, poor white women did work in the fields when family circumstances or their husbands dictated, but the colony did not tax them for it.) These child indentures varied in length, but white children usually became free at twenty-five. Illegitimate children and children of mixed race served longer (the latter to thirty-five), and their masters could extend their indentures for what they determined to be bad behavior.[17]

The economic needs of the families to which orphans were bound determined their occupations, their futures, and the kind of emotional upbringing they had. For the most part, families struggled to survive and expected the children they housed to contribute their utmost. There was little time for the examination or expression of feeling. Its articulation was not encouraged as a social grace. Even a century later in Virginia, rural women were supposed to work hard and repress much, including ill-treatment, disappointment, and grief.[18]

If Mary was a step away from the experience of poorer white orphans, she was a further remove from the bitter experience of enslaved orphan children, although they were her playmates. They lost their parents through disease as rapidly as—or more so than—white children did, but the laws of slavery and planters' deathbed desires also orphaned them.[19] The presence of so many small slave children and so few adults on Ball's plantation represents a confluence of the successive disasters that blighted the lives of African and African American children.

Joseph Ball had devised his will with no attention to any human connections enslaved parents or children might have had. In this brutal and formative period in Virginia, Ball guaranteed his bickering children the babies of enslaved girls not yet capable of having them.[20]

Ball's inventory listed the presence of two enslaved adults, Dinah and Tony, and three slave children of six years old, three of three years old, and three of two years old. Ball's inventory was completed in the fall of 1712, and by then his children had already taken their property. In Ball's will, he noted that he gave (again) his son, Joseph, an adult woman whose name was Murrcah and her "Increase." He had already given his daughters Ann Conway and Easter Chinn two of Murrcah's children, Jack and James. In his will, he insisted on their ownership of Jack and James and that "no other of her children therefore born to her body to be construed to belong to the said Joseph Ball by virtue of the said deed." Joseph Ball understood that his son, Joseph junior, apparently inspired by his cousin Richard Ball's suit to possess Bess and Hannah, had decided to try to reinterpret the word "Increase" retroactively to mean that he should get not only Murrcah's future children but also her earlier offspring, Jack and James.

Ball gave his wife, Mary, the slaves Dinah and Tony, who are listed in his inventory. His will indicates that there were a number of other slaves working under an overseer who were to remain working on the plantation to harvest that summer's crop before they were to be distributed among

Joseph, Easter, and Ann. In the records of the last tithe before this year, Ball was listed as having thirteen tithables (that is, people capable of field work: white and black men and black women over the age of sixteen) in December 1711. He and his overseer would have constituted two of them, so in addition to Tony and Dinah he would have had nine slaves sixteen years or over, plus the nine enslaved children he held, who were under the age to be taxed.[21]

To little Mary, Joseph left "my negro boy Tom" and "Joe and Jack that formerly were belonging to Joseph Carnegie deceased." He also gave to his wife, Mary, "the use of the girl Jenney that I formerly gave to my daughter Elizabeth Carnegie until my grandson Joseph Carnegie shall come of age at one and twenty and she my said wife looking after her children if she shall have any in the time for my grandson's future benefit."

Ball's arrangements for both Marys were generous from his point of view and risky from theirs. And to Tom, Joe, Jack, and Jenney, they were horrible in ways we can imagine but cannot know in each of their hurtful particulars. Little Mary received three slaves, one of whom was a child who would be—or had already been—separated from his mother. Joe and Jack perhaps account for the growth (one at a time over two years) in Ball's number of tithables because he had assumed the administration of his son-in-law Carnegie's will.[22] He had retrieved slaves that he had given to Carnegie, now that both his daughter and his son-in-law were dead. Mary would have to go and retrieve the nearly pubescent Jenney from her step-nephew and then "look after [Jenney's] children," should she have some, with what to her would have been the unpleasant prospect of giving them back to young Joseph at his majority. Jenney, meanwhile, was young enough to need a mother. When Joseph Ball Sr. gave "the use of" her to his daughter Elizabeth, she was presumably separated from her own mother. And now she was being retrieved from whatever ties she had managed to make in her years with the shrinking Carnegie family. Unless Dinah was Jenney's mother, she appears only as a forlorn pawn in Ball's last display of power, a power that reached beyond his grave to sadden and deprive not only Murrcah's and Jenney's lives, but also those of any children they would ever have.

The nine enslaved children enumerated but not named in Ball's inventory are an awful reminder of the desolation that Virginia testamentary practices enabled slave owners to wreak on the African and American-born slaves they bought and compelled to go here and there. Tony and Dinah might have been a couple, but they might not have been. They might have been the parents of three of these children, fewer, or none at all. They were, however, the only potential parents that remained to this huddle of family-less toddlers and children left behind when the harvest was in and, one by one, the Balls descended on their father's plantation and took away the adults.

The children would have been Mary's earliest playmates, but they would not have been swaddled, at least not with the approval of their owners and not in the way their owners understood the practice.[23] For one thing, mothers who did field work could not be permitted to waste time changing swaddling bands. The practice also demanded considerable fabric that most slave owners would have begrudged their slaves. And, philosophically, most owners would not have seen the importance of insisting on distinguishing the humanity of slave infants from their animal nature or making sure that their limbs developed perfectly. That said, slave mothers who worked in the fields and took their infants with them to nurse wrapped their babies as well as they could, with the fabric allotted to them to protect them as they lay, waiting for their mothers' toil to end, on the dirt.

Ball's collection of fabrics included flannel and "course broad linning," most if not all of which would have been for his slaves. Fabric was an expensive import and laborious to make and tightly rationed for slaves. Nineteenth-century observers noted that small slaves were barely clad at all. There is no evidence about the apparel of the senior Joseph Ball's slaves.

However, Joseph Ball's son, Joseph junior—little Mary's half brother—left more of a record. He moved back to Lancaster County, after being educated as a barrister in England, in the late 1720s. After a decade or so in the colonies, he, his wife, and their surviving daughter (two children had died) returned to England. He paid his nephew Rawleigh Chinn (the son of Easter Ball Chinn and Rawleigh Chinn) forty pounds a year to look after his Virginia properties. Ball specified to Chinn that the "breeding wenches have Baby clothes, for which you may tear up old sheets or any other old linen that you can find in my house . . . and let them have good midwives; and what is necessary." He allotted the slave children a coat of "Worster" (worsted) cotton or Virginia cloth (that is, a coarse homespun that would increasingly be made on plantations by slave women) and "two shirts or shifts of oznabrig [osnaburg]." He specified that slave mothers be given needles and thread to make their children's clothes.[24]

Some masters did not provide slave children or adults with shoes. An observer in 1732 noted that Afro-Virginians who worked in public houses were required to wash their feet, meaning they were shoeless. Later in the eighteenth century, a traveler noted that field hands worked barefoot.[25] But Joseph Ball instructed his overseer to make sure that his slaves had a pair of "good strong shoes, and stockings," and for those who worked with the animals or in damp places two pairs.[26]

Joseph Ball's child slaves were not baptized. Planters and slaves alike still believed (or hoped, in the case of slaves) that Christianity meant freedom; an early justification for enslaving people was that they were not Christians. Although the House of Burgesses and courts made it clear several times, beginning in 1667, that this was not the case, planters generally refused baptism and religious instruction to their slaves.[27] Some ministers and planters excused themselves on the basis of the difficulty of preaching to slaves unlikely to speak English. This was a period of high importations of slaves from Africa: 7,840 between 1700 and 1709; 6,275 in the next decade; and 12,700 in the following ten years. However, historians believe Africans quickly learned the basics of survival English. Slave owners with so many angry and desperate bond people to both extract work from and pacify were more concerned with security than with spirituality, although later some came to view religion as a route to security.[28] There is no mention of religion in Ball's Letterbook, nor did George Washington in the mid-

and later eighteenth century give religious instruction to his slaves. One of the latter's slaves, Ona Judge, who ran away, complained that slaves at Mount Vernon received no "moral instruction, of any kind."[29]

||||||||||||||||

THE SLAVE POPULATION in Virginia had been growing fast for the previous thirty years but not through the reproduction of slave families. By 1680, the slave birthrate had begun to approach natural increase—a condition that is recognizable in part through a normal sex ratio of slightly more female than male children. From the early seventeenth century, planters had been buying small numbers of slaves from coastal traders coming from the Caribbean. But after 1680, planters began buying more and more Africans directly from transatlantic traders. At the time Ball's inventory was taken, the number of slaves in the colony was about 19,500, and the number of Africans in that population was 10,161, or more than half.[30] Planters preferred to purchase male slaves and quickly unbalanced the even sex ratio. It did not return to equilibrium until 1770.[31]

Planters' desire for males helped drive the slave birthrate sharply down after 1680. And the effect of the harrowing Middle Passage on surviving women was to weaken their ability and desire to reproduce. Fully 25 percent of captives never even lived to disembark in the New World, and others were sickened and driven to desperation by capture, loss of family, uncertainty, starvation, and brutality.

Orphaned by the deaths and sales of parents, slave children lived in a culture in which kinship and obligation could no longer structure or give much meaning to their lives, while grief was everywhere and comfort rare. We cannot know what this group of parentless children received by way of hope or solace at the hands of Mary Johnson Ball. But the seventeenth-century English working men and women who came to the New World were largely used badly here, and there was little in the culture to suggest that they should empathize and give succor to strangers still less fortunate. The legal protections for the physical and religious well-being of white orphans did not extend to African and Afro-Virginian children, nor was the word "orphan" used to describe the parentless ones.

Enslaved women who were able to bear children usually had children every two years and sometimes as often as yearly. They were likely to start giving birth in their mid-teens, unlike white women, who usually began in their twenties. Given the mortality rate of slaves in late seventeenth- and early eighteenth-century Virginia, death had no doubt taken at least some of the parents of the enslaved children in Ball's possession. The sudden drop to two tithables in Joseph Ball's inventory and the rapid increase in those of Joseph Ball Jr. from ten to thirteen in 1713 means that some of the children's parents ended up with him.[32]

While slave children could lose their parents from sale or the vagaries of property distribution after their owners' deaths, they could also lose parents because of owners' whims. When Joseph Ball Jr. returned to Great Britain with his wife and daughter in the 1730s, he took two enslaved toddlers, a boy, Aaron, and a girl named Martha. He left Martha's mother to labor in the fields of Virginia, and perhaps Aaron's as well. He later wrote that he raised the children "tenderly" and dressed them well, apparently using them as "pets" like those aristocratic families that had portraits of their children painted with child slaves in jeweled collars along with fetching dogs, wearing similar collars. Aaron wore livery that Ball later gave to one of the enslaved men on his plantation. That Ball the barrister did not "need" these children as workers in Great Britain is borne out by the fact that in 1754, when his daughter had grown beyond childhood, he sent the young man and woman back to work in his colonial fields.[33]

Little Mary, then, spent her earliest years in close companionship with black toddlers whom her family fed, clothed, sheltered, and to some degree protected at the same time that they began to work them. A few decades later, her son George Washington's famous young colleague Thomas Jefferson wrote his well-known remarks on the effects of slavery on the children of slave owners. "The parent storms, the child looks on, catches the lineaments of wrath, puts on the same airs in the circle of smaller slaves, gives a loose [*sic*] to the worst of passions, and thus nursed, educated, and daily exercised in tyranny, cannot but be stamped by it with odious peculiarities."[34]

Jefferson described "the whole commerce between master and slave [as] a perpetual exercise of the most boisterous passions, the most unremitting despotism on the one part, and degrading submissions on the other. Our children see this, and learn to imitate it; for man is an imitative animal." Joseph, who meticulously cared for certain of the physical needs of his slaves while twisting their lives to his profit and personal vanity, was in no way an exceptional slave owner, and Mary's childhood observations of the "commerce between master and slave" were unremarkable for her time and place.[35]

She could probably not have articulated the meaning of owning one of her playmates or her family's ownership of these nine companions, but family possession of little ones offered her the chance to play out in her childish relationships the dominance her parents exercised over all the Africans on their plantation. The child slaves were not yet economically valuable, but they were learning the defensive lessons of how to portray themselves as possessions just as little Mary was learning the feel of owning. They offered a kind of inimitable companionship that invited Mary simultaneously to intimacy and to domination as these children rapidly became aware that they were required to absorb aggression without retribution. These relationships trained the owners' capacities for command without any requirement for empathy, while they trained the owned in guardedness and a detailed knowledge of their owners.

Critics and admirers both have commented on Mary's unembarrassed exercise of authority as an adult. Mary's status in those formative and porous years as a slave owner at or before her third birthday, and her daily intimacy with her independent mother, contributed to her air of command. Slave ownership became integrated early into her sense of who she was, a white Virginian, commander of property in people.

3

BRUISING
THE SMALL SPIRIT[1]

By DECEMBER 1712, a little over a year after Joseph Ball's death, Mary's mother married Captain Richard Hughes.[2] Hughes, like Ball, was an active and ambitious man in local politics but less rich and successful. During Mary's marriage to Ball, her husband had frequently encountered Hughes in court. Hughes and Ball had served on a jury together in June 1710, and they had assessed the estate of Ball's son-in-law John Carnegie. Hughes had also sued successfully to recover money from Carnegie's estate. Assessing and serving as a juror were the first steps a striver took to climb the ladder of political influence. He was in court at almost every session. He oversaw the building of a road by his property on Cherry Point in Northumberland County.[3] (Hughes's farm lay just north of Lancaster County on a creek that poured into the Potomac River. It was very close to George Eskridge's home on the Potomac.) Sometimes Hughes served as churchwarden, giving evidence against mothers of illegitimate children. He litigated to recover debts, and as tobacco inspector, an important and lucrative position, he collected levies and made sure the hogsheads of tobacco did not contain sand, stones, and rotten tobacco.[4] He arbitrated disputes out of his home on Cherry Point.

Without a family, it would have been hard for Hughes to advance his ambitions much further. Marrying solidified a man's social standing and improved his economic situation.[5] Mary's considerable experience as a manager of households, frequenter of the courts, and mistress of slaves and her skills that included dairying, sewing, preserving vegetables and meat, cooking and overseeing food preparation, medical care, and textile production would all be at his service.

Men's, but particularly women's, work had diversified since the seventeenth century. Some families began to grow more than tobacco in order to participate in the expanding local barter markets that were emerging in the Chesapeake. Hughes owned the labor of at least one indentured woman, Eleanor Garvey, and two women slaves. Hughes's possession of these women meant that Mary would not have had to do field work. For Hughes, marrying the shrewd, hardworking, and personable widow of a wealthy man made sense in every way.[6]

From Mary Johnson Ball's point of view, the marriage made sense as well. She was alone with a bit of land surrounded by the property of her stepson, who, she had reason to believe, would be unfriendly. She had some years of labor from an indentured woman, two slaves, and another to retrieve from a step-nephew in addition to however many—if any—of the enslaved children went with her. She was perched precariously in the house that her stepson would want. While widowhood promised her an independent legal identity and ownership of her own land and slaves, a husband would help her to coerce her slaves to turn a profit and support her in the legal battles she and Hughes knew were looming. A marriage beckoned in this siege atmosphere.

In the summer of 1712, Hughes went to court to secure his legal rights against Ellen Cranford, his indentured servant, who had had a child with an African man. The court lengthened Cranford's time of service—probably by five years—and would have forced her child to serve until he or she reached thirty-five years instead of twenty-five as it would have been for a white child. (In 1691, after Bacon's Rebellion, in which blacks and disgruntled whites had fought together against the elite of the colony, colonial authorities enacted a number of measures to discourage alliances between the races, including a prohibition of cross-race marriages and penalties for children of mixed couples.)[7]

In December 1712, Joseph Ball, little Mary's half brother, recently returned from England, sued the newlyweds for a debt, and they responded by countersuing in July 1713.[8] They used the chancery courts that were available in Virginia after 1645. These courts, dealing specifically with inheritance, were more flexible than regular courts and were intended to mitigate some of the harshest effects of coverture[9] on married women in an area where wives daily became widows.[10] In August 1713, young Joseph Ball won a little over four pounds in damages from Richard and Mary. At that same court, they sued Ball for trespass.[11] That Hughes paid taxes in Lancaster County in 1713 suggests that he and Mary, little Mary, and her half siblings Elizabeth and John Johnson were probably staying in the house at Corotoman in the year or so immediately following the death of Joseph Ball. Ball probably came onto Mary's dower property, which her marriage had put into jeopardy.[12]

Until 1713, Richard Hughes figured frequently in the Northumberland County court records. Ball's will did not stipulate that Mary had to leave if she remarried, but precedent—and probably the numerous Balls on the court—favored that interpretation. The wording in Ball's will suggests that he anticipated problems with his son, asserting that Mary be able to enjoy her dower rights "peaceably . . . during her Natural life."[13] The court continued the trespass case into 1714 and finally dismissed it when Hughes did not appear to prosecute his suit—not surprisingly—because he died in January or February (still called 1713 in the Old Style that was used in the record books) of that year.[14]

Little Mary had little time to adjust to the loss of her father before having to recognize a new authority in the house. Her mother's rapid marriage and Mary Hughes's and her new husband's maneuvers to secure their joint property in the face of Joseph Ball's calculations would have generated a tense atmosphere. The family moved to Hughes's home at Cherry Point in this period, a distance of perhaps twenty miles from the Corotoman home in Lancaster County, or a horseback ride of about three hours. Mary Hughes started showing up in the Northumberland records in 1713/1714, when she put Hughes's will in for probate.

Hughes's farm at Cherry Point, near the Potomac, sat very close to the home of George Eskridge, whose path often crossed Hughes's in court and whom Mary Hughes already knew, because he often appeared in court in Lancaster County where her late husband Joseph Ball had officiated. She no doubt knew that he represented Hannah and David Fox and later Richard Ball in the suits over the slaves James, Hannah, and Bess and their "encrease." She would describe him later as her "trusty and well-beloved friend."[15]

No sooner had the Johnson-Ball-Hughes family settled itself on Cherry Point than a commotion occurred in the neighborhood. Little Mary's stepfather and her mother's "well-beloved friend" presided over the execution of a slave at Cherry Point. That her stepfather and Eskridge carried out such violence must have impressed itself powerfully on Mary, who would have been five or six years old.

‖‖‖‖‖‖‖‖‖

GEORGE ESKRIDGE, a wealthy and well-connected planter-attorney who became a member of the House of Burgesses in 1705, would play an important role in little Mary's life. He accumulated 12,444 acres of land in four counties between 1703 and 1739 and scores of slaves.[16] In his first year as a burgess, he helped pass complicated legislation that confirmed a 1692 law for the "Speedy and Easie Prosecution of Slaves Committing Capital Crimes."[17] This law directed that slaves be tried locally in a specially convened county court of oyer and terminer in which the local magistrates were commissioned specifically for that purpose, instead of being taken to Williamsburg and tried before the General Court as white servants continued to be. Eskridge was elected to the House of Burgesses in the middle of a decade in which white Virginians purchased eight thousand captive Africans. Afraid of the Native Americans they were evicting from their lands, Virginians were rapidly importing unfamiliar people whom they feared even more.

People dragooned from Africa made up about 90 percent of the slave population, and unlike most of the slaves who had been born in Virginia, they bore marks of their heritage that included ritual scars, braids, and filed teeth. They made music and played drums at night; they spoke unfamiliar languages; they were angry, traumatized, frightened, and often recalcitrant. They resisted. They ran away. White Virginians imagined that they were plotting revolts, and sometimes they were. William Byrd I wrote in 1736, summing up the colonists' willingness to do whatever was needed as they enslaved more and more Africans, "Another unhappy effect of many Negros is the necessity of being severe . . . then foul means must do what fair will not."[18] The years roughly between Eskridge's arrival and 1740 were increasingly inhuman as the English perfected colonial slavery.[19]

Before the passage of the second part of the "Speedy and Easie Prosecution" bill, Virginia law excluded all testimony of slaves except for the confessions or testimony of Christian slaves taken under oath. Because most slaves were not Christians, this law made it very unlikely that they could bear witness in court. The 1705 statute, revising this law, explicitly excluded all "popish recusants convict, negroes, mulattoes and Indian servants, and others, not being Christians" from being "witnesses in any case whatsoever."[20] *All* slave testimony was now excluded.

For Eskridge, who often served as colony prosecutor, this piece of legislation made his professional life more expeditious. All he had to do to prosecute an enslaved man or woman was gather together some white male accusers. Of course, it also made his life as a slaveholder more secure. Eskridge and his fellow burgesses understood that to dominate kidnapped Africans, they had to render them helpless before the law.

On February 19, 1713, Eskridge, public prosecutor for Northumberland County, announced his suspicion that one Daniel Conolly (or Connell), an indentured servant, Prince, an Indian slave, and Jack, an African slave belonging to Richard and Mary Hughes's neighbor Elizabeth Bankes, had borne "off a Ship in the River of Cone" (that is, Coan, not far from Sandy Point, where Eskridge lived). Eskridge further accused Jack and Prince of theft and "feloniously burning a Ship called the Nightingail of Biddeford."

On April 1, 1713, at a separate session from the regular court days, Jack came to trial and pleaded not guilty.[21] Eskridge called a number of men from his neighborhood, including Richard Hughes, to testify against him. On April 3, the court convicted Jack of burning the ship *Nightingail* and five hundred pounds of merchandise on board. Eskridge then accused him of burglary and felony—breaking into a house and stealing a hundred pounds of tobacco worth ten shillings. All crimes over five shillings were capital crimes. Jack's second trial was on April 6. The court convicted Jack and sentenced him to hang, explaining that it had followed the protocol laid out in the "Action for the Speedy and Easie Prosecution of Slaves Committing Capital Crimes." The court also convicted and sentenced to death the Indian slave Prince. Daniel Conolly, who was suspected of involvement in these crimes as well but was not subject to the "Speedy and Easie Prosecution" and could testify in his own defense, was sentenced to be whipped twenty lashes and then nineteen more. The justices agreed that Conolly was thoroughly bad: "a stubborn, pilfering, unruly servant, A NIGHT WALKER, Companion of negroes and greatly suspected likewise a Concealer of their thefts and Evil practices, being also of a very lewd life and bad behavior." But they were constrained to permit him the legal protections due to Englishmen, and these saved his life.

Jack was hanged on April 14, 1713, at the Cherry Point plantation of his owner, Elizabeth Bankes. The colony estimated her slave's value at thirty pounds for the purposes of reimbursing her for her lost labor.[22] Some parents found executions instructive for children, and Richard and Mary might have taken little Mary and her older siblings to this remorseless, nearby example of slave law. On June 17, Eskridge read to the court the governor's note pardoning the Indian slave Prince, thus saving the colony the expense of reimbursing his owner.

The historian Kathleen Brown has calculated that slaves convicted of some sort of violation belonging to women had a 50 percent chance of being executed, while those belonging to men had only a 20 percent chance. Such slaves had a substantially greater chance of being convicted as well. Women owners were also disproportionately represented among those with slaves who came before the courts. It is an open question whether slaves owned by women were more likely to act rebelliously or whether planters were more likely to see single women as incapable of proper discipline—or both.[23]

Adapting to white violence against blacks asked Mary to insulate herself against the shock of witnessing others' agony by accepting the need to punish a potentially dangerous and alien labor force. Children accommodate what they witness by assenting, under the guidance of those they trust, to the world around them as it is. Accommodation cordons off the development of empathy, a favorite subject of English moral philosophers, novelists, poets, and playwrights.

Two days after Jack's execution, Richard Hughes initiated in the Northumberland court five suits for debt against men of small estate for amounts of tobacco ranging from 980 pounds (worth about five pounds sterling) to

2,661 pounds of tobacco (or about thirteen pounds and three shillings). Hughes had not been feeling well for some months[24] and, complaining of weakness, had made out his will in 1712. He managed to survive the busy court season in the early summer. The third-time widow Mary Hughes brought his will to probate in February 1714.

Through this brief marriage, Mary was trying to secure her family's economic stability. Her small daughter had to cope with a new father and a move—possibly hurried—from her familiar home. Her mother and stepfather were tense about conflict with her half brother. And then her stepfather became ill and died.

There is no record of Hughes's feelings about little Mary or hers about him. Patriarch of the blended Johnson-Ball-Hughes family, Hughes had much on his mind during the event-filled months of his marriage. Colonial fathers usually gave minimal time and attention to their very young children, especially girls—especially stepdaughters—and he might have had a relatively small impact on Mary.

Little Mary would have seen scenes she was already familiar with—a man lying sick, visitors eddying around his bedside, her mother and possibly Dinah or Abba, one of Hughes's slaves, tending him. There would have been the washing of Hughes's body, a shroud and coffin, a burial, sermon, and gathering. She, her mother, and her siblings would have put on mourning again. They and their neighbors, prominent among them the Eskridges, would have noted the brevity and fragility of life and talked about the new sorting out of property that would begin.

When he died, Hughes, like Ball, left words of his affection for his wife; he left her and her two older children, John and Elizabeth Johnson, everything he owned. Hughes left Mary's mother a life interest in his house on Cherry Point and the 160 acres it was on, allocating the house and land to her daughter Elizabeth, after her mother's death. In addition, he left to his widow and eventually Elizabeth his slaves: "a negro woman called Abba and a negro girl called Winney" and a mulatto called Darby, as well as money to purchase a "breeding negro." He also had had the indentured servant Eleanor Garvey in his employ until she became free.[25] To John Johnson, Mary's second child, he left 600 acres and six head of cattle when he became an adult.[26] He bequeathed young Mary, now around six, nothing, presumably because Joseph Ball had already provided a secure future for her, although it is also possible that he did not like her. Hughes behaved generously to his acquired family, although they were not kin.[27]

Now experienced in these matters, Mary Hughes presented her husband's will to the court as executrix. She called for an appraisal of his estate.

Young Mary had lost a second father by the time she was six years old. Her relationship with her mother would have buffered her from this loss. As she had in 1711, Mary Ball Hughes held center stage in the 1714 drama of her husband's death, and little Mary would no doubt have tried to give her as little cause for further grief as possible. This new family crisis would have contributed to the child's growing store of apprehension about the durability of the adults surrounding her.[28] It also would have accelerated her acquisition of the appearances of maturity, although that maturity might not ever gain much depth.[29]

Religious writers counseled preparation for the death that awaited everyone. Mary was becoming familiar with the ritual Christian words around her as adults tried to celebrate the mysterious claim that in death a soul reunited joyfully with God.[30] It is easier to imagine that she registered these deaths as sorrowful interruptions to normal life, not occasions of glorious transcendence. Mary would live to see conditions improve and Virginians' lives lengthening, but she prepared for her own maturity in a harsh landscape where mortality was relentlessly high.

Controlling fear and grief can produce numbness that is likely to go unquestioned because it easily doubles as good behavior. Adults, preoccupied with their own feelings and the practical demands that death made on them, would require no explanation of feelings from a quiet child who seemed to be practicing obedience to God's will.

Frightened children are likely to be angry children, and given Mary's position in her family, dependent girl-child of a newly widowed mother, Mary would not have wanted or been permitted to express her distress and conflict to her mother. Among slaves, however, Mary did not need to restrain her feelings or her aggressive impulses. Southern parents encouraged aggression in boys and did not curb it sharply in girls, as northern parents were likely to do.[31] Perhaps some of her fright and dismay emerged in aggressive activities against her slave companion Tom, James, or Jack or Hughes's Winney.

Apart from mourning her third husband, Mary Johnson Ball Hughes occupied herself after her husband's death with court battles and managing the Cherry Point farm. She hired William Dulaney (also spelled Delaney) to oversee her workers and dispense punishment. She had six captives, who included the two adults Hughes left her and Dinah, Tony, and probably Joe and Jack, retrieved from the young Joseph Carnegie. Young Mary's Tom would have been still too young to do field work. Mary's mother had the slaves grow tobacco, along with corn and beans to feed everyone.[32] As a widow, she was now legally able to litigate and strive for small advantages over others. She added to her friends another man trained in law, David Straughan, who helped appraise the estate of one of her dead husband's debtors.

Richard Hughes, in his last sally in court before he became too unwell, had gone after Matthias Chatwood for debt in June 1713, but as of July he had not paid up. Chatwood had apparently been appointed constable but died in office. Mary, picking up Hughes's suit where he had left off, called for an appraisal of Chatwood's estate. David Straughan and others found him to have an assortment of dilapidated implements and livestock, an "old" mare, six pigs, an "old" chest, a pestle, three "old hilling hoes" (for tobacco), a bedstead, a pail, and a scattering of other objects, most also described as "old." In addition to Chatwood's estate, Mary sued a roster of farmers, some of them more than once. One of Hughes's former creditors, William Bear, sued Mary for outstanding wages. In 1716, the court summoned her to pay William Bear what he was owed.[33]

After Richard Hughes's death, young Mary learned from her mother, no doubt more by example and watching than through lessons and explanations. As a tobacco planter, Mary Hughes was busy around the calendar making difficult decisions, each one crucial to the survival and quality of her tobacco. Preparations began in December or January, when the slaves put manure or ash on the small area where they would plant tobacco seeds and cover them with branches to protect them from frost.[34] Beginning in April and continuing through the summer, slaves transplanted these seedlings when ready—one of many difficult judgment calls the planter had to make—to hills that they had heaped up with hoes in the tobacco fields. Slave children might carry the plants to the fields, and experienced workers transplanted them. Transplanting was a tricky process and worked better when it rained, which helped the roots come up without tearing.

Once settled into their mounds, the plants needed weeding three times a summer. Slaves had to remove the devouring worms and pinch off the plant tops to prevent flowering, which drew energy and nutrients away from the leaves. Shoots had to be pinched for the same reason. In September and early October, the tobacco needed cutting—not too soon when the leaves were too moist to dry properly and not too late to avoid the possibility of frost ruining the plants. Slaves hung the cut plants first on poles in the fields and later in the tobacco shed to cure. The moment to cut, too, was hard to select; a rainy spell could make leaves rot. The tobacco was ready, or "case," when it was dry but still flexible. Stripping the tobacco and packing it could go on until December.[35] Some planters then had slaves take the stems from the tobacco leaves in addition to pulling them off the stalks before packing the crop, leaf by leaf, and pressing it ("prizing") after each layer (being careful not to crumble it) in huge hogsheads that weighed a thousand pounds when filled. Slaves rolled the heavy-laden hogsheads downhill to the nearby river to be shipped. Mary Hughes, with a relatively small crop, did not ship from her home as many planters did, so she probably had an arrangement with Eskridge to transport her crop to his plantation and ship from there.[36]

Planters could use one spot for tobacco for only about four years before the soil became too depleted for subsequent crops. Writers on the subject suggested that a planter needed 50 acres for every worker, in order to have enough land for cultivation and enough extra to lie fallow. Mary, with 160 acres and six hands, had enough to grow tobacco as well as the corn, wheat, and beans she needed to feed her dependents.

The adventurous and determined Mary Hughes developed a client-patron relationship with her neighbor George Eskridge. He was Mary's closest counselor and sometimes her lawyer. She came to have a relationship with him that resembled the one that Eskridge would have with Augustine Washington and that George Fairfax would establish with Lawrence and then George Washington. It was common in Virginia, but almost exclusively between men.[37] Mary Hughes profited from Eskridge's protection and advice, although he did not share business tips and land deals with the widow.

Mary Hughes took advantage of the relative fluidity that death had forced on Virginia. But even as she appeared in courts, witnessing, suing, and being sued, the public spaces she inhabited were closing their doors to women. Little Mary's mother had fought her way up in Virginia and put her children in a position to surpass her socially and economically, while it was becoming more and more unusual for women to use the tools that Mary Johnson Ball Hughes had struggled to acquire.

Young Mary learned to read and write in these years, adding on one and possibly two accomplishments that her mother did not possess. Although young Mary could write, she wrote with an inelegant hand and spelled erratically. In the eighteenth century, mothers typically taught children to read but not to write. Little Mary probably learned reading from her half siblings. The girl would have had to learn writing from a "writing master."[38]

Mary's education and experiences would not mark her as an upper-class woman. She did not master the ability to express refined feeling in an aesthetically pleasing way, on paper and orally, failing to acquire a central accomplishment for women of the elite. She was not trained to display "sensibility" as other girls of her father's class increasingly were.[39] Her education—at least as she demonstrated it in her few remaining letters— was better than but not dissimilar to that of indentured girls, taught to read by studying the Bible. That said, all but the most elite Virginia girls learned more about housewifery than about literature.

As mechanical printing became the dominant mode of public communication in the eighteenth century, the quality of one's handwriting became a writer's presentation of his or her social rank. Mary's inability to write a flowing script betrayed her humble origins.[40]

Mary early learned the skills of the household by observing and helping her mother and older sister. She watched and helped as they sewed and supervised slave women doing the work of the garden, the kitchen, and the dairy.

After her mother's death, Mary inherited a dozen napkins and two "diaper" tablecloths that were worked with the initials "M.B." (Diaper was an expensive and absorbent cotton or linen with a repeating pattern of diamonds or flowers.) It is not clear when they were made, but it is possible that Mary's mother along with Elizabeth and young Mary worked on them together and/or that they were the product of sewing lessons for the little girl. Embroidery, like working samplers, blurred the distance between literacy and illiteracy for girls and women with the leisure to learn it.

At about five years old, Mary began girlhood without the oversight of a man in the household. She witnessed her mother's independence, a woman choosing her own activities, litigating, and directing the education and tending to the physical and material interests of her children. This was simply how things were to Mary, who would have had, as yet, little sense that their household arrangements were unusual. Mary, being young and female, owed some deference to her older half brother John Johnson, but he, too, was dependent on their mother and did not have a patriarch's weight in the household.[41] Demanding and expecting obedience and having exacting standards for work characterized her own later life as a mother and slave owner. She learned these things at her mother's knee, observing her strong and open exercise of authority at home.[42]

Mary's early youth would have been usually free. White southern girls in this period had much the same kind of physical freedom as boys. They were encouraged to play outdoors, to enjoy the hours of light.[43] Mary became a good dancer and a good horseback rider, learning on her mother's Dragon and Rush. She was a strong and healthy girl.

While Mary was under her mother's tutelage, her half sister married, tightening the bonds between her family and the Eskridges.[44] Elizabeth married Samuel Bonam of Westmoreland County, who had a farm on the Potomac. Bonam was the nephew of George Eskridge's first wife, Rebecca Bonam. Samuel was apparently in his late forties or early fifties. Parents in the Chesapeake often did not live long enough to exert traditional control over their children's marriages, and young people had some latitude in marrying. Mary Hughes and her friend George Eskridge likely facilitated the marriage of Elizabeth and Samuel. Elizabeth, with the prospect of inheriting her stepfather's land at Cherry Point, was a good match for Bonam, whose land in Westmoreland was not very far from either Cherry Point or his uncle Eskridge's home at Sandy Point.[45] At the time of his death, only six years later, Bonam bequeathed a black walnut desk and a silver tumbler, suggesting that he had prosperous connections if he himself had not been very wealthy.[46]

In late 1720, when Mary was about eleven, both Mary Hughes and her son, John Johnson, became sick, possibly from the same illness. David Straughan, Mary Hughes's friend, helped John to make out his will in October 1720 and wrote Mary's on December 17, 1720. John Johnson was able to sign his, and Mary made her mark, consisting of three vertical lines. Both mother and son described themselves as "sick and weake in body."[47]

Mary, now about eleven or twelve, was old enough to help tend her brother and her mother during the long and unhappy fall and winter of 1720–1721. She had help from her sister, Elizabeth, and could also rely on the enslaved Abba and Winney and possibly others. Visitors first grouped around John and then the ailing widow Hughes: the Eskridges, Bonam relatives, perhaps some Balls, and other friends from Lancaster and Northumberland. The mood at home would have been somber and anxious as John and Mary suffered, and young, worried Mary and Elizabeth tried to keep them comfortable. Abba, Winney, Dinah, Tony, Joe, Jack, and Tom would have been worried as well, because death probably meant sale or other dismaying changes that would disrupt whatever equilibrium they had managed to establish in their time at Cherry Point.

As Mary Hughes was dying, she told her young daughter that she was going to leave her "a young mare and her Increase." The girl must have received this promise torn between excitement at the prospect and terrible dread about the circumstances that were bringing it to her. Young Mary had only her newlywed sister to help her through this grievous time, and Elizabeth was distracted by her own grief and the demands on her of her husband and new household.

Mary died first, in February 1721, then John.[48] John left to his sister Mary the landed property that their mother had just willed to him. Mary Johnson Ball Hughes had designated her executors, George Eskridge and John Johnson, to choose the location for her burial. Eskridge was left to make the decision. Mary and Elizabeth once again put on first mourning.

Richard Hughes had left the house at Cherry Point to Mary's daughter Elizabeth after Mary's death, and Mary had confirmed that in her own will. She added a suit of black-and-white calico. She wrote that it had been "part of [her] own wearing apparel." Clothing was precious in and of itself, as well as a unique reminder of its original owner. In this case, the suit carried Mary Hughes's legacy of intimacy. Mary Hughes made some special bequests to her younger daughter, including the rich bed furnishings that her husband Joseph Ball had left her, most of her clothing, two gold rings, linens, kitchen utensils, and the "good paceing horse."[49] Mary also instructed Eskridge to buy her daughter a plush silk sidesaddle. She confirmed her promise to give Mary a mare and whatever foals she produced. She stipulated that the estate purchase her a "likely young Negro woman" on her eighteenth birthday, which would bring to four the number of Mary's slaves. It would also give Mary a slave who could produce other slaves for her. Richard Hughes and Joseph Ball had both recognized the importance of enslaved women for creating wealth, and Mary Hughes embraced this lesson as well.[50] "Likely" meant many things at the time including attractive, healthy, and likely to reproduce. Finally, John's death transferred the six hundred acres that his mother had left him in Stafford County to Mary Ball.

Mary Hughes specified that her estate spend twelve pounds securing her daughter's land, knowing that now that Mary was doubly orphaned, she would be extremely vulnerable to men's claims against her Ball inheritance. As an extra protection, she put Mary "under the Tutelidge and governorship of Captain George Eskridge, during her minority," describing him as her "trust [sic] and well beloved Friend." Everything else she owned she passed on to Mary.[51]

The property arrangements unfolded as both wills were probated in July 1721, and Joseph Ball II continued to litigate with the estate of Mary Hughes over his father's properties.[52] Over that spring and summer, the new shocks settled in on Mary.

When Mary's mother died, she abruptly ended the girl's years as the focus of her care—or of anyone's. Entering adolescence, Mary had lost a father, a stepfather, a half brother, and a mother. The historians Anita and Darrett Rutman observed that such losses as hers were at the extreme end of the scale measuring "the mass trauma and disruption of childhood" that then hung over life in the Chesapeake.[53] Trauma was Mary's normality.[54] The fact that many shared these trials did not lessen Mary's pain or grief or relieve her in the coming years of the limited security and comfort she suffered as a girl.

Mary's dubious preparation for these new deaths was earlier ones. Early losses often mean a harder time coping with subsequent ones.[55] Mary had only her half sister to help her in her misery and forlornness. After the death of their mother, Elizabeth made Mary feel welcome in her home and gave her what affection and security she knew as an adolescent.

Mary Hughes had reinforced Mary Ball's position as a young slaveholder in her will with her promise of the "likely" enslaved woman. Such a woman would work for her and "breed" for her as Richard Hughes had specified of the slave he wanted his estate to purchase for Mary's mother. In losing her father, Mary had become the owner of two men and a boy. When she lost her mother, she came into the future ownership of a young, strong woman. Death brought Mary irreparable loss, as well as human property. Mary's mother's death both isolated Mary and added to the number of people who surrounded her—as possessions.

Mary's acquisition of identity as a propertied Virginian braided together emotional pain with material gain and enhanced command. Under the shock of countless deaths in this period, white Virginians gave obsessive attention in their wills and inventories to each hog, bag of grain, bucket, hoe, and length of chain that would remain after them. Wealthy colonists taking stock in their inventories and reshuffling objects, acres, years of service owed by workers, enslaved men and women, and their imagined enslaved babies have a ritualistic quality, as if these manipulations could mitigate the terrors of death. The legal battles that so frequently ensued from these rearrangements registered the aggression that accompanied and distracted the bereaved from their losses.

Apart from being attempts to ward off the blunt trauma of death, these arrangements and rearrangements reflected the struggles for consolidation and preeminence among families that began in the late seventeenth century and would become more and more pronounced over the decades to come. Mary Johnson Ball had tasted the life close to the top in her years with Joseph Ball. As a mother, she worked tirelessly to protect her children's, but particularly her youngest daughter's possibilities for becoming part of the world she had briefly enjoyed. As a single mother, she labored to enhance little Mary's choices in joining a wealthy clan. Richard Hughes's legacy to his stepchildren resonates with that lonely man's desire to solidify and thank his acquired family at a time when a few assorted people huddling together gave enhanced meaning to his world. His widow brought her suits and left her legacies knowing that if the remnants of her family would succeed, it would be through the possibilities of a decent dowry for her orphan daughter.[56]

At her young age, Mary had mastered the catechism and the tenets of Anglicanism. The adults around her would have encouraged her to derive the prescribed religious lesson from her brother's and mother's deaths, to try to focus on their translation to a better world through the loving intercession of Jesus Christ. This behavior would have won her the approval of the half sister and brother-in-law on whom she was suddenly dependent, now that she no longer had a mother. Her mother's home, Cherry Point, now came into the hands of Elizabeth and Samuel Bonam.[57] It was strenuous work to keep her feelings in check and to put a stoic face on the gravest loss of her short life. Her prolonged exercise of will would not make her flexible or deeply empathetic in future intimate relations.

In late 1721, William Dulaney, who had been familiar to young Mary as her mother's overseer, sued George Eskridge, the executor of her mother's estate, for unpaid services. Mary's brother Joseph Ball considered overseers "a parcel of slubbering sons of bitches," but Dulaney had been a part of Mary's world on the Cherry Point farm.[58] The court determined in October 1723 that the estate owed him twenty-one pounds and ten shillings for a year's work. The court permitted Dulaney to recover this in tobacco, corn, beans, wheat, and salt. The damages were substantial for a household with a relatively small workforce. Eskridge, as executor, would have charged the estate fees, further draining the resources going to Elizabeth and any surplus to buy the "likely" slave for Mary.[59]

George Washington often wrote later that imaginary feelings of material want plagued Mary in her older years.[60] But the loss of so many adults in such a short time, including the mother who had been the one constant force in an unstable world, could easily have created powerful feelings of want and of an insufficiency of guidance and protection. The familiar

Dulaney, suing her mother's estate and recovering damages, must have been a terrible affliction. He had to come to Cherry Point and leave Mary's home with 697 pounds of tobacco and nine barrels of corn and bushels and half bushels of wheat, beans, and salt—all precious provender—a deeply unsettling sight.

The central supports in her short life had washed away. A child's identification with a parent intensifies with that parent's death and would have resulted in severe worry and fear of her own death.[61] Mary was terrified of thunderstorms. According to family tradition, a close friend was struck by lightning while eating. Her fork and knife were reputed to have melted. Some historians have used the utensil-melting detail to question all or part of the story's validity, while others have given the fear credence.[62] It seems plausible that Mary might well have associated an incident involving lightning and a friend's death to explain the panicky feelings to which all these deaths made her prone. Her mother's death and the others she had endured might have produced little effect on her surface but left terror and grief imperfectly suppressed just below. Mary's stoical repression of sorrow and fear could easily have generated sudden and debilitating attacks of anxiety.

In her last years, when Mary was spending much time at her daughter Betty's home in Fredericksburg, she disappeared one evening during a thunderstorm. Betty found her upstairs on her knees praying. She got up and told Betty that she had been "striving for years against this weakness, for you know, Betty, my trust is in God; but sometimes my fears are stronger than my faith."[63] Mary's lifelong efforts to contain her fears for herself and for others would give her a memorably stoical veneer but leave the fears running loose below the surface.

Losing a parent is likely to make a child regress as grief occupies the energy that would normally be absorbed in growth. In the best of circumstances, a remaining parent or substitute will understand this need and tolerate it. Mary was just entering puberty, and her mother's death might have inhibited the sexual and romantic restlessness that initiates adolescence.

But she could not comfortably become more childish and rely on her sister to understand and comfort her, because Elizabeth was preoccupied with her new household responsibilities and taking over the management of Cherry Point. Mary's need to allay her sensation of free fall in the absence of her mother and the cultural sanctions against uncontrolled behavior would have combined to make her suppress strong displays of emotion. Her most immediate emotional task was to attach herself as firmly as possible to her older sister, to become indispensable to her. Her need to ensure her spot in a household that no longer belonged to her mother would probably have directed her away from the socializing that was increasingly a part of the lives of young people her age and toward the household management that would make her an asset, not a burden.

4

MARY, HER KIN,
AND HER BOOKS

LIZABETH JOHNSON BONAM GAVE the bereft girl shelter and affection. Mary named her first daughter Elizabeth, and late in his life George treated her descendant with his careful but real generosity, doing his best by his mother's kin. But from this time on, Mary had to raise herself, and she did so by working hard and making herself useful.

During his presidency, George Washington shared responsibility with his sister, Betty (Elizabeth), for his orphaned niece Harriot. He gave the girl advice that would have guided his mother at this point in her life as well.

He told the fifteen-year-old that because her "fortune [was] small—[to] supply the want of it . . . with a well cultivated mind, with dispositions to industry and frugality—with gentleness of manners—obliging temper—and such qualifications as will attract notice, and recommend you to a happy establishment for life." He went on to describe "many girls'" experience, which seems to conform remarkably to that of his mother. "Many girls before they have arrived at your age have been found so trustworthy as to take the whole trouble of a family from their Mothers; but it is by a steady and rigid attention to the rules of propriety that such confidence is obtained."[1] Mary practiced industry and frugality. On her own, she cultivated her mind and learned the "rigid rules of propriety" and manners from her kin.

Throughout her life, Mary kept up with the numerous Ball clan doings. Virginians identified strongly with their extended families. They ascribed character traits to themselves and others collectively (the Carters, for example, were considered haughty). They used the word "cousin" to indicate affection and intimacy as well as shorthand for many degrees of kinship.[2] In her later correspondence with her brother Joseph, he regularly asked for news about their surviving relatives, nieces, and nephews.

The death of Mary Ball Hughes made an opening for the growth of an affectionate, paternalistic relationship between Joseph Ball and his half sister. After settling their father's estate, he returned to England before 1716, and he and his wife, Frances, had three children there before he came back to Virginia in about 1720. Ball took his role as vestryman seriously and remained in that position until 1739, with transatlantic trips interspersed.[3] He became a significant supporter of the church in his and Mary's community.

Ball became part of a transatlantic movement to strengthen the Anglican colonial church, increasing recruitment of ministers from London. The Virginia clergy at this time were largely Scots (the Church of England had been disestablished in Scotland in 1688) and Huguenots (refugees after the Revocation of the Edict of Nantes in 1685). In 1723, Edmund Gibson ascended to the position of bishop of London, taking over responsibility for the colonial ministry. He initiated a survey of colonial ministers. The Reverend John Bell, who had been ministering to both Christ Church and St. Mary's Parish, where the Balls attended, since 1712, noted that there were about three hundred families that worshipped with him, that his territory was about forty miles by eight, and that he conducted services every Sunday and on Good Friday. He observed that his parishioners were mostly white and that he did "nothing" toward the conversion of blacks and Indians, despite Church of England enthusiasm for missionary work of this type.[4] Two years later, a survey revealed that fifteen of one hundred parishes in the colony were vacant.[5] The Society for the Propagation of the Gospel in Foreign Parts, established in 1701, was also working to build up the church in the colonies. Between 1723 and 1729, 22 percent of recruits for the ministry were from Virginia. Between 1730 and 1739, 33 percent were Virginians.[6]

Joseph Ball took a personal interest in expanding the colonial base of the Virginia ministry. Ball was back in the colonies after completing his studies at Gray's Inn. (He had been called to the bar in 1725 or 1726.)[7] In 1729, Ball pushed a proposal "concerning a certain number of young gentlemen, Virginians born, in the study of divinity, at the country's charge . . . and on his prayer ordered to be certified to the General Assembly." The church permitted him and his cousin Major James Ball (1678–1754) to build a gallery in White Chapel Church for their families as long as it was decorated like the adjacent gallery.[8] In Joseph, Mary had a substantial counselor and very visible supporter of the church.

If her brother projected respectability, her sister Easter revealed Ball family secrets. Right after Mary's mother's death, Easter Ball Chinn sought legal relief from decades of marital violence. Her husband, Rawleigh Chinn, whose receipt for 190 acres from Joseph Ball Mary Johnson had witnessed in 1702, had been abusing Easter and having an affair for several years with the widow Margaret Ball Downman, a cousin of Easter and Mary's. Margaret and Rawleigh had three sons. Easter made no reference to the liaison, perhaps because it was not grounds for a separation if the man was at fault, as was the case in Massachusetts. Chinn does not seem to have concealed his activities and later left land, slaves, furniture, and livestock to these children, but not, conspicuously, to Downman's children by her husband. Easter testified that her abuse began before Mary was born, but she left her husband only in 1722 after almost two decades of marriage.

Easter swore at Lancaster County court on July 11, 1722, that she was pregnant and feared her husband Rawleigh Chinn's assaults and refusal to provide for her and her unborn child. Chinn brought several friends to testify for him, and the court dismissed Easter's case. She sued one of Rawleigh's character witnesses for perjury, but the court also dismissed these charges. Her case finally got the court's attention when Rawleigh Chinn "redicul[ed] in his authority" one of the magistrates, Easter's younger and Mary's older brother, Joseph Ball. Chinn also sued Joseph Ball for assault and trespass. Chinn, in turn, was sued for fighting with several people. Having dismissed Easter's charges against Chinn and his friend, the court reversed itself and granted Easter a legal separation and twenty-five pounds sterling a year or four thousand pounds of tobacco.

Not even Easter Chinn's high status and the presence of several Ball family members on the Lancaster court could move the magistrates to interfere with the rights of her husband until Chinn called the authority of his magistrate brother-in-law into question. Twenty years later, Chinn granted a final twenty-five pounds sterling to Easter, provided that she not seek her dower third from his estate. Easter Chinn died in 1749, estranged from all of her children but Ann. She left her daughter and namesake, Esther Shearman, what was left of her estate.[9] In a chilling epilogue, twelve years later in 1761, Mrs. Ann Conway Chinn died. Her father, Colonel Conway, called a jury to examine her body because he suspected that his son-in-law, Thomas, Rawleigh Chinn's son, had killed her by "beating & abusing her."[10]

Divorce was not a possibility in the southern colonies where the established Anglican church counted marriage a sacrament, not a civil contract, as Dissenters did. There were no ecclesiastical courts in the colonies to intervene in marriages; the only possibility for a divorce in the Anglican New World was an act of Parliament, and no Virginian attempted this feat. A few couples, like the Chinns, formally separated, and from time to time a wife petitioned successfully for support. Far more wives sacrificed the support and left, if they had anywhere to go. For a wife to be successful in acquiring court-ordered support, she had to convince the authorities, against her husband's word, that her life was in danger. Easter contended that Chinn was beating and starving her. But only when Chinn attacked her brother did the magistrates act.

In England, a husband's authority to inflict punishment upon his wife was reined in somewhat by the interventions of neighbors who would be likely to see excessive violence against wives as destabilizing to their community. In Lancaster County, however, neighbors lived far away from one another, and in the absence of a powerful state and the presence of thousands of restive and angry Africans and Afro-Virginians, magistrates knew that it took strong patriarchal authority to maintain the status quo.[11]

In England, wealthier women, like Chinn, were often less willing to complain of violence in the home than poorer ones were. Easter Chinn had endured twenty years and several pregnancies before making a complaint. She might have been reluctant to come forward because she feared the publicity.[12] She also might have been unwilling to come forward because Virginia had enacted legislation against "brabling women" in 1662. The law asserted that women's talk often constituted slander, and because wives had no legal existence in themselves, their damaging talk caused their husbands to pay the fines that they incurred. It stipulated that women could be ducked (that is, tied to a stool and plunged underwater) for slander if their husbands could not or did not wish to pay their fines. The statute asserted the mendacity of women and established a severe—and humiliating—punishment if their talk was found to be without basis or "disorderly." The burden of proof was heavy, and the consequences harsh for a woman who challenged the authority of a patriarch.[13] We have seen how little import the court gave Easter's words until Rawleigh Chinn had the poor judgment and/or sufficient alcohol to attack his justice of the peace brother-in-law.

With unusual courage—or feeling unusually desperate—Mary's elder sibling testified to her high-living husband's frequent brutality.[14] Family talk would have circulated Easter's problems and Rawleigh's behavior long before she went to court. But the details of violence and abuse became a public topic shortly after Mary's mother's death, a time of exhausting emotional overload for a girl entering puberty, already a moment of charged sensibilities and volatile emotions. She could not have missed the striking contrast between her widowed mother's autonomy and her married sister's confinement and abuse. Heavy emotional losses spliced with family tales of many years of beatings accompanied her entry into a womanhood that might have seemed neither uniformly safe nor inviting.

Before Easter's case was resolved, in the heat of July 1723, Elizabeth had little Samuel Bonam, her first son. Mary, about fourteen, would have helped her sister at the birth of her nephew.[15] If Elizabeth felt strong and warm, if she had good color and was not unhappy, humoral medical theory (based on the idea of maintaining the proper balance among the four humors) predicted she was carrying a boy.[16]

Mary, at the time of Elizabeth's giving birth, was old enough to have absorbed the medical and philosophical lore that regarded the uterus as "unclean, filthy, and foul" and potentially as a "breeder of poison." Medical writers described the womb as performing a dirty, excretory function whether the product was unclean menstrual blood, the afterbirth, or amniotic fluid. Writers portrayed childbirth as a great "evacuation," confirming with scientific authority what the doctrine of Eve's sin laid out theologically: that a holy intervention was necessary after the female mess, disorder, and corruption of childbirth.[17] The almost complete silence of early colonial women on childbirth indicates their discomfort with the topic.[18]

Although Mary might have witnessed and helped at other births, she would have had a privileged place performing the rituals and duties attendant on her sister's delivery. They had both lost the mother who should have been there to educate and comfort them. Mary's experience confirmed her membership in the world of women by the early age of fourteen or fifteen, because she had witnessed and assisted at both death and birth. Through religious ideas, medical lore, and her family's use of the law, she had also absorbed a large dose of ideology that underpinned women's subordination.

Six weeks after the birth of Samuel, religious tradition called Elizabeth to the local church, where the Reverend John Bell would have read a psalm giving thanks for Elizabeth's safe delivery and said some prayers including the Lord's Prayer, thus purifying, or "churching," her after childbirth. In some accounts, churching was the occasion for a jolly women's get-together for eating and drinking; other accounts stress the mother's humbling need to be cleansed after the pollutions of childbirth.[19] This ritual sanctioned her and her husband's resumption of sexual relations and her return to public worship. In the six weeks before churching, Mary would have had much to do looking after her sister and the new infant and running the household.[20] As her son wrote at the end of the century, she was "found so trustworthy as to take the whole trouble of a family from their Mothers."

IIIIIIIIIIIIII

MARY'S BROTHER-IN-LAW, Samuel Bonam, witnessed a deed in 1724 with his uncle George Eskridge, a year after his son, Samuel, was born.[21] But in February 1726, he became sick and wrote his will, leaving all his land to his son, Samuel, and to the child his wife was carrying (who apparently did not survive). He designated his powerful kinsman George Eskridge as guardian of his children, something Eskridge was accustomed to, because he was overseeing the adolescence of Mary.[22] He also left to his young sister-in-law Mary a "young dapple gray riding horse."

After this death, Mary and Elizabeth had to look after young Samuel and the household and to repeat to one another the Anglican mantra not to indulge in grief but to remember life's brevity and the eternal peace and beauty of salvation. They would have washed Samuel's corpse and with the help of the Eskridges buried him. Afterward, neighbors and kin would drink wine and eat biscuits with them.

Bonam's bequest expressed real affection for his wife's young sister, gratitude for her help in the household, and the confidence that a horse would be a welcome gift for the capable and enthusiastic rider she had become.[23] First her mother and now her brother-in-law recognized and encouraged her physical strength, daring, and independence. Mary, vigorous and strong, enjoyed her horses and developed a lifelong love of the beauties of the Virginia countryside. These were no small gifts given the long string of sad and frightening events that had punctuated her life. George, like his mother, would enjoy horses, becoming a famously gifted horseman.

Bonam's legacy to Mary now made her the owner of three horses and her mother's elegant silk sidesaddle. The Virginia gentry admired good horsemanship, and although both men and women rode, it was less common among women than men. Mary cared about horses throughout her life. Older gentry women, including Mary in later years, were more likely to use a carriage than a horse. As the gentry grew richer and more established, young women rode horseback less frequently than their predecessors, usually traveling in less sporty and exposed ways.[24]

Few documents associate women with horses, a pairing that was all but universal among men. Visitors to Virginia observed that "everyone" owned a horse and that Virginians rode even short distances rather than permit themselves ever to be seen on foot. A Swiss visitor, in 1701, predicted that "it must be a poor man who cannot afford [a horse]."[25] And Devereux Jarratt, who trained his brother's horses, confirmed that observation, noting that he was so poor that he had neither a horse nor a saddle.[26] As one historian has noted, "Without a horse, a planter felt despised, an object of ridicule."[27]

When Mary was a girl, hunters captured the small, hardy, and swift wild horses that still roamed Virginia. They would wait until April, when the horses were hungry, and tempt them with corn. Girls rode those "light-footed" Virginia horses, which by the 1750s would be bred with English horses of Arabian descent.[28]

Planters usually had a hired hand or slave tend their horses. Mary might have enjoyed exercising her own horses; George would enjoy the challenge of breaking them in. George would later regard the exercise of riding as essential to his health. There is no quotation from Mary saying this, but she seems to have instilled this idea in her children.

The gentry girls who rode for pleasure and exercise bought riding clothes through Virginia and London merchants. Mary's plush silk side-saddle had the pommel moved slightly to the left of center and curved to secure the rider's right leg. Women wore some sort of overskirt, boots, and cloaks to protect against dust and cold. They also sometimes wore panta-loons under their skirts to provide a layer between the chafing and sweat of the horse and their legs.[29]

Around the time Mary learned to ride, an adequate horse cost three to eight pounds sterling, or about twenty-five dollars.[30] By the later eigh-teenth century, a good racing horse cost as much as seventy-five dollars.

The traveler who noted that only a very poor man in Virginia did not have a horse observed that Virginians "never ride them in a walk, but al-ways in a gallop, as if a deer was running." A Jamestown minister memo-rialized the "Planter's pace" as "a good sharp hard gallop."[31] Another observer described the gait as a canter and was surprised to see how well women, too, kept their seats. Doubtless Mary, whose mother had prom-ised her a good "paceing horse," rode at the Virginia speed. Riding side-saddle at a gallop made her equestrian feats even more daring.[32] On horseback, she would have been able to visit kin and friends, keeping up with Ball relatives to the west of Cherry Point in Lancaster County or vis-iting George Eskridge's plantation nearby when her sister could spare her. (Eskridge's second wife was only eight or nine years older than Mary, and they had a daughter just a bit younger.)[33] It took about an hour to cover seven miles.

George's skill on horseback was legendary. Jefferson said that "he was the best horseman of his age, and the most graceful figure that could be seen on horseback."[34]

Mary became a graceful dancer, as well as a rider, a pastime she enjoyed well into her fifties. Between 1722 and 1727, Robert Carter, who lived across Corotoman Creek from where Mary was born, hired a dancing master to come once a month from Williamsburg to give his children and others a day of dancing instruction. Colonel James Ball, Joseph Ball's cousin and Mary's first cousin once removed, who lived on Joseph Ball's side of the creek, brought the same teacher for his children. Because dancing was even more important for girls than for boys, George Eskridge, closer to home than James Ball, doubtless had a dancing master for his daughters. He was a frequent visitor at Robert Carter's and would have known the dancing master. There would have been many good opportunities for Mary to learn the minuet, country dances, jigs, and reels locally, particularly because she was mobile.[35]

In addition to housewifery, riding, and dancing, Mary began her tiny but precious collection of devotional books in these years. Given Joseph Ball's embrace of the mission of the church and his paternal interest in Mary, it seems likely that he gave her the first of these.

Mary was nineteen or twenty in 1728 when she wrote her name into John Scott's *Christian Life, from Its Beginning, to Its Consummation in Glory*, first published in London in 1681. Joseph Ball traveled to England frequently. Men were much more likely than women to order English products like books both from Great Britain and from local merchants. Ball, like other gentry men, knew that education for girls in this period was about moral training, not intellectual achievement. Scott's volume provided a moral framework for life—a proper gift from a self-consciously Christian older brother and vestryman to his considerably younger and poorer orphan sister.

Scott's advice would have served a young woman particularly well when she became marriageable, as Mary now was. Protestants saw conversion as a useful prelude to the subjection required for women in marriage. Scott's volume recommended Christian virtues like meekness, resignation, and humility that a wife would need if she hoped for a peaceful marriage in a patriarchal world. Mary emphasized humility to herself, her children, and her grandchildren, as they would recall.

Scott did not direct this book at a female audience.[36] The wealthy planters Robert Carter and William Byrd also had copies of the work.[37] Mary would later come to own James Hervey's *Meditations Among the Tombs*, which was written for women, but Scott and her later favorite, Matthew Hale's *Contemplations Moral and Divine*, she taught to her boys and girl alike.

Mary's orphan status was less remarkable at twenty than at twelve, but it had left her with years of unasked questions. An Anglican divine's pages could have answers and guidance that children with parents could get more easily. George's fascination at a slightly younger age with the *Rules of Civility and Decent Behaviour in Company and Conversation* provides a parallel. Both adolescents had gaps to fill in occasioned by parental loss.

Scott's text resonated with Mary's need for solace. He warned his readers that some of them would need more than average patience and fortitude to get through life. Besides the everyday difficulties, "it may be your lot to take up the Cross too, and to follow your Saviour through a dark lane of suffering . . . and then you will need a world of Patience and Courage to . . . fight your way to heaven if ever you come there." Mary could have recognized herself in Scott's description of a Christian who had already had to take up her cross. Scott's work offered the special comfort of describing loss and sadness seriously and recognizing that it required special fortitude to traverse painful times.[38]

Scott's seventeenth-century prose and thought offered instruction, not recreation or escape. Mary was born before the rapidly growing popularity of fiction. She was even born before the publication of most of the conduct manuals for women. Her reading experience did not resemble that of women a generation later, like the future Martha Washington, who grew up with novels. Martha and many young gentry women enjoyed romantic stories that encouraged them to imagine themselves in thrilling situations with impetuous lovers. Mary read Scott slowly, ruminating on his teachings and applying them to her life. He wrote as her superior and instructor, not an exciting friend. She would not model her spoken and written English on the self-consciously witty or well-turned phrases of novelists or take, as young girls would in the later eighteenth century, a romantic alias and adopt an arch writing style.[39] She would, instead, turn what happened to her into moral and religious lessons for herself and for her children and grandchildren, who remembered them vividly. Her intimacy with her favorite texts shaped both her observations and her language.

Scott advised his readers to read and reread his book many times. George Washington and George Washington Parke Custis (George's step-grandson) recalled that Mary pored over Matthew Hale's *Contemplations Moral and Divine* and read it to her children and grandchildren. She probably developed her reading habits with her first book.[40] Repetitive reading gives comfort, and rehearsing familiar aspirations and homilies can calm and focus the mind. The Anglican Isaac Watts, famous for his book of hymns, among other writings, called memorized words "a constant furniture, that [Christians] may have to . . . think upon when alone."[41] Devotional reading lodged precepts of modesty, industry, obedience to superiors, obedience from inferiors, and the constant awareness of God in Mary's mind. It gave her easy access to a template for responding to events and thinking about the problems and circumstances that faced her.[42]

Scott's suggestions for private devotions in the morning and evening include instructions for closeted prayers (the texts of which he provided) and for ways to express "thanksgiving" and "repentance" and to experience "humiliation." Martha's grandson George Washington Parke Custis specifically remembered her as an older woman retiring for private devotions: "Abstracted from the world and worldly things, she communed with her Creator in humiliation and prayer."[43] Scott recommended that Christians frequently examine their actions for fear that they might heedlessly fail to tax themselves with sins they had committed. He advised taking a tally every evening to "censure the actions of the day."

Scott advised that "we should humble and abase ourselves in our own eyes [and] be touched with a sense of our vileness, [knowing that] God stands off at the Stench of our Abominations not withstanding all his Benignity towards us."[44] (Seventeenth-century Virginians were quite likely to have Puritan authors alongside Anglican ones in their libraries, but this grew less common in the eighteenth century. Scott employed the stinging language of Puritans.)[45] Elsewhere he added that we should keep in mind "the little Reason we have to be proud of any Personal Accomplishments, whether it be of Body or Mind, to strut like Esop's Crow, in these borrowed feathers, which are wholly owing . . . to the Divine Bounty."[46] The *OED*'s 1639 quotation from the Puritan divine William Whately expresses this understanding of the word. "That is true humility to have a meager esteem of himself out of an apprehension of God's greatness." Mary and her generation would have given this meaning to humility, and her personal struggle would have been to reveal the sin and corruption of her human nature when isolated from God.

By the middle of the next century, when Mary was in middle age, the word had taken a secular meaning. The *OED* quotes David Hume in 1757 describing humility as "dissatisfaction with ourselves on account of some defect or infirmity." This meaning of "humility" no longer invites the reader to compare herself with God and instead shifts to one's unhappiness with oneself. The word no longer conveys a religious truth. George Washington, who was, not coincidentally, deeply preoccupied with humility and its other side—pride, honor, and reputation—would come to understand the word differently from how his mother did, that is, as a secular revelation of inadequacy or failure and to be avoided at all costs.

This book gave Mary much guidance. Private devotions were extremely significant to religious Virginians. As one historian observes, they seem to have had a "'hidden piety' of holy conversation, private prayer . . . and biblical reflection."[47] Home prayer and religious contemplation especially helped women for whom it was often difficult to get to church or visit the minister—either because of distance or because of domestic duties. Guidance from books and tracts substituted for pastoral advice on how to order one's days in a godly fashion, on prayers for different occasions, on how to regulate one's behavior in ways agreeable to God. Virginia law recognized the obstacles to frequent church attendance by requiring church attendance only once every month in the seventeenth century and amending that already relaxed rule (by New England standards) to once every two months in the early eighteenth century.

Scott discouraged sectarian thinking and did not fuel inter-Protestant fighting that had so recently (only forty-odd years before publication of his book in 1681) resulted in civil war. As a twenty-year-old in a colonial, Anglican society with sprinklings of Quakers, Huguenots, and Presbyterians, Mary had contact with varieties of Christians. But she would probably have cared more about Scott's thoughts, written with immediacy, intimacy, and directness, about how to behave in a very stratified society, how to think about death, and how to carry on a continuous and sustaining religious life without much external guidance. But it is significant that the authors of all of Mary's books were "latitudinarian"—writers who stayed clear of the "schismatic" way of the sixteenth and early seventeenth centuries.[48] Her son famously avoided sectarian religious thought.

Scott's social and political views would have been familiar to Mary. He based his text on English, not colonial, society. Scott, like Locke, wrote about the necessity for a social contract for the protection of people and property, invoking rationality as the way to understand God's purposes. He saw God's hand in the creation of worldly inequality.[49] Scott did not envision mobility in this world, where rank indicated one's obligations to superiors and inferiors. He recommended that Christians be "peaceable" in their "states" and "relations," carrying themselves modestly "toward those that are *Superior* to us in our Society" and behaving "condescending[ly] to all that are *Inferior*."[50] Scott's worldview flattered slave owners and justified coercion if their inferiors did not obey with alacrity.[51] Scott's comments on hierarchy and obedience helped obscure the distinctly non-Christian work of slave management. The closest he came to taking on the brutality of inequality was to comment that a good Christian should not *"oppress* or *overreach* [others] or to deal so *hardly* by them as either not to allow them any share of the profit . . . or not a *sufficient* share for them to subsist and Live by, is an injurious Invasion of that natural Right" to life.[52]

Scott exhorted good Christians to pursue their callings with energy and persistence.[53] Mary's mother's life exemplified the zealous stewardship of her goods in the pursuit of her calling. "The holiest service that we doe is an honest calling, though it be but to plow or digge, if done in obedience and conscience of God's commandment." Mary embraced vigorous activity, as did her eldest two children. *Christian Life, from Its Beginning, to Its Consummation in Glory* was the earliest volume in Mary's precious library and a beginning guide to her own thought and behavior.

Mary's brother Joseph Ball's later instructions to his overseer exhibit the ways Scott's teachings could produce a bizarre mix of inhumanity and solicitous concern. Ball's letters capture something of the way slaveholders in Mary's family held together their awareness of Christian teachings and daily violations of them. Ball's repetition and careful details blend his business acumen with his desire to be "condescending" in providing for "my Negroes." "I would have you make the overseer take care that they have good wood enough always at the door, especially in cold weather . . . a good fire is the life of a Negro. . . . The Coarse Cotton . . . was designed for Blankets for my Negroes: There must be four yards and a half to each Blanket. They that have not two Blankets already; that is one tolerable old one, and one pretty good one, must have what is wanting to make it up. Four and one half yards in a blanket. And every one of the workers must have a good suit . . . not to scanty nor bobtail'd. . . . I would not have you think that once reading it [my instructions] over, when you first receive it, will be sufficient. I must desire you to read it over now and then; else I am sure you will not know what I would have done."[54]

71

Ball wanted his nephew to treat his letter like a devotional text, reading it repeatedly and looking for its deepest meanings—marking the slave owner's anxiety about both caring properly for his human property and his own conscience. George Washington would often advise his managers on how to read his extraordinarily detailed instructions as well.

〜〜〜〜〜〜〜〜

HISTORIANS HAVE SEEN Puritans as the foundation of the industrious, thrifty, pleasure-deferring bourgeoisie and ushers of capitalism. But Scott, the Anglican, describes the business of life and the business of religion as identical, sometimes using metaphors that Puritans used of banking and credit to make his points.[55] "To mind our own Business is part of our Religion, and 'tis that particular part to which God's Providence hath called us." He goes on to explain that if we are unfaithful in our own worldly business, that makes us bad servants of God and that no one should be "maintained in their Sloth and Idleness." A Christian who spends too much time in his church or closeted in prayer and fails to tend his garden, family, or business is a poor servant of God. For Mary Ball, caring for her sister's household, and eventually her own, would have, in Scott's judgment, equal value with her sequestered devotions. In a slave society, it was easy for slave owners to find themselves maintained in sloth and idleness. Mary would not be among them.[56] Nor would her children George and Betty.

Scott's book offered a range of supports for Mary at a time when she had much complex and painful experience to make peace with. These particular challenges had to produce unease in a young, parentless woman of marriageable age. Mary's identity as a young propertied woman (and graceful rider of horses) would have provided her with an anchor in the otherwise choppy waters of her youth. Scott's text would not have challenged Mary's developing command of her slaves, so crucial to her sense of who she was. It would instead have affirmed her brother's oft-repeated and self-serving descriptions of his obligations to his human property.

The Reverend John Scott confirmed the righteousness of Mary's industry, command, oversight, and frugality as prudent stewardship during her passage on earth. These activities matured and groomed this tall, serious girl to have a role in the ruling class.

5.

MARY BALL,
AUGUSTINE WASHINGTON,
AND MATTHEW HALE

HEN MARY WAS ABOUT TWENTY-TWO, in March 1731, she married the thirty-six-year-old widower Augustine Washington. Augustine, like Mary, descended from a seventeenth-century Anglican immigrant who had come to Virginia to make his fortune. Augustine and his grandfather Captain John Washington shared restlessness, energy, acquisitiveness, and a short life span. The Washingtons, much like the Balls, used their wits, their connections, and the courts to accumulate land and slaves and hang on to them. Augustine (1694–1743), or Gus, had been orphaned young like Mary. His father, Lawrence, died in March 1698, at thirty-eight, when Augustine was three. Lawrence had bequeathed a quarter of his property to his three children and his wife, Mildred Warner, daughter of the Speaker of the House of Burgesses, with special bequests to other family members and friends.[1] He had made his wife and his cousin John Washington of Stafford County his executors.

Soon after his death, Lawrence's widow, Mildred, married George Gale from a wealthy ship-owning family in Whitehaven in northwest England. The couple crossed the Atlantic with one or more slaves to Gale's home in Whitehaven in 1699.[2] In May 1700, Mildred, fearing she might not survive childbirth, made her will. Right after bearing a daughter, she had her as well as her slave Jane baptized. Mildred died in January 1701, as did her infant girl carrying her name and the enslaved child.[3] Young Jane had traveled thousands of miles to die without any family nearby. Both Mildreds and Jane were buried in Whitehaven. George Gale, to whom Mildred had given custody of the boys, enrolled them in the Appleby School in Cumbria. By his seventh year, Augustine and his younger brother lost their remaining parent. Before her death, Mildred had made over to Gale one thousand pounds and divided the rest among him and the children.

Back in Virginia, the boys' cousin and Lawrence's remaining executor, John Washington (of Chotank, a stream in what is now King George County that flows into the Potomac, where that branch of the Washingtons had a plantation), took an interest in the parentless boys and in their inheritance. He sued their stepfather, and George Gale returned to Virginia in 1702 with the boys, where he won custody of them. John won on appeal, however, and Gale brought the well-traveled boys back to John in 1704. John Washington's suit, like that between William and Joseph Ball and Joseph's mother, Hannah Ball, challenged the right of a widow to dispose of property inherited from her spouse. In both cases, the court eventually decided to deny the widow's wishes. John Washington prevailed long after, but the absence of a final settlement left the boys' inheritance disputed for years to come.

While John Washington's suit and assuming guardianship smack of self-interest, his victory and the stories he told about it would certainly have impressed on the boys that their stepfather had tried to make off with their legacy from their parents. At the time Augustine wrote his own will, he guarded his children against the eventuality of Mary Ball Washington's remarrying.

Augustine Washington had achieved his majority—normally twenty-one for men—by 1715 and married the sixteen- or seventeen-year-old orphan Jane Butler shortly thereafter.[4] Augustine began married life as a planter with 1,740 acres and soon acquired the positions of justice of the peace and magistrate of the county court of Westmoreland. He began construction on a house at Pope's Creek, flowing into the Potomac in Westmoreland County, northwest of Northumberland County, not far from Chotank. In 1716, Jane bore her first child, Butler, a boy, who did not survive. She bore Lawrence in 1718, Augustine in 1720, and Jane in 1722 or 1723. In 1726 or 1727, the family occupied Wakefield, the imposing home with several outbuildings that Augustine had completed at Pope's Creek.[5]

At about the time Augustine and Jane Butler married, George Eskridge, made a widower in 1714, married Elizabeth Vaulx. Elizabeth Eskridge and Jane Washington had the same mother but different fathers. As deaths and remarriages rotated the kaleidoscope of relationships, Augustine and Eskridge became brothers-in-law.[6]

Friendship and kinship secured the political and business partnership of the brothers-in-law. Eskridge as a deputy escheator helped Augustine with his inside knowledge of sales of valuable land for which no heirs existed. Augustine busied himself acquiring slaves, adding to the number his wife brought with her. In 1722, he was charged with failing to list twenty-one tithables on whom he should have paid taxes.[7] In his will two decades later, he disposed of approximately fifty-four enslaved people. In 1726, he and Jane sold off some of her land in Westmoreland. Jane, according to the law protecting the dower property of wives, was examined separately to confirm that she was not being coerced into selling her property. Eskridge simultaneously sold off acreage. In March of that same year, Augustine bought 450 acres in Stafford County, northwest of Westmoreland, running between the Potomac and the Rappahannock. Augustine's land, on Acco- keek Run, near the tract that Joseph Ball had left Mary, had iron ore on it and signaled his entry into that business.[8] Eventually, Augustine ac- quired a total of 4,756 acres.[9] Eskridge, too, was buying land in Stafford County—purchases of 934 acres, 612 acres, and 1,115 acres.[10]

In 1727, Eskridge saw to it that the House of Burgesses entertain a bill for the encouragement of ironworks. The bill passed on March 30, 1728, with the governor's approval.[11]

Eskridge, as the more substantial of the brothers-in-law, played patron to Augustine's client, but Augustine supported Eskridge when and how he could. As sheriff of Westmoreland County, Augustine administered elec- tions in 1727. Eskridge served for a long time on the powerful Committee of Privileges and Elections, which regulated voting.[12] In 1727, the House of Burgesses received a complaint from Thomas Barnes, a merchant of Washington Parish[13] in Westmoreland County, stating that Sheriff Augus- tine Washington had denied Barnes the chance to have a poll or a voice vote, thus giving the incumbents, Eskridge and Thomas Lee, their seats with no contest. Barnes complained that Washington promised him a poll, but as the weather grew bad, Washington simply declared Eskridge and Lee the winners. According to the rules, the sheriff had the final say about when the polls were to be closed, but citizens could appeal to the House of Burgesses, as Barnes did.[14]

The decision of the committee of burgesses who met to deal with Barnes's complaint found that the election was fair. Barnes, on the next day, declared that he was "unfeignedly sorry for the offence that he has given this House." He paid a fine along with his apology.[15] The account in the *House Journal* reported that the incumbents were heavily favored, but Es- kridge was on the committee overseeing elections and had the power to shape the outcome of the story.

At the end of May 1727, Jane and Augustine deeded a number of slaves to their young sons, Lawrence and Augustine, putting them in trust to George Eskridge and a relative of Jane's.[16] Moll and her children including a boy named Lawrence, one girl named Frank, and her future children would be "for the proper use of Lawrence Washington." And Bess and her children (a girl named Bett and a boy named Guss) and girls named Priscilla and Little Sarah, along with their future offspring, would go to Augustine Washington Jr.[17] Augustine could recall his and his brother's unresolved legacies, his parents' early deaths, and the confusion and bitterness that material disputes added to his grief. This transfer "acknowledg[ing] the natural love and affection" Jane and Augustine had for their sons added immeasurably to their slaves' confusion, bitterness, and grief.

Jane and Augustine, like Joseph Ball and other wealthy Virginians, saw to it that their deaths would load their children with the riches of enslaved women and children, securing their membership in Virginia's upper echelon. Jane and Augustine put into Lawrence and Augustine's grasp the most important control seized by white lawmakers over Africans. White boys who owned black girls owned the sexuality that was both at their personal command and a source of their future wealth. White males dominated all females in Virginia, but polite rituals and paternalistic vocabulary did not disguise their power over black females, nor could protective relatives or legal dodges diminish it.[18]

In 1725, John England, a British Quaker and colonial representative of the Principio Iron Works, began negotiating with Augustine Washington to bring him into some kind of partnership in Principio.[19] They agreed to work together without a contract. In 1726, Washington leased about sixteen hundred acres of his land to Principio, and the company built a blast furnace there. In 1729, he traveled to England, returning with a contract drawn up in March 1730.[20]

On his return, in May 1730, he found to his sorrow and shock that Jane had died the previous November. Although there is no record, it seems probable that in the absence of parents the Eskridges had looked after young Lawrence, Augustine, and Jane. Eskridge, after all, was trustee of the boys' slaves and brother-in-law and friend of their father and his wife, Elizabeth, the children's aunt.[21]

Augustine and Jane seem to have had an affectionate marriage. As a mother, she had borne many brushes with death, which could increase women's piety. Jane owned the popular devotional book by Matthew Hale that would become Mary's mainstay, a book that opened with a lengthy chapter on why it was beneficial to consider one's "latter end." In a stripped-down form, Hale advised readers to face death and misery, embrace them, and let them remind you to lead a life free from hankering for worldly joys, success, honor, and luxuries that distract you from serving God. When Augustine left for England, Jane had to face at least a year apart from him as well as worries about the dangers that would attend his sea voyages. Matthew Hale's writings might have been of some comfort, although the death she had to face would be hers, not his.

Principio needed Augustine to respond to its queries about iron ore, but absorbed in his grief, he wrote instead about Jane's death.[22] George and Elizabeth Eskridge comforted their kinsman and helped him think about remarrying someone to run his home and care for his children. Very probably, Augustine already knew Mary from the association both of them had with Eskridge. If the Eskridges hosted their Washington niece and nephews at Sandy Point, Mary might well have helped Elizabeth Eskridge with the care of three extra children.

Mary and Augustine made a very common kind of marriage—between people who were interconnected in many ways, people whose lives and families had been reshaped more than once by premature death. Augustine, like Mary's father, Joseph Ball, needed someone to take care of his household, and Mary needed to marry. There was no other option for her. She moved from a life of service in the modest home of her sister to a life of service in the grander home of her husband.

Some of George's biographers have described Mary at twenty-two as old for marriage, but she was within the normal range for a bride.[23] A strong, healthy young woman with light-colored hair, clear blue eyes, and a pleasant voice,[24] Mary made an attractive pair with Augustine, also tall and strong at thirty-six, and remembered as genial and well-disposed.

A genial man must have been very welcome to Mary. Husbands, as she knew, came in varying humors (bilious, melancholic, phlegmatic). Her husband would not only set the tone of the days of her life from then on but also control her property and activities. Of course, a superficially genial man might turn out on closer inspection to have a bad temper; perhaps Rawleigh Chinn had seemed jolly to Easter on first encounter. But Mary was acquainted with her future spouse and his temperament from Eskridge's recommendations, from reports from his sister-in-law, and most important from spending time with him in the winter of 1730–1731 before their marriage.

Authors of advice to women discouraged passion and advised them to choose men they could obey, because they would have to.[25] John Scott condemned "the sensual pleasures of animals" and urged that behavior be "rational and well-grounded."[26] Given Mary's experience, she probably did not anticipate a love match, but certainly hoped that hers would be a loving marriage. She had to be grateful at her good fortune in finding a wealthy and well-connected spouse after her hardworking years on a small farm.

Passion without reason frightened parents and moralists. Around this time, Alexander Pope's controversial *Essay on Man*, praising the passions and self-love as natural and indeed sources of good for society, began to circulate in the colonies. Ultimately, a majority of Americans in the new nation would come to accept this view, but those who claimed the right to assert emotion would be the socially powerful, that is, white, property-owning men. Mary would not be among them.[27]

Mary must have looked forward to being in charge of a household of her own, although she would be isolated from her sister. Augustine, like her brother Joseph, had crossed the Atlantic more than once and had acquired much more education and worldly experience than Mary had. His wealth was comparable to her own father's and would provide her with a secure spot in the Virginia hierarchy, not at the very top, but high up the ladder. These attributes would have contributed to her willingness to imagine obeying him.

Marrying Augustine would fulfill the common hope of young Virginia women to join themselves to wealthy families. Mary would be helping Augustine to further the interests of his own family, and she would participate in that project. Eventually, she would make it entirely hers. Members of this generation of Virginians emerged from families battered by death and often divided by the Atlantic. They sheltered survivors and labored to reconstitute ties and extend new ones. Mary's mother's relationship with George Eskridge and *his* relationship with Augustine heightened the sense Mary must have had of the rightness of this union. The marriage promised to strengthen kin ties for a young woman who had experienced more of their weaknesses than many. Mary had always lived in reconfigured families; there was nothing unusual about joining another one. Her new family would consist of Augustine and his two motherless adolescent boys and little girl, Jane.

Espousals, publication of the banns, execution of the espousal contract, celebration, and consummation made up the five steps of marriage.[28] The espousals meant the parents' or guardians' or principals' negotiations of the property exchanges that the marriage would put in motion. By law, Mary did not need George Eskridge's approval of the match, because she was over twenty-one,[29] but she would have been very unlikely to marry against his wishes. (If she had, they would hardly have named her first son after him.) Eskridge had protected Mary's two pieces of property and the slaves she owned since her mother had died. Because both Augustine and Mary were orphans, Eskridge doubtless felt sure that he was fulfilling his obligation to Mary and her mother by seeing her married to his brother-in-law and protégé. No one else seems to have been involved in coming to this agreement, although in some cases as many as five groups were parties to a marriage settlement.[30] Mary retained title, although the paperwork would disappear, to her father's bequest of land that abutted Augustine's ironworks and those of Principio.[31]

Mary owned several slaves, although it is difficult to tell exactly how many. She had inherited Joe, Jack, and Tom from her father, and her mother's will stipulated that one be bought for her from the estate proceeds. There are no records about whether this took place.

After the principals had come to terms, the couple either got a license through the county clerk or posted banns three successive Sundays in church, waiting to see if anyone objected to their union. Because Augustine had been a justice of the court, he could have supplied the license himself. This required posting a bond and paying fees. (Mary and Augustine would have had to post banns in two churches because she was from Cople Parish and he from Washington Parish in Westmoreland County.) Posting the banns was to prevent underage couples from marrying without the consent of their elders or masters (if they were indentured servants). Banns also helped to prevent marriages of an incestuous closeness of blood—something Virginia had legislated against in May, just before Augustine was returning home. (These degrees of kinship did not outlaw first-cousin marriage, a very popular form of Virginia union.)

Mary and Augustine married on Tuesday, March 6, 1731, shortly before Lent, a time of year when the church prohibited taking vows. (Marriage was supposed to take place in church and on Sunday, but few occurred on Sunday.) Celebration of the marriage itself had to take place between 8:00 a.m. and noon. Virginians usually married at the home of the bride. This might have meant Eskridge's Sandy Point in Mary and Augustine's case.[32] The Reverend Walter Jones,[33] the minister of Cople Parish, where Eskridge was vestryman, would have come to his home. Vigorous partying followed the ceremony, with guests eating, drinking, gossiping, dancing, making jokes, bawdy and otherwise, then eating and drinking and dancing some more. Mary's sister Elizabeth would certainly have been there, as would her brother Joseph and his wife, Frances. A Ball sister like

Hannah Ball Travers might have shown up to celebrate Mary's good fortune. In the evening, the revelers, with varying degrees of ribaldry, would have wished the couple well as they retired to bed.[34]

||||||||||||

TWO VERY SMALL gold rings of Mary's lie in a small box of her few remaining possessions at Mount Vernon. She received two rings from her mother and a mourning ring from her stepson Lawrence after his death. It is possible that her daughter, Betty, might have taken one at the time of her mother's death because her mother instructed her to take two or three articles of her "wearing apparel," before they were divided among the granddaughters.[35] It is possible that Augustine gave her one of these rings. Or, because a gold ring once given was not to be removed except ritually, perhaps her family interred Mary wearing her wedding ring. Early modern men and women saw the ring finger as a direct channel to the heart.[36]

We have only indirect access to the emotional content of Mary and Augustine's life together. The presents he gave her, like several fashionable tea sets, communicate affection and comfort. The fact that she conceived children steadily, every two years or less, indicates that their physical connection was continuous. Her two oldest children made comfortable and affectionate marriages, and the others did as well as far as the scantier evidence shows. This is suggestive, not, of course, dispositive.

As a kind of mute declaration of intent, Mary signed her name in one of Augustine's first gifts, Jane's devotional book: Matthew Hale's *Contemplations Moral and Divine*. She signed directly below the signature of her predecessor, Jane Butler.

Augustine wished for a pious successor to his first wife. If Mary harbored hopes to be recognized for her individuality, she would have been disappointed. But there is no reason to assume that she cherished such desires. Her identity, to use a word that did not then mean what it does now, emerged from and merged with those of her kin, those she took care of and those on whom she depended. Marriage re-centered her on an enlarged map of mutual responsibilities. Religion provided the vocabulary for her psychological and emotional life.[37]

Some combination of the facts that Augustine gave it to her, that it had belonged to the beloved wife who preceded her, and that it resonated deeply with her experience made *Contemplations* the most important book in Mary's life. By signing her name in it, she confirmed the significance of this charged bequest. Her later life shows that it guided her days.

Hale's long first chapter on the rewards to come from thinking about "our latter end," of course, had a special resonance for Mary. And now Mary was taking the place of the young, dead Jane in the household and bed of her husband. Death could never have been too far from Mary's thoughts as she entered her childbearing years. Recently, she had witnessed her sister Elizabeth lose at least two children. Finding an author who could make her fears useful to her spiritual growth and to her daily performance of her duties promised to give her comfort and to endow her new rounds of obligations with steadiness.[38]

Hale weaves through his book the theme that each Christian must and can bear his or her burdens cheerfully. He writes of the importance of accepting contentedly pain, frustrations, bereavements, and reverses. To complain about one's misery is to challenge God's judgment. Hale assures the reader that not only can she find resignation, peace, and even cheer in the face of the greatest woes, but she must; it is her Christian duty. She who came to marriage already burdened needed these lessons. Her children and grandchildren remembered her teaching from Hale. She would have taught them these lessons among others. As a sixteen-year-old, George used these arguments on his repining sister-in-law. As an old man, George urged these arguments on his aged mother. Mary began circulating Hale's lessons, and they returned to her.

Hale's work became her greatest teaching tool. She made his thought part of herself and part of her children's thinking. Hale's focus, like Scott's, on maintaining a distance from absorption in the honors and luxuries that life offered reinforced in her both moderation as a consumer of the increasing array of things that eighteenth-century Britain offered and an inclination to pay little attention to worldly success and its symbols.[39] She strengthened her habits of industry and frugality; she tried to train her children to stewardship rather than power.

Historians have criticized her for having little interest in later life in George's victory over the British and election as president. She lived through the Revolution day by day with her daughter and son-in-law, always waiting for news from the rest of the family, so it is impossible to conclude that she took no interest in George's activities. Her step-great-grandson George Washington Parke Custis remembered her saying that all George's triumphs brought with them too much "flattery; still George will not forget the lessons I early taught him—he will not forget himself, though he is the subject of so much praise."[40] Whether she said those actual words or something similar, the point she made is completely consistent with the values Scott and Hale sustained. Emerging from the blighted landscape of her early years, she believed in humility in the face of God's perfection and her own sins. She spared her praise.

Success in this world was of no account in meriting eternal life in the next. If praise overwhelmed George and made him forget his lowly position in God's universe, his glories in battle and in civic life would not have been occasions of praise, but would have destroyed that which was important in him. Mary was clear about this. And George, whose God seems to have been a bit more distant than Mary's, struggled to retain a sense of proportion about his own importance, from youthful self-aggrandizement and hypersensitivity to a sharply controlled maturity that left observers marveling at his restraint in the face of temptations to power.

Hale's *Contemplations* engaged many, if not most, of the moral themes of Mary's life. Like Scott's volume, the book shaped her interior life beyond simply giving her a way to see that keeping thoughts of death and affliction near at hand could be a sturdy staff for her. I do not suggest that Mary lived faithfully by the maxims of Hale's and Scott's books. I only argue that these texts provided reference points and principles that she embraced. No doubt she did not live up to her favorite writers' standards. No doubt she had contradictory desires that confused her and led her in inconsistent directions. But these sanctified authors supplied her with principles to move with some confidence into a position of authority in the household of a middle-aged widower. As best she could, she passed these principles on to her children.

6.

WIFE AND MOTHER

⁀Ɡ̶FTER THEIR MARCH WEDDING, Mary and Augustine moved to Wakefield, where Jane and Augustine had lived at Pope's Creek. Augustine's wooden house, fifty-eight feet long and nineteen feet wide, with chimneys at both ends, contained eight rooms and eight fireplaces. From the big house, the Washingtons commanded the people and activities in the smokehouse, distillery, spinning house, slave quarters, drying sheds, and other outbuildings.[1] Mary was now a plantation mistress.

In the first days of her married life, Mary would have looked to see what was in the larder and had the slaves combine it or had them make pancakes for a traditional Shrove Tuesday dinner, in preparation for the semi-fasting that Virginians did during Lent. Anglicans were supposed to give up sweets, meat, and dairy during Lent. According to Virginia ministers, they did not rigorously adhere to the ideal, but for the observant, recipes from the most widely circulated cookbook featured varieties of pea soup made without the customary bacon, ham, or mutton, as well as fish and various vegetarian soups. Mary would probably have done what Augustine wanted. Of the two, she was the more devout, but not necessarily scrupulous about rules and observances. She would probably not have brought a recipe book with her, because her mother had been semi-illiterate. Perhaps she inherited one with the keys to the larder and store cabinets at Pope's Creek.[2]

Shrove Tuesday was traditionally a day in which boys threw cudgels and stones at a cock that was tethered to a stake or buried in the ground up to its neck. It is not clear whether this "almost universal" practice in rural England continued in Virginia.[3] In England by the 1740s, writers were beginning to point out that it was cruel.

At the time of Mary and Augustine's wedding, thirteen-year-old Lawrence Washington and eleven-year-old Augustine (also called Austin) Washington attended the Appleby School in Cumbria, Great Britain, where their father had studied. Mary took into her full-time care the sad, bewildered, motherless nine-year-old Jane.

Mary well knew how little Jane felt. A planter in Stafford County, recalling his childhood losses, wrote to his mother in 1698, "Before I was ten years old as I am sure you very well remember I look'd upon this life here as but going to an Inn, no permanent being." But he dreamed up this metaphor long after he was nine.[4] Hale's and Scott's devotion to the benefits of contemplating our own end and the ephemeral nature of life was of much less use to a child reeling from the loss of a parent than to a grieving adult. Mary's training in stoically carrying on might not have helped dispel Jane's woe.

The young Mrs. Washington characteristically solved problems by working hard, and she would have begun to introduce Jane to housekeeping responsibilities. Mary was likely a more hands-on housekeeper than Jane's mother had been, because she came from humbler origins. From Mary's point of view, Jane was of an age to be responsible for some household tasks in the kitchen or the cowshed and the vegetable garden. While Jane might have found employment dulled her loss, she might also have resented her stepmother's expectations of discipline and industry.

Mary now commanded or, in the words of one slave owner, tried to make slaves of the people she and Augustine owned.[5] Jane knew them better than Mary did. Jane and the enslaved at Wakefield would have had to adjust to Mary's no-nonsense style of management, frugality, and incessant activity. The slaves at Pope's Creek numbered between twenty and twenty-five, including Bess, Bett, Priscilla, Little Sarah, Moll, and Frank, whom Jane had put in trust for her sons. An inventory of house slaves taken at the time of Augustine's death some ten years later mentions Lucy, Sue, Judy, Nan, Betty, Jenny, Phillis, and Hannah. The men included Jack and Jack (at least one of whom probably came with Mary), Bob, Ned, Dick, Toney (who might also have come with Mary if he was Tony of Tony and Dinah), Steven, Jo (valued at one shilling), London, George, and Jcumy.[6] Richard Hughes's slaves, Abba and Winney and Darby, went to Elizabeth in the settlement of Mary Ball Hughes's estate. They were listed along with "negro Tom," who might be the Tom whom Joseph Ball had willed Mary in 1711. James Straughan, Elizabeth Bonam's second husband, who died in 1740, also listed Dinah, who was probably the Dinah whom Joseph Ball had left his wife.

It is possible that the three young boys and men that Mary's father had willed her had all died. Fifty percent of white children died before reaching the age of ten, and the mortality rate was higher for slaves, who had demanding work, less care, less food, fewer clothes, and more exposure to the weather. They were especially vulnerable to anemia, cholera, tuberculosis, and influenza.[7]

Mary oversaw the production of home brews at Wakefield. The water in eastern Virginia was bad, and Virginians consumed on average a gallon of ale daily. Everyone thirsted. Joseph Ball ordered his plantation manager to "let the Negroes have what [cider] will do them good; but more for feasts."[8] Doctors thought alcohol good for the health. It was less expensive than milk, and in the warmth everything made from fruit started to ferment right away, so there was little choice.[9] In Virginia, women largely brewed for home consumption. There was little commercial market for liquor in early Virginia except in the labor-intensive business of running a tavern.[10] Mary's father had left his still, a costly apparatus, to his son, so Mary had to learn her skills at Wakefield.[11] She oversaw the distillation of pears and apples, peaches, and persimmons to make, respectively, "perry" (cider from pears) or cider from apples, brandy from peaches, and beer from persimmons.[12] Ale came from homegrown corn and molasses from the Caribbean. One Virginian ale started with a mix of water and crushed or whole corn kernels that was then fermented, making a sweet drink with a bite.

Mary became pregnant in June, but she would not have been certain until "quickening," or when she could feel the baby move—between four and five months—sometime in September. Given the constancy of her pregnancies, she and Augustine enjoyed what medical experts recommended: a regular sex life. In the seventeenth and eighteenth centuries, women's desire was taken for granted once it was aroused.[13] Sexual desire was believed to heat men's and women's bodies, although men's were thought to be inherently hotter. In early modern thought, both men and women contributed seeds formed by blood to create the baby. Orgasm released the seeds from both men and women. A woman's orgasm both released her own seed and sucked the man's into her. Writers advised men and women, but men particularly, not to make love lazily or feebly, lest from lackadaisical conception the resulting child not enjoy robust health. Experts thought that sexually inactive or unsatisfied women suffered from greensickness, or a longing for orgasm. Medical writers warned that greensickness among married women could inhibit reproduction and damage health, while it was a source of jokes about virgins. Writers advised husbands to give their wives frequent, enthusiastic sexual satisfaction.[14]

Mary's sister Elizabeth, who had married James Straughan after Samuel Bonam's death, was probably pregnant with one of her two girls at around the same time as Mary's first pregnancy. Mary would not have lost the freedom of horseback riding until quickening. Before that, she could have taken one of her horses and ridden much of the day to the familiar house at Cherry Point to talk to Elizabeth. She could have used affection and guidance in her new adventures—marriage to Augustine, pregnancy, household responsibilities, little Jane, and her relations with the numerous bond people who were new to her. Further pregnancies and growing household duties would keep her homebound in future years. And after quickening, medical writers discouraged vigorous physical exercise.[15]

As Mary gained weight and her shape changed, she would have loosened the strings of her bodice for comfort, revealing her chemise underneath. She would have worn a sack, a comfortable, loose, waistless garment that decades later became identified as a dressing gown—only for wear around the house. In this period, however, women wore them when and where they wished. Women did not distinguish between lingerie and outerwear in the seventeenth and early eighteenth centuries as they would later. Mary continued to dress comfortably, according to the practice of her generation, long after refined society had ruled that women should put on fussier and more elaborate clothes to appear in public.

Stepping up in social class meant higher standards for bodily cleanliness. The early eighteenth-century mistress was to appear in spotless linens and keep her family in them. Medical writers considered linen against the skin a good cleaning agent, better than daily baths, which were not common. Linen was thought to brush away the pollutions of the body—of which women accumulated the greatest and most varied share—and elite men and women typically changed their underclothing often. Mary would already have known about using buttermilk to bleach linens, but her marriage brought more linens to tend and more critical scrutiny of them, along with more enslaved laundresses to wash and iron them. As the scholar Kathleen Brown has observed, "Elite women, in particular, bore the pressures of supporting emerging class distinctions as well as overcoming an age-old presumption of their inherent filth." These pressures would grow and become a source of tension through Mary's lifetime.[16]

Colonial women had an average of eight children, more than their contemporaries in Europe. Women regarded childbearing as their duty and destiny. Some women knew how to limit childbearing. Some extended the intervals between babies by prolonged lactation.[17] A few knew about and sometimes used abortifacients and occasionally practiced infanticide. But the colonies punished abortion and infanticide and extolled the virtues of prolific women.

Women were, however, less enthusiastic about uninterrupted childbearing than men were. In the later eighteenth century, women privately discussed the health hazards of many pregnancies and thought some "Lords of Creation" should abstain from sex to protect their wives.[18] The Quaker Elizabeth Drinker expressed a feeling that resonated with many, including Mary, apparently, who, contrary to pervasive local practice when widowed, never remarried. Drinker wrote, "I have often thought that women who live to get over the time of Child-bareing, if other things are favourable to them, experience more comfort and satisfaction than at any other period in their lives."[19] Thomas Jefferson was well aware of the extreme dangers birth placed on his frail wife and watched her die after one of her excruciating deliveries.[20] But religion, the law, and men agreed on women's biological destiny and husbands' sexual rights. In Virginia, where some men referred to their wives as "breeders," men took pride in their wives' fertility.[21] Mary did not challenge her duty to bear children during her marriage, and her constitution was up to the task.

Although Mary had witnessed Elizabeth survive childbirth and knew enslaved women who had successfully given birth, she also knew of women and infants, free and slave, who had succumbed. Mary saw one of Elizabeth's babies die. Augustine's mother had died from complications of giving birth to a child who also died. While colonial women bore an average of eight children, only four of them were likely to survive to the age of ten.[22] (Five of Mary's six survived to adulthood.) Statistics for slave mothers are unknown even in the better-documented nineteenth century, but one-fifth of white mothers died in one eighteenth-century community, while slaves, exhausted by work and undernourished, died at a higher rate.[23]

First-time mothers feared death in childbirth, and for some the terror never diminished. Mary had Matthew Hale and John Scott to consult, although their advice to make peace with the possibility of death could not calm her more incarnate fears.

Mary moved through her circuit of duties and chores with perhaps less speed but more certainty as she came to know the house and Augustine's slaves better. In Virginia, tradition taught that pregnancies could go terribly wrong if a mother did not get what she craved.[24] The idea also circulated that mothers suffering a fright or experiencing an unnaturally strong desire might mark or deform their children.[25]

At Christmas 1731, Mary, feeling bulky, presided over her first celebration of Christ's birth at Pope's Creek. Ministers preached against rowdiness and gaming in remembering the birth of the Savior, but work—even slaves' work—stopped for the day, and feasting and drinking, dancing and play took over. Throughout the days until Twelfth Night, or the Epiphany, when the three kings made it to the manger, Virginians gave parties. They foxhunted, danced, drank, and ate together. Ministers offered Communion first on Christmas and three other times during those festive days. Twelfth Night concluded with a bang-up party, the high point of which was the cake. Martha Washington's granddaughter later recorded her grandmother's recipe that begins, "Take 40 eggs."[26] Mary's preparations would have been more modest, but she carried the keys and oversaw the festivities. In both cases, slaves performed the work.

In late February, when Mary began to feel contractions, her sister Elizabeth, depending on her obligations, might have come for her first delivery. Mildred Washington Gregory, Augustine's sister, and Catharine Washington, his sister-in-law, living in the vicinity, probably helped. Augustine paid a midwife because male doctors were still not welcome at the bedsides of laboring women. Attendants were friends or relatives, likely on a social plane with the laboring mother.[27] Mary's slaves provided food and drink for the women who gathered. She could have had some wine or cider to ease her pains, while her companions drank and chatted. By the time of delivery, the midwife and just one or two others would have remained. She could have given birth in a number of positions, sitting on a chair or small stool. She probably did not deliver lying down. The midwife cut the umbilical cord—its length of humorous interest, as indicative of the future size of the infant's genitalia.[28] Mothers like Mary had ready a set of childbed linens, probably in damask, to wear when presenting the infant at the "sitting up" visits of friends and relatives.[29]

The boy was born at 10:00 a.m. on February 22, 1732,[30] and although there is no written proof, his parents clearly named him for George Eskridge. Virginians liked the names of warriors, knights, and kings, and George was among their favorite. Tradition in Virginia very strongly favored the continuation of family names. Lawrence and Augustine had already been covered, and John would have been the logical next choice. The couple's joint and individual attachments to Eskridge induced them to introduce his name into the Washington line, extending their clan connections.[31]

Wealthy women like Mary spent the month after birth in bed. After the midwife went home, slaves made sure Mary stayed warm; that meant, in February and early March, a roaring fire, tightly drawn bed curtains, and piles of blankets. Slaves prepared her foods like red meat, eggs, wine, and ale to restore her strength. Mary had time to gather her energies, establish her milk, and nurse her infant.[32]

Thomas Comber's *Short Discourses upon the Whole Common-Prayer* bears both Mary's and Augustine's names. Comber devoted a section to the churching, or thanksgiving and purification, that Mary would have undergone about six weeks after the birth of George. This ceremony praised God for helping a woman survive childbirth. It also marked her ready to resume her religious duties and sex with her husband. Churching originated in a Jewish ceremony described in Leviticus and had to undergo some Christianizing to make it acceptable to Anglicans. Comber interpreted the ritual by denying that anything "but Sin makes any person unclean under the Gospel"; that is, childbirth itself did not make a woman impure, contrary to Jewish thought. According to Comber, a mother's distress in labor was the proper punishment for Eve's original sin.[33]

Although Comber wrote that it was "absurd" to perform such a ceremony at home instead of praising the Lord in public, the prominence of the Washingtons might have pressured the minister to visit Wakefield. Pastors in Virginia complained about making these house calls.[34] The Puritans prohibited churching during the English Civil War, but it seems women liked it, and with the Restoration much of the English Anglican population took it up again. It might never have been suspended in Virginia.[35]

Whether at home or in church, a minister would have begun with the Lord's Prayer and gone on to Psalm 116 or Psalm 127 or both. Comber suggested a prayer for new mothers based on Psalm 116 that recalled the pain and fear of childbirth and described the experience as being as close as humans come to the pains of hell: "I prayed earnestly in my late danger. . . . I could scarce speak I was so faint, but [he inclined his ear to me] and heard my inward and secret groans . . . the pains that are the most terrible next to those of hell violently got hold on me . . . and he was pleased to hear me . . . he was righteous in laying this punishment of the first Sin upon me, and it was purely his free Mercy to support me, and take it off from me."[36] Mary and other mothers could only have appreciated the commendation of bodily suffering, an almost unique instance of positive public attention to the female body and experience.

Because Mary had given birth to a boy, Psalm 127 was a natural (and prophetic) choice:

Sons are a heritage from the Lord,
children a reward from him.
Like arrows in the hands of a warrior
are sons born in one's youth.

Blessed is the man whose quiver is full of them.
They will not be put to shame
When they contend with their enemies in the gate.

The rector of Washington Parish, the Reverend Roderick McCullough, baptized George. Because he was a boy, he had two godfathers, Captain Christopher Brooke and Beverly Whiting, who was the brother-in-law of Augustine's brother, John Washington, and was married to Catharine Whiting.[37] Augustine's sister (George's aunt), Mildred Washington Gregory, became his godmother. George's white brocaded silk christening gown had a rose-colored silk lining.[38] Mary probably nursed George until he was about seven months old and then either gave him to a slave to wet-nurse or started him on food. She became pregnant in October 1732.[39]

Mary and Augustine's next child was a girl, born June 20, 1733, at about 6:00 a.m., whom Mary named after her sister Elizabeth. Conveniently, George Eskridge's wife was also Elizabeth, so she would have been gratified by the name as well. Around this time, Mary's sister Elizabeth gave birth to a second girl, whom she named Mary. Both Mary and Elizabeth and their children managed to escape death from pleurisy, which felled many in the spring of 1733.[40] Elizabeth followed the expected routine, naming her first daughter after herself and her second after both her mother and her sister. Mary, however, named her first daughter after Elizabeth, and never named a child after herself (and/or her biological mother), although she bore another girl. Augustine had named his second son Augustine and his fifth son John Augustine. Mary underlined the strength of her love for her sister. Perhaps the decade or so she spent with her blurred earlier memories of her mother, or perhaps the comparison favored Elizabeth. Perhaps it was an act of self-effacement.

Over time, little Betty became the mainstay in Mary's life. Betty and her mother lived near each other all of their lives, so there was no need for correspondence. They expressed their affection in exchanges of food and clothing, helpful visits, care for each other's health, gifts of work and the products of work, commiseration, and intimate talk about kin, health, religion, and neighbors.

After the arrival of Betty in June 1733, Mary probably nursed her for seven or eight months before becoming pregnant with Samuel, born on November 16, 1734. Mary's former brother-in-law Samuel Bonam, who had been kind to her, might have been the origin of this name. By Samuel's birth, Mary's deliveries should have been becoming somewhat less frightening and somewhat easier.

Mary started dressing George and Betty and later Samuel, after their swaddling months, in petticoats and an undergarment or shift of white linen—or more than one, depending on the season. On special occasions the boys might wear a broad, square collar called a falling band to distinguish themselves from girls. But otherwise, Mary dressed her boys and girls indistinguishably until she put George into breeches at about six. Gentry boys and girls also sometimes wore padded corsets to teach them proper carriage.[41] These would have been made at home. Mary made or oversaw the making of the children's clothing, household linens, and slave clothing, although Augustine had the final say over the latter.

She would not have put diapers or underwear on the toddlers. This made it easy for them to relieve themselves. They used chamber pots inside and could go outside in warmer weather. Small children might use walking stools to get around and learn to walk, but parents did little about toilet training in this relatively unregimented age.

Mary had just recovered from Samuel's birth and reassumed her duties when Jane Washington, by now about twelve years old, died. It might have been one of the childhood illnesses like measles that took her. George did not contract them as an adult, so he must have survived them as a child. Perhaps it was diphtheria, which George is known to have survived as well.[42]

It is unclear how strong a bond Mary forged with Jane; her pregnancies and births came quickly, and her duties were many. Jane alone among Augustine's children with his first wife was Mary's daily charge, and she would have taken that responsibility seriously. The girl's orphaning echoed her own. If Jane had not enjoyed helping her stepmother and caring for her new siblings, she would have been an unhappy child. Jane might have had trouble adjusting to a mother less polished than her own. Augustine seems to have been largely interested in his two older boys. There is no record of his feelings for Jane, nor of any provisions for her like his slave trusts for her brothers.

Jane's death in January 1735 ushered in a troubled year for Mary. In May, she became pregnant. When she was in her fourth month, about the time she would have begun checking for signs of the baby's quickening, Augustine moved the family about fifty miles north to an isolated spot then called Epsewasson where the Little Hunting Creek flows into the Potomac. He had slave cabins and a mill built there.[43] Later, Lawrence Washington would inherit this spot and name it Mount Vernon for the admiral under whom he served in the British navy. Epsewasson was closer to Augustine's and Mary's lands containing iron ore in Stafford County than Pope's Creek had been, but it was close to little else.

On the convoluted Virginia shoreline, the Washingtons now lived about two days' ride from Pope's Creek and about three from Cherry Point. The new house sat so far away from the road that the Washingtons could not hear passersby.[44] The distance between Mary and Elizabeth made visiting difficult.

In that same year, 1735, John England, the short, tough Quaker ironmaster and manager of the Principio Iron Works, died.[45] England had left his and Augustine's ironworks, according to Principio's historians, "in the very front rank of American colonial iron enterprises" (which, however, were quite small scale).[46] He had managed the ironworks' day-to-day operations. Epsewasson, thirty miles from the mine, remained a day's ride away for Augustine to supervise the laboring slaves and indentured servants who extracted the ore.

The Washingtons had only recently moved into Epsewasson when news arrived of the death of George Eskridge in October. Eskridge, a bridge to Mary's fractured past, had befriended and counseled her mother. He had long been a friend and protective neighbor, uncle of her sister Elizabeth's first husband. Mary's mother had relied on him, and her daughter inherited her confidence in Eskridge, extending it to—and eventually sharing it with—her husband.

To the fatherless Augustine, Eskridge had offered counsel and become a senior partner and patron in their push toward greater wealth and status. When Augustine's wife died, George directed him to a new marriage and to reengaging with life. Male writers idealized male friendship in this period, contrasting it with women's presumably less disinterested and jealousy-prone attachments. In Virginia, male friendships prevailed in which self-interest and kinship reinforced each other. A friend, wrote an eighteenth-century philosopher, "is our boon companion, or joins with us in our pleasures and diversions, or encourages us in our business, or unites in the same scheme, or votes the same way in an election, or is our patron, or dependant, who we hope will help us in rising to preferment or increasing our interest."[47] The deaths of John England and George Eskridge shook Augustine's security, leaving him without two very important supports in his life.

Augustine, indebted to Eskridge in so many different ways, would probably have made the trip to Sandy Point to share his grief with his former sister-in-law, Elizabeth Eskridge. Mary, on the other hand, six months pregnant, would certainly have wanted to go but might not have attempted the trip. Her sister Elizabeth in all probability would have attended.

Mary delivered her next child, John Augustine, in January 1736, bringing the number of small children in the house to four: three boys and

Betty. At Epsewasson, Mary was farther from those who had helped her at her previous deliveries. Augustine's Washington cousins at Chotank lived not far to the north. They doubtless helped, in particular Augustine's sister, Mildred. (Mary would name her next daughter after her.)

Mary had her hands full running the household, particularly when Augustine was away at the ironworks at Accokeek and in England in 1736. She acted the "deputy husband."[48]

When John Augustine was about ten months old, it was beginning to be cold weather again, and his father decided to make a trip to England to clarify his position within the iron enterprise. Augustine left sometime in late 1736 or early 1737 and stayed through the winter and early spring. When he returned from Great Britain in early 1737, he narrowly escaped death by "gaol fever." Many of his fellow passengers, convicts being transported to work in the colony, as well as the ship's captain, perished.[49] He was home in time to read the notice of his arrival in the new publication *The Virginia Gazette* in July 1737.[50] Augustine managed to get a contract from his partners in London giving him one-twelfth of the proceeds of the company.

On his trip, Augustine visited his older sons at the Appleby School. His eldest son, Lawrence, either came back with him or returned shortly thereafter. Augustine must have felt the want of a male companion and someone to share his business interests, having lost Eskridge and England.

Augustine, who had endured an Appleby education, wanted to have his sons experience one.[51] The boys learned through harsh competition and "through mixing with others of the same social class in the raw." One educator published a treatise recommending attending cockfights as a way to help boys to become brave. "The cock was a preeminent symbol of masculine fortitude and sexual prowess, praised for the courage and resolution with which he fought to the death, however badly wounded." School authorities did not organize games at boys' schools, but they generally applauded the winners of the fights endemic among students. Schools enforced rules against gambling and drinking with flogging. English schools for gentry boys worked to produce men who were physically courageous and who displayed aggression, indifference to pain, and an unwillingness to back down.[52]

Lawrence and his younger brother, Augustine junior, returned with educated speech and poise. Augustine senior intended this education for his younger sons as well. Meanwhile, George and the younger children played among the slaves. Mary recounted a dream many years later that wound up in Mason Weems's hagiographic biography of Washington. She dreamed five-year-old George was following a particularly skillful enslaved man named Dick around as he plowed the fields, with his own toy plow made of a cornstalk.[53] For Mary, born at the sterner end of the eighteenth century, it was a good dream. It pictured what would be her son's great interest in husbandry. After George retired from commanding the army, he wrote to the renowned British agricultural innovator and author Arthur Young, "Agriculture has ever been amongst the most favourite amusements of my life," adding humbly, "though I never possessed much skill in the art."[54]

Most white eighteenth-century Virginians, wealthy or not, objected to their children's intermingling with slave children. Some of the wealthy used the company of slaves as a reason to send their children—mostly boys—to school in England, where they would not pick up words, speech patterns, and what William Byrd referred to generally as "nothing good" from their slaves.[55] George Washington, years later, hired an overseer who wished to keep his white children apart from the black ones who hovered around the kitchen and main house at Mount Vernon.[56] Augustine also wanted privileged companions for his boys and the supervision of educated men.[57]

By 1738, Lawrence, Augustine's firstborn by Jane Butler, was about twenty or twenty-one—a man, legally grown or only months away from it.[58] He had as much education as his father had had and displayed the mother-country polish that ambitious colonial parents desired for their children. Lawrence helped Augustine with his farms and iron production.

Mary's brood of small children filled up her days with activity, care, and the small pleasures they brought. Much of the happiness she experienced as an adolescent depended on the affection and care of her half sister. The hunger of her babies for her affection and her body gave her ongoing sweetness—something she had not had. She was a disciplinarian, but the love of her children was a welcome satisfaction. Betty's children remembered their grandmother and their own mother as sweet and loving. It seems clear that Mary, while a demanding and strict parent, enjoyed her little ones.

When not preoccupied with her household, her husband, infant, toddlers, and children, Mary must have had complicated feelings about Lawrence's return. He was only about six years younger than she, yet his presence meant another ambiguous authority in the household. He, not George, was the first son of the household, and although Mary schooled herself not to aspire to worldly honors and riches, it might have been hard to see Lawrence slip into the role of Augustine's oldest and distinctly advantaged heir. Her mother, after all, had spent her last years trying to guarantee prosperity for her children in the menacing shadow of Joseph Ball Jr., who occupied the same privileged dynastic position as Lawrence. As Augustine's second wife, Mary was well aware of the many negative associations that attached to the word "stepmother." Her own mother had stirred the enmity of her father's family with her claims. Augustine's family had worked hard to nullify the effects of *his* mother's second marriage and the actions of his stepfather. On the other hand, she could not have missed the parallels between George's attraction to Lawrence and her own bond with her sister Elizabeth. The age difference was similar. They were half siblings with much in common and real affection growing between them.

Mary looked protectively after the children's safety and health. She worked to produce respect and obedience in them. Virginia children learned early to behave according to formal rules that included bowing to their parents and addressing them as "sir" and "madam." George addressed his mother in his later letters as "Honourd Madam," which writers have pointed to as a sign of his lack of affection. But Washington was a punctilious young man, and his mother had raised her children to respect her and Augustine, not to place affection first as later eighteenth-century parents would begin doing. Placing affection first is more familiar to us, but it undercuts the primacy of respect and its corollary, obedience. George reflected that, just as his step-grandson reflected the same thing in addressing his grandfather as "Honoured Sir." Lawrence addressed Augustine as "Hon'd Sir," suggesting that Augustine prescribed the form.[59] George usually signed himself "Yr most Dutiful & Obedt Son," sometimes adding "affectionate." In 1793, Washington's friend Burgess Ball, the husband of a favorite niece and a notably affectionate father, received letters from his son addressed to him as "Honor'd Father."[60]

Virginia parents trained their children in modesty and courtesy. At the same time and contradictorily, children, particularly boys, were praised for strength and willfulness. Virginians perceived and named this paradox: bending the will against itself.[61]

Mothers in the early eighteenth century were to have relatively little to do with raising their boys after they were six or seven years old. Sending her boys away to school measured a gentry mother's capacity for stoicism in service of her sons' own good.[62] Fathers and moralists generally thought that it was salutary for boys to be away from maternal softness and under the control of someone willing to use the rod. Locke, whose *Some Thoughts Concerning Education* was immensely influential in the eighteenth century, deplored education through force. He recommended, however, that fathers cane boys with gradually growing severity to make them strong. This was to be done not with rage but with love.[63]

Mary, who was home considerably more than her husband, influenced her sons' upbringing more than a typical Virginia mother would have. George later said he remembered little of his father. Augustine served as vestryman between 1735 and 1737, publicly upholding the family respectability and power. But he was away much of that time in England and, when in Virginia, often at Accokeek. Mary saw to the children's domestic religious training. Wealthy Virginians, living at a distance from their churches, took over or shared a number of functions with the ministry, reflecting both their relative isolation and their notable devotion to family over religious community. Thus, gentry brought ministers to them when they could to marry, to baptize, and to bury. Fathers read the Book of Common Prayer morning and evening and catechized their children. Mothers did this in the absence of fathers. Mary discharged these pious duties.[64]

Mary would have kept Betty indoors more than her boys, particularly after she reached the age of five or six. Betty would have watched—and begun fumblingly to participate in—the activities women in her household performed, like cooking, gardening, taking care of the poultry, managing the dairy, cleaning, making and mending clothes, spinning and weaving fabric, and knitting. However, one of George's childhood companions re-membered Betty traipsing along after her older brother and his friend on their explorations. She learned to be a good horseback rider, like her mother and brother. Mary trusted her oldest boy with his sister. She no doubt re-membered her pleasure and independence as a young girl horseback rid-ing in the countryside.[65]

The piety that characterized Mary from an early age corresponded to the principles of Scott and Hale. Rather than producing appealing timidity and deference, these ideas apparently contributed to infusing her with in-ner authority. Although Mary's favorite moralists recommended *practicing* the virtues of piety, obedience, and humility, they did not counsel women to *display* them in a feminized form. Later authors like the Reverend James Fordyce, who published *Sermons to Young Women* in 1766, recommended dramatizing meekness and submission as attractive to men: not laughing too loudly, not reading fiction or poetry, not displaying wit, and suffering in silence if their husbands were unfaithful. The books that Mary collected did not advise flattering and reassuring men. She did not learn to—or per-haps care to—display her piety as a way to show herself uncertain and in need of guidance. On the contrary, her piety gave her certainty, and as she grew older, she also grew in gravity, rooted in her religious convictions.

George's cousin and playmate Lawrence often visited Epsewasson and later Ferry Farm. Many years after, he remembered that he "was ten times more afraid [of Mary] than I ever was of my own parents. She awed me in the midst of her kindness, for she was, indeed, truly kind. I have often been present with her sons, proper tall fellows too, and we were all as mute as mice; and even now, when time has whitened my locks . . . I could not behold that remarkable woman without feelings it is impossible to describe. Whoever has seen that awe-inspiring air and manner so characteristic in the Father of his Country, will remember the matron as she appeared when the presiding genius of her well-ordered household, commanding and being obeyed." Historians have often cut off this quotation to leave out the phrase about how kind Mary was. If she was imposing, children also found her kind. At the end of her life, her grandchildren experienced both awe and love for this woman.[66] They are not incompatible.[67]

In September 1737, after Augustine's semi-miraculous return from England, Mary became pregnant for the fifth time. Charles was born the following May. Mary apparently did not experience major problems carrying and bearing her children, but some historians say that she had lost most of her teeth by the time she was older. Many women often lost a tooth or two during or after pregnancy. Carrying a child slightly depresses the immune system and increases the likelihood of gum disease—an inflammation and the most common cause of tooth loss. James Gordon of Lancaster County (father of the woman who married Easter Ball Chinn's abusive son) noted in his diary the gum and tooth troubles that coincided with his wife's pregnancies. (Gordon wrote that when his wife's tooth bled, they applied a mixture of spider's web and turpentine to it, a remedy that even for the time seems particularly nasty.)[68] George lost his teeth in middle age. Periodontal disease is exacerbated by what we would now think of as improper care of the teeth, something that was probably not uncommon in the eighteenth century, although George's account books show that he ordered many, many toothbrushes from Great Britain.

In the spring of 1738, Augustine became interested in a property—or rather several adjoining tracts on the Rappahannock River, not far from

Fredericksburg—that would also locate him nearer to his ironworks. On the property, a pair of ferries operated across the Rappahannock from the countryside into Fredericksburg, eventually giving the place its name: Ferry Farm, although this designation started to be used only after the Washingtons had moved on.[69] Mary would spend more than thirty years of her life there, and it was there that George and his siblings would grow up. Augustine bought the property in November 1738, and the family moved there in December.[70]

7

PEOPLE AND PROPERTY
AT FERRY FARM

*O*NE AND A HALF STORIES HIGH, the dark red wooden Ferry Farm, of Georgian design, sat on the top of a slope that looked down to the river. Wealthy Virginia patriarchs lived on rivers to transport their tobacco and liked sweeping views of the water running by their plantations. The front entrance was high off the ground, with stairs to the door. Relatively spacious—fifty-four feet by twenty-eight feet—built on stone foundations with large chimneys at both ends, the house resembled Wakefield, and Mount Vernon would have a similar look. There were two large public rooms in front, facing the river, wood paneled, with wood-decorated fireplaces. Elite Virginians aiming for elegance favored abundant displays of good, well-worked wood. Two bedrooms were in the back of the house, behind which enslaved people worked and trash was tossed out the back door. Upstairs, two dormitory-like rooms under the roof made flexible bedrooms for the four boys.[1] The Strother family, from whom Augustine bought it, had built it in about 1727 or 1728.[2] Through the 1720s and '30s, Virginians demonstrated their status through the number of buildings they constructed and used rather than the quality of any particular one. The Washingtons had ten structures at Ferry Farm. The wealthy went to brick mansions later in colonial America than they had in Great Britain. Augustine's houses—Pope's Creek (Wakefield), Epsewasson (later Mount Vernon), and Ferry Farm, with their slave quarters, kitchens, spinning houses, tobacco-drying sheds, stills, dairies, and smokehouses—spoke of his high standing.

Mary would enjoy living just across the Rappahannock from the lively trading center, where all kinds of people stopped and gossiped about friends, kin, neighbors, commerce, and politics. The earliest settlers of Fredericksburg built homes on fifty-acre plots. Germans, French, Scots, Dutch, Italians, Flemish, Scandinavians, and Bohemians took advantage of the town's location just before the falls on the Rappahannock, the last stretch of the river that large ships could navigate. The House of Burgesses confirmed the establishment of the town after it had been settled, by an act in 1727. They permitted the town to hold public markets and fairs and denied residents the right to let their pigs and goats run free in the streets. Merchants built warehouses and wharves up along the river's edge, and the city became a center for all kinds of colonial and imported goods. Augustine's ironworks had been one of two operating in the vicinity (the other was Governor Alexander Spotswood's, begun in 1715).[3] All along the riverbanks were quarries of sandstone, limestone, slate, and granite. The town attracted doctors and lawyers and schools and began to offer cultural events.

Fredericksburg expanded its boundaries five times between settlement and 1769. By the 1740s, it was provisioning settlers moving west to the Piedmont and Shenandoah Valley. Eventually, an eight-way road system radiated out of Fredericksburg, connecting it (for the very adventurous) with places as far away as Boston and St. Augustine.

Mary stepped into and strengthened kin and social relationships that the Washingtons already had with prosperous merchant and entrepreneurial families of Fredericksburg including the Lewis, Willis, Thornton, and Mercer families. Visiting, entertaining, business, and marriage would tie the Washingtons more closely to them.

Mary and Augustine's proximity to Fredericksburg made it easier for them to participate in the great expansion of British consumer goods at low prices now available. Architects and customers designed homes like Ferry Farm to provide an emerging new commodity: privacy for family members. Ambitious homeowners now designated some rooms as public, where others could admire their elegant purchases.

Archaeologists believe that the Washingtons kept the furniture that the Strothers left behind. When Mary died, she had a "best bed" and other furnishings that seem to have been an improvement on the Strothers' leavings. The Strothers did not leave behind the soft pink elegant wing chair, trimmed in green, made by a Scottish artisan, Robert Walker, who set up a workplace in King George County.[4] Possibly Augustine's gift for Mary, the chair announced taste and wealth.[5] The mahogany chair (a luxury wood that people trading directly with Great Britain had access to), upholstered in costly pink worsted damask with green trim, had four legs (not two, which would have been the cheap way) with a scallop shell at the "knee," finishing in carved raptor's claws clutching spheres. Wings from the top down the sides protected the sitter from drafts.[6] Mary's costly chair might have been on public display in her bedchamber, because those rooms still sometimes doubled as salons or public rooms. The chair first sat at Ferry Farm and later came into the possession of Betty. Whoever its purchaser, the chair unabashedly crossed over the moral line that many colonists and later citizens of the new republic drew, distinguishing "comforts" from "luxuries."

Mary loved tea. The Washingtons left remains of at least three different styles of imported tea sets, one white stoneware, in a "molded basket pattern" made in 1740, another more elaborate from the 1750s, and a third, later set of porcelain.[7] Mary and Augustine purchased tea and teapots, and she continued this practice throughout her long stay at Ferry Farm, teaching Betty the intricacies of the tea rituals. As a little girl, Betty owned at least one pewter teaspoon with her initials on it. Under Mary's guidance, she was beginning to mime the elaborate performances surrounding tea drinking.[8]

In addition to Betty's pewter spoon, archaeologists have dug up a very large number—more than two hundred—ceramic wig curlers of all different sizes at Ferry Farm. There was no wig maker in Fredericksburg, so it was up to Augustine's slaves to care for his wigs and eventually for the wigs of his sons.[9] The wig curlers represent the largest domestic find of its kind. The Washingtons' slaves did their wig tending in the back of the house.

Elite boys began wearing wigs around seven years old, so George and possibly Samuel were already wearing wigs by the time they moved to Ferry Farm. Wig wearing, developed in part to combat head lice—or some say to cover scabs and disfigurements from syphilis—became fashionable in the mid-seventeenth century and required a shaved scalp. When not wearing a wig, boys and men kept their heads warm with caps, usually white. Slaves washed, curled, and applied pomade and powder to the Washingtons' wigs—ideally once a week, although they might not have been so fastidious. Unclean wigs, however, repeatedly treated with pomade could attract lice and mice. Most people desired wigs made from human hair, which were the most expensive. Sailors usually used ones made from wool, to withstand extremes in weather. A wig maker, Abigail Peake, announced herself open for business in Yorktown in 1751 and might have attracted the Washingtons as customers.[10] George Washington gave up wig wearing at a certain point and merely had his own hair powdered.

At Ferry Farm, Mary had the chance to plan and develop her garden, a pastime that gave her much pleasure and provided herbs for cooking, greens for "salletts," and ingredients for medicines. She gardened throughout her long life. She and George would share a strong interest in growing things and in the pleasures and beauties of flowers, shrubs, and bushes. Spacious beds for Mary's herbs, flowers, and vegetables extended out behind Ferry Farm.

A traveler in Virginia in 1732 noted that Virginians tended to be tall and thin and that the gentry customarily had five main courses at their tables for the family and whatever travelers should happen by. They usually served a plate of pork with greens, a "Tame fowl . . . or a plate with Beef, Mutton, Veal or Lamb"; sometimes a "Pudding" might be served as well as a dish of "Venison, Wild fowl, or fish." Drinks included "Smal[l] beer made of molasses, with Madera Wine [and] English Beer [is] their liquor. . . . They have good Cyder but will not keep it, but [instead] drink [it] by pailfulls."[11] Mary, who was herself tall, made sure to have an array of hearty food on her table for her family and for stoppers-by.

⁙

THE WASHINGTONS AND other wealthy Virginians were making and increasing their fortunes growing the special, sweet-smelling tobacco that could be grown only in patches of rich soil along these waterways.[12] These men had a disproportionate share of political and economic power in Virginia from their tobacco, which could be priced higher than the less desirable oronoco that was grown more widely.[13]

The Washingtons held roughly twenty slaves at Ferry Farm, in addition to the slaves they had put in trust for Augustine and Lawrence who apparently remained at Pope's Creek and Epsewasson, respectively, working on crops there.[14] These moves had required much of the slaves in the way of packing and carrying. It had also torn the "home" slaves from their previous two "homes" and whatever comforts they had devised as well as from any relationships they might have established since leaving Wakefield.

The Strother family, who had lived at Ferry Farm before the Washingtons, had owned twenty-two slaves and had built accommodations, such as they were, that sheltered the enslaved people that Augustine and Mary brought. Archaeological investigation places their dormitory across the road that now cuts through the original property. The excavations at Ferry Farm show that slaves lived in a wooden structure about a hundred feet north of the main house, also facing the river. There is no evidence of a chimney, and the exact dimensions of the building are not determinable. In the Chesapeake, when slaves built their own cabins—which was not the case at Ferry Farm—they used mud to fill the chinks in the walls. The floors were dirt. Frequently, cooking was done outside.[15]

At Mount Vernon, years later, foreign visitors were appalled at the level of material poverty in which slaves lived—far worse, they noted, than any European peasant—but they noticed in the general void of furniture and amenities that some slaves had teacups and a teapot, clearly hand-me-downs from the big house. We don't know what, if anything, filtered down to the Ferry Farm slaves in the way of ceramic or glass.

Mary and Augustine's slaves probably kept whatever possessions they had in underground pits, sometimes protected with a lining of stone or brick, as was done on several other Virginia plantations.[16] Slaves often had two such pits, one for food, such as tubers and corn, to protect it from rats and other foragers, and another for objects.

A very few slave owners gave locks to their slaves—usually relatively privileged ones—so they could protect the possessions they managed to accumulate. Joseph Ball was among them. Mary no doubt heard from him or her nephew Joseph Chinn about his unusual arrangements for a young enslaved man and woman whom he sent back from Great Britain to Virginia to work in his tobacco fields after raising them as house servants and attendants to his child. Ball instructed Chinn to have cabins built for them with a lock on the door of the young woman's home. With his usual precision, he spelled out the size of the cabins and the "gentle" breaking in they were to have, completely unaccustomed as they were to long hours of agricultural labor.[17] Ball wanted to protect the possessions he and his family had provided to his British-raised slaves and keep the young woman from unwanted sex. Locks on slaves' doors symbolize two precious items— private property and privacy—that masters almost universally denied to slaves.[18] We don't know what Mary made of her brother's experiments with his slaves' lives. She was committed to hierarchy and obedience. His favoritism could have encouraged disobedience and contradicted the simplest reading of black subordination. But she might have had favorites herself. The records do not help us understand.

With the exception of Jcumy, the names of the slaves on Ferry Farm sound Creole, but the historian Lorena Walsh has determined that most were Africans, bought in the years when the trade was still filling the Chesapeake with "outlandish" people.[19] Washington gave them names he could pronounce and to which they had to answer. These were probably not their only names. As John Mbiti has written, "There is no stop to the giving of names in many African societies."[20] Emerging characteristics and particular circumstances or incidents called for additional names that would have probably remained unknown to the Washingtons. These slaves would very likely have named their own children.[21]

Although archaeologists have yet to excavate the area in which the slaves lived at Ferry Farm, they have found in the main house a reddish bead of carnelian. It has a hole in the middle and eight facets. It lay in the root cellar, an area seven and a half to eight feet belowground, beneath the hall where one of the two chimneys stood. Another of these has been found in Barbados, and one at the Calvert estate in Maryland. The carnelian was part of the British Empire's production and circulation of goods. India produced it, as well as the colorful cotton Indians made for sale in Africa. The bead belonged to one of the slaves who worked in the house. Someone who had survived the Middle Passage might have brought it, or it might have come on an enslaved woman or man from the Caribbean. One observer at a slave sale in the Caribbean saw slaves decorated with beads that were apparently given to them by their captors.[22]

Carnelian beads signified high status among the Yoruba, who were captured from what is now Nigeria.[23] Historians identify the Yoruba (and the Igbo, another Nigerian ethnicity) as having been brought to *southern* Virginia, not one of the ethnicities whose members usually wound up on Northern Neck plantations. The beads that have been recovered at Mount Vernon, found much more commonly in this area as well, were blue.[24]

Slaves used beads for ornaments, of course, but they also used them as grave goods, placing them with the deceased to accompany him or her home. Enslaved West Africans generally regarded death as rather like life, but better, and they saw the place where the dead exist as the home to which everyone goes. Funerals facilitated entry into this world. In their own societies, Africans did not bury slaves with free people, nor were slaves expected to enter the spirit home. However, because nearly all Africans were enslaved here, they hoped for a better future for those who died in bondage far from home. Grave goods like tobacco, pipes, food, drink, and favorite objects accompanied the buried in what is now Ghana, in Barbados, and very likely on the Washington farm. Evidence elsewhere suggests that the presence of many Africans meant many grave goods, and as the first generation died off, so did the number of grave goods.[25]

William Grove boarded two slave ships in Lancaster County in 1732 and noted that the boys and girls were naked and the men and women largely so. "Some," however, "had beads about their necks, arms, and Wasts, and a ragg or Peice of Leather the bigness of a figg Leafe." He watched while a Virginia woman came aboard to inspect the Africans, to "examine the Limbs and soundness of some." Grove described these ships as being from "Angolo," signifying broadly West Africa south of the equator, and the other from "Guineau," or north of the equator.

At home, Grove's hosts gave the ten "stark naked" men and women they had bought "Coarse Shirts" and "Drawers." He said they cost twenty pounds, making no distinction between the men and the women. His companions allotted their slaves "a peck of Indian Corn per Week, which stands the master 26" shillings a year in addition to ten yards of brown linen at five shillings, and a pair of shoes for three shillings. The slaves were "allow[ed] to plant little Platts for potatoes or . . . Indian pease" and beans.[26] At Mount Vernon in the 1780s, George allotted his slaves a heaping peck of corn a week.[27]

Some Northern Neck planters preferred Africans from the Senegambia, the Gold Coast, and Upper Guinea rather than farther east and south.[28] Joseph Ball's old neighbor Robert "King" Carter, the man who bought the largest number of slaves in Virginia—and his son John—would not accept slaves from Angola because, they reasoned, the voyage was so long and their captivity so "sudding & surprising . . . that the people will be Afraid to Venture on them [ships] again."[29] Seventy-five percent of the slaves brought to upper Virginia in the eighteenth century came from the Senegambia and that region that is now Guinea-Bissau, Ivory Coast, and Ghana. However, although the Carters expressed a preference for slaves from these regions, they got what they wanted largely because the merchants who kidnapped slaves for them came from Liverpool and specialized in slaves from this area. Bristol and London slavers worked the southern Virginia market and trafficked in people from the area that is now Nigeria and Angola.

Four-fifths of the Africans who were forced into slavery in Virginia until 1750 were herded off ships on the York River and the Rappahannock River, where Ferry Farm was located. The Washingtons' move to Fredericksburg placed them where Virginia's wealth and power were most concentrated.

8

"AS SPARKS FLY
UPWARD"[1]

IN THE FALL OF 1738, about the time Augustine was looking over Ferry Farm and deciding to move, Mary became pregnant for the last time. In June 1739, she gave birth to Mildred Washington at nine at night, the only one of Mary's children to be born at Ferry Farm. Named for Augustine's sister, she died in October 1740 at sixteen months.

Mary had no more children. She was only in her early thirties. Augustine was in residence, although he was not around very much. He spent considerable time working on the house at Epsewasson, destined for

Lawrence. His frequent moving of houses and his travels convey a restless spirit as he pursued continuing land deals and largely unavailing efforts to improve his situation in the iron industry. The losses of Eskridge and England contributed to Augustine's anxieties and workload.[2]

Mildred's death was probably preceded by an illness that taxed Mary's endurance and left her exhausted. She might have found scarce comfort for the loss of a daughter, who had survived infancy and was beginning to walk around and exert her tiny charms. Mary was in a stronger position to withstand the shock of the death of a dear one than she had been years before. Yet Mildred's death, interrupting Mary's string of healthy births, grieved her, calling up old, unwelcome sensations of fear, helplessness, and despair.

In 1735, the Quaker Susanna Wright had written a poem about the death of a little girl. The feelings and hopes she evoked could not have been too different from Mary's:

> 'Twas thus the Poppet ceas'd to breathe,
> The small Machine stood still,
> The little Lungs no longer heave
> Or Motion follows Will.
> . . . .
> Now to the silent Grave retir'd,
> Its Organs moulder there.
> . . . .
> Thy harmless Soul releas'd from Earth,
> A Cherub sings above,
> Immortal in a second Birth,
> By thy Redeemer's Love.[3]

On Christmas Eve, not three months after Mildred's death and after the family had been living at Ferry Farm a little more than a year, it caught fire. The fire, while contained in one corner of the house, destroyed family plans for Christmas and Twelfth Night celebrations, as well as Augustine's financial security. Augustine wrote to an English friend that the fire had been serious and had set him back.[4] George Washington mentioned it to David Humphreys, his first and official biographer, as among the significant events of his early life. Mary had a memorable dream about the fire, a version of which wound up in Parson Weems's *Life of Washington*. Mason Locke Weems, an Anglican minister, wrote the wildly popular and unreliable 1809 biography of Washington to eulogize the late president and instill good behavior in boys and girls. Weems wrote that his source for the dream told him that Mary had recounted it often late in her life and that she had retold it just a few weeks before she died. Weems's thirdhand account is our only source of Mary's story, however, and we must approach his account cautiously.[5]

Weems wrote that she dreamed of "a kind of roaring noise on the eastern side of the house. On running to see what was the matter, I beheld a dreadful sheet of fire bursting from the roof." When her husband and the servants proved ineffectual, she screamed for George. George came running. When he saw the flames, he was not frightened but happy. He told his mother, "Oh, Ma! Don't be afraid: God Almighty will help us, and we shall soon put it out." His bravery inspired everyone around him, and soon a ladder arrived, and George threw the water that the slaves brought him on the fire. The flames, however, did not go out, and the fire roared on until, in Mary's dream, an old man appeared with an iron rod in his hand and a wooden trough that he gave to George to throw water on the fire. This did the trick, and in time they extinguished the fire. After this, when everyone else was happy, George ("showing no more of transport now than of terror before") was sad at the damage that had been done. But after thinking a bit, he announced that they could build a much better house that would last forever.

I am inclined to accept as fact that Mary often shared some version of this dream and that Weems would have been more likely to twist it to his evangelical ends than to actually invent it. The fire did happen; Augustine and George both left strong responses to it. Two elements in the dream plausibly reflect on Mary's state of mind at this time. First, of course, the fire distressed her greatly. Second, George figured boldly in her imagination. Placing George at the center of Mary's dream certainly served Weems's purposes, but it seems to me to overlap with her concerns as well. She dreamed this after the fact—when is unknown, but most likely when George had proved himself an important aid to her as a widow.

Weems desired to make Mary's dream politically prophetic in addition to fitting into his invented interpretation of the characters of Washington's parents: the father, a pious evangelical who gave George his first religious lessons; his mother, suitably tender and fond. The truth was different. Augustine was not notably religious, while piety shaped Mary's world. (Indeed, Lawrence de Butte, the pastor of the Epsewasson, or Washington Parish, congregation had sued Augustine and other congregants for failing to live up to their obligations to him.)[6]

Mason Weems might have played fast and loose with the details; certainly his interpretation depends on using them creatively. He asserted that the old man was a stand-in for Benjamin Franklin, the fire the Revolution, and that rebuilding meant producing the new nation. It suited Weems's purpose that George saved the house and that he remained precociously calm and competent in the face of a threatening fire. Most of all, Weems wished to give George's role in the dream glorious significance for the Republic.

Mary located George prominently in her imaginative life, reflecting his consistent presence in her life while she performed as a deputy husband and later became a widow. In the dream as Weems quotes it, Mary lauded little George's bravery, calm, and good sense—something observers have said she did not often do. Perhaps Weems intervened to make her seem fond and doting, or perhaps narrating a dream to people other than George permitted Mary to praise her son more freely than her scruples usually allowed. In any case, Mary's dream recalled a terrifying evening that closed a sad year.

Whatever her dream meant, she must have felt for many months much as did Anne Bradstreet, whose house burned in 1666. Before being able to reconcile herself to the destruction as God's will, she had to name and mourn its details:

> *Here stood that trunk, and there that chest,*
> *There lay that store I counted best.*
> *My pleasant things in ashes lye,*
> *And them behold no more shall I.*[7]

In early 1740, young Lawrence Washington heard news of Admiral Edward Vernon's naval victory over the Spanish forces in Panama. Vernon's forces, sailing from Jamaica, had attacked and taken Portobelo. This military victory in the War of Jenkins' Ear between Britain and Spain helped revive the historical appeal to honor of British military life, which had dimmed after the English Civil War.[8] Vernon's win encouraged Lawrence and a number of other young Virginians to vie for commissions in the British navy, applying to Virginia's governor, William Gooch. Gooch rewarded Lawrence, George recalled, with a commission and appointed him "Senior Officer" of the Virginia troops raised for the "American Brigade" including some few volunteers and convicts to fill out the levy. He sailed in the fall of 1740. As Washington remembered, "He was scarcely of age when he went on this expedition."[9]

Lawrence was joining one of the most violent and hierarchical institutions of a violent and hierarchical age. As an officer, of course, he was protected from lashing and other harsh punishments, unlike the men under him, but subject to the caprices, arrogance, and bad judgment of his many superiors as well as the diseases he would find in the hot and humid Caribbean. Mary came to dislike the military, starting with the experiences of her stepson. She witnessed her husband and oldest son admiring Lawrence's pursuit of a commission. They supported his ambition to come back with an impressive rank. In Mary's view, that meant little or nothing.

Later in the year, Lawrence Washington returned from the Caribbean.

Governor Gooch's recruiting goal had been three thousand volunteers. Only sixteen hundred returned. An enormous number had died of disease— primarily yellow fever. Lawrence, living in close, steamy quarters with thousands of others, might have been exposed there to the tuberculosis that later killed him, if he did not have it before; it afflicted many of the Washingtons.

Lawrence's personal adventure strongly impressed George as the family read aloud his letters. Lawrence wrote that the enemy had killed about six hundred of them but that disease had taken many more. "Vast changes are had in each regiment; some are so weak as to be reduced to a third of their men; a great quantity of officers amongst the rest are dead. . . . Our Regiment has not rec'd that treatment we expected but I am resolved to persiver in the undertaking. War is horrid in fact but much more so in imagination. We there learned to live on ordinary diet, to watch much and disregard the noise or shot of cannon."[10] Perhaps George found that an exhilarating challenge.

Lawrence concluded by sending his respects to his "mother," that is Mary, his aunt, his brothers and sisters, and others. Similarly to George's later closings, he concluded his letter, "I am Hon'd Sir, Your ever dutiful son, Lawrence."[11]

Mary's later dread of war had its roots in Lawrence's experiences in the Caribbean. Augustine, trained like his son at Appleby and on Virginia slave plantations to aggression and domination, would have admired Lawrence's courage and apparent ability to control his fearful imaginings in the face of war. To observers like Mary, the voluntary risks soldiers took, but also the horrible and useless loss of life through disease, were incomprehensible. Young men like Lawrence might have been home raising families, running farms, and warding off the dangers that worried white Virginians—like fires, slave insurrection, and Native American violence. Mary no doubt recorded Lawrence's details about the loss of men and officers, the "ordinary diet," and the regiment's indifferent treatment despite Lawrence's high expectations.

Even in Virginia, much less the Caribbean, the British navy noted high levels of morbidity through the late seventeenth and early eighteenth centuries. In 1740, one British ship, wintering over in Norfolk, lost sixty-two men to disease, a statistic that had not improved since the time of Mary's birth. Sick seamen were often quartered with locals who were willing to accept money for the risks and work they undertook. In 1747, a young British officer wrote to his superiors about the "miserable condition of the sick and Wounded seamen, belonging to his Majesties Ships on the Virginia Station [and] . . . the fatall Consequences that attends Epidemicall Distempers, Sweeping off the Choisest and Ablest Seamen."[12] It could not have escaped Virginians' attention that the navy, and marine life in general, bred disease, particularly after Augustine's escape from "gaol fever" only three years earlier.

Mary had support in her low opinion of the military. Augustine's first cousin John Lewis, a wealthy Fredericksburg merchant,[13] thought Lawrence had made a particularly bad choice by going into the navy and wrote him so: "I cannot see what delight you take in such a life[.] I heartily wish you safe here with that so wish'd for title, so much design'd to be gained in the field of Battle, but I think may as deserved be acquired at home in the service of his Country, County, Parish & neighborhood in peace and Quietness." To reinforce his point, Lewis listed all the wealthy and eligible young men and women of Lawrence's acquaintance who were coupling, knowing it was a subject of hot interest to the young man. He mentioned that Miss Randolph (a wealthy heiress) was "yet single though many offers has been made her, it is reported . . . that she stays for you, but not believed by many, for the dangers of war and a sickly climate no person can depend upon."[14]

Richard Yates, a friend of Augustine's, wrote to him in 1741 to commiserate on the calamity of the fire but to congratulate him on Lawrence's survival. He sent Augustine "joy on your son's happy escape out of the midst of a danger that prov'd fatal to so many about him."[15] Mary's daughter, Betty, would later marry John Lewis's son Fielding, confirming her mother and future father-in-law's preference for men who stayed closer to home.

Listening to Lawrence's letters (those that arrived—he said he had sent many, but only one survives) confirmed Mary's membership in an "Atlantic family" that strengthened its distant connections by writing. Her brother Joseph's many trips to London to study law gave her a taste of being in a family with far-flung members. By the time she listened to Lawrence's elegantly written letters and saw his fine hand, she belonged to the family circle that collectively cared about his news, relished his ability to conjure up sights and sounds, and appreciated his reactions. Mary's imaginative world would likely have grown through this literary performance of "familiarity"—the rhetorical creation of a heightened feeling of affection, interest, and investment in family and kin. Letters like Lawrence's, the product of a British education and reading essays and novels, displayed the sensibility and narrative skill that were increasingly required to denote high status. Comfortable and easy expressions of love, reminders of connections over distance, the awareness of the perils and rewards of distance itself, all were part of absorbing Lawrence's tales and receiving his youthful wisdom and affection.[16] She was getting a glimpse of the entertainment that letters could provide as well as their distorted relationship to the actual letter writer. Mary had to integrate her acquaintance with Lawrence as a pleasant enough young man whose linens she was responsible for keeping clean with the confident and seemingly mature author of adventurous letters. She might have registered the fact that his persuasive representation of himself might be at odds with the youth she knew.

Lawrence's letters demonstrated to her the ways in which extended families scattered all over used the warm, codified language of familiarity to sustain their bonds. This, to a woman who had lost so many, would have been instructive. Mary's letters would never resemble Lawrence's, and she might well have felt her inferior education in light of the young man's virtuosity with a pen. For Mary, the disjuncture between genteel behavior and her own experience and feelings would increasingly make her ill at ease in elite society with its proliferating refinements.[17] She might also have sharpened her ambitions for polishing her own children.

While Lawrence was in the Caribbean, James Straughan, Mary's brother-in-law, whose brother had drawn up her mother's and brother John's wills and married her sister Elizabeth, died in March 1741. He left a small estate for his widow and their two daughters, Mary and Elizabeth, of which Elizabeth became the administrator.

In July 1741, Mary's sister Elizabeth married Thomas Tobin, who moved to Cherry Point. But Elizabeth, beloved of Mary, died herself six months later. Her death, in January 1742, came a little more than a year after the death of Mary's daughter Mildred. Elizabeth left her daughters under the guardianship of two friends. In a later settlement, the guardians charged the estate for a coffin for little Mary Straughan, who died some time before January 1746.[18]

After the loss of Mildred and the fire at Ferry Farm, the loss of her Elizabeth was a brutal blow for Mary. This was an irreplaceable intimacy, a lifelong companion and guardian, now of middle age, who had sheltered her when their mother died, labored with her at domestic chores, and helped her learn to manage a house. It was a relatively egalitarian bond, but from Mary's standpoint it had the added warm layer of the slightly older woman's care for her younger sibling. Mary and Elizabeth helped each other out at births and deaths and undoubtedly discussed the most private moments and decisions of their lives. She was the only person who shared Mary's earliest memories and remembered the relationships that had formed them both. However affectionate her relationship with Augustine might have been, it was an unequal one and would not have provided the warmth, mutual recognition, and spontaneity that she had shared with Elizabeth. Mary would have had a long and hard time recovering from the grief that accompanied the death of Elizabeth.

At the time of Elizabeth's death, George acquired *The Sufficiency of a Standing Revelation in General, and of the Scripture Revelation in Particular* by Ofspring Blackall and signed his name in it.[19] He kept the book his whole life. According to the scholar Kevin Hayes, he was about nine years old when he put his signature on the frontispiece of the book, the age he was, more or less, at the time of Elizabeth's death in January 1742. Two other signatures precede his: Robert Wickliff's and Samuel Bowman's. Because of the timing of the arrival of the book and the similarity of the names Bowman and Bonam, I believe the book came from Elizabeth's estate. She and her first husband, Samuel, had had a son, Samuel, in 1723, and he survived until 1739. It seems a reasonable supposition that little Samuel inherited the book from his father and wrote his name in it twice by the time he was sixteen. At the time of Elizabeth's death in 1742, her only living child seems to be Elizabeth.[20] Until Robert Wickliff is identified, the story remains speculation, but given the many spellings of early eighteenth-century names (for example, Mary Johnson Ball [Hughes, Hews, Hues, Hewes]; and Elizabeth Johnson [Bonum, Bonam] Straughan [Toben, Tobin, Toby, Tobey]), Elizabeth's limited education, and the early demise of her husband and son, it seems very likely to me that the book belonged to Mary's affectionate brother-in-law, went to his son, Samuel, and somehow Mary gave it to George as an important memento from her sister.

Mary's gift of the book to George would have confirmed the boy's connection to Elizabeth and Mary's love for her. When, many years later, George received a plea for help from Mary's half niece Elizabeth Straughan for her daughter Sarah Haynie (later called Sallie or Sally), he responded with generosity, calling up his memory of his mother's tenderness for her sister and her sister's daughter and namesake.[21] George Washington, as an old man, still felt an obligation to honor that loving bond. He wrote to his nephew Rob Lewis that he must look after the old woman and her daughter.[22]

In 1742, the year of Elizabeth's death, young Augustine (or Austin) Washington arrived at Ferry Farm after his years at the Appleby School. He had hoped to become a lawyer but, in Lawrence's absence, returned to help out his father with his scattered properties. Austin was of an age to claim the slaves his father and mother had put in trust for him, and he began to farm and use his slaves at Wakefield, where George had been born. From Mary's point of view, here was another well-educated, ambitious youth to claim the attention and resources of her husband and to challenge her children for pride of place. He would also be, however, a significant resource to her as a widow.

By the time Austin arrived in Virginia, Mary was about thirty-three. She would bear no more children. Grief over the relentless losses—Eskridge, Mildred, James, and Elizabeth—darkened her first years at Ferry Farm.

9

THE WIDOW WASHINGTON

IIIIIIIIIIIIIIIIIIIIIIIIIIIIIIIIIIIIIIIIIIIIIIIIIIIIIIIIIIIIIIIIIIIIIIIIIIIIIIIIIIIIIIIIIIIIIIIIIIIIIIIIIIIIIIIIIIIIIIIIIIIIIIIIIIIIIIIIIIIIIIIIII

*I*N JANUARY 1743, Mary and the family welcomed Lawrence home from the Caribbean. The family rejoiced in his survival. In preparation for Lawrence's return, Augustine had often been away, working on the house he would give his son.

Early in 1743, Augustine senior and his brother, John, initiated a court action to settle a boundary dispute between them that they could not agree on themselves "as well as to prevent all such happening in the time to come." This boundary question dated from their childhood, when their uncle John had retrieved their estate from their stepfather, George Gale. Perhaps Augustine was feeling his own mortality in bringing this long-standing uncertainty finally to a resolution.[1]

That spring, a little over a year after Elizabeth had died, Augustine complained of pain in his stomach. Mary knew well the potential for illness to turn disastrous. This would be another one of those times. On April 11, when eleven-year-old George, according to George Washington Parke Custis, was visiting his cousins at Chotank, Augustine and Mary called in friends, including Robert Jackson and Anthony Strother, to witness Augustine's will. He declared that he was "sick and weak" but that his memory was perfect, as was his "disposing" sense.[2] Mary had to go through the final, sad drill. If Augustine wished, she would have called the Reverend James Marye (anglicized to Maury) to visit and give Communion to Augustine. In his memoir, Custis repeated a family story in which the dying Augustine declared it was a good thing that he had never hit anyone in anger because he was so large and strong that he would have killed his antagonist. The blood of another would have weighed on his soul. As it was, he said, he was at peace with all men.[3] If Augustine said it, it seems that he had bent his will back on himself successfully, as members of the Virginia gentry were trained to do. It also marks his awareness of the aggression close to his surface.

Suddenly Mary—shocked and grieving—had to collaborate with Lawrence to organize a funeral for Augustine. Augustine wished to be buried in the family graveyard at Bridge's Creek in Westmoreland County, where his first wife lay.[4] Mary and Lawrence had three days to get Augustine's large body transported over the poor roads to the shore of the Potomac.[5] Mary would have made sure that a group sat at night with Augustine's shrouded body.[6] Mary and the children put on some kind of mourning, probably all black first mourning. Augustine might have had a lay service because they were permitted for private burials.[7]

At the time of Augustine's death, Mary's children ranged in age from George at eleven, Betty at almost ten, Samuel at eight, John Augustine at seven, to Charles at almost five. Mary made her way through the ceremonial days, offering refreshments to friends, family, and neighbors in Fredericksburg. Whatever her feelings, she had to hold herself together and look after her brood.

Augustine left a businesslike will, without endearments. Lawrence received Mount Vernon and the ironworks. Augustine left Wakefield to Austin, and George was to inherit Ferry Farm when he became twenty-one. Augustine willed Mary five slaves (one more than those with whom she probably came) in lieu of her dower rights, which would have been one-third of the slaves. The will directed that if she asked for her full dower rights, any additional enslaved people would come from among those bequeathed to her sons. She retained the two parcels of land that she had brought to the marriage. She would receive the crops from Bridge's Creek that would later go to Austin and the right to work that land for five years, as well as crops from Ferry Farm and from land on Chotank Creek that would eventually be going to Samuel. She was to share with her children all those things (personalty) not specifically bequeathed. Because George would be taking over Ferry Farm, she was, within five years, to build herself a house on a tract called Deep Run in King George County.[8]

Augustine's will instructed Lawrence to give Betty four hundred pounds from his profits at the ironworks. Lawrence was also to buy three slaves for Austin. Augustine left Betty two little enslaved girls: "a negroe child, Mary, the daughter of Sue," who, in a subsequent division, was given to his widow, and a girl named Betty, the daughter of Judy, also designated for Mary Washington.[9] These children would stay with their mothers until Betty married, about seven years later. Most of the slaves at Ferry Farm would stay put for the time being. Seven years down the road, a family council would divide up the fifty slaves among Mary, George, Samuel, John Augustine, and Charles.

Augustine had amassed about ten thousand acres and purchased a large number of slaves. He set his sons up well—but unequally, with smaller shares for Mary's youngest boys. Children of well-off planters between the

1730s and the 1770s were lucky because the value of their fathers' property had grown considerably in those years.[10] In particular, the value of slaves, especially Creole slaves, had appreciated, that is, the "increase" that Augustine's sons enjoyed and would continue to enjoy. (Plantation owners wanting to buy enslaved people complained of high prices.)[11]

Mary was to oversee the education and manage the properties of her sons until they reached maturity. (Betty was not included in this, because she received no real property, just cash and two slaves, and Augustine ignored her education.) If Mary were to remarry, her husband would be charged with providing security for the boys' estates and managing them responsibly. If he did not provide security and deliver the estates properly to the boys at maturity, management of the estate would to be taken away from him and Mary.[12]

Augustine settled his best holdings on his sons by Jane. He made no sentimental bequests to Mary and pitted her desires to look out for her own interest against her desires to look out for those of her children. He specified that she be ready to be out of Ferry Farm in five years, long before George would arrive at twenty-one. He also set any desire she might have had to remarry against the possibility of losing control of her boys.

Augustine had fathered her five children and had restored her to the barely remembered status and privileges of her earliest years. He was Mary's regular sexual partner for twelve years, although it is possible that their sexual relationship had ended or in any case slowed down as many as three or four years before he died. While Mary doubtless felt sadness at Augustine's death, it was probably a different kind of grief from the one she had felt for Elizabeth, whose death ended a connection that reached deeper into her experience and spirit.

Whereas husbands and wives had sometimes gone visiting together in the early eighteenth century, their lives grew increasingly distinct in the period in which Mary and Augustine were married. Men participated in recreations like racing, cockfighting, politics, gambling, billiards, and talking at the tavern—all accompanied by drinking. Men hunted.[13] Men largely did the shopping at local markets, and women remained at home.[14] George remarked that he saw his father relatively little; the same would have been true for Mary.[15]

She had grown up to operate independently inside a complex of formally but often not emotionally dependent relationships. Mary's history of emotional shocks and lack of a father probably undermined her ability to develop much of a trusting intimacy with her husband. Early eighteenth-century marriage, designed for the comfort and convenience of men, did not require or even encourage that kind of intimacy. Loving intimacy might occur in these marriages, but they were not conducive to it, nor did all partners seek it.[16] Augustine, significantly older, wealthier, and better educated than she, made the decisions, at least when he was around. His power over her and her obligatory deference to his authority would have hindered reciprocal intimacy, shared confidences, and mutual understanding. In her youth, Mary had depended emotionally on Elizabeth. She would later depend on Betty.

Along with sadness and shock, Mary might well have felt panic. Augustine's abrupt death split his estate into parts, subtracting the majority of its income. Lawrence and Austin now received returns from the crops of the best lands on the Potomac: Wakefield and Mount Vernon. In addition to a large drop in income, there were ongoing expenses for the other properties and maintenance of the enslaved workers. The loneliness of widowhood and its attendant financial and familial worries pushed her toward somberness and anxiety. The constant companionship of her religious texts might have relieved the anxiety but probably augmented her sober watchfulness.

Her life as a widow, lacking whatever small and large pleasures that Augustine provided—the company, the affection, the sexual intimacy, the babies, and the gifts—became austere. As a young woman, she enjoyed good health, fast horses, dancing, and companionship; as a young wife and mother, she had few financial worries, a strong, active husband, several small children, and a series of bustling households to manage. After Augustine's death, Mary's load of responsibilities and innate refusal to give way, fortified by her religious convictions, seem to have made her, as Lawrence Washington of Chotank remembered, externally, at least, awe inspiring.

Her mother's example could not have been far from her mind when she thought about her future duties. Now, suddenly, she found herself at the center of the family, like the one she had watched disintegrate as a child. She would do her best to protect her five surviving children and to consolidate her family. She redoubled her efforts to watch over the children she had borne, clothed, catechized, fed, and trained. George, Betty, Samuel, John Augustine, and Charles would be very close to each other as adults, visiting, helping, advising one another, naming their children after one another—and Mary—and acting as godparents to multiple members of the next generation. They would do all this work, or "kin keeping,"[17] in part, because Mary taught them the Virginia ethos well: family above all.

10.

SINGLE MOTHER

|||||||||||||||||||||||||||||||||||||||||||||||||||||||||||||||||||||||||||||||||||||||||||||||||||||||||||||||||||||||||||||||||||||

That as much as I am but a steward, I will be very
careful that my management of my trust may
be such as will bear my Lord's scrutiny.

—MATTHEW HALE, *CONTEMPLATIONS MORAL AND DIVINE*

ARY FOUND HERSELF in the mid-1740s with five young
children, ranging in age from five to eleven, living on a medium-
sized farm on mediocre soil. Her stepsons had established themselves elsewhere. Austin, twenty years old in 1740, lived at Pope's Creek with his
wife, the former Anne Aylett, about sixteen, and their daughter, Jane. On
July 18, 1743, within three months of his father's death, Lawrence, who
was living at Mount Vernon, married his wealthy neighbor Anne Fairfax,
ten years his junior.[1] Anne's father, Colonel William Fairfax, managed the

enormous Fairfax land grant and lived at Belvoir, bordering Mount Vernon. Lawrence picked up where Augustine had left off, improving the house in which Mary had lived into the basic structure that would become George Washington's Mount Vernon.

Lawrence's marriage allied him to the wealthiest and most important family in the Northern Neck. Indeed, the Privy Council, in 1745, recognized the claim of the proprietor (Thomas Culpepper, Lord Fairfax, 1693–1781) to more than five million acres of Virginia and the quitrents due from these lands. (This meant that for land speculators, as George Washington would be, land purchases had to occur *beyond* the now legally established limits of the Fairfax proprietorship.)[2] If, despite his years away at school and in the British navy, Lawrence felt at all unmoored by the loss of his father, his marriage into the most powerful and prestigious family in Virginia anchored him.

During Mary's married years, class divisions became greater, defined by material possessions, dress, and hospitality, as well as more finely articulated genteel behavior that displayed a cosmopolitan acquaintance with the Atlantic world and its culture. Women drew praise for their piety and familial instruction in morality as well as their social grace and charm. The two did not necessarily fit well together, particularly in Mary's case. Just as Mary entered into single motherhood, she faced a rising set of costly social expectations for keeping her children in the upper class.[3] Her income sharply diminished, she aimed at keeping the doors of the ruling class open to her offspring.

Mary improvised educations for her eldest two. She scrabbled together months of school here and tutoring there for her elder children, establishing a pattern for her younger children. She worked to make up for her lack of funds through connections and the arts of sociability.

The older children apparently spent (George possibly in 1747) some time in school with the Reverend James Maury across the Rappahannock. The son of Washington's cousin Lewis Willis remembered his father telling him about George's studiousness with occasional eruptions of play, particularly with one of the "largest girls." This apparently astonished his companions. Willis also recalled times that he and George and Betty would enjoy the outdoors together, which perhaps made George think romping with girls was normal.[4]

George spent considerable time at Wakefield at Austin and Anne's. After his father's death, he seems to have attended a school in Westmoreland County run by Henry Williams. He also spent time with his cousins Lawrence and Robin Washington from Chotank, located on the route from Fredericksburg to Pope's Creek (Wakefield). Washington later remembered these cousins in his will, calling them the "acquaintances and friends of my Juvenile years." He made a lifelong bond with another cousin, Lund Washington, who would manage Mount Vernon while George was commander in chief. After Augustine's death, George often visited these relatives and wrote letters to them as an adolescent.[5] George later remembered his "defective" education and being tutored. Mary could not have paid for a tutor, so perhaps he meant Williams.[6]

Mary allowed George to visit Mount Vernon and enjoy the company of the well-mannered Lawrence, his in-laws, and his circle of friends. He spent many happy days and evenings at Lawrence's in-laws' neighboring home, Belvoir. (After the Revolution, when it was in ruins, George wrote that he couldn't bear to look at it when he "considered that the happiest moments of my life had been spent there.")[7] About fourteen years older than George, Lawrence offered his little brother companionship, continuity with his father's line of the family, and a model of elite masculinity. Their relationship had parallels with the one Mary's half sister Elizabeth formed with the just-bereaved Mary at almost exactly the same stage in her life.[8] George passed stretches of nourishing time with his eldest brother, something Mary would have known from her own experience that he needed.

At twelve, a year after his father's death, George famously made a handwritten copy of a brief version of *Rules of Civility and Decent Behaviour in Company and Conversation*. The Reverend James Maury, who ran a school in Fredericksburg that George is said to have attended, would have known this book and been able to translate it, but scholars believe that George was working from an English edition.[9] In any case, the 110 rules gave instructions for decorous behavior, especially at table, and ranged from injunctions against killing vermin in company to deferring to others in conversation, from not speaking at too great length to not speaking ill of the absent. Controlling the body figured importantly: not cleaning the teeth at the table or puffing out one's cheeks or putting one's face too close to another and/or spitting on him. These kinds of warnings dotted the gentility manuals that circulated among ambitious colonials and offered behavioral guides to the young and uncertain.[10]

Much later, a youthful companion from the Pope's Creek area, Buckner Stith, reminded George that he and his cousin Lawrence had laughed at him for holding a wineglass by the bowl with his whole hand instead of by the stem. "But as I was five years elder than either of them, I thought I might hold the wine glass as I pleased."[11] (Archaeology at Ferry Farm shows that the Washingtons had stem glassware, an uncommon refinement at mid-century. George learned his lessons in elegance at home.)[12]

The *Rules* confirmed the social safety of George's natural tendencies to gravity and taciturnity ("reserve," as Washington himself described it).[13] To the fatherless child with a mother whose footing remained unsteady in her late husband's social class, these were important precepts. Touchingly, when George was suddenly deprived of a close example of proper male behavior, he looked to written rules that would guide him, especially in the kinds of social occasions that he was encountering through Lawrence. George's turn toward Mount Vernon and the Fairfaxes brought him into contact with people whose manners seemed assured, who spoke of matters that he probably did not always understand, who dressed and conversed more elegantly than he did, using humor and snatches of foreign languages. He wanted to be part of this world.

Mary's mother had not modeled surpassing elegance in speech or literacy. More than one of George's biographers have argued that Lawrence found Mary crude, illiterate, and pipe smoking. Lawrence's polish might have constrained his stepmother's behavior with him, particularly if he made her feel her own lack of sophistication. Certainly, such distaste would have communicated itself. She was, of course, not illiterate, and although she had not had a refined education, there is no evidence that she was crude. The word "respectable" is most often applied to her and to her Ball relatives like her half niece Sallie Haynie, whom George would help out in her old age. The word described women with good manners and reputations but little fortune. Archaeologists have found Mason's pipe fragments at Ferry Farm from the time George became a Mason and received a promotion, but they have not connected pipe artifacts to Mary. However Lawrence might have evaluated Mary's manners, he did not alienate her, and Mary in turn did not discourage George's relationship with Lawrence. She did not try to include herself in visits to Belvoir. She was aware of her own social limits. But she wished for more for her young. An impecunious, widowed mother, she stayed on the alert for opportunities for her children.

Mothers usually relinquished whatever control they had over their sons by the time they reached adolescence. Observers in Virginia were struck by the independence of gentry young men who, at fifteen, commandeered transportation and slaves and took the liberty to go where they desired and do what they wished. The young British diarist and traveler Nicholas Cresswell observed, "There is very little subordination observed in their youth. Implicit obedience to old age is not among their qualifications."[14] Usually with the approval and encouragement of their fathers, sons seized early opportunities to hunt, shoot, fight, drink, and have sex with slaves and poor white girls. In the Carter family, old neighbors of Mary's from across Corotoman Creek, the tutor, Philip Fithian, seemed amused by the accusation that his student Ben had tried to rape the sixteen-year-old "buxom" slave Sukey. Later in the century, Richard Randolph read off-color books, sexually exploited a poor white girl, and spent money recklessly.[15] Martha Custis Washington's son Jacky would attend school with two horses and the enslaved Julius (who would have to be replaced with Joe because Julius became "spoiled" under Jack's management). He spent money with wild abandon, became engaged secretly at about nineteen, and dropped out of Columbia College against the wishes of his stepfather.[16]

Mary did not permit George the high-living adolescence most Virginia gentry boys enjoyed. Much later, David Humphreys in his biography of George cited the latter's dismay over wealthy youths being educated in England and, if left in Virginia, being "in danger of becoming indolent & helpless from the usual indulgence giving a horse & a servant to attend them, as soon as they could ride; if not imperious & dissipated from the habit of commanding slaves & living in a measure without controul." George noted that if his father had not died, he would have gone to school in England.[17] Humphreys credited George's self-control and his misfortune in losing his father with helping him to resist the debilitating temptations for young white men from slaveholding families. Humphreys was unable to see the influence of Mary in George's development. But it was Mary who kept him from "living in a measure without controul." She did it in part by including him as a principal adviser on problems of farm management and consulting him about the family's straits. She began to share responsibili-ties with him for thinking about running the farm that would be his. In the void opened by Augustine's demise, she treated George seriously as a man and as a religious being. Scrupulous, thrifty, and observant, she ex-acted a strict accounting from him, literally and morally, and he kept the habit as a son, planter, military man, and political leader. George respected her moral authority and adopted much of her philosophy as his own.

Mary's extreme shortness of cash meant that she could not afford many activities useful for George on entering manhood at the elite social level. She could not afford to pay for the dancing lessons George wanted, though she knew how essential this skill was in Virginia society. Mary advanced him the money. He noted in the account book he began keeping at fifteen that he paid her back the three shillings for the "Musick Master."[18] The dancing master would teach him genteel postures and attitudes to strike in company, invaluable for dancing but also for self-presentation. In the minuet, for example, those postures, formal bows, and "correct" walking constituted the dance itself. In portraits of Washington and others of the era, the men place their legs and feet in these prescribed ways.[19] (He would become an excellent dancer and search carefully for a dancing master for Martha's children.)

Archaeologists have identified the hinge of a card table at Ferry Farm. George and Betty and their brothers clearly socialized at home as well as at Belvoir and Mount Vernon. Mary made it possible for them to entertain and enjoy themselves at games like whist, one of George's later favorites.[20]

George shopped for Mary in Fredericksburg, buying a glass ring and some ribbons. In later years, he remained a strict accountant. He also became known at a young age as the one in the family who actually possessed some cash. His brothers, including Lawrence, borrowed from him.[21]

Mary oversaw the maintenance of the wigs for all four of her sons, now of wig-wearing ages. They were for sale in Williamsburg by 1720 and after 1750 at Yorktown, but they were expensive—anywhere from a little over a pound and a half to more than three pounds, and then there was the powder and the pomade. Gentlemen usually had more than one wig. No doubt, the boys could share, but head sizes differed, and it was extremely embarrassing to have a wig slip or fall off. When George was twenty, he bought his younger brother a gray wig for a little more than seventeen shillings. Samuel would have his portrait painted in another.[22]

At her mother's side, Betty acquired experience in the kitchen, spinning room, dairy, and gardens earlier than she might have if the family had had less need for purposeful labor. Or if Betty had had a mother who valued work less.

Betty spent enough time at the Reverend Maury's school to learn to write with a more rhetorical flourish than her mother did.[23] She wrote in an attractive and legible hand, with style beyond what is required simply to communicate information, although her spelling, like her mother's and Martha Washington's, was imaginative. She also picked up the emotive, elite style of the time. Writing to George in 1779, after a visit to Martha at Mount Vernon, she exclaimed rhetorically, "Could I of found you there it would of Compleat'd my Happiness, O when will that Day Come that we shall meet again?"[24]

Betty must have learned something about writing from reading Eliza Haywood's *Female Spectator*. Some time after 1746, when it became available, Mary acquired the collection of articles written by the actress, dramatist, and novelist. Although officially directed toward girls and women, it also could serve as a guide to the adolescent sexual behavior of both sexes. Many of the essays stress reason in the choice of lovers and illustrate the evil consequences of choices made from passion (on the part of either young people or their parents). Similar to the British newspaper stories of the period that found their way into *The Virginia Gazette*, Haywood described the dangers to women of violence and rape that lurked at balls, at masquerades, and in seemingly innocent friendships. Tales of girls' seduction and violation are paired with happier narratives of young women's reasoned selection of honorable men for husbands and sober brothers protecting the virtue of their sisters.

Haywood also insisted that parents not coerce their children to marry against their desires. Ideally, a young man and woman raised with affection and reason will exercise both in choosing a partner. Haywood thought bringing young men and women together socially would give them experience to judge carefully. She wondered if "Miss Eagaretta [would] have ever condescended to marry the greasy Footman that ran before her Chair, had he not been the only Man her over-careful Father had permitted her to speak to."[25]

Eliza Haywood did not limit her articles to cautionary tales for moral training of the young. She also wrote about the joys of reading and observing nature in a scientific way. Influenced by Locke and Bacon, Haywood illustrated her works with women studying, learning, and meditating on the implications of what they observe. She rejected those male thinkers who said that a woman should be confined to the "Management of her Family; that is to give orders concerning the Table, take care of her Children in their Infancy, and observe that her Servants do not neglect their Business."

Instead, she argued that "true Philosophy as well as Religion will shew us better Things. . . . Let us then devote some Part of our Time to Study and Meditation. *When the Mind is worthily employed,* says a great Author, *the Body becomes spiritualized; but when we suffer a Lassitude to benumn our Faculties, the very spirit degenerates into Matter."*

Haywood's ideas on moral training, education for boys and girls, and the value of natural philosophy correspond to Mary's. They also correspond to George's, and in 1764 George also owned a copy of Haywood's *Epistles for the Ladies.*[26] It would have made useful reading for George, who, as a teenager and young man, enjoyed a few passionate flirts. Betty was on the verge of marriage and very likely would have found Haywood's support for continuing female education appealing. Certainly, Mary encouraged socializing as good education for her children. No greasy footman married into her family; all her children married up.

Mary saw that Betty's education balanced work and social accomplishments. She wanted Betty to marry well, and she labored to provide her daughter with the poise, polish, and household skills to compensate for a small dowry. She could not afford many of the consumer items pouring into the market, but she added many inexpensive accoutrements to the necessary table, board, and tea services already at Ferry Farm. Tea services combined displays of status and leisure along with comfort.

Shards of seven successive teapots testify to Mary's commitment to giving her children, but particularly Betty, an essential social skill. Tea tables and tea boards held the several teapots that contained different kinds of tea, and Mary and Betty would share the rituals of presenting tea and food to family and visitors correctly. Both Betty and her brothers attended tea and learned its lexicon of proprieties, such as the gesture indicating that one had had enough tea.[27] When Mary served tea, and instructed Betty to do the same, she provided the warm setting for a family performance of respectability and sociability.

The eighteenth-century tea table was a very widespread, informal center of genteel women's power, a kind of semipublic space within the home where women and men discussed fashion, reading, friends, family and neighbors, power relations between the genders, and increasingly politics. It is unlikely that Mary would have talked politics, but her children would have. She would have exchanged gossip and details of agricultural and town life. Her children began developing their conversational styles: deference to their mother and, in George's case, reserve and watchfulness. Betty learned to serve, welcome friends and family, and speak about family and local matters in a familiar but not too familiar way, and with the humor, practicality, intelligence, and sensibility that her letters reflect and her children remembered.[28]

Mary's tea table training helped her children behave gracefully with elite young people. Leisured Virginians compared tea flavors, teapots, dishes, and styles of serving.[29] Mary's children learned at her tea board how tea should taste and what should be served with it. George was devoted to tea throughout his life. He wrote a send-up of what he named "The Bread and Butter Ball" in 1760, when he encountered tea and coffee that the "drinkers could not distinguish from Hot water sweetened." On the table, he wrote archly, "abounded great plenty of Bread and Butter." George, accustomed to a better spread—like his mother's pound cake—teased the hosts of the ball for providing nothing else.[30] During the constitutional deliberations, tea was often the only activity that made it into George's diaries.[31] Betty would have taken tea with her friends and relatives, including her cousin Catharine Washington, who became the first wife of the family friend Fielding Lewis. Catharine's mother, Catharine, Betty's aunt, had died in 1743, and Catharine, who was twenty-one in 1745, had moved to Fredericksburg. After the death of Catharine, Fielding might well have pressed his desire to marry Betty over tea.

To ornament the house that friends visited for tea, Mary bought a few small stoneware figurines displaying the vices such as sloth and gluttony. These, too, were inexpensive and displayed the family's taste and individuality.

Mary instructed Betty in needlework, the skills in stitching that she had acquired as a child as well as fancywork that required a tambour hook. The tambour hook found at Ferry Farm came from England and had a horn handle decorated with flowering vines, leaves, and a parrot—all designs that tambour workers liked to replicate.[32] Betty held a frame with stretched fabric in it, hooked thread from beneath it with the tambour needle, and pulled it through. It demanded less skill than embroidery and became an extremely popular women's ornamental accomplishment in late eighteenth-century Virginia. When Mary helped Betty learn, tambour hooks and stitching were still quite rare in the colony.

Mary and Betty spent considerable time reconfiguring items of cloth-ing to get the maximum amount of use from them. Producing cloth was still very time-consuming, and women's clothing was largely handmade, although men's clothing was beginning to be standardized. Mid-eighteenth-century women's clothing was complicated and worn tight, requiring careful fitting to the body. Betty and Mary could use their fancy needle-work skills on hand-quilted petticoats that were designed to show at the front opening of a gown and below the skirt where it was folded up to re-veal fine designs. These quilted petticoats, like the figurines and tea services, displayed individuality, taste, and the workmanship of hands with leisure and servants to accomplish the household's many more basic sewing needs.[33]

Years later, when George and Betty serially sheltered their orphaned niece, Harriot, they wrote displaying their identical views on Harriot's be-havior with her clothing. They warned the girl against wearing inappro-priately dressy clothes around the house on ordinary days and thoughtlessly leaving her clothes balled up and wrinkled about the house. They praised her for preserving, mending, and using garments with care and attention. After observing her for a while, Betty wrote to George, "I must in Justice to Harriot say she Payes the strictest regard to the advice I give her and really she is very Ingenious in makeing her Clothes and altering them to the best advantage."[34] Mary's lessons outlived her.

Mary tried to see that not only George but also Betty had diversions.

She permitted her to accompany George when he visited Lawrence, in whose houses prosperous people gathered. Betty visited Mount Vernon with George at least once, when his stepbrother was in England in 1749, and probably more often. Young men and women made these kinds of visits—often of a week or more—to socialize respectably and to find mates.[35]

||||||||||||

SOMETIME IN 1746, Lawrence decided that it would be a good thing for fourteen-year-old George to go into the British navy or to learn commercial seafaring and become a captain. An able-bodied seaman earned about twenty-four shillings every twenty-eight days, a fairly high wage for the time. Lawrence was probably imagining George as a midshipman, who would earn a bit more but, more important, would probably become a lieutenant in two years if things went well. A midshipman had to behave and dress like a gentleman and enjoyed the significant class privilege of being allowed to walk the quarterdeck. He also would have had the company of some fifty other boys between the ages of about six and eighteen who routinely sailed on navy ships literally to learn the ropes.[36]

Lawrence thought the choice was unlikely to find favor with Mary. Mary, who had not so long ago absorbed Lawrence's frightening letters about his maritime adventure in the Caribbean, had a new reason to be opposed to a naval career for George. Thomas Fairfax, an officer in the British navy and prospective brother-in-law of Lawrence's, had died just the month before Lawrence and his sister Anne's wedding, in a battle with the French off the Indian coast.[37] The British navy enlisted many orphan boys about George's age. However, about one-third of the fourteen-year-old recruits did not survive their first two years of exposure to disease and the other rigors of British navy life.[38]

Proceeding cautiously, indeed duplicitously, Lawrence, his father-in-law, William Fairfax, and a number of their friends, including Robert Jackson, a Fredericksburg merchant, a vestryman, and one of the executors of Augustine Washington's will, raised the possibility with mother and son separately.[39] William Fairfax passed through Fredericksburg in September 1746 and wrote to Lawrence that he had not yet seen Mrs. Washington but he had spoken to George, who "has been with us and says he will be steady, and thankfully follow your advice as his best friend. I gave him his mother's letter to deliver with caution not to shew his." William Fairfax mentioned that Dr. Spencer was often at Ferry Farm, and he would try to get him to put in a good word for the plan.[40] The letter for George, presumably describing the delights of a sailor's life, has not survived.

Several substantial men—the agent and relative of an English lord, a local merchant and friend of Augustine's, Mary's stepson, and other friendly observers—tried hard to manipulate the boy and the widow. They drew George into their conspiracy and encouraged him to join them in softening up and working around his mother. George pledged to "thankfully follow" Lawrence's advice as his best friend. In claiming Lawrence as his best friend, George pledged himself to a relationship of primary importance upon which depended his advancement in life. As Keith Thomas has written, "A faithful friend was a strong defence . . . [in a] hostile world. The private correspondence of the early modern period is preoccupied with the creation and maintenance of such alliances; . . . the language employed was that of benefits bestowed and gratitude returned."[41] George's circle of would-be patrons invited him to enjoy male solidarity—a state that he would enjoy off and on throughout his life. But they failed to convince Mary.

Robert Jackson wrote to Lawrence in September 1746 that Mary seemed more predisposed against the idea. "I am afraid that Mrs. Washington will not keep up her first resolution—She seems to intimate a dislike of George's going to sea, & says several persons have told her its [*sic*] a very bad Scheme. She offers several trifling objections."[42]

Mary wrote to her brother Joseph Ball for advice in December 1746. Ball responded in May 1747 with a resounding no. His letter confirmed her decision. Ball wrote, "I think he had better be put apprentice to a tinker; for a common sailor before the mast has by no means the common liberty of the Subject; for they will press him from a ship where he has 50 shillings a month and make him take three and twenty; and cut him and staple him and use him like a negro, or rather, like a dog."[43] There is some doubt that this letter reached her before she had made up her mind. She might also have heard the story—possibly apocryphal—that George Eskridge had been pressed onto a ship as a young man, and it had cost him eight years of freedom. When she got Ball's letter, she knew exactly what Ball meant by his comparisons of sailors with dogs and blacks. Mary played her part in sustaining the abject condition of blacks, at the same time she, too, was without the "common liberty of the [British] subject."[44] Washington later recalled that his packed bags had to be retrieved from shipboard. He also recalled, tellingly, that his mother's "earnest solicitations" had won the day. George described his mother as not commanding him to stay home but beseeching him.[45]

This rare, incompletely documented incident of one of Mary's decisions about her son has played a disproportionate part in numerous damning depictions of her. Many biographers have interpreted Mary Washington's reluctance to let George follow Lawrence into the British navy as a midshipman as, at best, a sign of her "fondness" or weak-minded love for her eldest son and, at worst, a demonstration of her possessive, overprotective, and emasculating attitude toward him.[46] Douglas Southall Freeman wrote, "Mistress of much or of little, mistress she was resolved to be, and in nothing more certainly than in deciding what should be done by her first-born, her pride and her weakness. She would hold him fast, safe from the temptations of a sailor's life and from the dangers of the frontier. Lawrence might counsel and plan, but she would decide: George was her son, not Lawrence's."[47] Freeman's belittling view of Mary Washington as controlling and overly protective, which echoes that of Samuel Eliot Morison two decades before,[48] has strongly influenced subsequent historians. (In fact, she did not try to keep him safe from the frontier.)

There is no evidence that Mary—on her side—took part in a power struggle with Lawrence over her son, although Lawrence was underhandedly trying to influence George to resist her. If she had been trying to diminish Lawrence's influence, she would have tried to curtail George's access to him, and she did not do that. On the contrary, she permitted George in March 1748 to go on a lengthy and potentially dangerous surveying mission of the Fairfaxes' western territories, precisely to the frontier from which Freeman claimed she was trying to keep him.[49] Lawrence does not seem to have held her decision about the navy against her. He agreed, when he went to Great Britain the following year, to visit her brother Joseph. He brought back gifts on his return. Jack Warren, a historian steeped in the Washington records, thinks Mary's refusal shows Lawrence's lack of influence on George rather than the very powerful bond that Freeman and others have assumed existed between them.[50]

Most important, it is hard to dispute her good sense in keeping her fourteen-year-old son out of the British navy, a singularly dangerous institution in the eighteenth century. While many of Washington's biographers have overlooked this point, some have noted, at least, that if George had become an officer in the British navy, the Revolution might have taken a different turn.

Mary stands out from many white southern mothers in continuing to have influence over her son in his mid-teens, a time when adolescent boys pushed off. George did not, nor was his older brother's enthusiasm enough to make him break away. Duty, rebellion, and the tension between the two dominated this complex young man's spirit during much of his life. It seems that Mary's principles of dutiful obedience to religiously ordained obligations and the suppression of impulses that threatened these values warred in George with an aggressive, restless, and risk-taking spirit. In prosecuting the Revolution, he would find a way to blend these two antagonistic parts of his character guiltlessly.

Mary assumed that she both could and should have some control over the behavior of her children, partly from her belief that it was for the best but also because eighteenth-century parents generally had a less fatalistic attitude than parents of an earlier era. White Virginians of Mary's generation had an increasing sense of their own ability to control, with rationality, their strong emotions. Their use of reason seems to have helped them extend their control to their surroundings. In the seventeenth century, Cotton Mather, for one, wrote several times about his children's falling into the fireplace and being scorched. Rather than put a screen up, he analyzed God's various reasons for punishing him. Seventeenth-century diaries are full of these kinds of stories, written by parents who relied on teaching their children to be obedient and to learn to love God as a way to keep them safe. Eighteenth-century adults saw themselves as more capable of controlling not only their strong feelings but also their environments. Mary's devotional books all counseled the use of reason to combat sadness, fear, and anger. The emphasis on stoicism in the face of unhappy events simultaneously encouraged the development of self-control. And this, historians think, helped lead believers to take those matters that they could into their own hands.[51]

MARY TOOK PAINS to make her children safe, but contrary to Freeman she was not an overly protective mother. Custis's memoirs of Washington's early youth include a story that resembles the famous cherry tree tale enough to seem as if it were its basis, except that it involves George risking danger.

Mary had a number of "blooded," or specially bred, horses that she liked. Among them was a sorrel of a "fierce and ungovernable nature" that "resisted all attempts to subject him to the rein."[52] According to the story, several hardy riders had attempted and failed to break the horse. Early one morning, George told his companions that he would ride the horse if they would help him put a bridle on it. They briefly immobilized the horse and put a bit in his mouth, and George mounted. "The struggle now became terrific to the beholders, who almost wished that they had not joined in an enterprise, so likely to be fatal to their daring associate." The two fought on, and it seemed that George was beginning to subdue the horse's resistance when it suddenly gathered all its power to make a final plunge using all its strength and just as suddenly fell and died. George was unharmed.

At breakfast, Mary asked them if they had seen her blooded colts, especially her favorite, which she had heard had become quite large. After a pause, George answered, "Your favorite sorrel is dead, madam." George told the story: that the colt had been unridable, that George, in trying to ride it, had struggled, and that the horse had exerted itself so much that it died. In Custis's narration, Mary's cheeks became red with anger, but she controlled herself and said, "It is well; but while I regret the loss of my favorite, *I rejoice in my son, who always speaks the truth.*" It's not hard to imagine Mary, the talented horsewoman, admiring the courage it took for George to try to break the colt while simultaneously being angry at its death. Her effort to find a moral rather than a material perspective on this loss of a young, promising colt resonates with the Anglican thinkers she read who put acceptance of loss above the things of this world. Perhaps her anger and her forgiveness did not happen at the same time. She had a "high temper"; perhaps she lost it.[53] We will never know.

We do know that George enjoyed subduing difficult horses all his life. Jeremy Prophet, an enslaved man of George's brother John Augustine, who then shared him with George, remembered a particularly wild horse named Starling that George raised years later. "He no let nobody ride or break him. When he tree year old, he bring him one Sunday morning, and say he gying to ride him. I look out; I 'xpect ebery minute he git he neck broke, but when he sling he leg over, he dare, no git him off. . . . I don't say no better dan he, but I neber seed none." Jeremy told this story at ninety.[54]

Mary groped for a way to set George on a rewarding and safe path. In the rest of Joseph Ball's letter rejecting the navy, he told her what he thought George should do: "A planter that has three or four hundred acres of land, and three or four slaves, if he be Industrious, may live more comfortably, and leave his family in better Bread than such a master of a ship can. And if the Planter can get ever so little beforehand, let him begin to . . . buy goods for tobacco and sell them again for tobacco . . . but he must never pretend to buy for money and sell for tobacco. I never knew any of them but what lost more money than they got; neither must he send his tobacco to England to be sold here and goods sent him; if he does, he will soon get in the Merchants' debt, and never get out again."[55] Ball was well aware of the high yield to be had for substantial planters. Ball himself, now an absentee farmer, lived "comfortably." He was also thoroughly knowledgeable about the debts that tobacco cultivation and the colonial trade system could lead to. Mary took his advice seriously.

The death of Augustine had abruptly pointed George toward a practical education, not the classical one his brothers had enjoyed. George's lack of educational polish would be a source of embarrassment for him, but Mary gave him what education she could, and he made the most of it. He practiced with his father's surveying gear and learned the mathematics and geometry to become the surveyor of Culpeper County at seventeen, the youngest surveyor ever.

George had to learn his mathematics to some extent on his own because basic arithmetic was not a skill widely taught in Virginia schools. Oddly, Virginians became interested in mathematics and statistics before their famously calculating Puritan counterparts in New England. Even so, as late as 1755, Fielding Lewis (who would become Mary's son-in-law) and Robert Jackson had to advertise for someone to teach the skills in Fredericksburg, so absent was it from the curriculum for young people. As Patricia Cline Cohen, historian of numeracy, has written, "Increasingly what colonial administrators measured was what they thought they should *control*." A push for control and measure came with smallpox epidemics in the early and mid-eighteenth century, and merchants generally needed mathematics. But planters, who incurred large debts and urgently needed accounting skills, seem to have eschewed them. Not George, however. Land was, of course, something he already wanted to control, and the evidence of his precise accounting coincided with his avid study of geometry and mathematics.[56]

Equivalent in social prestige to being a lawyer, a surveyor in Virginia could bring in an income of a hundred pounds annually and, of course, would make George knowledgeable about available lands. The College of William and Mary appointed surveyors, and the General Assembly regulated their fees, which rose over the eighteenth century. Lord Fairfax's patronage and William Fairfax's position on the Governor's Council greatly enhanced George's prospects for an appointment. Most surveyors served a long apprenticeship before getting a colony appointment, and George never even studied surveying formally. He presented his commission to the Culpepper authorities on July 20 and took his first assignment there two days later, earning him two pounds and three shillings. He also copied deeds for landowners. The cash fees he earned often made him the member of the family who enjoyed some liquidity—of which his siblings availed themselves.[57] In his first period doing surveying, he was also engaged in Bible study. A note from a very early memorandum book reads, "If you cant find it in the Book of Ezekiel look for it in Israel."[58]

The years after Augustine's death made George closer to his mother than he might otherwise have been. He acquired the habit of shouldering responsibility and began trying on a judicious voice of authority in these years. His ideas and tone seem steeped in those of Matthew Hale. In a letter to Lawrence's wife, Anne, in 1749, he told her he hoped that while Lawrence was away in Great Britain, she would "make Use of [her] Natural Resolution and contentedness as they are the only Remedys to spend the time with ease & pleasure to yourself."[59] Hale described contentedness as the most desirable state of mind and one that a Christian must strive for. George's precocious moral advice (he was seventeen when he wrote this letter to his seemingly sophisticated twenty-one-year-old sister-in-law) echoed Hale's recommendation to adopt a "cheerful submission to adversity" and the author's belief that it was a lesson that could be learned. In Hale's view, contentedness ultimately derived from an easy conscience and gratitude to God for what one has. George, eager to look mature but not overly pious, marshaled the behavioral advice and did not invoke the religious thought behind it.[60] If Mary was given to moral summations and lessons, so too was her son and in phrases strikingly similar to those of her favorite books.

As a newly widowed mother, Mary encouraged her eldest son and daughter to help and advise her. In the early modern period, particularly in agricultural societies like Virginia, age was not the marker that it came to be. Mary included Betty in her daily activities, as she herself had been both apprentice and companion to her mother and sister. The choice of her older children for these responsibilities had less to do with their actual ages than with their birth order and gender, as well as Mary's sense of their characters and capacities. George, as a young male with an unusually serious bearing, was destined for autonomy and responsibility. Betty, as the only girl, alone could acquire and carry on her mother's valuable knowledge and skills and share her intimate concerns for her other children as well as their mutual understandings of being female in a patriarchy.

11

MARY'S STEWARDSHIP:
SCRAPING BY

‖‖‖

This World is a place for our duty and employment,
and we must use all honest care and lawful means
to preserve our lives and our comforts.

—MATTHEW HALE, *CONTEMPLATIONS MORAL AND DIVINE*

*I*N 1748, LAWRENCE AND ANOTHER EXECUTOR of Augustine's will sold a tract of Ferry Farm back to its original owner, Anthony Strother, reducing the land available for Mary to cultivate. The will had provided for this sale if it would benefit George. It put 110 pounds in his pocket—or a future pocket.[1]

Because she and her family no longer received income from Augustine's other plantations, Mary's crops had to produce whatever cash there would be for the family as well as feed everyone, including about twenty enslaved men, women, and children. Mary grew some combination of tobacco, corn, wheat, oats, flax, rye, and vegetables and raised pigs, sheep, beef, and hens on Ferry Farm.[2]

Mary inherited Augustine's overseer, whom she had to manage. Her mother's and brother's experiences, in addition to whatever complaints Augustine might have expressed—and no planter failed to complain about overseers—already filled her head with suspicions and criticisms. In 1745, Joseph Ball, in one of his passionate letters from Great Britain, from where he was trying to manage his plantation manager, congratulated Joseph Chinn, his and Mary's nephew, for firing his overseer, "a sad sleepy headed fellow; you can't well get a worse."[3] When Ball wrote to him about the deaths of a number of his slaves, he speculated that Chinn had not provided them with sufficient fires, alcohol, and medical attention, but worse, "you let unmerciful overseers beat, and abuse them inhumanly, and break their hearts."[4] Under Mary and her overseer, the enslaved Bob had the position of driver, that difficult, divided responsibility, pitting his loyalty to his fellow workers against his desire for survival and safety.

During her years with Augustine, Mary had more leisure and luxury than at any other time in her life, but her habits were formed in less comfortable circumstances, and she believed in productive activity. Marriage to Augustine shielded her from necessity and full-time management. Now she had to run things. Mary was up to her new job.

To show her command and limit the mistakes she anticipated, Mary spelled out her orders, trying to leave little room for initiative or omissions. Her grandson reported that as an old woman after she moved off Ferry Farm, she continued to carry her own keys to the supplies on her remaining land. A slave would drive her "about her fields, giving her orders, and seeing that they were obeyed." On one occasion, an agent to whom she had given directions about a particular piece of work chose to execute the job in his own way. "The lady, whose *coup d'oeil* was as perfect in rural affairs as that of her son in war, pointed out the error. The agent excused himself by saying that 'in his judgment the work was done to more advantage than it would have been by his first directions.' Mrs. Washington replied, 'And pray, who gave you any exercise of judgment in the matter? I command you, sir; there is nothing left for you but to obey.'"[5] Her firstborn son wrote almost identical sentiments more than once in his life. Four days before he died, George wrote, "I cannot forbear to add, and in strong terms; it is, that whenever I order a thing to be done, it must be done; or a reason given at the time, or as soon as the impractibility is discovered, why it cannot."[6]

Historians have used Custis's story to paint Mary Washington as an unreasonably demanding plantation mistress.[7] The judgment against Mary comes, of course, from ideas about how women should behave, not the ugly realities of slave or worker management.

Mary had been both female and an owner of slaves all her life. From her earliest years, she needed to bear herself in the world with convincing authority. When she was widowed, the habit of command was particularly useful to her. A woman's authority invited challenge, and Mary knew that she would have to show herself capable of commanding her manager if she was to have any credibility as a farm mistress. Slavery could not survive without force. Mary knew from long experience that a woman plantation owner could not back down before a hired hand, particularly in front of slaves.[8] This behavior put her at odds with myths about the inherently gentle disposition of (white) women that were increasingly widespread in novels and books and had come to be used to distinguish the elite from the rest in southern colonial society.[9] Custis used the anecdote to highlight Mary's planter expertise and strength, but Freeman wished to show that she was no lady.

Mary saw to it that slaves put the corn in sometime in April or May. Corn, like tobacco, required slaves to hoe up little hills in which to plant it. Moles and birds attacked corn, and the plants had to be weeded.[10] Slave children sometimes worked shooing away the crows, blackbirds, and other corn eaters. Sometimes they also thinned out the corn seedlings.[11]

Some planters sowed their wheat in among the corn where the land was already plowed. Wherever Mary had the slaves sow her rye, grain in general was the crop that, once planted, tended to take care of itself until harvest. In Virginia, farmers could grow two wheat crops a year. George recorded in his diary cutting his first crop of wheat in July and sowing rye in September.[12] Relatively work-free, wheat eventually became the crop that planters like George Washington used to try to extricate themselves from the debt cycle that tobacco produced with its high labor demands, its almost continually falling prices, and the growing stranglehold that British merchants had over extravagant planters.[13]

The 1750s were very dry years, and crops were thin.[14] In May 1753 and again in 1754, Mary had to defend herself against charges that she was growing inferior tobacco, or tobacco from suckers—secondary shoots coming up from the main plant. Throughout the eighteenth century, tobacco inspection to distinguish high-grade from lower-grade leaves roused strong feelings and even violence. When prices of tobacco dropped, as they had cyclically since the turn of the eighteenth century, and then again in the 1720s and the 1740s, officials tried to remedy the situation by allowing less tobacco on the market and regulating its quality rigorously. The Virginia Inspection Act of 1730 required all tobacco to be inspected at warehouses. Smaller farmers in several counties rallied against the law and its agents and burned warehouses. The law pitted smaller farmers against richer ones, who could better afford to lose a bit of their crop. Tobacco from the Northern Neck was famous for its aromatic flavor and quality. The laws also aimed to protect that reputation and maintain the distinction between it and the lower-grade tobacco grown along the shores of the Potomac. The law seemed to work. In the 1750s, tobacco prices were on the rise and would continue to climb until the depression that followed the Seven Years' War, but planters were increasingly in debt. The King George County deputy attorney John Lewis charged Mary and a number of other tobacco growers with the offense of including inferior tobacco in their shipments. She did not show up for the first trial. At the second, a year later, a jury exonerated her and her fellow defendants.

These charges displayed Mary's position among the middling farmers who were trying to get by, not the wealthy who could afford these challenges. Mary needed to call on her grit in the face of setbacks and humiliations. Scrappy and tough like her mother, she stood up for herself. Whether it was this legal unpleasantness, trying to coax good tobacco during the dry decade of the 1750s, or some other reason, she had stopped growing tobacco by 1760. That year, she wrote to her brother that the captains did not call on her, "as I don't ship tobacco."[15]

Mary's mother had grown flax at Cherry Point farm. Mary, too, would grow flax despite its challenges and the three seasons required to raise and process it. Great Britain had long encouraged the cultivation of flax, and Virginia and Maryland had actually passed a law requiring farmers to grow it, but the seeds were hard to come by, and the laws had to be repealed. When seeds became more available, most colonists chose not to raise it as a commercial crop, because it required considerable skill and time that most farmers preferred to expend on tobacco when the prices were not depressed, as they were not from the 1740s until the Seven Years' War.[16]

Flax had to be left to decay and then pounded and combed before the "hard outer shell released the fibers within." The harvested crop went through several poetically named stages. Once "breaked," the fibers had to be "scutched" or "swingled" with a double-sided scutching knife to remove bits of bark and woody pieces left in the fibers. Then they had to be "heckled," or "hackled," with a heckle board and iron comb, on which a heckler (or hechler) combed the coarse fibers, removing the short ones, which became oakum for filling cracks and seams on boats, with the rest becoming linen fiber.

Only at that point could the fibers be spun into thread and then woven into linen. Once spun, it might be bleached with buttermilk to make it white and increase its value. Or it could be left in its natural brown color to clothe the poorest members of the establishment.[17] With her flax crop, Mary could produce rough linen or osnaburg for slaves to wear.

Mary cared for her horses with particular attention. Jeremy Prophet, who witnessed George breaking a horse, remembered that in the 1750s

Mary had two dun-colored horses that she used only for her carriage. They were, he recalled vividly, very hard to handle and extremely "pranktious." "She wouldn't let um ever go to mill, and when dey was turned out, she always had um turned out in de bottom land, below de house, whare she could see um all de time."[18] Mary protected her favorite spirited and hard-to-handle horses from drudgery and took pleasure watching them enjoy their freedom along the river in front of her house.

During the third quarter of the eighteenth century—that is, when Mary took over Ferry Farm—"the annual gross revenue per hand" rose in Virginia overall by about five pounds from the previous quarter. "Slaves suffered disproportionately, since it was primarily their leisure that was sacrificed."[19] Mary's neighbor downstream on the Rappahannock, Landon Carter, had his slaves working many nights on various tobacco tasks like hanging tobacco plants to dry on poles, stripping the leaves off the stems and binding them into bundles, and stemming the tougher leaves. Several times, Carter remarked that his workers "labored till the moon went down."[20] Slaves had only the evening for whatever cooking, child care, socializing, and resting they hoped to do, so these steady encroachments on the little leisure they had were bitter.[21]

Whether or not Mary ratcheted up her work discipline, she probably shared her brother's tightfistedness toward slaves. Ball's sentimental impulses and gestures to favorites did not blunt his hard-edged understanding that he had purchased men and women to make himself a very good life, and he would make sure that they did that. There is no reason to assume that Mary felt any differently.

Joseph angrily rejected his slaves' request that in their free time they use some of his fallow land to grow wheat for themselves. Ball wrote to Chinn calling the proposal a "very pretty fancy that they shall have a share of everything that is made for me; and besides that I must find them ground to make wheat for themselves . . . you will allow no such liberty . . . let them swap some of their corn for it . . . they shall have none off my ground."[22]

In May 1749, Mary's corn stores were particularly small. George wrote to his brother Lawrence that he didn't have sufficient corn to nourish his thin horse for a long ride.[23] (He thought perhaps later in the season things would be better. These were the years that he later remembered with pain as being the poorest in his life.)[24]

A year later, the records show that Lawrence paid his brother Austin eighty-seven pounds and ten shillings for 180 barrels of corn for Accokeek and the workers there. That same bill noted the sale of 30 barrels of Mary's corn to Austin. When Mary's children were older, the siblings would all do business among themselves. In this case, Mary clearly needed cash and turned to her stepson who had just done a much bigger deal with his brother.[25]

The shortages at Ferry Farm probably came from scarce harvests, but planters generally believed slaves were stealing their crops as well. Mary's brother instructed his manager about protecting the corn. "Encourage," he wrote in 1743, "the overseers to make a good deal of corn and let the folks have their full shares; and . . . lock up the keys of the folks' cornhouse; for else they will sell it, and starve themselves; as they did when I was away in England before. They may let them have the key whenever they want corn to use, and then take it away again."[26] Later, George complained repeatedly about his slaves' thefts of plantation produce. Perhaps Mary's slaves were able to smuggle off more corn than they had when Augustine was in charge. Cereal sales (including corn) in Europe were growing in the eighteenth century, and there was always a ready market.[27]

If Mary punished her slaves for theft, we do not know what she and her overseer agreed on for disciplinary measures. Her brother wrote to Aaron, the enslaved man whom he sent back to work on his Virginia plantation after growing up in Great Britain, "You were very saucy while you were in Britain and resisted me twice. There must be no more of that; for if you offer to Strike your overseer, or be unruly, you must be tyed up and Slasht Severely and pickled [have his wounds doused with brine]; and if you Run away you must wear an Iron Pothook about your Neck: and if that don't tame you, you must wear Iron Spancels till you Submit." (Spancels were fetters used on the back legs of a cow to keep her still while milking her. An iron pothook was a long rod of iron with a large hook on the end for holding a pot over a fire.) After this set of grotesque threats, Ball ended his letter to Aaron, "Take warning and don't Ruin yourself by your folly. I recd. Your Letr. If you will be good I shall be yr. Loving Master, Jos. Ball."[28] Ball dispensed exhortation and menace from his imagined command post of a good Christian. He wanted to be a loving master, as Christ was to the faithful. But if provoked by Aaron's resistance, the loving master would have no choice but to slash and pickle.

Mary might not have shared her brother's desire to convince individual slaves that she was a "loving" mistress. As a woman, she would have had her hands full impressing on others her authority. Also, as a mistress in daily contact with household slaves, she had to delimit carefully the intimacy she shared with them. The enslaved Sue ran Mary's kitchen for many years—a crucial position. Mary depended on her fully to realize her daily goals and to underpin Mary's identity as the competent mistress of Ferry Farm. Mary had to pass endless hours in Sue's company without blurring their relative social positions. Sue, as much as anyone, knew Mary's habits, desires, temper, and thinking. Family members kept few enough of Mary's notes and thoughts, but the archive says nothing about Sue.

At the time that Mary was widowed, the high importations of Africans had just trailed off. In 1740, black inhabitants of the Chesapeake colonies constituted 28 percent of the population, and by mid-century Africans were four-fifths of the slave population.[29] At about that time, Africans in the Chesapeake region began to reproduce themselves in numbers that kept their population expanding from births, not from importations. This had never occurred among New World slaves. And it would not happen elsewhere in the South for six more decades.[30] Creole women were usually healthier than their African predecessors. They also approached parity with males in the population for the first time, crucial if a population is to reproduce itself. Many had eight or nine children over a lifetime.[31] Although enslaved women consistently had lower market prices than males, Thomas Jefferson observed that other masters regarded "a woman who brings a child every two years as more valuable than the best man on the farm."[32]

A group of twenty slaves, large for its time, was not large enough for all adults to find partners. Some of these slaves might have already formed attachments with slaves at Wakefield, at the iron foundry at Accokeek, where both men and women worked, or at Mount Vernon. They also might have found companions in the neighborhood of Fredericksburg, a growing town, only a short distance from the farm. Slaves could reach relatives and friends through an ever-expanding network of paths and roads that were too numerous for white Virginians to control. By the eve of the Revolution, "nearly every county between the Rappahannock and James Rivers as far west as the heads of navigation was more than half black."[33] Joseph Ball restricted the number of visits one of his married slaves could make to his wife on a neighboring plantation to once a month, leaving it to her to make the long trek if they wanted to see each other at other times.[34] How Mary's slaves fared, what kinds of relationships they were able to make, and how far afield they made marriages are unknown.

Mary considered building herself a house on Deep Run, on land that Augustine had divided between George and Samuel, according to Augustine's plan. She wrote to her brother Joseph asking if she could use wood from his plantation to build a house. Joseph approved of her plan to move out of Ferry Farm. But, more liberal with advice than with help, he wrote in May 1747, "As for timber, I have scarce enough for my own Plantation; so can spare you none of that, but as for stone, you may take what you please to build you a house."[35] After his refusal, her plan stalled.

She and George became alarmed in 1749 that a neighbor was planning to petition to shift the ferry across the river. George, worried about this possible infringement, wrote to Lawrence that access to the ferry would run "right through the very Heart and best of the Land. . . . I think we suffer enough with the Free Ferry." Lawrence was a member of the House of Burgesses, and perhaps that was sufficient deterrent. The neighbor does not seem to have made the petition.[36] In 1750, Mary's ability to draw income from the crops at Bridge's Creek was finishing according to the terms of Augustine's will and reverting to her stepson Austin.

During these difficult, poor years, Mary, a widow in her early forties with five children to feed and clothe, might well, by Virginia custom, have remarried. Dr. Spencer, a Fredericksburg physician who Robert Jackson and Lawrence had hoped would put in a good word with Mary about George's entering the navy, visited her frequently. He might have been a suitor.[37] In Mary's society, single men actively looked for women to manage their homes, look after any children they might have had, and increase their holdings. Although it is a commonplace that widows remarried as a rule in this world, a historian of the subject argues that many widows "seldom considered remarriage a viable option." They preferred not to remold themselves to the inevitable demands of another man. Widows and their children created habits of mutual emotional sustenance and material help. Remarrying would be very likely to upend those arrangements and expectations. Mary had four sons and a daughter for company, help, and affection. She found rich comfort in Christian teachings and private reflections. Most white widows in the mid- to late eighteenth century walked similar religious paths. Whether Mary knew or sensed it, the roles for married women were narrowing after mid-century. Certainly, the broad range of activities in which she had been engaged as a widow would narrow for her with a second marriage.[38]

If she had remarried, she would have been legally under the direction and control of her husband, who might or might not have respected her property rights. The property her father had left her could be in jeopardy. The court records are full of cases of husbands illegally withholding their wives' property. George, over the years, would be involved in more than one such case in which he tried to aid wives, often remarried widows with some property, whose husbands were despoiling their estates. Mary's mother's prolonged widowhood at the end of her life blazed a path—a desirable one in light of the tumultuous legal battles between Mary Johnson Ball and Joseph Ball after she married Richard Hughes. By remarrying, Mary Washington would put at risk her chances to retain custody of Samuel, Charles, Betty, George, and John Augustine. Her own marriage, whatever its emotional tone, had meant children every one to two years and the duty to submit; she would not do this again.[39]

While historians have noted Spencer's visits and assumed he was courting Mary, he might also have been visiting in a professional capacity, because George was ill in the fall of 1749. He described it as "Ague and Feaver[,] which I have had to Extremety." This description almost always means malaria, something George (and most Virginians) suffered from throughout his life. He would use home remedies until he learned about the "bark," or quinine. The ague and fever initiated a long series of illnesses that would afflict George and terrify his mother over the next years.[40]

12

MID-CENTURY:
A WEDDING, A MURDER,
A FAMILY DEATH

ARY MUST HAVE TAKEN INCREASING satisfaction from George's youthful accomplishments. His careful ways with money, energy, and industry, like her own but with a white man's array of choices, began to relieve her of the burden of his support. His activities also began to shift their relation away from his dependency on her to a collaboration between her and her patriarch in training. Surveying jobs paid in cash, making George the one in the family who had a little cash in his pockets.

In March 1748, he made a surveying trip with his friend and patron, George William Fairfax, eight years his senior. The two young men rode northwest from Alexandria along the Potomac, west across the Shenandoah Valley, and up to Winchester in the Blue Ridge, continuing on farther. They stopped at taverns but sometimes preferred the ground to the tavern insects. They met German-speaking settlers, whom the first-time traveler George found stupid for not speaking English. One memorable evening, George witnessed an Indian celebratory dance. When they returned in April, George had developed an appetite for the fertile lands he had traversed beyond the Alleghenies.[1]

Although George spent time at Mount Vernon and Belvoir, his principal home was with Mary, who continued to provide care for his health and necessities. As mistress of Ferry Farm, she was responsible for the health of everyone resident there. During 1748, there was a smallpox scare in Fredericksburg, and Mary and her family surely curtailed their visits to town.[2]

Mary followed common medical practice, adhering to the philosophy of maintaining a balance among the four humors by purging and drawing blood from and/or giving emetics to people with symptoms thought to derive from an excess of certain kinds of fluids. Joseph Ball's letters about medicine display his belief in good supportive care that strengthened the patient, but neither Ball nor Mary nor George revolted against heroic dosing. Her brother thought that when the slaves were sick, they should have "a good fire, good meat and broth" and be bled and vomited. "I think both to be proper in most cures."[3] He was generally suspicious of doctors and probably resentful of their fees, but Mary relied on their help.

Mary bought medications for purging that medical practitioners recommended like "Julip," "asafedita" (a sulfurous-smelling herb), "purging pills," "antimon powder" (antimony, a substance that caused vomiting, as well as depression and other unpleasant effects), igneth, a mercury compound (used for purging), and various clysters (or enemas). Other familiar drugs included the anesthetic opium and alcohol cordials that were often mixed with powerful purgatives.[4]

George Eskridge
(1660–1735), friend
and patron to, and link
between, Mary Ball and
Augustine Washington
(COURTESY OF VIRGINIA
HISTORICAL SOCIETY)

Rebecca Bonum
Eskridge (1665–1715;
Mrs. George), aunt of
Samuel Bonum, Mary
Ball's brother-in-law
(COURTESY OF VIRGINIA
HISTORICAL SOCIETY)

Mary's view: The
Rappahannock River
in front of Ferry Farm
(COPYRIGHT © ENRICO
FERORELLI)

A reconstruction of the Washingtons' Ferry Farm,
in Fredericksburg on the Rappahannock, Mary's home for many years
(COURTESY OF THE GEORGE WASHINGTON FOUNDATION)

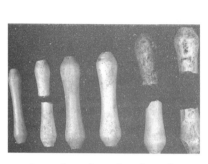

Just a few wig curlers from the
trove found in the backyard
at Ferry Farm

(COURTESY OF THE GEORGE
WASHINGTON FOUNDATION)

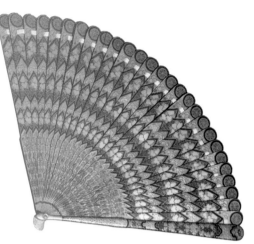

A fan, attributed to Mary Washington

(COPYRIGHT © ENRICO FERORELLI)

1 inch

1 cm

The back of a tambour
hook, used for ornamental
stitchery, owned by
Betty Washington Lewis,
Mary's second child

(COURTESY OF THE GEORGE
WASHINGTON FOUNDATION)

Mary's tea table,
photographed at her
Fredericksburg home

(COPYRIGHT © ENRICO
FERORELLI)

Lawrence Washington (1718–1752), George's older half brother,
son of Augustine Washington and his first wife, Jane Butler

Betty Washington Lewis
(1733–1797), Mary's second child
and only surviving daughter
(JOHN WOLLASTON, OIL ON CANVAS, 1753–56;
COURTESY OF MOUNT VERNON)

Colonel Samuel Washington
(1734–1781), Mary's third child
and second son
(JAMES ALEXANDER SIMPSON, AFTER
JOHN HESSELIUS, OIL ON CANVAS, 1855;
COURTESY OF MOUNT VERNON)

Charles Washington (1738–1799), Mary's
fifth surviving child and fourth son
(JAMES ALEXANDER SIMPSON, OIL ON CANVAS,
1855; COURTESY OF MOUNT VERNON)

George Washington (1732–1799), Mary's first child

(CHARLES WILSON PEALE, OIL ON CANVAS, 1770; WASHINGTON-CUSTIS-LEE
COLLECTION, WASHINGTON AND LEE UNIVERSITY, LEXINGTON, VIRGINIA)

Martha Dandridge Custis Washington (1731–1802),
Mary's daughter-in-law, and George's wife

(JOHN WOLLASTON, OIL ON CANVAS, 1753–1756; WASHINGTON-CUSTIS-LEE
COLLECTION, WASHINGTON AND LEE UNIVERSITY, LEXINGTON, VIRGINIA)

Mary Washington's last home (after 1770), Fredericksburg
(COPYRIGHT © ENRICO FERORELLI)

Kenmore, Betty and Fielding Lewis's Fredericksburg home, very near Mary's home
(COPYRIGHT © ENRICO FERORELLI)

After Dr. Spencer's visits to Ferry Farm ended, Dr. Sutherland paid a number of calls. He bled and gave a cordial to a "negro wench." He bled the enslaved Tom and drew a tooth from a "Negro fellow."[5] (Two enslaved men named Tom, one owned by Charles and one by Samuel, lived under Mary's dominion at Ferry Farm.[6])

Mary still probably took responsibility for keeping George as neat and stylish as he liked to be, along with the rest of her children. He itemized the clothes he packed on a visit to the Fairfaxes in 1749–1750; they included seven shirts, six linen waistcoats, six bands, four neck cloths, and seven caps.[7] Thanks to Mary's enslaved women, he dressed in spanking-clean white linens crucial to his appearance as a civilized man of wealth.[8]

The long-ago inventory of textiles in her father's estate and her store accounts in Fredericksburg show Mary's lifelong connoisseurship of fabrics. She made fine distinctions among them, artfully deploying their characters and strengths. George learned about textiles, their properties, and their care at his mother's house. As a young man, he had a deep acquaintance with the variety of available materials and their uses, bringing this knowledge to bear on his own meticulously chosen wardrobe and on the uniforms he would design for himself and his troops. George ordered from his London tailors and designed outfits with striking confidence. Betty, too, learned these skills at home as mother and daughter sewed for the family and used their ornamental talents for Betty's first-day-of-marriage dress. But George's unusual expertise draws attention to this widespread but undervalued female achievement.

As Mary followed George's growth, she facilitated Betty's maturation as well. In March 1750, Lawrence Washington returned to Virginia from Great Britain, after seeking medical advice for his tuberculosis.[9] During the trip, he visited with Mary's brother Joseph, bringing back a letter and a present to his sister.[10] Joseph sent her a "tea chest, and in it six silver spoons, a silver strainer and tongs." Betty's initialed pewter spoons paled beside Ball's handsome gift. He had also sent her half a pound of green tea and a canister of Bohea[11] (an extremely desirable Chinese black tea) as well as a boxful of sugar that was already broken, "so that as soon as you get your chest you may sit down and drink a Dish of Tea."[12] Betty now had the beginning of an elegant selection of teas, which she could serve from the variously shaped teapots Mary was acquiring. Refined hostesses offered tea drinkers a choice out of differently shaped pots that were believed to suit particular types of teas.[13]

Joseph Ball's gift to Betty was a showy, stylish welcome to womanhood. It also constituted a large part of her dowry. Just two months later, Mary had the pleasure, relief, and sadness of seeing Betty Washington married to the widower Fielding Lewis, son of the Fredericksburg merchant John Lewis. Mary gave her permission, no doubt joyful that Betty would be living so close by. Catharine Washington, Fielding's first wife and Betty's friend and cousin, had died in February 1750, after the birth and December death of her third child, Warner. The widower had two small children for whom to care.[14] Fielding had worked from about 1746 at the store of the Fredericksburg merchant Charles Dick before going to work in his father's store. (Dick rapidly became a substantial merchant.[15] Mary and Charles Dick were both godparents of Fielding's first child, John, and had been friends since Dick had arrived in Fredericksburg shortly after the Washingtons.)

Betty was not quite seventeen in 1750, about six years younger than her mother had been when she married, trained in the same household habits and skills but with only one mournful family shock in her memory. She was close to her mother and to her siblings, especially George. Her intelligence, family feeling, affection, humor, ability to cope, and deep attachments come through in her actions and letters. She was tall like her mother and apparently looked like George, enough so that later in life she would wear a cape and hat and trick people into thinking she was her famous brother. Tradition has it that she wore white satin and heels with sparkling buckles at her marriage, held at Ferry Farm. George is said to have come back from western surveying to give her away. A remnant of Betty's white silk "second day dress" remains at Kenmore, the imposing plantation she and Fielding later designed in Fredericksburg. Mary or Betty or both had embroidered red flowers in baskets for this ceremonial outfit to wear on her first day as a married woman. Betty moved into Fielding's house in Fredericksburg.

This was not an adventurous marriage for either partner; the families were close, and Betty had often visited the Lewises, taking the ferry across the river into town or coming by after school from the Reverend Maury's. Mary was already the godmother of little John Lewis (born 1747), and George the godfather of Frances Lewis (born 1748). Betty's cousins included the children of her aunt Mildred Washington Gregory Willis and the immense colonel Henry Willis, offspring of perhaps the most prominent couple in town. She knew little John and Frances Lewis, Fielding and Catharine's children, well. She had undoubtedly helped at Fielding's home with the children between the birth of Warner and his and Catharine's deaths. Catharine's illness and death and Betty's and Fielding's shared sadness brought them close.[16] As George and Betty advised their niece Harriot, much later, Betty developed a helpful disposition and the skills to manage a household in the absence of much of a dowry. In addition to Joseph Ball's fortuitous tea service, Augustine's will gave her two enslaved girls, one of whom would be parted from her mother at Ferry Farm.

Like her mother and her grandmother before her, Betty married a widower with children. She took after Mary in the regularity of her ability to conceive and her physical strength in recovery. Of her eleven infants, eight survived childhood. Multiple godparenting among Mary, the Washington brothers, the Lewises, and the Dicks diagram the closeness of these bonds: Mary, already godmother to Lewis's son John, served as godparent to two of Betty and Fielding's children, George to two, his wife, Martha, to one, Charles to three, and Samuel to one.[17]

Betty and Fielding would have a close, affectionate marriage as well as something of a business partnership. When Fielding bought a ship, he named it the *Betty*. They co-signed land transactions, and their joint initials went out on the barrels of tobacco that they shipped.[18]

For Mary, Betty's marriage meant the sacrifice of a much-loved companion who had shared her work, thoughts, and worries. But it also kept Betty nearby and meant that mother and daughter could continue to see each other and exchange advice, affection, and household products. Mary was always close at hand when Betty gave birth.

Perhaps the friends encouraged each other in matrimony, or perhaps it was coincidence, but Charles Dick married the same year as Fielding Lewis. Mary would probably have attended the wedding festivities with Betty and Fielding.[19]

In the fall of 1750, two enslaved men belonging to Mary disrupted the provisional peace in the quarters at Ferry Farm. Harry, an enslaved man who worked in the fields, was convicted of killing another slave, Tame. The court recorded the latter's name twice with that spelling, but it is possible that if he were African, it could have been turned into Tom on the Washingtons' lists, because two Toms then worked at Ferry Farm. Neither Tame nor Harry appears on the list of Mary's or her children's slaves made up at the time of Augustine's death or on Augustine's list of "negroes at the Home House." Mary probably did not have the money to acquire slaves in this period, but it is possible that Lawrence had allowed her to use men belonging to him.

The violence was close-up and frightening for everyone but particularly for the enslaved men and women on the plantation, who all lived together in a large wooden building. Mary, too, was probably frightened. Harry told the court of oyer and terminer on September 7 that he was innocent, but the five magistrates, listening to the (white) witnesses, decided he was guilty. They ordered him to be returned to the jail in King George County and hanged by the sheriff on October 10. (The sheriff and executioner, John Champe, also often served as a magistrate. His daughter Jane would be the first of young Samuel Washington's five wives.)[20] The magistrates ordered that the value of Harry to be paid to Mary was thirty-five pounds.

In the absence of records, we do not know how Tame died. Harry might have been accused of poisoning Tame, or the death might have been more violent. The two might have had ethnic differences, reasons for jealousy, or a dispute known only to them. Harry would have had to have a white witness to exonerate him. In the absence of a fair trial, including enslaved witnesses, we cannot know if he was acting in self-defense or if he did it at all.[21]

Murder among slaves was unusual but not unheard of. In 1761, Colonel James Gordon, who lived near Mary's very first home in Lancaster County, purchased Tom, a miller. Tom soon became sick. He told Gordon he was afraid that Gordon's slave Sambo had poisoned him. Some time later, Gordon's slave Scipio said he was poisoned. Gordon wrote that it gave him "some uneasiness, as there has been a difference between Tom & him." Apparently, both recovered.

Masters particularly feared poisoning and fire as special weapons of angry slaves. The widowed Mary would have felt unusually vulnerable to the menace of slave violence. A speedy verdict and immediate punishment might have left her worrying about her reputation in the community as a good manager. If she remembered the slave who was hanged so long ago at Cherry Point, she might also have remembered that his owner was a widow. The slaves of widows were more likely to be convicted of crimes and more likely to be executed. The community might well infer that widows had less control over their enslaved people.[22]

On the last day of October 1750, the family gathered at Ferry Farm in the presence of John Champe and other witnesses to divide up their slaves according to Augustine's wishes. George was eighteen and was beginning to acquire his first properties in the western part of the colony. He would want slaves to clear and cultivate that land, and he would mention some of the men and women he acquired that day in his correspondence about his plantation in Frederick County. Mary was confirmed in the ownership of Ned, Jack, Bob, Sue, Jane, Jack, "a child," Ned, Prince, Phillis, Judy, and Will. The sons all received eleven people each, although for the time being those of the younger boys would remain at Ferry Farm with them.

The family apparently divvied up its human property according to the total evaluation of each group of slaves. By this measure, George noted that he came out eleven pounds ahead, Austin eighteen pounds ahead, and his younger brothers received by small amounts too little.[23] It is painful to imagine the cold appraisals that accompanied this exercise.

Betty had become pregnant immediately after marriage and bore her first baby nine months later. Mary was near her young daughter throughout and had the satisfaction of helping Betty—and Betty had the comfort of having her mother—at her delivery. Mary became godmother to their first child, Fielding, born in February 1751.

Lawrence's tuberculosis had weakened him enough that he thought he should not risk another Virginia winter. In September 1751, George accompanied his brother to Barbados, whose balmy climate they hoped would improve his failing health. Not only did Lawrence's health not improve while in Barbados, George also came down with smallpox. He spent three weeks in bed there and left for home on December 22, leaving Lawrence behind to pursue his cure.[24] According to the journal he kept on his trip, he sailed through Christmas, squalls, thunder and lightning, storms, snow, and "mountainous sea," finally arriving early one morning in the York River, where a pilot boat took him ashore.[25] He stopped by Ferry Farm on his way to Mount Vernon.[26] George brought the journal he had kept for his family and friends to read. Mary would have heard about the brothers' adventures from their letters home, but if there were any to her, they no longer exist. The uncertain mails might have brought news of George's illness at the same time as the news of his recovery. If not, Mary would have suffered terribly over George's possibly deadly encounter. After her son arrived safely, Mary twice purchased "a large box of ointment" from Dr. Sutherland (soon to be a fellow Mason of George's), who administered it. She also bought purging medicine that might have been for him as well.[27] The ointment was for whatever scarring the smallpox had caused, although it did not erase the traces of disease from his face. Doctors and laypeople alike considered a hearty purging useful for most complaints. On recovery, George, of course, was immune, a great advantage for a man who would have a long career in the military.

About the time George arrived home in December, Mary was probably savoring the fact that he had won a suit against one of two Fredericksburg indentured servants. He had taken them to court for stealing his clothes while he was washing in the Rappahannock the previous summer.[28] Fielding Lewis, Robert Jackson (a friend of Augustine's and one of the men trying to interest Mary in the British navy for George), and Charles Dick were all magistrates on the court, so it is not surprising that things went George's way or that Mary would have heard the news as soon as—or sooner than—the verdict was announced.[29] The convicted Mary McDaniel, too poor to pay a fine, endured fifteen lashes on her naked back. Mary might have witnessed McDaniel's flogging. Because mother and son were both jealous of their property, it is easy to imagine their shared pleasure in believing that justice had been served.

Lawrence returned from Barbados very unwell. Mary and all her sons visited him in his wasted condition at Mount Vernon in June. In conformity to Augustine's will, Lawrence deeded to George three lots of land in Fredericksburg.[30] Not long after (July 12, 1752), Lawrence summoned witnesses and dictated his will, commencing with his salute to "the uncertainty of this transitory life." He left fully half of his land and some of his wife Anne's that she had agreed to contribute, in addition to some stock— to be sold to pay off his many debts. He left half his slaves to his wife and, eventually, to his two-year-old daughter, Sarah Washington (born in 1750), particularly singling out a slave named Moll and her three children. If his wife were to die, the slaves would go to his brother Austin, to whom he left large parcels of land. He left his remaining slaves to be divided up among family members without any provision for keeping husbands and wives or parents and children together. He left Betty some land to be claimed after his wife's death, for which George was to pay her 150 pounds. He left Samuel 450 acres in addition to another parcel.[31] His executors included his brothers George and Austin, his father-in-law and brother-in-law,

William and George William Fairfax, and two friends.[32] George, who much later expressed horror at his brother Samuel's indebted estate and his brother Charles's poor management, had a long, close look at a complicated and debt-ridden estate.

Lawrence left his wife, his executors, and his "mother-in-law" each a mourning ring. Lawrence's wife's stepmother, Deborah Clarke, was dead at the time he made out his will, and the mother-in-law he indicated was his stepmother, Mary Washington.[33] Mourning rings typically contained a lock of the hair of the deceased. Distributing mourning rings singled out for affection and respect significant figures like wives and siblings. Mourning rings in their Catholic origins were gifts to the living to pray for the dead to reach heaven. Because Anglicans did not believe prayer after death would make a difference in the ultimate destiny of the deceased, mourning rings became instead fond messages to the living and tokens soliciting remembrance. It was neither an insignificant gesture nor a mechanical one.[34]

Lawrence's sweet memento to Mary says that she and her elder stepson maintained good relations, despite what a number of George's biographers have argued to the contrary. She had made him welcome in the home she shared with his father when he returned from Great Britain. She shared with him a desire to advance her fatherless children to adulthood with as many opportunities as possible. She let her son risk his life to care for Lawrence on his sad, fruitless search for health in Barbados.

In December 1752, about six months after Lawrence's death, his widow, Anne, married George Lee of Westmoreland County. In marrying, Anne forfeited half of the slaves Lawrence left her, totaling twenty adults and eight children, who came to be property of the Washington siblings.[35] This meant eight more enslaved workers for George.[36] By 1752, George Washington, at twenty, was an independent planter and the owner of two thousand acres in the west who also earned income—and early opportunities to purchase desirable land—through surveying.

The process of selling off lands satisfactorily and paying creditors took time, and it was three years before Lawrence's estate was settled. In the meantime, the death of Lawrence and Anne's little girl Sarah had changed property relations once again. In 1754, George leased Mount Vernon and seventeen slaves from his former sister-in-law for fifteen thousand pounds of tobacco a year. A provision in the agreement stipulated that for every male slave who died, Washington's rent would be reduced by a thousand pounds of tobacco (unless Cesar, who must have been elderly or unwell, died, in which case the reduction would be only five hundred). For every slave woman who died, the rent would go down by eight hundred pounds.[37] Given the enthusiasm of planters for slave "increase," the price difference seems to reflect either shortsightedness or sexism, or both.

While George was increasing his holdings of slaves and land, Betty and Fielding were enlarging their family. Mary's son Charles was godfather to their second child, Augustine, born in January 1752. If Betty nursed her babies, it doesn't seem to have delayed her pregnancies. Mary would have taken satisfaction from seeing her family grow and her children prosper. They were, she would have thought, using "all honest and lawful means to preserve [their] lives and comfort by [their] honest care and diligence."[38]

13

MARY AND GEORGE'S
SEVEN YEARS' WAR

||||||||||||||||||||||||||||||||||||||||||||||||||||||||||||||||||||||||||||||||||||||||||||||||||||||||||||||

Legions, legions of Disasters, such as no Prudence can foresee,
no Care prevent, lie in wait to accomplish our Doom. A starting Horse
may throw his Rider; and at once dash his Body against the
Stones, and fling his Soul into the invisible World.

—JAMES HERVEY, *MEDITATIONS AMONG THE TOMBS*

ARY ACQUIRED A NEW BOOK in the 1750s: James Hervey's *Meditations Among the Tombs*, published in 1746. The British book was reprinted in Boston and Philadelphia, and the Virginia bookseller William Hunter, publisher of *The Virginia Gazette*, had a hundred copies of the work in stock in 1751. It rapidly made its way into the hands of Virginia backcountry merchants.[1] Mary wrote "Mary Washington her Book" in both volumes of it. Under her name is a second signature, "Mary Washington," and below that "Lewis." "Lewis" is written on the flyleaf of her book, suggesting that Betty or one of her children or grand-children claimed it after Mary died. Hervey directed it specifically to women, unlike Mary's other devotional books. One historian has written that Hervey "excited the religious feelings of colonial American women (and men) more than any other during the second half of the eighteenth century."[2] Mary's religious feelings were already excited, but she found in Hervey guidance for getting old. She was in her mid-forties in the mid-1750s, getting on toward old for the era; her children were growing up fast and would all set up homes of their own by the end of the decade. Like Hale, Hervey reminded her to prepare for the end of her life, but he set his guidance in one of her favorite locations: gardens. "While the Hand is cupping the transient Beauties of a Flower, the attentive Mind may be enriching itself with solid and lasting Good."[3]

In the early 1750s, Mary was preoccupied helping with Betty's frequent pregnancies and births. Her first grandson, Fielding Lewis Jr., arrived in February 1751. Mary was godmother, as was Frances Gregory Thornton, the mother of Mildred, who would soon marry Charles, Mary's youngest. George was godfather with Robert Jackson. In January 1752, Betty delivered their second son, Augustine.

From 1751 until the end of the decade, Mary struggled with powerful fears about George's health and the military career he was entering on. Hervey's messages, similar to those of Matthew Hale, offered lessons to Mary about death, duty—hers and others'—the worthlessness of worldly honors, and the importance of stewardship. "How mean," wrote Hervey, "are these ostentatious Methods of bribing the Vote of Fame and purchasing a little posthumous Renown" through military glory. "The only infallible way of immortalizing our Characters is . . . to gain some sweet Evidence that our Names are written in Heaven."[4] Informed by her own fear of loss as well as her devotional books, she tried hard but without success to keep her beloved son from putting himself at risk.

When George recovered from smallpox, he built on and shared the knowledge he gained from surveying to increase his holdings and help others invest in lands in the western part of the colony. He and his brother-in-law Fielding along with many other kin and friends had similar ambitions. Fielding would come to finance a number of George's purchases and operations, profiting himself, at least for a time, as well. George's career as a political and military leader developed directly from his familiarity with the western lands and his (and his colleagues') insatiable appetite for them.

Fredericksburg's location made it a gate to western Virginia and to the greater Ohio valley. In 1747, a group of wealthy Northern Neck men who at different times included Lawrence and Austin Washington; Robert Dinwiddie; Thomas, Richard, and Philip Ludwell Lee; Gavin Corbin; William Thornton; John, John junior, James, and George Mercer; George Mason; John Lewis; George William Fairfax; and Dr. Thomas Walker came together to form the Ohio Company, the first of a number of companies to acquire and develop lands in the Ohio valley. George's name does not appear in the company's minutes, but his own familiarity with the contours of the Fairfax grant in Frederick County gave him unusual practical knowledge of the area, and his early acquisition of land there put him in the forefront of prospective developers. In 1750, George acquired a tract of land along the Bullskin River in Frederick County in the Shenandoah Valley. He called it the Bullskin Plantation, and George's slaves soon produced corn, wheat, and tobacco.[5]

Governors of Virginia had been pushing the need for the British to secure these desirable lands from the French for many years. On July 4, 1744, Virginia (then under the governorship of William Gooch) and Maryland signed the Treaty of Lancaster with the then Five Nations of the Iroquois to buy the Ohio valley from them while letting them use the warriors' path that traversed the land north to south and recognizing their rule over the Delaware and the Shawnee. Very few of the Shawnee or Delaware who lived there were actually at the council that signed away this land.[6] In any case, despite the grandiose claims of the Iroquois and the self-serving British recognition of their primacy, most groups of Indians did not acknowledge the Iroquois' right to dispose of this land. The treaty had not produced peace, allies, or the hoped-for conditions for white purchase and settlement.[7]

In 1748, Governor Gooch applied to Great Britain for funds to pacify the west side of the Blue Ridge for British settlement. At first, this request was denied, but in July 1749, Lord Halifax approved the formation of the Ohio and Loyal Companies, granting initially two hundred thousand acres to the Ohio Company on the south side of the Allegheny River, providing for one hundred families of settlers, and promising to erect a fort for their security. The company agreed to settle one hundred families, promote the fur trade, and make it safe for British commerce with local Indians. Halifax promised another three hundred thousand acres when that happened. Meanwhile, Sir William Johnson, commissioner of the Indians in the north and an adopted Mohawk (Iroquois), kept the Virginians aware about the moves of the French. In 1753, Governor Dinwiddie received the king's orders to repel the French by force, and he received cannon and shot for "his" fort in the Ohio valley.[8]

George had met Governor Dinwiddie[9] through connections made on his Barbados trip with Lawrence. George was eager to succeed Lawrence as adjutant of the Virginia militia and solicited the position that Lawrence's death had left vacant. Dinwiddie divided up the Virginia forces, and George became major of one-quarter of the colony's militias, for which he received a hundred pounds a year.[10]

The British had managed to get an agreement with some Indians ratified in 1752, permitting the British to build the two forts that the Crown had already promised to the Ohio Company. But the French were busily solidifying their claims to the same area.[11]

London ordered Dinwiddie to evaluate the French presence and plans and to resort to force if they were intransigent. George knew this area from his surveying, and his ambition and military appointment made him the logical person to explore the French project. On October 31, 1753, at the meeting of the Governor's Council in Williamsburg, Dinwiddie gave the twenty-year-old George, adjutant general for the Southern District of

Virginia, orders to visit the French and a stipend of 150 pounds. He was to protest their erection of forts and to demand a reply from them about their intentions toward land the English claimed. On this journey, Washington encountered Tanaghrisson (George Washington called him "Tanachari-son"), known as the Half King, an ally who was wavering in his commitment to the British because they were trying to settle the western lands. Tana-ghrisson, born a Catawba, was captured in an Iroquois mourning war and reared a Seneca. He had suffered much from wars with French-allied Indians and was desperate to keep the French out of the Ohio valley.[12]

George Washington journeyed west to the French forces on the Ohio, arriving at Fort Le Boeuf on December 11, discovering the fort well es-tablished and plans for another one downriver at Logstown. These were part of the new governor of Canada Marquis Duquesne's plan to erect a chain of forts to secure French control of the area. Washington asked the French their intentions and why they had seized the goods and house of an English trader. A French spokesperson answered that they had orders not to "suffer any English subjects to settle on his master's country."[13] George Washington returned through terrible winter storms, miraculously escap-ing drowning and frostbite, with the unyielding French response. He re-ceived the gratitude of the House of Burgesses and fifty pounds for his exploit.[14]

The next step was military engagement. George again offered Gover-nor Dinwiddie his services in the fall of 1753. In March 1754, he received a lieutenant colonel's commission from Dinwiddie, who asked him to lead a group of militia to go to the Ohio valley to build forts and to hinder simi-lar French activities there.[15] With no military experience but much desire for it, George went to the Ohio valley again, with 160 men, including Tana-ghrisson. On May 28, Tanaghrisson discovered a French encampment. Although accounts vary, one of George's Indian allies testified that when George saw them from his position above the encampment, he opened fire, and his troops followed suit. The Virginians killed a number of soldiers. After a pause, when their leader, de Jumonville, seemed to be trying to initiate a truce with Washington, Tanaghrisson singled him out as representative of French perfidy and killed him with tomahawk blows to his head. He then reportedly washed his hands in de Jumonville's brain. After the murder, the Indians under Tanaghrisson massacred the French soldiers whom Washington's men had wounded. Washington, the French, and assorted observers offered competing versions of the skirmish. The French survivors insisted that they were coming in peace to treat with the colonials but that Washington had never allowed them time to make a case. The French regarded Washington's behavior as knavish and murderous. Washington defended himself to Dinwiddie and others by saying that the French were acting in bad faith and had "bad hearts," as the Half King expressed it. Fred Anderson, a historian of the war, argues that Washington's description of what happened was self-serving and inaccurate.[16]

Washington immortalized his excitement at witnessing slaughter and surviving in a postscript to his favorite brother, John Augustine. "I fortunately escaped without a wound, tho' the right Wing where I stood was exposed to & received all the Enemy's fire and was the part where the man was killed & the rest wounded. I can with truth assure you, I heard Bullets whistle and believe me there was something charming in the sound."[17]

Throughout George's services to the colony, Mary followed his progress and that of military conflicts not only through him and John Augustine but also through Fielding Lewis's and Charles Dick's roles as confidants and later as commissaries to Washington's troops. Through her daughter and increasingly well-connected son-in-law, she followed the struggles between the government at Williamsburg, Washington, and his officers over management and money.

The king of England, George II, reportedly said that if Washington had heard many bullets, he would not have written such a message. If Washington's words reached King George, Mary certainly heard them.

In a small town filled with her kin and friends, it would have been hard for Mary not to hear of the Half King's bloody dispatch of de Jumonville and that in George's surveying and travels with various Delaware, Shawnee, and Iroquois, he was known as Conotocarious, a dubious honorific meaning "Town Wrecker." Colonel John Washington, his great-grandfather, had originally earned this title when, at the order of Governor William Berkeley, he visited the Doeg and Susquehannock Indians in 1675, to investigate a pair of incidents in which several Indians had been killed trying to recover their stolen property. In revenge for these deaths, they killed an Englishman. Washington, contrary to Governor Berkeley's orders, called up 250 Maryland militiamen in addition to some Virginians and proceeded to the fort to confront the Susquehannocks and Doeg. Washington and others demanded the Indians' story and, finding it did not satisfy them, murdered the five sachems who had emerged from the fort to talk. When Governor Berkeley protested the murders, the Virginians accused the Maryland men of the killings and vice versa. No one ever determined the truth. Doeg, however (as in Dogue's Run), was a substantial tract of land, some of which John Washington acquired and George would inherit. Berkeley's defense of the murdered Indians united colonists against him and helped ignite Bacon's Rebellion.[18]

George inherited that warlike moniker proudly. He developed military respect for Indians, and the name distinguished him among them and gave him a certain status among the older, experienced colonial frontiersmen as well.[19]

Mary, however, came from a farming background with no family tradition of military service or any particular reverence for it. That her son had been exposed to fire and enjoyed it was unsettling enough. That his partner in this failed military expedition was an Indian—or a savage, as she and George both would have called him—who tomahawked a French officer to death and enjoyed dipping his hands in the corpse's brains was infinitely worse than unsettling. Mary Washington's view of Native Americans resembled George's (at that time in his life) and that of the community in which she lived. To most colonial Virginians, Indians had no culture or civilization. Their widespread rejection of Christianity assured Virginians of their inveterate barbarity. And this incident would have confirmed Mary's belief that Indians were of a savagery that made them utterly different from men and women of European descent. She would not have seen Tanaghrisson's theatrical act of revenge in the context of the rapid European extermination of Native people. For Mary, the relevant information from this incident was that her son's military endeavors paired him with men she viewed as crazed and bloodthirsty and seemed to bring out in him a pleasure in recklessness.

Around the time George's letter arrived, Mary received a visit from young Carolus Gustavus de Splitdorff, a volunteer serving under George who was helping to deliver French prisoners to Dinwiddie. George sent him to his mother to see to any needs she might have while he was away. Thus Mary received a respectful report of George's unchanging dutifulness, as well as firsthand testimony about her son's bravery, competence, and survival.

At more or less the same time, George got news of his mother from Daniel Campbell, a merchant in town close by on the Rappahannock. Campbell and other Scottish settlers had founded a Masonic lodge in October 1752, and George had joined in November. Fielding Lewis, Charles Dick, and Colonel John Thornton would soon join.[20] Campbell reported to George that he saw his mother and friends and family "frequently" and that she and everyone were well. He added that he had "the honour to dance with her, when your health was not forgot."[21] In toasting George, Fredericksburg friends congratulated and celebrated with Mary. Although she was terrified by George's exploits, she knew he was safe. She received public compliments about her son and could enjoy his successes and dance to them. Among possessions attributed to her is an elegant fan, just right for such convivial occasions. She could share in the community's pride in her son after her terrible fears.

In July 1754, Washington fought another battle with the French but with a different outcome, at Fort Necessity. This time French soldiers, under the brother of the assassinated de Jumonville, overpowered the

Virginians, who were without Indian help. Washington lost thirty men, and seventy others were wounded. He signed terms of surrender on July 3, 1754.[22]

Dinwiddie subsequently ordered a reorganization of the Virginia troops, deciding that all colonial officers could advance no further than the rank of captain. Washington, to the immense but premature relief of his mother, decided this represented a step down for him because he had been commissioned as a colonel (two ranks above captain). Feeling dishonored, he resigned his commission in October 1754.[23] Mary would not have been reassured, however, had she known his full feelings about his resignation. He wrote that he declined his commission "to obey the call of Honour, and the advice of my Friends . . . and not to gratify any desire I had to leave the military line. My inclinations are strongly bent to arms."[24]

In December 1754, Mary welcomed George home. That winter, he met with his brothers to divide among themselves the slaves that Anne Washington's marriage to George Lee had made theirs. At the same time, George · entered into a lease with George Lee for Mount Vernon and for the rental of eighteen slaves.[25]

Mary's relief about George's safety and his refusal of Dinwiddie's proffered captainship did not last long. General Edward Braddock arrived in the colony only a few weeks later, in February 1755, to fight the French and Indians in the Ohio valley. In March, he invited George to be a member of his military family. Being attached to Braddock in this way would allow George to sidestep the embarrassments of rank that had prompted his resignation from service with the colonial forces. George persuaded his trusted brother John Augustine to manage Mount Vernon while he was away, and he consented to Braddock's offer.

Mary, terrified at the prospect of George's service with Braddock and privy to his plans with John Augustine to take over his plantations, traveled the fifty-odd miles from Fredericksburg. She appeared at Mount Vernon around April 1 to express her fears. Her surprise visit made him late for a rendezvous with Braddock. He wrote that many visitors including his mother, "alarmd at the report of my intentions to attend your Fortunes," made it impossible for him to keep his appointment with Braddock and his party punctually.[26]

Mary had lost many people in her life, and she could not bear to lose this capable son whom she loved and on whom she depended. This incident began the numerous farewells that made her sure each time that she would lose him to battle or illness. In 1789, when Mary was suffering from the breast cancer that would kill her, Betty wrote to George that their mother was "perfectly resign'd" to her death, but "she wishes to here from you, she will not believe you are well till she has it from under your Hand."[27] Mary had witnessed four years of George's illnesses, beginning with "Ague and Feaver . . . to Extremety" and smallpox, and then, in 1752, he "was taken with a Violent Pleurisie which . . . reduced [him] very low."[28] His siblings suffered from tuberculosis, and one historian speculates that this may indicate that Washington had it as well, contracting it from Lawrence. The evidence about tuberculosis is inconclusive, but Mary's growing aversion to military service cannot be understood without taking George's fluctuating health into consideration.[29] A mother distant from a beloved child who is suffering can only suffer herself, and Mary's imagination for George's suffering was highly developed.

Mary's anxiety for George's health and safety motivated her to drop in unexpectedly, but her favored clerics helped shape her thinking about George's behavior. In Matthew Hale's view, a good Christian was content with the station to which God had assigned him, and striving for higher status and achieving it "could do us harm, would undo us, would make us luxurious, proud, insolent, domineering," and, worst of all, "forgetful of God." George's desire for military glory betrayed his lust for the honors and rewards of this world and his inadequate estimation of those of the next life. The temperate man moderated his desire for glory, like all the other passions. "Honour, and applause, and successes, and glory . . . [are] poor, empty, insipid things" in the final accounting. Hale insisted that the good Christian "provide for [his] Families and relations."[30]

Mary hoped that George might study his conscience for pride and the irresponsible shaking off of his stewardship of his and the family's property and the futures of his younger brothers. She knew that women had little to say about the activities of their adult sons. After her failed attempt to change his mind, her subsequent attempts lost vigor and soon appear to have stopped. She knew that the strong bond between them meant that they would carry on their obligations to each other regardless of their disagreements. George knew this too, knew that he was free to do what he wanted, but that his bond with his mother was deep and permanent and would continue despite their differences. George wrote to his mother three times between his departure and the completion of the battle, always respectfully and always attentive to her needs, knowing how much she suffered over his choice and communicating in his own way that he would still behave as the head of their family. He no doubt found her appearance at his door inconvenient, but he also knew it was an expression of her lifelong concern for him.[31]

Before he left, Mary, George, and John had discussed the possibility that joining Braddock would mean he would be treated as an inferior among the British officers, because regulars had precedence over colonial military of the same rank. George had just resigned one commission over the rank question; it might be foolish to step into another possibly humiliating appointment. Mary had apparently worried that he would have to be on his guard and stiff, arguing that by remaining at Mount Vernon and continuing to run the plantation, he was able to spend time in the company of kin and others with whom he was easy and affable.[32] George's letters to the family reassured them that Braddock and his military family included him with a pleasing, pronounced lack of ceremony.[33] George noted to Mary that in joining the Braddock circle, he was being treated with "a complaisant Freedom which is quite agreeable to me: so that I have no reason to doubt the satisfaction I hoped for, in making the Campaigne." He described finding a cherished familiarity that was typically shared among friends and family. He added that he intended to make the most of the acquaintanceships he made on this expedition and imagined that his great reward would be experience, because it was not likely to be wealth or rank.[34] Ever ambitious for the family's advancement, he urged John to call frequently and be otherwise attentive to his neighbors at Belvoir.[35]

Mary was at Mount Vernon when Washington set out in May with his body servant, John Alton, his brother John Augustine, and a young enslaved boy of fifteen or sixteen years old named Jeremy. Jeremy had been a gift from John Bushrod, John Augustine's future father-in-law. John and George seem to have shared the services of this enslaved man they both valued. John Augustine went as far as the Bullskin Plantation, which would be part of his responsibility in George's absence. (In Jeremy's account, he accompanied Washington on Braddock's expedition, but his account is confusing and unconfirmed by other evidence, so I have omitted it, although it is worth reading.)[36] Mary and George had discussed her immediate plans, and he urged her to spend much of the time when he was away at Mount Vernon with John, "where I am certain everything will be ordered as much to your satisfaction as possible."[37]

In June, Mary wrote to him through the merchant Charles Dick asking for a German worker and a quantity of butter. George could not supply either. He was not in the area where the German immigrants lived and was at that time unable to provide his troops with enough butter. Historians have seen her requests as grasping and insensitive to his new status and concerns, but Washington seems to have found them innocuous. When he was in the backcountry on military duty, he supplied his troops from merchants and farmers. He knew where to get things. He also answered letters about his brother Samuel's real estate plans and his own tobacco crop. No one has criticized his brothers for intruding on his mission with these kinds of concerns.[38]

By the early summer of 1755, Mary's second son, Samuel, who had a house in Fredericksburg, had married and taken possession of his lands on the Chotank Creek, leaving her alone with Charles at Ferry Farm. Samuel was the first of her boys to marry. He wed Jane Champe, the daughter of the magistrate who had had the enslaved Harry executed. George confirmed on June 14 that he would be agreeable to dividing the family lands at Deep Run, where Samuel and Jane lived. Samuel asserted his solidity as a married man and landholder in the wake of the deaths of his father and half brother by having John Hesselius paint his and Jane's portrait.

The son of the Swedish painter Gustavus Hesselius, the portraitist had made a "painting tour" in Virginia in 1750–1751, and on his return trip some years later he painted the newlyweds. Like other men, Samuel made this investment at a significant step on his path to maturity. One historian has written that portraits, which were the only kind of art that Americans bought in this period, certified "the movement of family substance in an orderly, prescribed manner. . . . It cement[ed] the social hierarchy and . . . reminded family members of the facts of authority and duty, of the rules being followed, of the family line in operation, of chaos and litigation avoided, of family acquiescence in the all-important arena of money."[39]

Samuel's showy purchase carried more than one irony. Jane was only the first of Samuel's five wives. She died soon after their marriage, apparently because of a difficult childbirth. (In 1758, he would marry, confusingly, Mildred Thornton, the cousin of the Mildred Thornton whom Charles married.) The same year Samuel married Jane, he was engaged in a lawsuit against Governor Dinwiddie's secretary, who was also a merchant.[40] Rather than rules being followed and chaos and litigation avoided, Samuel would live recklessly, horrifying his prudent older brother with his posthumous debts and disordered estate. His sister, Betty, would have to clothe, feed, and raise his impoverished orphans.[41]

News of Braddock's disastrous failure at Fort Duquesne and death just preceded George's letters describing the event. George, assuming his mother and brother believed him dead along with so many others, wrote immediately to both. The news traveled by July 11 to Cumberland, Maryland, and was confirmed on the thirteenth. George had been so extremely sick with dysentery for weeks before the battle that he had to be carried in a wagon to the site. When the battle exploded, his weak and painful condition made him ride with a cushion on his saddle. However, excitement and adrenaline powered him with remarkable reserves of strength and energy. George fought courageously, rallied the remnants of survivors, and commanded the retreat. He did all of this despite his suffering and with his other two aides-de-camp out of commission.

On July 18, George wrote to his mother and brother and Governor Dinwiddie.[42] The only reassuring aspect of his letter was that it proved he was alive. Throwing sensitivity for her feelings to the wind, perhaps intentionally, he exulted in how close to death he had come. He cited the number of bullets to pass through his cloak (four) and the number of horses shot out from under him (two). In his letter to John Augustine, he went beyond what he might have thought of as a toned-down version for his mother. "But by the all powerful dispensations of Providence, I have been protected beyond all human probability & expectation . . . although death was leveling my companions on every side [I] escaped unhurt." He spared Mary no distressing details about his illness. "I am not half recovered from a violent illness that had confin'd me to my Bed, and a Waggon, for above 10 Days; I am still in a weak and Feeble condn which induces me to halt here 2 or 3 Days in hopes of recovg a little Strength, to enable me to proceed homewards." Because of this, he would not be able to stop by and "have the pleasure of seeing you" until September unless "it be in Fairfax," that is, Mount Vernon.[43]

George's eagerness to describe his near-death experiences and the dramatic adjectives (especially "violent") he favored in characterizing his illnesses create the suspicion that he took some pleasure in upsetting his mother. He wanted her to know how much he had suffered. It was one fiber in the bond between them.

From Mary's standpoint, she could breathe in relief that he wasn't dead and take anxious pride in his remarkable courage, skill, and tenacity. She might have been one of her brother's sources of news praising her son, because Joseph Ball wrote to George lauding his military prowess. "It is a Pleasure to me to hear that you have behaved yourself with such a

Martial Spirit in all your Engagements with the French. . . . God prosper you." Then he added, using his status as uncle for leverage, "I desire you, as you may from time to time have opportunity to give me a Short Account how you proceed. As I am your Mother's brother, I hope you can't deny my Request."[44] Nonetheless, George seems to have denied his request. George's account of his illness left Mary little peace.

George recovered enough in September to consider accepting command of the reorganized Virginia Regiment, despite complaints about inadequate money and confusing command structures. His health continued to be poor throughout the fall. He was restricted to a jelly diet and missed the care—and jelly recipes—of his sister-in-law Hannah Bushrod, who was away. (His diet would have consisted of "calve's foot jelly" and other gelatinous soups made with bone marrow, not sweet jellies.)[45] Perhaps he sent on to his mother George Mercer's "compliments" for her from South Carolina, or perhaps he was too distracted and sick.[46] During his convalescence, he calculated the financial losses and humiliations he suffered in his last three military exploits, including horses and health. He steeled himself to refuse anything but an adequately recompensed command in which he was fully in charge. He heard from his cousin Warner Lewis that the General Assembly wanted him to command the Virginia Regiment to protect Ohio valley settlers from the Indians raiding them as a result of the British defeat.

Mary protested. To his mother's protest, George wrote that he would try not to go to the Ohio region again but that he could not turn the position down "if the command is pressed on me by the genl. Voice of the country, and offered on such terms as cannot be objected against, . . . it wou'd reflect eternal dishonour upon me to refuse it; and that, I am sure, must or ought, to give you greater cause of uneasiness than my going in an honourable command; for upon no other terms will I accept of it if I do at all."[47]

He would later use the honor and public sacrifice argument with Martha when offered the command of the Continental army. He told her that he could not honorably refuse to serve when called. "You may believe me . . .

that so far from seeking this appointment, I have used every endeavour in my power to avoid it. . . . It was utterly out of my power to refuse this . . . without exposing my Character to such censures as would have reflected dishonor upon myself . . . this I am sure you could not, and ought not to be pleasing to you." Washington combined an evocation of the personal honor of reputation, an aristocratic ideal, with that of sacrifice to a civic cause.[48] He did not mention to either mother or wife, of course, his "inclination" to arms or the pleasure and satisfaction he derived from combat and command. Washington's disingenuous argument to Mary that the call came from the country, given the amount of time and energy he had spent pursuing a military career, was in keeping with his later political practice that if one wanted public office, one must not openly seek it but meticulously arrange to have it thrust upon you. He portrayed himself as the passive recipient of a call that he could not refuse, although Mary knew well that he worked assiduously to see that the terms of the call were to his liking.

In the winter of 1755–1756, George had been in Winchester with his troops for months, and Mary grew suddenly worried, having had no news from him. Jeremy Prophet recalled that George had told the family that he was going, and if they didn't hear from him in nine months, "dey must give him up."[49] When her worry came to a boil, she sent a man to Mount Vernon as fast as he could ride with a letter for John Augustine to come to Ferry Farm. John ordered Jeremy to get horses ready to leave early the next day. They left in the bitter cold and managed to get to Ferry Farm by nightfall. Mary, who was favoring a lame leg and walking with the aid of two sticks, greeted them. In Jeremy's memory of this incident, she called out, "O Johnny Washington, Johnny Washington have you heard any news of George Washington? His time's run out, no papers, no news, no nothing of him. He's dead—he's dead—go and seek him, dead or alive— bring home his bones if nothing else."

Jeremy remembered that there was deep snow everywhere, but "John so fond of . . . George, and de old lady, he go foot sooner dan turn back." Two days later, they were struggling up a road west of Alexandria when they saw a man coming down the mountain on horseback with "his right leg over de pummel of de saddle, woman fashion, wid a broad piece of paper in his lap reading, and de bridle reins loose in his fingers." Wearing only a jacket and "moccasin gaiters, his beard mighty long," George recognized John before his brother realized who it was. Soon they were dismounted and "talk, talk." George called out to a man behind him leading horses; he produced a little table and meat and every amenity "down to [a] pepper-box." The brothers sat at the table to eat, but it was so cold that Jeremy put his meat and bread in his pocket, "and dare was dat man wid notting but his roundabout jacket and . . . his great-coat close by on de pummel of he saddle . . . dat man he no more mind cold dan a stone-fence."[50]

George went to Mount Vernon, and Jeremy and John went to Fredericksburg with a package of letters from George. They arrived that evening with the news of George's safety. After reporting on George's shaggy appearance, they went to Betty and Fielding Lewis's house with the same good news. George himself showed up the next day, "dashing down de road. . . . And den drew a such rejoicing, for de old lady was fondest of George of all de boys." Jeremy noted that "the gin'ral had a face like he mother."[51]

James Kirke Paulding (1778–1860), a writer and secretary of the navy under President Martin Van Buren, took down Jeremy Prophet's testimonies when George had become the new nation's icon of all virtue. It is not surprising that Prophet emphasized George's physical endurance, but as Paulding said, the portrait of Mary's adoration of her son did not conform to the Mount Vernon view in which Martha Custis Washington, sweet and congenial, was the antithesis to the slightly embarrassing and stern Mary. Mother and daughter-in-law differed in significant ways, and Martha's strong control of the family politics at Mount Vernon as well as of the family papers has not been kind to Mary's reputation.

In 1756, John Augustine, while managing Mount Vernon for his admired older brother, married Hannah Bushrod, daughter of John Bushrod, a friend of the deceased Augustine Washington. Her family lived on the Bushfield Plantation at the confluence of the Potomac and the Nomini Rivers in Westmoreland County. John Augustine would manage Mount Vernon for George until 1758. Hannah and John Augustine's first two children were born at Mount Vernon. They named their first—probably in 1757—Mary, a precious tribute but sadly short-lived. Hannah Bushrod had weak health later in life; perhaps it began with childbearing. No doubt Mary's care when they were together at Mt. Vernon, like that she gave Betty and her half sister Elizabeth, endeared her to her daughter-in-law.[52]

With the departure of Samuel and the imminent marriage of Charles, the enslaved men and women Mary used to produce her crops endured ongoing separations from one another, and some were taken from working the crops at Ferry Farm. That year, Mary prepared for the wedding of her youngest son, Charles, who was nineteen and wanted to marry his cousin Mildred Thornton. In May 1757, Mary had to borrow five pounds from George, so short of cash was she, trying to run Ferry Farm, with its depleted soil and a shrinking number of laborers.

George returned to Fredericksburg in September 1757 for the funeral of Colonel William Fairfax, his patron.[53] At the time of his return, the widowed mother of Charles's intended bride, Mildred, had learned from Augustine's will that if Charles were to die while he was still a minor, his property would go to his brother George. Mildred Thornton's mother wanted George to waive his rights in favor of Mildred. George wrote to his mother at the end of September that Mrs. Thornton misunderstood his principles if she thought he would take advantage of Mildred, but he agreed to sign a document as long as it was limited to this matter.[54] He might have been more than a trifle offended because he had made a gift to Mildred's brother John, two years before, of a building lot in Fredericksburg. In the marriage settlement for the two minors, Fielding Lewis became Charles Washington's guardian, and John Thornton, Mildred's uncle, became her guardian, each giving security of two thousand pounds. The marriage went forward. Charles and Mildred took up residence in Fredericksburg.[55]

Services and chores went both ways between the mother and her son.

At the time of Charles's wedding, George asked Mary to buy him 250 yards of osnaburg, 200 yards of cotton, and 35 pairs of plaid hose for his slaves at Fielding's store and, if he didn't have them, to get them from Robert Jackson. (The family usually bought osnaburg imported from Germany from the local merchants.)[56] John Alton, his servant, came to Fredericksburg from Mount Vernon with a cart to take the goods home.

George spent another interval in Winchester with his remaining troops and returned to Alexandria very sick with dysentery in November 1757.[57] He wrote to an official in late January from Fredericksburg, "I lingered a long time under an illness which obliged me to retire from my command (by the Surgeon's advice, and with the Governors approbation;) and that I am yet but imperfectly recovered from." He seems to have been home at Ferry Farm when he wrote, so his mother fully appreciated his debilitated and frightening condition.[58]

On February 6, a friend from Williamsburg wrote that he was delighted to hear from him because he had had news that he was dead and many had been made sad thinking about his loss of life.[59] (George was not too ill to order some "worked ruffles" for his shirts, card tables, playing cards, almonds, raisins, and currants, and "if workd ruffles should be out of fashion send such as are not." He subsequently canceled the ruffles.)[60] John Augustine and Hannah, still at Mount Vernon, were the other family members most closely concerned with George's health and the closest witnesses to it. On February 20, George wrote that he had tried to set out from Mount Vernon to Williamsburg but "found I was unable to proceed, my fever and pain increasing upon me to a high degree, and the Physicians assured me that I might endanger my life in prosecuting the journey." In early March, he set off for Williamsburg gingerly and in stages, stopping in Fredericksburg to consult with Dr. Sutherland and meeting with two others. Again Mary seems to have tended her ailing son while praying for his recovery.[61] George wrote of his condition, "My constitution I believe has received great Injury, and as nothing can retrieve it but the greatest care, & most circumspect Conduct."[62]

By the very end of March, his health was sufficiently restored that he was actively courting the widow Martha Dandridge Custis and visited her in Williamsburg.[63] He had probably known her for some time. Although family legend has it that they met and fell in love instantly, this seems extremely unlikely in view of his well-documented and overlapping infatuation with Sally Cary Fairfax (Mrs. George William). George wrote the spirited wife of his close friend love notes at about the time that he began courting Martha Custis.[64]

Virginians openly discussed the financial holdings of prospective spouses, and Martha's enormous wealth—about eighteen thousand acres worth some forty thousand pounds and 84 slaves of her own along with another 160 or more that would come to her children—would have been no secret to George. At the time he courted her, he had been in debt for some time given falling tobacco prices, skimpy crops because of the dry weather, and rising prices for his purchases. Martha Custis was an attractive young widow who also represented a promising solution to his economic embarrassments.[65]

After arranging things with the widow Custis and ordering himself some very fine clothes, Washington returned to Winchester. Over the next months, he tried to keep the morale of his men up, although many were ill.

The greatest danger Washington incurred in his last months of service in the west was on November 12, 1758, from the friendly but deadly fire of a party under his friend Colonel George Mercer, who was sent out to help him (or the other way around, Washington later reversed the newspaper account). Thirteen men and three officers died as a result. Washington approached the firing Virginia troops and with his sword knocked their rifles into the air to stop the killing. He did not include this horrible incident in his report to Governor Francis Fauquier, nor did Mary probably know this story. George seems to have decided his services were no longer needed when the French abandoned Fort Duquesne, leaving the English in possession in November 1758. His impending marriage would secure his economic future and replenish the losses that he had incurred serving Virginia.[66]

In October 1759, Mary and others received the welcome news that Quebec and Montreal had surrendered but that General James Wolfe had died in the conflict.[67] Mary wrote to her brother Joseph with misplaced satisfaction, "Thear was no end to my troble while George was in the Army butt he has now given it up."[68]

By December 9, 1758, Washington was sick again on his trip home from the west. By the time he set off for Williamsburg to see the governor and to marry, he had recovered. He left Mount Vernon with Miles Richardson and Jeremy Prophet carting all his trunks in a "little wagon." They made it partway to Fredericksburg when the front left wheel of the wagon crashed with what Jeremy described the "monstrous heavy trunks" on it. George rode on ahead to his mother's. Miles stayed with the trunks, and Jeremy rode as fast as he could to Ferry Farm. Jeremy remembered that "when old misses see me come widout de trunks, she was *stuffed*, a tell you— so she says, 'take my two duns, Jerry, and start by daybreak, wid de two forewheels o' de carriage, and bring de trunks and wagon.'

"When I seed she was in sich a fluster 'bout de trunks, I goes off and I gits de wheels and de duns, and off I goes a cracking, I tell you." The wheels wouldn't fit, so they lashed the trunks onto the "axletree, and bed of de forewheels." Miles got on top, and they had twenty-four miles to accomplish before daybreak. The duns, Jeremy observed, had never moved anything but Mary's little carriage. They were the "pranktious" duns that preened in the bottomland below the house so she could enjoy the sight of them.

When they managed to get to Ferry Farm, Mary, who had helped save the day for her son, was delighted and had them rest. George said to take the trunks to Fielding and Betty's house. From there, Fielding Lewis told them to take the trunks onward toward Williamsburg. "Den Miles he ride on de trunks, and I ride a fine horse belonging to massa." They made a cold, long journey, George occasionally flying by standing up in his stirrups with two slaves behind him. He called them a ferry to cross the York River. He crossed first on a river that looked "mighty ugly, all white, and de wind blowing like great guns, and it was a freezing hard." Miles and Jeremy took the horse ferry, six hours "in de boat, half leg deep in water—come on darker and darker—de men pull and pull, but de shore seem as if he done gone. . . . I stood upon de head of de boat, wid de bridle-reins of my horse over my shoulder—if de boat sink, I hang to de horse, I say to myself. . . . When we got to shore, I feel glad, I tell you—'Twas Christmas Eve.

"As we pas de winder, I see in, and I seed de gin'ral in de big chair jis so,—and dare was de lady jam up to him jis so—an' he had de lady's little daughter on he lap. Aha! You feller, say I to myself, dat what you come for trough de cold, eh! . . . Next day I hear de people say de gin'ral got he nose frost-but; and when I seed it look red, I right glad, cause he ought to have some ob de pain, as he got all de fun—ha!ha!"[69]

Jeremy's account refines the portrait of Mary's almost feverish desire to be helpful to her son. She no doubt hoped that with the end of his military service and his marriage he would settle into planter life and relieve her worries. For a while, he did.

George and Martha married at her house on the Pamunkey River on January 6.[70] George brought Martha to Mount Vernon, arriving on April 7, 1759. He wrote to John Alton to get the house ready when he was on the road from Williamsburg. A week later, he noted that he had paid his "mother's Sue," who ran Mary's kitchen and household at Ferry Farm, six shillings and seven and a half pence. Whatever services Sue performed for George, either at Mount Vernon or at Ferry Farm, helped him welcome his exacting new bride home.

Mary had to contend that summer with a drought that stunted her corn and oats and meant continuing cash shortages.[71] She presided over a diminished Ferry Farm and the Quarter (the land her father had left her on the Rappahannock, two plantations downriver). Because the children were all married and dispersed, they had also dispersed their enslaved people and put them to work on the lands they had inherited. Mary, who now walked with some pain, would have more difficulty managing her overseers and increasing trouble breaking even.

14

BETWEEN THE WARS: KIN, CONSUMPTION, CONFLICT

The Rule *and* Measure *of* every good man . . . *That [God] would*
supply him, not with curiosities or delicacies, but with necessaries;
and will give [him] bread to eat and rayment to put on.

—MATTHEW HALE, *CONTEMPLATIONS MORAL AND DIVINE*

*M*ARY'S HORIZONS, NEVER VERY WIDE, narrowed to Ferry Farm and her family during the 1760s. After the flurried preparations for George's wedding, she had time to reflect on her children's worldly positions. All her sons were now wealthy farmers, married to women richer than they, and George's marriage had made him a grandee. Her son-in-law, Fielding, prospered in business. He named his trading schooner *Betty* both from affection and because of her important role in his business. Mary's nearby children visited her and one another often.

Young Charles and his wife, Mildred, built a house in Fredericksburg and had their first child in 1758, George Augustine. Charles would soon become a vestryman at St. George's Church and join the town's community leaders. Mildred bore Frances in 1763. Two other children would follow.

Mary closely followed the health of her family. Betty and Fielding had had six children by 1760, although several had not survived childhood. In April 1759, Betty gave birth to Mary Lewis, to whom Mary Washington was godmother. The little girl died the following Christmas Eve. Their son Augustine had died at four years, Warner at eighteen months.[1] Samuel's first wife had died, but he married again to Mildred Thornton, the cousin of Charles's wife (with the same name, to add more confusion to a family dedicated to getting the most out of a small selection of names). Mary's daughter-in-law Martha had come down with measles in January 1760 but was feeling well by June.[2] Mary's stepson Austin sent a momentarily optimistic report on his uncertain health.[3]

In July 1760, Mary wrote to her brother Joseph in response to a letter from him complaining that she did not write often enough. She pleaded that she wrote infrequently not for "wante of a very great Regard for you and the Family"; instead, because she did not ship tobacco, "the Captins nevr Call one me soe that I never know when they come or when the[y] goe." Mary kept a protective eye on his property, close to hers on the Rappahannock, and warned him that "Captain Newton has taken a large peace of ground from which I dear [dare] say if you had been hear yourself it had not been Don[e]." She caught him up on local friends and kin and concluded, "Give my love to sister Ball and . . . I am Dear Brother your Loving Sister Mary Washington."[4]

Her brother never received Mary's contrite letter. She learned of his death when Ball's son-in-law returned her letter to her. In Joseph Ball, Mary lost a hectoring, opinionated brother/father figure, a fixture of her life for more than fifty years. His education and the authority he habitually assumed had carried weight with her, and his occasional transatlantic news and questions about her long unseen relatives linked her to a past few else knew or cared much about. His death shifted the existential ground under her feet. She achieved the lonely distinction of being the last survivor of her generation of siblings.

In January 1761, George and some family members—but probably not Mary—attended the funeral of Anne Fairfax Washington Lee, Lawrence's widow.[5] As a teenager, George had counseled his sister-in-law when her husband was away, and Mary had cared for Lawrence and celebrated his marriage into the most important family in the colony.

Six months later, news of George's ill health would have frozen Mary with fear if she heard the whole of it. News from Mount Vernon might not have been very detailed, but her other children would have known, and over the months of his illness they would have had difficulty keeping it secret. Of his condition, George later wrote to a cousin, "I have in appearance been very near my last gasp—the Indisposition . . . Increased upon me and I fell into a low and very dangerous State— . . . I once thought . . . I must sink in spite of a noble struggle but thank God I have now got the better of the disorder."[6]

George and Martha went northwest to Berkeley Springs in Berkeley County to take the waters in that beautiful high valley on the Potomac, hoping for a respite. He purchased eight ounces of liquid laudanum and eight ounces of crude opium to ease the pains and fevers he endured.[7] Only by November was George convalescing.

A few months after George's recovery, Mary's stepson Austin, who despite the hopeful news he had sent about his illness, died. Mary had never been as close to Austin as to Lawrence, but she remembered the arrivals of the adolescent boys fresh from their English school and how she introduced them to their new landscape and their unfamiliar young siblings.

These deaths and illnesses gave intensity to Mary and her children's intra-family activities. Historians have argued that George visited Mary infrequently and unwillingly. The record says otherwise. George, the de facto family reporter, filled his diaries with entries about family visits, made and received, gifts given, money dispensed and earned. They learned from each other. In the mid-1760s, Mary and Betty taught George a new technique for planting potatoes under straw.[8] Mary, her five children, and their spouses supported and expressed affection to one another through letters, visits, circulating goods, and gifts. They kept each other (selectively) informed of their doings, health, comings and goings. The siblings scrupulously named their offspring after one another and their parents.

Many days passed in which family members socialized exclusively with kin. One day, George received a visit at Mount Vernon from Samuel's former father-in-law. He then went to his mother's at Ferry Farm and found Samuel there. The next day he and his brother went to Fredericksburg. He returned to his mother's for the night during a sleet and snow storm.[9]

As stepfather to the Custis children, George worked to acquaint them with their Fredericksburg relatives. He wrote to his stepson Jacky's schoolmaster that he was bringing Jacky back from school briefly so that they could "embrace the oppertunity of seeing his Relations for a short space."[10] George brought the family to Fredericksburg for the fair in June 1761.[11] The family spent Christmas together in Fredericksburg that winter. In November and December 1769, George visited his mother, apparently with Martha and Patsy, Martha's daughter by her first husband.[12]

Mary's especially close relationship with Betty carried over to her children, whom she cared for, sewed for, and instructed. She treated her grandchildren to quotations from Matthew Hale and small pieces of pound cake. Tradition has it that when she knew George was coming, she would bake a large pound cake and cut it in half in order to not be extravagant. She would store half of it under the head of her curtained bed. She would present half the cake to George and his friends. Family came to call it the ritual of the "halved-cake."[13]

Concern for the next generation brought the adults together. On the last day of July 1770, George, Martha, and Patsy arrived at Mary's after visiting Jacky at school. Patsy suddenly became very ill. She had suffered from epilepsy for two years, and George thought that she had not only a seizure but also malaria. George brought his friend Dr. Hugh Mercer from Fredericksburg to Ferry Farm, where he bled and treated the girl. George, who had been keeping a record of her seizures from the end of June, wrote that this was "very bad." Mary and the enslaved Sue served the family lunch (called "dinner," the midday meal) on August 1. On August 2, Patsy and Martha ate at the Lewises, transferring there when Patsy improved sufficiently. This made it more convenient for Dr. Mercer and easier for Patsy to play with the young Lewises and Charles and Mildred's children. George shuttled back and forth between Ferry Farm and Fredericksburg during the nine days of Patsy's convalescence, keeping his mother abreast of Patsy's recovery, staying with her some nights and others with Betty and Fielding. Mary had not witnessed the girl's agonies before, because she had not visited Mount Vernon in the two years since they began. Sharing the stricken adolescent's misery with her parents was as difficult as trying to ease the pain of the worried parents. Mary could only provide food and shelter and counsel resignation to God's will.[14]

While George continued to see his mother, Martha spent less time with her, and the couple did not include her in life at Mount Vernon. It is impossible to tell whose choice this was. Mary helped George get ready for his wedding with a whirlwind of activity but did not attend the festivities themselves. She had been lame in the winter of 1755–1756, according to Jeremy, and perhaps that became a permanent disability. She did not leave Ferry Farm much under normal circumstances. Nothing tells us whether she felt shut out of the social life at Mount Vernon.

George and Martha were constructing a life at Mount Vernon as one of Virginia's first couples. They might have wished to close ranks against the more joyless aspects of George's past. Mary's hardworking and abstemious presence might have felt like a reproach. She had been born of unstable fortune and formed to survive. Beyond tea pouring, Mary had few parlor tricks. She was neither very polished nor elegant, nor even particularly cheerful. She dressed frugally, and her conversation was not sprightly. John Locke thought that the secret to being pleasing was having a regard for other people's feelings and finding "the most acceptable and agreeable way of expressing that disposition." But the new demands of gentility for smooth and pleasing conversation easily put people at odds with their inner thoughts and feelings. Mary was more likely to speak her mind than turn a stylish compliment.[15] James Paulding wrote approvingly that she had a "great simplicity of manners," something the Marquis de Lafayette would echo after visiting her many years later. She was courteous, but not elaborate, and put on little show. Perhaps her son and daughter-in-law found her behavior too blunt for their taste.[16]

By the time of George and Martha's wedding, wealthy planters took more and more enslaved women and men from field work to labor in the household, where they created increasingly elegant scenes of domesticity and hospitality. The Washingtons had ten enslaved workers in house-related tasks, so Martha could spend some of her time in more ornamental activities and with her children in intensive child rearing. Martha's oversight of Mount Vernon reflected the new emphasis placed on domestic luxury in clothing, food, and entertainments.[17] According to one recent historian, in the 1760s and '70s, the Washingtons had as many as 400 guests a year at Mount Vernon. In 1768, there were at least 130 overnight guests.[18] Simultaneously, Mary was cutting back on display at Ferry Farm, shedding the obligation to dress formally, entertaining less, and continuing her rustic, hands-on management of her diminished estate.

Over the 1760s, Mary saw George expand the role of patriarch for which she had groomed him. George's spectacular marriage had solidified his position as the social and financial center of the family. Because Daniel Custis had died intestate, his affairs were complicated, but his widow, Martha, inherited some eighty-four enslaved men and women, who came under George's control at their marriage. Each of her two children would inherit another group of humans of the same number and land accordingly. Martha had been unable to pay off her late husband's debts and finally settle the estate. George immediately assumed the task of administration for Martha, himself, and his stepchildren, Patsy and John Parke Custis.

George would succeed in settling the complex inheritance in 1761.[19] An account keeper from adolescence, experienced from settling Lawrence's posthumous debts and holdings, George tracked income and outgo more assiduously than ever after his marriage.

Augustine and Mary both had in their different capacities seen their extended family as a kind of corporation and their sons as their junior financial partners. Betty's husband quickly became a central member of this circle, showing much greater economic sense than Samuel, John Augustine, or Charles. The family circulated financial advice, loans, and business possibilities. Members sometimes used or rented one another's slaves, as George had used Mary's Sue to help with Martha's arrival at Mount Vernon. They sold crops to each other or made helpful exchanges. Before the Revolution, George did not always infuse his financial dealings with a high ethical tone. He included his three brothers as front men in his clandestine plans to buy up lands designated as bonuses for the officers who had served under him. "In the whole of your transactions . . . do not let it be kno[wn that] I have any concern therein."[20] In 1767, he lent his brother Samuel 425 pounds.[21] By 1771, George noted that he had lent Samuel 525 pounds, and about half that amount to Charles.[22] He gave his mother-in-law 35 pounds in April 1760.[23] In November of that year, he gave Mary 15 pounds, something he did every few months—sometimes 15 pounds, twice 3 pounds, once 8 pounds, and once 6, as well as smaller amounts.[24]

Although the sums George reluctantly doled out to Mary were very small compared with what he lent his brothers, Mary's requests for money began to irritate him. George's biographers have accepted without question his annoyance with his mother over money. As a result, they have almost uniformly described Mary as grasping and a bad manager. Only George's aggrieved notes and letters remain, but putting her money requests in the context of some of the important and intertwined changes that affected their relationship in the 1760s makes it harder to see them solely as the self-serving and groundless pleas of an aging, selfish woman.

All of Mary's children, and particularly George, visibly accelerated their consumption of luxury items, "curiosities and delicacies," in these years. Credit was easy, and planters took advantage of it. Marriage to Martha gave George access to much very easy credit.[25]

During the 1760s, George, like many other planters, was making increasingly extravagant purchases, even as his tobacco bought less in Great Britain.[26] George observed and facilitated Martha's extravagances with his orders to London merchants. He disapproved of her indulgences with Jacky but decided that he could not interfere in this relationship. She had, after all, brought to him her enormous estate.[27] He continued to acquire land and enslaved men and women, hoping to outrun his substantial debts (nineteen hundred pounds in 1760[28]) with increased production and more efficient methods, but the strategy failed.

Jacky enjoyed just the kind of imperial adolescence that George would later say few planter boys survived without serious damage to their characters.[29] George worried that Jacky was spoiled, and after a few months at school he and Jacky's teacher decided that even his slave, Julius, was "spoiled" by the experience of attending him at school. George and Martha replaced Julius with the apparently less corruptible Joe.[30]

Mary did not see the remarkable improvements or beautiful furnishings at Mount Vernon, but she later heard from Betty about George and Fielding's competition to decorate their mansions with the most enviable mantelpiece sculptures and to use the finest workmen.[31] Mary certainly witnessed the spectacle George enjoyed creating with his new six-horse green coach—or "chariot" as he called it—ordered at remarkable expense and lengthy back-and-forth with his London procurer. Until things turned sour with Great Britain, he would enjoy offering dignitaries like Governor Dunmore the use of his elegant vehicle and his liveried attendant slaves.

George and Martha's rapid accumulation of costly goods set the pace for the whole family's—except for Mary's. Mary did not order from London, but shopped at Fredericksburg stores. Fragments of her accounts remain. She mainly purchased fabric that she turned into clothing for herself, Betty, and her grandchildren. She bought German osnaburg for slave clothing, and muslin, silk, "net sheeting," " best Drogheda" (a kind of wool especially for upholstery), thread, buttons, pins, two crystal ones, "figured" ribbon, buckles, "best white sheeting," calico, and "black Barcelona." She purchased a little bonnet for a granddaughter. She bought flour, salt, nuts, pepper, cloves, ginger, and cheese as well as cheese molds. The bills include charges for gin, turpentine, sugar, Bohea, and green and black hyson tea. Frivolities were few; there was a necklace for sixteen shillings and nine pence, the "best fan," a "black satin bonnet" (in 1769), and a silk purse, amid purchases of shot and powder, five hundred nails, candles, and a pair of candlesticks. She also bought a dictionary either as a gift to a grandchild or to help her with spelling and reading. She bought snuff and a snuffbox, again perhaps as a gift or perhaps for herself, although no one ever recalled her taking snuff.[32] Unlike her younger sons, but like her daughter, she died with very few debts, which her estate easily paid off.

Samuel, on the other hand, after witnessing George's splendid green coach, wrote to William Lee, a London merchant, about one for himself. In November of the following year, Lee wrote to Samuel, "I have after a great deal of trouble at last got you a second hand chariot . . . not a bad bargain." He enclosed a bill of fifty-two pounds and fifteen shillings. He was also trying to supply Samuel with indentured servants and a weaver for his land claims in the west. Meanwhile, he wrote, "It is impossible to carry on any business here, without money, of which I have not a great deal, I must beg you will not fail to make a full remittance," and urged him to send his tobacco along as well. Samuel had not paid by the summer of 1771, the year George noted that Samuel owed him 525 pounds, nor had he shipped his tobacco through Lee. (By contrast, George ordered a new coach in 1762 for 162 pounds for Fielding Lewis, who paid him promptly.)[33]

Richard Henry Lee, William's brother in Virginia, wrote to William that "J. A. [John Augustine] Washington liked flattery, try him." He also encouraged William that Samuel Washington, as well as some others, "deserves to be carefully cultivated." William replied that as to J. A. Washington, "You can do more with [him] than I can,"[34] but continued to work with Samuel, who seems to have been unable to stop buying things, particularly if his older brother, George, his mother's favorite, had them.[35]

George would later explain very cogently to George Mason the pressures on him and other members of his class to continue to buy more and more expensive items. He described planters haunted by an unending need to demonstrate to one another how affluent and successful they were. In April 1769, George's thinking about injurious British policies led him to imagine a way to help colonial shopping addicts curtail consumption. He wanted to prevent local merchants from importing certain kinds of luxury goods. Apart from pressuring Great Britain to change its tax policies, he thought rich Virginians would benefit. The "penurious man," George reflected, managed to live within his means, and he might not like the new system with fewer choices, but the "extravagant & expensive man . . . is thereby furnished with a pretext to live within his bounds, and embraces it.—Prudence dictated economy to him before, but his resolution was too weak to put it in practice; for how can I, *says he*, who have lived in such a manner change my method. I am ashamed to do it: and besides, such an alteration in the System of my living, will create suspicions of a decay in my fortune, & such a thought the world must not harbor; I will e'en continue my course: till at last the course discontinues the Estate, a sale of it being the consequence of his perseverance in error."[36] George, the "expensive man," saw himself hurtling downward on the path he thought ruinous.

His mother had always argued that appearances and shows of finery and objects meant nothing in the great scheme of things. She no doubt understood the circular confidence game he and others were playing, and perhaps she criticized him for being unable to stop playing. George criticized his overseers, his slaves, his factors, Great Britain, and the demands of elite Virginians for his predicament. But within the family, where the debts were piling up, he took a measure of his irritation for the predicament in which he found himself out on his mother.

This was even though George understood that if Mary was not making ends meet, most planters did not either. He later wrote that Virginia farming was "rarely productive."[37] George tried any number of efficiency schemes, crop experiments, plowing techniques, and reductions of slave rations before and after the Revolution, but never made his plantations truly profitable. Although George understood the consumption trap as well as the difficulty of managing an estate, he directed his ire about money at his mother, and she, not Samuel or Charles or John Augustine, all of whom died with many debts, has come down in history as greedy, whiny, and incompetent.

None of this is to argue that Mary might not have expressed her needs in guilt-inducing or even accusatory ways. Perhaps the phrasing of her requests needled him in a spot still painful from remembered maternal sermons. But she was acting in ways predictable and familiar to him and that he had responded to matter-of-factly in the past. After the Revolution, he complained to her of being seen as a "delinquent" son, which enraged him and produced lengthy missives of self-defense to her and others.[38] Both mother and son were tightfisted, and both believed fervently in their own views of their mutual obligations. Mary's thoughts on these matters have not survived, and except for a few plaintive notes about her poverty there is no way to know how she approached her high-living son and why, exactly, it made him so angry. She might have lectured him on the meaninglessness of wealth and luxuries in comparison with his duties as patriarch and shepherd of the family. Or perhaps he knew the script so well that he could recite it himself. He had his own copy of Matthew Hale by 1764.[39]

In the very last year of George's life, he had an interchange with his overseer that seems to articulate the raw, weary exasperation that sometimes throbbed between mother and son. George and James Anderson exchanged letters—too many from George's point of view—about farm questions. Finally, George wrote, "It is not my wish to hurt yours or the feelings of any man . . . but . . . I can scarcely ask . . . any question . . . but what your sensibility is affected. This, & not being able to open my lips upon subjects very interesting to my pecuniary concerns . . . without receiving a long letter by way of reprimand for Scolding . . . I ever have, and ever will, deliver my opinion in matters which relate to myself or my business: and it is needless to be repeating over and over again the favorable opinion I have so often expressed in writing of your Industry, zeal & honesty."[40] George, perhaps as Mary had, understood he was causing pain but asserted his right to keep hammering away. And he had little patience for injecting ritual praise to blunt his criticisms.

George's upbringing, which he later praised, bonded him and his mother in a profound but not always comfortable way. Raised to be frugal, he enjoyed participating in Martha's expenditures but felt ambivalence about it. He might have found a safe outlet for his ambivalence in complaining about Mary's wants.

When he was president, George wrote, "I never again will have two women in my house when I am there myself."[41] He was referring to the time he had spent living between Martha and the wife of his nephew George Augustine Washington. But it also suggests that he could manage a peaceful life with Martha, while the pulls of two strong women disturbed him, and marriage put his complex allegiance to his mother under new strains. Martha found in George an indefatigable manager who happened to be inclined from his relationship with his mother to avoid confrontation with women. But avoiding confrontations with two strong women simultaneously was more than he wished to do.

Compounding the tension between George and Mary was her occupation of Ferry Farm, which Augustine had willed to him. While she consumed almost nothing, compared with her sons and daughter-in-law, she was profiting from *his* property and costing him the occasional small handout in addition. He wished to be the dutiful son he, Virginia society, and

Mary agreed was his proper role. His own contradictory impulses toward luxurious living and penny-pinching imprisoned him, as did his fiercely legalistic approach to his rights. Patriarchal law shaped and supported his growing sense of the illegitimacy of Mary's requests, indeed of her chosen way of life.

One of Martha's cousins and close friends whom she visited when she came to Fredericksburg, the wealthy widow Mary Dandridge Spotswood Campbell (1727–1795), had a husband who left her wealthy in land but increasingly poor in cash. Her struggle to hold on to her estate from creditors and later from her son, Alexander, went on from the 1760s into the 1790s, by which time she was complaining to her daughter of lacking the money to buy her slaves shoes and to buy wood to keep warm. She worried that her son was attempting to sell off some of her lands and her "dower negroes." Mary Campbell's worries, which she no doubt shared with Martha over the years, made George look very good by comparison, but legally Alexander Campbell's claims were not unusual. He and George were longtime friends and were doing business up to the end of George's life.[42] The law nourished and often validated the exasperation of sons who wanted and felt entitled to the property of their widowed mothers.[43]

George and Mary contended for decades over relatively small amounts of money—at least small to him. His indebtedness, her desire to remain on the farm where she had lived most of her life, and the marital tensions that he displaced onto his strong, complicated bond with his mother reliably generated friction between them.

IIIIIIIIIIIII

IF MARY'S RELATIONSHIP with George became tenser in these years, hers with Betty and Fielding grew closer, despite their novel—to Mary— hope to facilitate slave education. The effort has only Fielding's name on it, but it is extremely unlikely that he would have founded a school for enslaved children without Betty's approval. The Fredericksburg school, begun in 1765 and modeled on the one in Williamsburg that had lasted ten years, would teach literacy and the basics of Anglicanism.

Some urban slave owners, particularly merchants, valued literate slaves more than they feared them. In the early nineteenth century, a number of merchants owned between fourteen and nineteen slaves each. The warehouses on Sophia Street where slaves and merchandise were loaded and unloaded required workers. Stores required laborers to move the stock. Ore from the local iron mines had to be shipped along the Rappahannock to the docks near Fredericksburg. Skilled black watermen, blacksmiths, carpenters, rope makers, shoemakers, tanners, cabinetmakers, seamstresses, cooks, and coopers all worked in town. Slaves mixed, intermarried, and enjoyed some leisure with the tiny free black population. They lived in quarters set back from their owners' houses, small but often of similar design. They had to carry passes to move about in town except for "Free Alley," which was apparently under sufficient surveillance from the houses along it.[44] In Fredericksburg, slaves were sold or hired out on the block, also used as a carriage mounting block at the corner of William and Charles Streets.[45]

Fielding served as vestryman at St. George's Church, built in Fredericksburg in the year of George's birth.[46] He encountered the ideas of Dr. Thomas Bray, an Episcopal minister who had come to the colonies in the early eighteenth century. Bray thought that blacks were "barbarous and heathen" and that there was nothing wrong with slavery, but he believed the enslaved had souls that needed attention. He organized an association that worked to persuade ministers to baptize and educate slaves and supply them with Bibles and devotional materials. He died in January 1729 or 1730, but his association carried on this work.[47]

Fielding thought a school to teach literacy was a "pious design" and worked with the Reverend James Maury of St. George's to recruit the school's first sixteen children, ages five to eight. Charles Washington, a vestryman at St. George's by 1770, was not party to this project. By September 1765, Fielding wrote that the students were already beginning to "read prettily." He received books from Anthony Bacon in Maryland, brother of the Reverend Thomas Bacon, whose sermons to slaves were popular among slave owners because they recommended, over and over, obedience to masters and paying attention to the masters' interests.[48]

The boys and girls learned to pray and to read the Bible. The girls also practiced sewing, knitting, and embroidering. A year into the project, Lewis saw that slave owners would not leave their slave children in school long enough for them to achieve much. Lewis proposed closing the school to any who would not commit to a five-year program for the youngsters. The authorities told him to do the best he could, not officially weighing in on the five-year requirement. By 1768, Lewis's school had only nine students who attended constantly and thought he would have only four the coming summer. He worried that soon there would be none because he had observed that the owners withdrew them as soon as they could read or were old enough to care for the younger black children at home. He promised to continue paying the schoolmistress her twenty pounds a year and hoped that some children would continue.

His British correspondents responded indignantly, ignorant of the long reach of slavery. "Are They so weak as to imagine divine providence send the Blacks among them merely to cultivate their Lands and do the severest Drudgery for their Masters worldly profit only without any regard to the Spiritual Welfare of the poor slaves? . . . Our Willingness to instruct the Negroes at our own Expence not only leaves the Master who refuse to have 'em instructed without Excuse but must involve 'em in very great Guilt."[49] Fielding discontinued the school and was not, as far as it seems, paid the outstanding thirty pounds for his effort.[50] If Mary discussed Fielding's school with him and Betty, she might have approved of a practical motive for it, but it seems more likely that it was a subject that they did not discuss much.

Meanwhile, the Reverend Jonathan Boucher, who was teaching Jacky Custis at his school in Caroline County and in correspondence with George Washington, baptized slaves in substantial numbers. He had observed the problems with trying to establish a school and instead gave the books that the associates sent him to those free blacks and slaves who were Christians and who could read.[51]

Mary and George seem to have imagined that a moral system based on obedience to their authority would benefit the slaves. George made this explicit later. He directed the enslaved Frank to be forced to do a job or "Idleness" would "ruin him."[52] George repeatedly used the word "duty" to his slaves in the 1780s, a word he used endlessly as military commander as well.

Mary found support for her belief in Hale's and Scott's works. Both theologians argued that moral systems without the superstructure of Christian theology were good enough for heathens. Mary knew that Christianity was the one thing needful for eternal life. Hale offered her a way to think about those whom she did *not* consider appropriate for religious instruction. Hale's title—*Contemplations Moral and Divine*—indicates the two planes on which his advice took place. The less exalted, moral plane was a good beginning for those who were not Christians—"considering how far by the help of these [moral reasons] many Heathans (that had not the true knowledge of God revealed in his Word and Son) advanced in the practice of these Virtues."[53] Mary believed in enforcing certain kinds of moral behavior because she saw it was useful for slaves, even though they were not capable of becoming Christians. If they improved in practical virtues like obedience and industry, they would better help Mary provide.

For Mary, like almost all slaveholders, if a slave was not interested in her moral system, violence could justifiably produce obedience. However, as she grew older, elite behavioral standards were beginning to mark her as unladylike. Younger elite women like George's wife, Martha, grew up at a time when wealthy Virginians began to believe that it was unwomanly to wield coercion openly. In fact, George established a rule at Mount Vernon that prevented slaves from complaining to their owners of treatment at the hands of overseers. Thus Charlotte, personal maid to Martha, after two whippings, *threatened* to tell Martha about what happened to her, but Martha herself did not have to either punish her or even know about her beatings. Mary grew up with few buffers between her and getting work out of her slaves.

The historian Thavolia Glymph has argued that planter men and historians have largely trivialized white women's violence, portraying it as a kind of aside to the slave system and a sign of the impulsivity of slave-owning women. To the contrary, she argues, white women's violence in support of slavery was widespread, necessary to maintaining the institution, and not so much impulsive as routine. As one nineteenth-century slaveholding woman mused, "'Amiable' elite women . . . moved in and out of the costume of the 'southern lady.'" Pro-slavery ideology downplayed the resistance of slave women that helped occasion white women's violence, depicting it as bad character and the inability to learn, rather than resistance to slavery. And white women's violence has been similarly downplayed in the interests of maintaining the myths of the primacy of patriarchs and the inherent gentleness of white women.[54]

Mary, for a variety of reasons, had not bothered much with the costume of the amiable southern lady, while George's wife, Martha, did. At Mount Vernon, Martha set work quotas for her household slaves, but George would often issue the commands. Despite her remove from some of slavery's front lines, Martha's relations with her household slaves left her angry and perplexed enough that she wrote to Fanny Bassett Washington, wife of George's nephew, "Blacks are so bad in their nature that they have not the least gratitude for the kindness that may be shewed to them."[55]

Women slave owners used force, name-calling, and abuse to try to turn people into slaves. There was no other way to do it in the face of resistance, and while Martha, Mary, and other slave-owning women displayed different manners and behavior to their equals, they all had to struggle to enslave their slaves. But Mary was getting on in years. She could no longer physically intimidate slaves as she once had. Her imposing presence came more and more from her emotional and psychological strength, not from her strong physical presence and the power of her limbs. And an aging woman's psychological power could not stop a slave from resisting her.

George and his siblings discussed Mary's future together and with her over the summer and fall of 1770. In the early fall of that year, Samuel and his then wife, Anne Steptoe, moved to Harewood in Frederick County, removing them from the circle of children close to their mother.[56] Mary had spent a decade alone on Ferry Farm. Her advancing age and the likelihood of an overseer and slaves not serving her well concerned George. He later wrote that an overseer he deplored "has no more authority over the Negroes . . . than an old woman would have."[57]

In 1772, George pushed into action the project of moving his mother from Ferry Farm and taking over its management and that of her four hundred acres on the Rappahannock that Joseph Ball had left her half a century before. Tired of her requests for money, he was convinced that he would run Ferry Farm better than she could. George expected to get enhanced yield from these acres, because in the preceding decade he had been experimenting with crop rotation, manure, new crops, various plowing techniques, and techniques to get more labor out of his slave force. He was impatient to try these out on Ferry Farm and the Quarter at Little Falls (land left to her by her father). In his diary, he mentioned riding Ferry Farm repeatedly, and his wholehearted pleasure in the new project is unmistakable.[58] He took care to make sure that the ground for planting corn was broken up, as he did meticulously on his own plantations.

Mary agreed with George that he would take over running the Quarter and Ferry Farm. In George's later telling of the story, Mary picked out a house on Charles Street in Fredericksburg near the Lewises' planned mansion, and George made a down payment of seventy-five pounds.[59]

He started making the arrangement in mid-September 1771. Mary owned slaves working on both plantations, so George would rent them from her as well as paying her rent for the Quarter, which she owned. Charles and Lewis would do an inventory that would determine the annual price that George would pay in rent.[60] George gave the fields a proper survey on September 13, 1771. He advanced her precisely four pounds, twelve shillings, and six pence on money that he would soon pay her to buy her stock and rent her slaves and the Quarter (or Little Falls). Those sums would come to thirty pounds a year for the Quarter and ninety-two pounds a year for the hire of her ten slaves, who included six men and four women, five at Ferry Farm and five at Little Falls. The stock was worth another ninety-three pounds, eleven shillings, and eight pence.[61] George retained Mary's overseer, Edward Jones, and hired William Powell to look after the Little Falls Quarter.[62] Throughout October, he returned to Fredericksburg to see the Lewises and his mother and to supervise the work at the farm. He spent an unexpected October day at Mary's because he lost his horse. In November, he gave Fielding two hundred pounds to complete the purchase of the house on Charles Street where Mary would live the rest of her life.[63] George was busy fencing Ferry Farm and attending to details.

When George paid her what their agreement stipulated, he began doing it through Fielding or Lund Washington, George's cousin and manager, or in the presence of Charles or Betty.[64] For her new life, Mary had George order from his London purveyor a red cloak with a hood for "Tall Women" that cost ten pounds, two shillings, and one penny and a "riding chair" that cost forty pounds. George had the two items charged to his mother.[65] In April, Mary hosted her son in her new home and saw much of him in May. George was nearby in June and brought slaves from his Muddy Hole Farm to Ferry Farm for the July harvest. By July 18, the harvest was all in, and George had begun to set slaves to "ditch the swamp" at Ferry Farm. The slaves sowed wheat there in August. In September, he stayed at Mary's and gave her thirty pounds in the presence of Charles. Under George's management, Ferry Farm produced respectable numbers of bushels of wheat, although there are no figures from the previous year to compare with.[66]

The transfer brought them together often and gave Mary and George both relief from their conflict. George acted the dutiful son in a way that suited him and his talents and that he thought would allow him to be generous but also to turn a profit for himself. Making his childhood home profitable clearly filled him with enthusiasm and energy. Mary doubtless enjoyed the unusual amounts of time he spent with her and in discussing the improvements he was executing. Unlike George's brothers, she couldn't foxhunt or do deals with him, but she knew every inch of the land he was trying to reinvigorate. They had not collaborated closely since the years just after Augustine's death, and it must have pleased her to watch her son put his years of experience, practical mind, and excitement into the farm she had managed for nearly thirty years and her land at Little Falls.

Her white house in town was on a corner lot, with a sloping roof, two parlors in the front, and a dining room in back that looked out on a large garden. Behind were stables and an orchard.[67] The garden was her favorite spot. The long rows of tall blooms that extend back from the house today suggest her deep love of flowers. George hoped she would find peace here, and although he as much as anyone would make that impossible, Mary nurtured a garden that still breathes beauty into the house. With his well-developed ideas about and great love for landscape and plants, George must have enjoyed discussing her plans for her improved garden.

The cultivation of fruits and flowers, long an English and colonial pastime, was one that inspired eighteenth-century men and women, wealthy and not, with aesthetic and tactile pleasure. In England, poor women earned money weeding. Mary's mother might have had "weeding women" in her family or weeding in her future if she had remained in England. In Mary's household, slaves did that work. But she designed and ordered her garden according to her own taste and probably in accord with hierarchies developed by the well-established field of gardening literature that had been available for well over a century. Examples of garden design were all around her.[68]

In 1759, at the time of his marriage, George acquired his first and only garden book, Batty Langley's *New Principles of Gardening*, which advocated that gardeners move away from strict symmetry and extensive topiaries characteristic of European aristocrats and create more individually expressive landscapes. Mary's house garden was not large like Mount Vernon's, but her long beds gave her an endless project and a retreat. Without George's acres to transform, she used different kinds of flowers to express her artistry. Her garden allowed her to work and simultaneously to enjoy James Hervey's analogies and tales.[69]

Hervey's book helped Mary savor the garden's spiritual metaphors. He extolled the natural world and the cultivated one, giving his readers thought paths that connected their daily surroundings to divine themes for meditation. He took readers on garden strolls, warning them to get up early or lose the flowers' perfume and to ponder the humble daisy, whose beauty put expensive gowns, jewelry, and all worldly acquisitions to shame. Mary had tended her literal garden carefully throughout her years at Ferry Farm. Walking through her flowers and finding them saturated not only with beauty but also with God's love and the power to bring her thoughts to divine subjects was a welcome act and might already have been a familiar one.

As if picking up a conversation with Mary, Hervey opened his book with a reflection on a young boy in a church, gazing admiringly at a statue of a wounded soldier. The author wrote in the wake of Great Britain's victory over Spain in the War of Jenkins' Ear—Lawrence's war and the perhaps the source of the disease that killed him. In Hervey's commentary, a minister explains to the boy that dying for one's country has little moral value when compared with Christ's dying for the salvation of his enemies. This instance "of such disinterested, diffusive, and divine Benevolence . . . makes all that Heroes have achieved, and Patriots suffered, dwindle into Nothing, and scarce deserve our Notice."[70]

A scholar of evangelical texts like Hervey's argues that these kinds of authors assumed the "indwelling of virtue" in the reader and that the authors gave more importance to virtue than to literary merit. Religious reading's purpose was to encourage repentance, "not warmer sociability. It led to a better relation with God and the promise of Heaven, not heightened sensibility on earth and in society."[71] Mary's readings of Hervey as well as her other books were for her private edification, through which she tracked her spiritual struggles. They did not aim to "refine" her behavior.

Hervey worked over a series of themes close to Mary's experience and heart. He lingered long over the grief, misery, and confusion of widowed mothers and their children—their untold and irreplaceable losses of husband and father. He wrote of the terrifying torments of hell awaiting the mother who had failed to instill godliness in her children. As Mary saw her seedlings grow, she could employ the metaphors of the plant world to remember her years as a wife, widow, and mother and to imagine lessons for her grandchildren.

In late June 1773, George and Martha were devastated by the death of her seventeen-year-old daughter, Patsy. Eerily, it coincided with an early summer snowstorm.[72] Two weeks later, George took the bereaved Martha to Ferry Farm to distract her with his projects. At the same time that he ordered his mother's cloak and riding chair, he ordered a "genteel mourning sword" to commemorate Patsy. He sealed his letters with black wax in this period.[73] In Fredericksburg, Mary and the Lewises gave Martha their condolences.

15.

THE REVOLUTION:
A FAMILY AFFAIR

This World is a place for our duty and employment, and we must use all honest and lawful means to preserve our lives and our comforts by our honest care and our diligence.

—MATTHEW HALE, *CONTEMPLATIONS MORAL AND DIVINE*

*M*ARY ENJOYED HER COMFORTABLY FURNISHED new house, just a brief walk from Betty and Fielding's house downtown, filled with her grandchildren. It would be even closer to their mansion in progress, Kenmore, completed in 1775.[1] After she moved, George visited a number of times. She also found her way to what became her favorite spot beyond her garden, a rock formation near the Rappahannock on Fielding and Betty's estate, where she enjoyed sitting and reading. She sometimes took her grandchildren with her and read to them from the family Bible and explained ideas from Matthew Hale. She could also attend the younger reverend Maury's services alone or in the company of the Lewises or Charles and Mildred when she liked.

Her slave Stephen, described as elderly, served as coachman and gardener. In her stables beyond the garden, Mary kept a bay horse for her phaeton, a topless carriage that had a seat in front for the driver, and two seats behind. She also kept two black horses along with her "riding chair." In her last years, she had a housekeeper, Mrs. Skelton, who executed Mary's desires and oversaw her maid Patty and cook Bet, who had replaced Sue. Stephen and Bet were married and had two children.[2]

In theory, her arrangement with George meant she did not have to oversee her land and slaves, but every day when the weather permitted, Stephen drove Mary out to the Quarter to check on things. In the summer, she wore a straw hat with a broad brim that she tied with black ribbons. In the winter, she wore her shag cloak alternatively described as red and purple. She acquired a gold-headed cane to help her walk, although she continued to be vigorous for her age and, like her son, enjoyed exercise.[3] She kept up her routine because she knew herself as an independent plantation owner responsible for the stewardship of her property and "family," as planters liked to call their slaves. George was gone. She remained vigilant. And her distrust of overseers had deep roots.

Mary endured most of the uneasy years before the Revolution and the war years in her new house. She had heard George, Fielding, Betty, and others talk about their discontents with Great Britain since at least 1765, when the Stamp Act provoked fierce resistance in Virginia and in the Northern Neck in particular. A meeting of 115 men got together at Leeds Town downstream on the Rappahannock to reject compliance. Charles Washington and Lewis Willis both signed. Fielding was apparently not there, but he would soon be a leader of the resistance to Britain's tax policies. George Mercer, who had served under George at Fort Necessity, had just returned from Great Britain with the job of stamp collector. He arrived in Williamsburg two days before the Stamp Tax was to take effect.

A mob insisted that he resign, which he did the following day. Richard Henry Lee of Westmoreland County, Mary's birthplace, staged a hanging in effigy of Mercer. Virginians began to reevaluate what had been the prestigious and lucrative practice of participating in the imperial bureaucracy.[4] It was at this point that George started reading political pamphlets and began developing the connections between his financial difficulties and deliberate British policy.[5]

Mary never commented—at least in any document that has survived—on the events leading up to the Revolution or on the war itself except as it affected her crops and ability to feed her slaves and herself. Even though she was the mother of the most famous protagonist of the war, Mary suffered food shortages, inflation, fears, and social upheavals like other Virginians. If all politics is local, for Mary politics was also familial. Because she spent so much time with Betty and Fielding Lewis, who were at the center of colony-wide Whig communications, and because Mary worried about her first son, I make the assumption that she had to know in broad outline what the issues were, that she kept some track of local and state politics and had some sense of the progress of the war. She wanted peace, and she wanted her son and eventually her grandchildren home safe. And, although Mary might have preferred to wish a pox on Whigs and Tories alike, it seems inevitable that with George putting his life at stake, Fielding and Betty offering up their fortunes, and the whole family supporting the Revolution, she could not have remained wholly ignorant of or indifferent to the Whig cause. If the matter of taxation remained opaque or of no interest to her, British war tactics, particularly those of Lord Dunmore, encouraging slave rebellion would have pushed her to align with her family. The famous charge by Michel Guillaume Jean de Crèvecoeur, who heard from someone else that she was a Tory, makes no sense. That she did not like military solutions to problems does make sense. Perhaps these observers (who seem to have been French speaking) mistook the latter for the former.

The skirmishes between the burgesses and the British governors became more hostile with the arrival of Lord Dunmore, previously stationed in New York, who kept the representatives' sessions as short as possible.[6] In 1773, the burgesses established the permanent colony-wide Committee of Correspondence to share information and ideas with other colonies. After the Boston Tea Party in December 1773, and despite troubles between the assembly and the governor, George offered his carriage for Dunmore's use when he arrived, hoping no doubt to demonstrate his own power and respectability and to find some help from the governor in bringing military force to the disturbances between Indians and settlers in the backcountry where George and his friends and relatives had large land claims.[7]

Parliament meanwhile, in March 1774, made the extraordinarily provocative blunder of ordering Boston closed until the Tea Partiers paid for the cargo heaved into the Atlantic. That month, before the news reached Virginia, Charles Washington sponsored a puppet show with considerable punch and bumbo (rum, sugar, water, and nutmeg) at Weedon's Tavern.[8] Perhaps Mary attended.

In May, when the burgesses received the news of the Boston Port Bill, they called for a day of fasting and prayer "to inspire us with firmness in support of our rights." Dunmore dissolved the assembly. A rump group met in a nearby tavern calling for an August meeting of representatives of all the colonies.[9] George, hoping to enlist Dunmore's power to his advantage in the west, subscribed a pound for a ball to welcome Lady Dunmore while excoriating imperial policy in Boston.[10]

The Reverend James Maury in Fredericksburg held services on June 1, 1774, "devoutly to implore the Divine Interposition for averting the heavy Calamity which threatens Destruction to the Civil Rights of America."[11] After his sermon, Fredericksburg men created their local eleven-man Committee of Correspondence, including Fielding Lewis as chairman, Charles Dick, and Charles Washington. The Virginia Gazette, reporting on happenings at Fredericksburg, announced, "Credit is due to the Ladies for the Part they took in our Association, and it does Honour to their Sex: for no sooner were they made acquainted with the Resolution to prohibit the use of TEA, after the first of June, but before the Day came, they sealed up the Stock which they had on Hand, and vowed never more to use it till the oppressive Act imposing a Duty thereupon should be repealed. May their Example be followed by all the Ladies on this Continent!" Mary bought hyson tea on May 18, 1774. Perhaps she was stocking up, afraid of what was coming down from Massachusetts.[12]

Given that a substantial number in the Virginia Committee of Correspondence and the insurgents in general were either Mary's close kin, neighbors, or lifelong friends, it seems that she probably put away her beloved Bohea and hyson teas—at least in company. Certainly Betty would have joined the boycott.[13] John Harrower, the indentured Scottish tutor at Belvidera, the Daingerfield family plantation, about seven miles down the Rappahannock from Fredericksburg, noted enduring six months without tea.[14] George spent the night at his mother's later in June and made no mention of tea.[15]

||||||||||||

WHILE FREDERICKSBURG MEN and women were closing ranks against British punishment of Boston, provoked Indians and aggressive settlers in the west of the colony were threatening George's hopes for profits from his tenants there. During the spring and summer of 1774, George received reports from his overseer Gilbert Simpson that five hundred families had left his western lands in one week fearing the Indians. This was even though only one settler died, while nineteen Indians were killed. Simpson helped build a fort and decided to stay and fight rather than lose his claim. He bought a "Nise Rifel."[16] Valentine Crawford, whom Washington had sent out to settle his lands, wrote, agreeing with Simpson's assessment, that it was "as much the white people falt as the Indians." Crawford never got as far as Washington's lands, stopping on the way to build himself a blockade.[17]

George wrote to his friend George William Fairfax that while he didn't approve of the Boston Tea Party, he thought the British were failing in their duty to protect Virginians who had "a cruel & bloodthirsty Enemy upon our Backs . . . between whom & our Frontier Inhabitants many

Skirmishes have happened & with whom a general war is inevitable." Meanwhile, the British were "endeavouring by every piece of Art & despotism to fix the shackles of Slavery up on us." George expected Dunmore to protect the settlers whom he and his friends and brothers had placed on their lands to secure their claims to thousands and thousands of acres across the mountains. He also wanted Dunmore to settle in favor of Virginia, where the boundary between Virginia and Pennsylvania colonies lay.[18]

In July, Dunmore took twelve hundred troops on an expedition against the Shawnees. Some of the fighting was on Washington's claimed lands. In November, Dunmore made a treaty acquiring Kentucky and securing the land east of the Ohio. By the end of November, George learned that Indians had burned the homes and "improvements" he and the settlers had been making on his lands. He calculated the expense at precisely 1,568 pounds, 18 shillings, and 7.5 pence.[19] With peace, however tenuous, George immediately started assigning land and hired James Cleveland to organize settling it.[20]

His and his colleagues' claims to these lands depended on the revocation of the Proclamation Act that Britain had passed in 1763 prohibiting settlement beyond the Alleghenies. Parliament passed the act precisely to avoid future wars with the Indians, having already the problem of paying for the most recent one between Great Britain and France and its Indian allies. George's bounty lands under this act were illegal, as were the purchases by the Ohio Company and others. The Treaty of Fort Stanwix, in which the Iroquois had sold land beyond the line, seemed to mean that the Proclamation Act was no longer being invoked, but repeated appeals to London failed to validate Washington's and others' claims. In any case, the Iroquois had sold land that had never been theirs. In light of the Iroquois deception, the southern tribes like the Cherokee began to form alliances to threaten Great Britain with a major war if it were to condone further settlement. It did not. At the time of Dunmore's War, the claims of George, his brothers, George Mason, Richard Henry Lee, Patrick Henry, Thomas

Jefferson, and many other Revolutionary leaders were legally ambiguous, although Dunmore's Treaty gave the speculators renewed hope.[21] Independence would remove the ambiguity.[22]

Fielding, Samuel, Charles, and George approved of Dunmore's War against the Shawnees, as Mary would have. The family united in its belief in the sanctity of property ownership. Colonists also generally believed that imperial policy toward Native people was wrongheaded and failed to take into account what George called their "cruel and bloodthirsty" nature.

Mary had seen the streams of indentured men and women, like her mother, getting off the boats at Fredericksburg in the years before the Revolution, planning to make their fortunes. Twenty shiploads or more came up the Rappahannock in the years before the Revolution.[23] Virginia had shortened indenture from seven to five years to make immigration more attractive. Fielding hired sixty immigrants to work on Kenmore, his new house.[24] Speculators like George with lands in the west engaged them to settle and develop their lands to validate their claims and to provide a buffer against the Indians.

George was at Betty and Fielding's at the beginning of August 1774 when Mary learned about the latest decisions the men were making. That month, the burgesses voted not to export tobacco after August 10 and in November to cease importing a wide array of goods, excepting medicines and slaves. The convention elected seven delegates to the First Continental Congress in Philadelphia in September, including George Washington, Richard Henry Lee, Peyton Randolph, Patrick Henry, and Benjamin Harrison.[25] That convention also voted to set up a gun manufactory. It appointed five commissioners, but the two managers would be Fielding Lewis (appointed in absentia because from 1773 on he spent August in Berkeley at the springs)[26] and Charles Dick.[27]

George had come to believe the conflict would require armed resistance. In August, before he left for the First Congress, he wrote to Bryan Fairfax that "the Crisis is arrived and we must assert our Rights, or Submit to every Imposition that can be heap'd upon us; till custom and use, will make us as tame, & abject Slaves, as the Blacks we rule over with such arbitrary Sway."[28]

In September, George left for Philadelphia.[29] When the Continental Congress imposed its ban on imports, Fredericksburg and others towns organized themselves to comply. Fielding Lewis headed the committee in charge of enforcing the new regulations, working with Charles Washington, James Mercer, Lewis Willis, Charles Dick, and two Thorntons to rent a warehouse for contributions to the relief of Boston. They also checked the books of all merchants who might be inflating their prices on goods that were becoming scarce. They collected the recently banned goods, sold them, and returned the money to the merchants who had bought them, using the extra to buy relief goods for Boston. In January, they sent a ship with wheat, flour, Indian corn, and bread for poor, hungry Bostonians. Betty and Mary were in the middle of this heightened activity, looking after the children and worried and uncertain about a future that was largely out of their hands.

The First Continental Congress (September–October 1774) instructed counties to start organizing companies for defense, and Spotsylvania County selected Fielding Lewis as first lieutenant, in charge of drawing up the company's regulations. Hugh Mercer headed the mounted company. Mary, Betty, and Fielding would all have watched George reviewing the companies in Fredericksburg in February 1775. A month later, again in Fredericksburg, George gathered the boys of a local school, gave them punch, patted their heads, and asked if they would be willing to fight for their country.[30]

The answer to that question, if posed to adults, would have been "that depends on the terms," because colonial leaders conceived and implemented schemes that relied on poorer, non-slaveholding whites to defend the property and rights of rich slaveholders. Initial plans called for three tiers of military: a group called minutemen, who would be the elite in discipline and training to replace the old, preexisting, independent companies of volunteers; militia companies, in which all white men were to serve; and two companies of men designed to serve in the Continental army who would presumably come from among the very poorest in society. Virginia Whig leaders hoped in this way to fight the British but also protect the colony from rebellious slaves. To this end, they also appointed patrollers from among the militia to check any slave resistance, while exempting all overseers of four people who were tithable (that is field workers or slaves) from service.[31] These regulations placed the burden of combat and of slave control on the small landholders and the landless, those without much of a stake in the overall fight. The regulations changed over the course of the war, and resistance to them forced wealthier Virginians to extraordinary measures to get poor men to fight. The aggrieved populations were particularly strong in the west. These struggles destabilized power relations in the colony and emboldened those who were unhappy with the status quo. Mary as an old woman already had a tenuous hold on authority. As the war went on, her overseer would fleece her, participating in the widespread unrest and exploiting her particular vulnerabilities of age and gender.

In February 1775, as George was reviewing troops in Fredericksburg, Dunmore tried to convene the burgesses, but few showed up. Opposition members gathered in mid-March to nominate the same delegates as before to the Second Continental Congress, this time including as an alternate Thomas Jefferson. Mary, Betty, and Fielding would have seen George on his way to Richmond, where he heard Patrick Henry deliver his famous speech putting his liberty in the scale with his death. Washington ate with the Lewises both nights on his return trip at the end of March, when the family discussed material matters like exchanging workmen for refined additions to their mansions in progress. The Lewises and Mary also heard about Washington's appointment to "develop a plan for embodying, arming and disciplining" a military force. Perhaps he discussed with his sister and mother his minute design ideas for the gorgets, sashes, and round-rose-shaped gold fringe on the uniforms of the men who would serve in the local armed forces—the "rose to be a little broader than the double of the lace which it is on."[32] He saw John Augustine in April and told him what he would have told Betty, Fielding, and Mary in late March, that he would be devoting himself to the colonial cause for the next years.[33]

Before George left, he and Fielding made final plans to finish up some decorative work to their mansions.[34] At the end of April, Mary and George settled up several years of accounts and explained to Lund and Fielding their arrangements. The account included reckonings for a purchase of wheat and Charles's sale of corn from the plantation. George got a loan from Fielding to pay Mary what he owed her.

On leaving in June, George wrote to Martha, as he had to Mary so many years earlier, "It was utterly out of my power to refuse this appointment without exposing my character to such censures as would have reflected dishonor upon myself, and given pain to my friends—this I am sure could not, and ought not to be pleasing to you. . . . I beg of you . . . to . . . pass your time as agreeably as possible . . . [and] pursue any Plan that is most likely to produce content, and a tollerable degree of Tranquility as it must add greatly to my uneasy feelings to hear that you are dissatisfied, and complaining at what I really could not avoid."[35] This does not jibe with the portrait of Martha, the Roman wife, urging George to the fight. Nor is it strictly true, because George did everything but volunteer for the command. But it has the wisdom of Matthew Hale, who argued that each has the duty of finding "contentation" with her fate, and not to do so is to challenge God.

There is no record of Mary's goodbye. In a note three years later to Lund Washington (George's manager), Mary referred to Martha without George as "pore Mrs Washington," and no doubt she felt the same about herself. With age, Mary's grief at parting again from her son was perhaps attenuated. A family account says she complained about why men had to be fighting all the time, but there is no record that she remonstrated with George. She probably would have thought this to be Martha's role, not hers.[36] Before departing, he had provided for her with her comfort in mind.

Like so many who have gone to war since, the colonists thought the war would be quick. No one then, or even now, seemed to fully appreciate ahead of time what long wars do to societies. The leaders and their Whig supporters of this war called it a revolution but could anticipate few of the changes or challenges or the chaos that ensued. No one imagined the fear, insecurity, and poverty that the Revolution would bring or that it would be seven years before Mary would see her son again. Family tradition has it that Mary made a homespun cloth cover for the family Bible of blue and buff, the Continental colors that George had chosen. But experts at Mount Vernon think the cover was made in the nineteenth century.[37]

After George attended the Congress, he continued on to Massachusetts to head up the Continental army in June 1775, just after the Battle of Bunker Hill. In Massachusetts, he bought a tomahawk for seven shillings.[38]

Alarming and fast-paced news kept everyone in Fredericksburg keyed up. During the time that George was settling his and Mary's affairs, the news of Lexington and Concord arrived in Virginia, agitating Whigs. On April 21, Governor Dunmore had fifteen marines in the dark of night remove the colony's supply of powder near Williamsburg and put it on his boat. He also stole the locks off the muskets stored there. From having been popular for his war against the Shawnees, he suddenly became a villain.[39] In response to Dunmore's theft, Hugh Mercer summoned volunteers to Fredericksburg, and six hundred men showed up in hunting shirts, ready to march to Williamsburg. Mercer alerted George. But before there was action from Fredericksburg, Peyton Randolph issued a calming statement after Dunmore promised to restore the gunpowder. In Fredericksburg, the men met and decided to disband.[40] In May, Dunmore shipped some goods up the Rappahannock to his home at Berkeley Springs. The rumor circulated that the shipment contained the missing gunpowder, and Fredericksburg citizens opened up Dunmore's packs, finding only clothing, tools, and supplies of salted pork.[41]

Mary heard from Fielding and others including John Augustine toward the end of July about the success of the Battle of Bunker Hill. The Fredericksburg relatives also heard through Lund and others that Governor Dunmore was threatening to take Martha hostage. Neither George nor

Martha nor her family took this threat very seriously initially. John Augustine wanted her to move, but Colonel Burwell Bassett, George's brother-in-law, thought she was in no danger. Eventually, Martha changed her mind and went to Maryland to stay with Jacky and his wife, then to Bassett's, followed by a couple of stops in Fredericksburg in October and November.[42] After her travels, in November, young George Lewis, Mary's grandson, accompanied Martha north to Cambridge, Massachusetts, to spend the winter with George.[43]

Mary and all Virginia slaveholders received a nasty shock on November 7, 1775, when Lord Dunmore issued his "Proclamation." He declared a state of martial law and "require[d]" everyone who could bear arms to rally to the king's cause. He welcomed indentured servants, "Negroes or others," who could bear arms and declared them free.[44] Lund wrote to George saying he would make an example of any who tried self-liberation. He passed on the wisdom of a temporary worker who said, "There is not a man of them, but would leave us, if they believed, that could make the Escape . . . & yet they have no fault to find[.] Liberty is Sweet."

James Madison, on the Committee of Public Safety for Orange County, Virginia, wrote that slaves were likely to engage in insurrection if Britain and the colonies went to war. Already, he reported, slaves in one county had chosen a leader to guide them to the British, where they were to become free. Madison added that the slaves hoping for freedom had been dealt with. He concluded that it would be wise to keep this and other similar activities secret.[45]

If Mary had not felt strongly for the Whig cause before Dunmore's Proclamation, she undoubtedly espoused it afterward. She had no qualms or ambivalence about slavery. She saw any encouragement to self-emancipation or revolt as a menace. Mary lived with a few slaves at her home on Charles Street. George was paying her rent for those she still owned working Ferry Farm and her land at Little Falls. George no doubt expressed the feelings of the rest of his family when he wrote that Dunmore should be "instantly crushed" and that he was an "Arch Traitor to the Rights of humanity."[46] For Mary and all her male children, their right to own people was a right of "humanity."

A painter and indentured servant named Joseph Wilson, who worked on both Mount Vernon and Kenmore, absented himself from Fredericksburg and from his indenture and joined the British. He was wounded in the leg in a skirmish at Hampton, according to Lund, and with some other prisoners was confined in Williamsburg. Lund wished Fielding Lewis to sell his time to someone else in Williamsburg or bring him back to Fredericksburg and have him whipped before selling him to someone in the west. It is not clear what happened to Wilson, but his decamping from Mary's son and her son-in-law would have enraged her as well as adding to her uneasiness about the way the conflict was unsettling her known world.[47]

As Mary's world suddenly became more threatening, she learned that her fifteen-year-old grandson, and George and Martha's godson, Charles Lewis, had died the week before while staying with his uncle Samuel at Harewood in Berkeley County. She and Betty had to comfort themselves in the familiar ways, trying to become resigned, trying to keep occupied, trying to remember that the will of God was inscrutable and that young Charles was in a better place.[48]

Meanwhile, Samuel, despite his debts to George, ran questionable business ideas past him. He wrote that he wanted to buy a mill. George replied—displaying that tired, slightly irritated patience that would become his trademark tone to Congress and others in the ensuing years—not to lay out a lot of money to produce an item he wouldn't be able to sell. "Have you considered the times? Where are you to get a market for anything you raise? This in my opinion is no time for purchases."[49]

Around the time of Dunmore's Proclamation, Fielding established a "gun manufactory." He wrote to George that he expected to employ fifty men by January, and he hoped to be able to produce about twelve guns a day. He observed that few men were signing up for military service and that no one was paying anyone for anything.[50]

Heavy rains in 1775 and a poor corn harvest made the yield at Mary's Quarter small. In the winter, she and most Virginians experienced a dramatic shortage of salt, essential for storing meat and for providing to cattle.[51] The militias now needed large quantities of preserved meat. The colonies had imported salt from the Caribbean and Europe, but because of their own boycott by late 1775 they confronted a potentially devastating shortage. Lund had hidden the three hundred bushels of salt that were at Mount Vernon, and when people asked if there was any, he wrote to George, he said no. In Fairfax County and elsewhere, violence broke out over the salt scarcity.[52] The colony banned hoarding, and the price of this necessity rose rapidly and continued to increase throughout the war, from about a bushel of corn for a bushel of salt to three of corn for one of salt.[53]

In January 1776, Dunmore frightened tense Virginians by attacking Norfolk. Virginia troops defended the town, but three ships began, in the words of one of the British officers, "a dreadful cannonading . . . which lasted till it was too hot for the rebels to stand on their wharves." The attackers then landed and set fire to several buildings until "the detested town of Norfolk is no more!" A defender from North Carolina wrote that no men were killed, but several women, some with children, looking for shelter were.[54] It seems that Virginia troops did more looting than their British antagonists, but the colonials allowed the blame to rest with the British.[55] In March, Fielding wrote that there was not one house left standing in Norfolk.[56] Lund, ever the faithful accountant, observed that Norfolk in ashes would "make it more difficult to collect the money that is due."[57]

Mary received the news about Norfolk as well as hearing that the residents of Alexandria on the Potomac were every day expecting an attack. People were leaving town, and Lund was packing up china and glass in barrels in case of an onslaught.[58] George raged against the people who wouldn't stay and defend the town, oblivious to the resentment poorer Virginians felt over the conflict.[59]

In February, Fredericksburg itself, Fielding wrote to George, was preparing for the arrival of the enemy, "should any appear in the Spring."

Nine regiments, he expected, would be ready by the end of March.[60] Fewer materialized. They trained behind the tutor John Harrower's school. Some came from long distances. Most did not wish to have to go far from home and be gone long for training. They were, they pleaded, indispensable to their families' well-being and had no help at home beyond that of their wives, who in their absence would have to become slaves or go begging.[61]

From home, George was hearing things that must have filtered through the Lewis family as well. Charles Washington had the lucrative job of supplying the local regiments with liquor and wanted to use George's "Markee." He told Lund that he knew his brother wouldn't mind, but Lund thought it was "crazy" and said he was very "sorry Mr. Washington has apply'd for it. I do not like to lend it."[62] Mary would later complain that Charles, whom George had asked to look after her affairs at the Quarter, was doing nothing for her.

Meanwhile, in the west, to Lund's dismay and all the land speculators', some settlers "improving" the latters' lands began talking democracy. Lund heard that Cleveland, who had been hired to help settle the western lands, "has turned Politition" and was telling others not to pay rent and that the new regulations for conscription should be revoked. Cleveland argued for a return to the practice of companies of men electing their own leaders. He thought neither officers nor regulars should be paid anything and was outraged by the new rules giving officers eight times in pay what their subordinates were getting and subjecting them to significant new discipline. Lund reported him saying that "there is no inducement for a poor man to fight, for he has nothing to defend . . . and such like stuff that it vexes me even to relate." Lund hoped that his speeches would result in "the loss of his lif[e] for I would wish every Damn'd Vilian who meddles in matters he knows nothing off, may get Hang'd."[63] The growing poverty of the farmers who, because of the gentry's non-import-export policy, could not sell their crops added intensity to the Loudoun County resistance. At the same time, the colony was printing money, which was beginning to depreciate rapidly. Militia members by law had to accept pay in paper money. At least one landlord, Richard Henry Lee, was insisting on collecting his rents in hard currency, of which there was almost none. Some organized rent strikes. Tenants were being thrown off the land.[64]

These threatening, angry men across the colony challenged the wealthy who wished to resist Great Britain while holding on to their lands, mansions, and slaves and not fighting themselves. The conflict with Britain and who would fight sharpened Virginia's economic divisions that the elite had thought to blunt with Election Day and militia rituals, with overflowing punch bowls, patron-client relations that meant some mobility for a select few, and a subservient clergy preaching a theology of personal resignation. George and Lund were irate at talk of democracy. They thought overseers and subordinates of all kinds should do their work and listen to their betters. Mary believed this deeply.

Historians argue that the dramatic unhappiness of the small landowners and the dispossessed helped push the gentry not to delay declaring independence. They hoped that if they could resume exports and imports, money would start circulating again, and the menace of democratic revolt would dissipate. France would not trade with the colonies or come to their aid until they were independent.

Virginia's leaders also knew that they could not set up a government for Virginia until their status was clarified. Since Dunmore's proroguing of the assembly, there had essentially been no operating court system or functioning government. The Whig leaders believed once they could create a new system, they could quell the disorders and get on with things as they had been.[65]

Dunmore, after frightening Virginians along the Potomac, approached Fielding and other colonial representatives, offering to mediate between them and the Crown. Fielding said that "our Committee of Safety" knew his "abilitys and friendship" for the colony too well to work with his "insignificancy." Beyond that, he added, this was an appointment Congress should determine. Fielding observed that he and many others had been reading Tom Paine's *Common Sense*.[66]

In the spring of 1776, Virginians were debating the possibility of separating completely from Great Britain. Elite Virginians worried that the social divisions would grow when independence was a fact, but they hoped to restore some unity with a strong government and revived courts. In May, the Fifth Virginia Convention met in Williamsburg and voted to instruct the delegates to the Second Continental Congress meeting in Philadelphia that they should vote "to declare the United Colonies free and Independent States." Accordingly, in June, Richard Henry Lee proposed to the Congress at Philadelphia that all the colonies be "free and independent states."

The Virginia Convention meeting in Williamsburg produced a bill of rights and a constitution on June 29, 1776. The bicameral legislature every year would elect a governor; Patrick Henry was the first. There would also be a legislative council and a separate judiciary.[67] On July 5, the Virginians established their own state government; they excised from the Book of Common Prayer mentions of the king and royal worship. Over the next few months, the assembly would give exemptions from tithing to Dissenters, and at the end of the year the vestrymen terminated the Reverend Maury's salary. During the Revolution, the vestrymen could still levy taxes for the poor, but only for that purpose.[68] Mary, like the Reverend Maury, would probably have found these changes upsetting and disorienting.

Congress drafted, revised, and adopted the Declaration of Independence. Around noon on July 10, Mary heard tremendous gunfire coming from her neighbors, celebrating the news that Congress had declared the independence of the United States.[69]

That spring, Virginians captured three ships on the Rappahannock and herded them to the Fredericksburg wharves. Fielding conducted an inquiry and determined that they were British. Confiscated, they were sold in July. Fielding, in charge of Fredericksburg's protection, bought two ships and had them armed. One was rechristened the *Dragon*, and its crew came ashore, staying in Fredericksburg in August 1776. They caroused and assaulted a local so violently that they were arrested. General Charles Lee, an irascible but, in Washington's view, brilliant general, came to Virginia to organize the colony's defense.[70] Some men in his escort had smallpox, and Fielding and Charles Dick had their clothes burned after encountering them.[71] It was the first appearance of the disease in town during the conflict and would threaten Mary and others more than once. Often now, Mary's walks in town could be unsettling, and her retreat to her rock formation offered comfort.

In the fall of 1776, Mary encountered an influx of slaves and poor whites coming to town to learn to make linen. In October, a factory opened with a mill and a school where slave owners could have their bondsmen and bondswomen trained in exchange for six months of work.[72] The process would have been of interest to Mary, who had grown flax for years.[73]

In September, the Virginian Anne Terrell published in *The Virginia Gazette* an appeal to men to join her husband in enlisting in the Continental army. Mary Washington knew from Fielding, who was intimately involved in recruiting, that it was a struggle to fill the militias and her son's army. Terrell wrote of the British "conspiring with our slaves to cut our throats [and instigating] the savage Indians to fall on our frontiers," both fears Mary shared. No doubt she hoped Terrell's appeal would be successful, but most of the men who would fight in George's force were not slaveholders and unlikely to be afraid of death at the hands of slaves.[74]

Mary found comfort in Matthew Hale's teachings. No democrat or leveler, Hale insisted that there had to be rich and poor. If the rich shared their wealth with all, he reasoned, it would make everyone poor, and then there would be "no Artificers, no Labourers, no Servants."[75]

In town, the Reverend Maury preached a gospel of looking away from worldly affairs and to the path to eternal life to calm the social turbulence. John Harrower noted some of the texts he heard the Reverend Maury preach from—sermons the enslaved Stephen might have driven Mary to or to which she might have gone with Betty and Vestryman Lewis. Maury's discussions raked ground familiar to Mary, like his call for Christians to clothe themselves here on earth in the garb of immortality and thus snatch victory away from death when it would come (1 Corinthians 15:53). He counseled not expecting to discover more godliness in the rich than in the poor, who could, he assured listeners, be rich in faith (2 Corinthians 18). From John's First Epistle, he urged a life of active righteousness and loving one another rather than loving the things of this world. Occasionally, Maury tried to frighten his parishioners. His sermon from Isaiah 15 dwelled on the crying, howling, and screaming of the Moabites who had devoted themselves to wealth and worldly concerns, thereby calling down God's rage. Mary's reading of Hale and Hervey brought these lessons—or these variations on a theme—home to her in countless ways, and they had life-long resonance. Her commitment to a hierarchical world permitted her to imagine Christianity in the poor but probably not in the rebellious poor. As for eschewing worldly matters, the war was making that almost impossible as her struggle to manage the Quarter got harder.[76] She knew that Hale admired the man who asked for neither poverty nor riches, instead asking God to "feed me with food convenient for me."[77]

With time for her reading, Mary got chunks of text by memory. Ministers, including James Maury Sr., the Washington children's old schoolmaster, and the father of Mary's current minister in Fredericksburg, had recommended reading devotional books, marking them, learning and digesting them, bit by bit. The wisdom in them was to achieve salvation, and it was "the most useful, important and desirable wisdom."[78]

Mary continued to do the things she knew how to do and listened to the political news because it was also family news that was embedded in sometimes frightening and sometimes enraging information about the larger colonial world. She went about her daily rounds, visiting Betty, now in residence at Kenmore. She would sometimes walk with her turbaned maid Patty, who carried the sewing and knitting Mary worked on, including socks, which she and Betty would send to George for the soldiers. At the end of the day, Stephen would fetch them in the phaeton.[79] She continued to visit the Quarter in these months and years of political and physical conflict. Her granddaughter Betty was eleven in 1776, and her grandsons Lawrence nine, Rob seven, and Howell five. They, particularly Rob and Lawrence, vividly recalled their devout grandmother in her late sixties as the revolutionary activities of Fielding and Betty fed the growing tempest.

16

THE ENDLESS REVOLUTION:
WARTIME VIRTUE,
WARTIME WOE

*S*UCH NEWS AS THE FAMILY RECEIVED from George came while he was fighting in New York from late summer into the fall of 1776. The family was also following the fighting in the South, where in late September the Whigs were conquering the Cherokees, while the Creeks were maintaining their neutrality.[1] George wrote to John Augustine in late September of his endless trials with poorly trained, undisciplined, and unhealthy soldiers and with the short stints of the militias that undermined the morale of the Continental soldiers, enlisted for longer.[2] He barraged

Congress and colleagues with letters explaining the shortcomings of army recruitment policies, irresponsible methods of selection of officers, and painfully inadequate money and supplies. George wrote to his brother John, "In short, it is not in the power of Words to describe the task I have to act. £50,000 Should not induce me again to undergo what I have done." He wrote to Lund, "Such is my situation that if I were to wish the bitterest curse on an enemy on this side of the grave, I should put him in my stead with my feelings. . . . I tell you that I never was in such an unhappy, divided state since I was born." He asked Lund to keep this private, knowing that Lund's privileged information was of the most urgent interest. However, he added, thinking ahead to his place in history, "If I Fall, it may not be amiss that these circumstances be known, and declaration made in credit to the justice of my character."[3]

In October, the family knew from Samuel in Berkeley County that official reports of the martial behavior of the militias were false and that they would neither stay in camp nor fight.[4] By December, with New York in the hands of the British and the Continental army across the Delaware in New Jersey, George wrote to Lund that things were so bad, he wanted Lund to get his papers at Mount Vernon ready to ship to Samuel in Berkeley in case the British should send ships up the Potomac.[5]

The Battle of Trenton, the daring river crossing, and the troops' bravery in freezing cold and combat revived Whig spirits a bit, and Virginians were proud of their contributions. Brigadier General Hugh Mercer, a particular favorite of Mary's, was fatally wounded in the subsequent Battle of Princeton and died on January 12, 1777.[6] Just a day later, Thomas Jefferson, George Mason, and others gathered in Fredericksburg at George Weedon's Tavern to write new laws for the state of Virginia.[7] At the same time, the local court was meeting to expel those inimical to the Revolution. Several left, and in the ensuing exodus from Fredericksburg, Fielding acquired some real estate and another sloop. He used it to trade with the West Indies, importing salt, sugar, coffee, paper, and other products in short supply.

Fielding joined Charles Dick, George Thornton, and ten others in taking the oath of office of magistrate of the local court in March 1777. He continued to serve with Charles Washington as vestryman. Because Maury had lost his salary, he appealed at the March court to establish a gristmill to supplement his income.[8]

Brigadier General George Weedon, an old family friend and a main conduit of news between the camp and the family home front, casually announced to Washington in March 1777, when the army was encamped at Morristown, that he would see him in the summer, imagining that he was not needed.[9] Washington wrote to him indignantly, "Can you possibly conceive that my consent would be obtain'd for such an absence as this?" He continued that no one could feel for the "private Inconveniences" of the army's demands more than he did "because no Person suffers more by an absence from home than myself." But he could not indulge Weedon's hope to return to Fredericksburg.[10]

George felt his own sacrifices acutely. He wrote to family, Lund, and friends of his unique burdens and losses. His outbursts and his sense of abandonment and isolation carry a terrible anguish. They seem to echo his widowed mother's sense of her own overwhelming burdens and the expectations that her children, particularly George, should understand her plight and, ideally, pitch in. Clearly, neither mother nor son was the only one to use the images of self-sacrifice to arouse sympathy and motivate through guilt, but that George turned to this rhetoric often and spontaneously indicates the grand scale of his sense of injury and how easily available to him was the language of martyrs.

George wrote to Weedon that his feelings "were not a little wounded by perceiving that this passion [for being absent from camp] is more prevalent among my Countrymen, than any other Troops." He had to reorganize the army, and said, "I must attempt to do all these duties myself . . . if every officer would lay his hands properly to the work, and afford those aids which I have a right to expect. . . . But I shall say no more, nor will I oppose your inclination."[11] (George was also exasperated by the endless, and often preposterous, kinds of problems he had to solve. In May 1777, he was still trying to convince some officers that it actually was very dangerous for them to wear the handsome red uniform jackets they had had designed and made.)[12]

Samuel managed to provoke a rare if weary-sounding joke out of his sober brother while he was in camp in Morristown. He wrote asking for a portrait. George answered that he'd be happy to comply but that "two insurmountable obstacles offer themselves—the want of a Painter—and if a Painter could be brought hither, the want of time to sit."[13]

Each member of the Washington family faced a frightening problem that George faced on a grand—though not personal—scale: smallpox. John Augustine and his wife and children all underwent inoculations and recovered in 1777. But Samuel's fourth wife died from hers. When George heard the news, he assumed that the inoculation must have been botched, because "in general an old Woman may Innoculate with as much success as the best Physician, the whole Art lying in keeping the Patient rather low in diet and cool."[14] To Samuel, George sent condolences and advice "to make every Manly exertion" to "acquiesce to the divine Will."[15]

Fielding was inoculated in March 1779 and underwent the prescribed isolation during his recovery. Betty, however, contracted the real disease. George Weedon, back in Fredericksburg, reported that she "has it favourable." Mary, however, could not be persuaded to be inoculated, even though it [smallpox] was "in almost every House in Town & Country," and while she was extremely uneasy that she should get it, the certainty of suffering the powerful illness and living some time in isolation was more frightening than the possibility of contracting it by chance. (George Weedon supplied the quarantined smallpox people "with dried fruit.")[16]

At the end of July 1777, George made the acquaintance of the young, charming Marquis de Lafayette, who would become his lifelong friend and whose unstinting and richly expressed affection and admiration gave the older, phlegmatic-seeming man unqualified pleasure.[17] Lafayette, alone among Washington's colleagues, made a special trip to visit Mary and in his many letters afterward regularly extended his respectful attentions to her.

Mary had been aware for some time that her son had become a celebrity. When Ebenezer Hazard, appointed to inspect the colonial postal system, visited Fredericksburg, he made a special pilgrimage to Ferry Farm, thinking mistakenly that it was where George Washington was born.[18]

In August 1777, two hundred British ships showed up in the Chesapeake at the mouth of the Potomac, frightening the colony again. Betty's daughter, thirteen-year-old Betty, wrote her aunt Hannah Bushrod Washington that "Mr. Dick has lost several of his negroes since you were here, and Mrs. Taliaferro has lost four. We hear that the negroes on the river are going on board the enemy's ships in the Potomac very fast. I hope my Uncle George will take care of this, or some of them may go also." Mary, too, no doubt, worried about the possibility of "Uncle George's" slaves running for freedom, and hoped he would "take care of" it. Virginia was not in a condition to defend itself against invasion, and fortunately for the Virginians the fighting shifted north to circle around possession of Philadelphia.[19] The British eventually occupied the city after the Battles of Brandywine and Germantown. The Germantown encounter, among other things, resulted in George's making an enemy by approving the court-martial of an old colleague and political competitor, Adam Stephen.[20]

The family, meanwhile, celebrated the October marriage of John Augustine and Hannah Bushrod Washington's oldest child, Jane, nineteen, to William Augustine Washington, twenty, her cousin, the son of Charles and Mildred.[21]

That month Washington learned that Fielding had bought him a lot at "Warm Spring" in Berkeley County, where both had gone for rest and restoration. Among the first things the assembly had done was to legitimate land claims made in the trans-Allegheny region. Samuel wrote to his brother in part for assurance that he would be reimbursed if he were to build enough improvements to ensure Washington's ownership of the land. George told him that he didn't know what the assembly had decided were the minimum requirements for improvements, but wanted something "uniform and clever."[22]

The winter of 1777, Washington moved into the infamous winter quarters at Valley Forge for the coldest and most horrific months of deprivation of the Revolution. He wrote a stream of letters detailing the soldiers' pitiful hunger, their lack of clothes and blankets. Washington described to a seemingly inert Congress his "naked and distressed Soldier[s], occupy[ing] a cold bleak hill, and sleep[ing] under frost & snow without Cloaths or Blankets." George Weedon's troops were a mile from water and lived for days on frozen potatoes and bread.[23]

That same terrible winter, Fielding Lewis rode with Charles Dick and Ebenezer Hazard to procure funds for the manufactory. Fielding, despite his asthma, rode so fast both ways that he lost his companions, and they had to find their way alone. That same winter, Betty Lewis and some other relatives—perhaps her daughter, perhaps the children of Charles and Mildred—visited the Hessian prisoners taken at Trenton and released from Winchester to live in Fredericksburg. Ironically, the Hessians were housed very comfortably and joined balls and other entertainments in the town.[24] Mary might have met some of them at town receptions and certainly heard about their pleasant accommodations.

Drawing needy transients to Fredericksburg, Fielding and the other justices were handing out salt, purchased from a government fund, as well as powder for their guns. Fielding's gunnery was producing about twenty muskets a week fitted with twenty-inch bayonets.[25] Governor Patrick Henry, to expand gun production, encouraged the assembly to provide funds to buy Augustine Washington's old ironworks and the land that went with it—which was now George's. James Hunter, who was Fielding Lewis's competitor in the gun manufactory business, but also producer of iron objects like kettles for the army, purchased it for his expansion. Charles Washington got the commission to be keeper of the powder magazine at Fredericksburg, but four years later it was not finished, and he had moved to Berkeley County.[26] In 1778, a year later, Hunter wrote to George to purchase the land that Mary's father had left her near Augustine's so many years ago. George said that the land "had not been legally conveyed or properly secured to me by my Mother," so he could not do it, and if he could, he nevertheless wanted the pines, which were thick on the property. Not quite two weeks after that (May 21, 1778), Mary signed the property over to her son John Augustine "for the natural love and affection which she hath" for him.[27]

Lund wrote to Washington on Christmas Eve 1777 about how bad conditions were at Mount Vernon. The wheat was destroyed, the mill wasn't milling anything, and the corn crop was inadequate. Mount Vernon had to feed more people and horses than when Washington was in residence. He complained that Jacky Custis was keeping his horses there as well.[28]

In early 1778, Mary requested that Lund send her Silla, a valuable slave at Mount Vernon. Lund wrote to George that he was reluctant to do it because Silla was married to Cooper Jack, "and they appear to live comfortable together." In March, Mary wrote again to send Silla down, but Cooper Jack, wrote Lund, "Cryes and Begs, sayg he had rather be Hang'd than separated." Mary apparently expressed no scruples about separating the two. Her reasons for wanting Silla are not documented, but it is possible that her trusted cook, Sue, had died. Mary had confirmed her ownership in the 1749 family slave division. Sue went to Mount Vernon to coordinate Martha's arrival and would have been well along in years by 1778. Later in the month, Silla was still at Mount Vernon because the weather had been so bad. She and Jack were "much distressd about partg." Mary's note is missing, but it seems that the cruelty of her demand was not apparent to her.

Charles also asked for a "hand" and a horse, but Lund refused.[29] He wrote that Samuel was collecting rent from George's tenants. But Lund was "at a loss"' about how to retrieve the money.[30] A young officer on a mission to buy horses for the army in Virginia told George that he thought "publick Virtue and every thing else but a desire of keeping up Riches has left the old Dominion." George might have recognized it in his own family as well.[31]

George wrote to Fielding's son Andrew that he was convinced that the American cause would only fail through a "want of Virtue," by which he meant "Extortion, forestalling, and other practices which have crept in & become exceedingly prevalent. . . . To make and extort money in every shape that can be devised . . . seems to have become . . . an epidemical disease." In the same letter, he asked if the family had any lands that had been surveyed but not validated because of the Proclamation Act. He had five thousand acres and "several thousands more," and to not profit by them "would be rather hard on me . . . to be a looser."[32]

Jefferson hoped for regulations that would favor small buyers of the western lands, but these had not gained favor. The regulations that did pass in 1778 made it difficult to challenge the claims of the large speculators and no longer made free land available to newlyweds. The bill also abolished the old head rights system in the future but sustained those already surveyed, again reassuring Washington and other prewar speculators that they could hang on to and profit by their claims. The assembly believed it had to act fast to set up a system or the lands they wished to sell would be flooded with settlers who would take matters into their own hands. They disregarded Washington's apprehension that opening the lands up this way would attract men who might otherwise join up and fight to earn their postwar bounties. Edmund Pendleton told him it was too late, and they had to ward off the flood of expected squatters or be left with nothing at all to sell.[33]

George and Jacky Custis exchanged letters about the lack of virtue among their countrymen who were profiteering. Jacky wrote of people "depraved by gaming and every other species of vice, that virtue seems to have taken his departure from Virginia." Jacky's effort to enjoy the short-lived profits of inflation in selling valuable property apparently looked like stupidity to his stepfather rather than an absence of virtue. Jacky told George about a new tax on slaves that would cost them seven or eight shillings per slave at the new inflated prices at which they could be bought and sold.[34] By the end of the war, the tax would be thirty shillings or a pound and a half per tithable.[35]

George, Jacky, and other wealthy gentlemen complained about the extortion and lack of virtue among their fellow citizens, but the middling and poor saw it differently. The assembly had to abandon the draft because resistance was so pervasive and powerful. Legislators offered bounties of $300, but recruiters were adding on as much as $450 to persuade men to join. Some men unwilling to serve gave volunteers substitute money on top of their bounties. As Edmund Pendleton moaned to George, the "demon of avarice, and spirit of extortion seem to have expelled the pure patriotism from the breasts of those who usually compose armies." Washington wrote that instead of the 3,500 men he ordered, he had received only 1,242.[36]

Fielding, whose commitment to the Revolutionary cause ruined him financially, bought almost twenty thousand pounds' worth of Loan Office certificates, to be redeemed at 6 percent in three years. He would not live to redeem them. He was owed by then a little over four thousand pounds in money he had spent on the gun-making project.[37]

In May 1778, news reached Fredericksburg that France had joined the American cause. John Augustine heard from his brother that the French support of the colonists "must put the Independency of America out of all manner of dispute." The news gave the family relief, although the difficulties they faced intensified.[38] Ironically, the French brought hard currency to pay for their supplies, further debasing Virginia's circulating paper.[39]

Times were harder and harder in Virginia.[40] The assembly placed new levies on personal property, including male slaves over twenty-one. These were difficult taxes to enforce on a resistant public. At the same time, they issued 1.7 million pounds in paper money.[41]

Lund advised George to buy land, but he had no cash. George recommended bartering for the land, especially Negroes "or anything else (except breeding Mares and stock of other kinds). . . . I had rather give Negroes—if Negroes would do, for to be plain I wish to get quit of

Negroes." George was feeling the pinch of having too many workers and too little work for them to justify the expense of maintaining them. George's evolving ideas about slavery focused on its inefficiency and high cost. At the same time, he was increasingly unwilling to separate families. He learned that the price of corn had quadrupled. He wrote to Lund of going back to tobacco, "but what Am I to do—or how am I to live—I cannot Support myself if I make nothing."[42]

Mary sold her livestock and farm tools from Ferry Farm to George Weedon to raise a bit of money. Weedon was now managing it. His late brother-in-law Hugh Mercer had bought it from George, but then died in battle at Princeton before completing the sale. Weedon offered to buy it— in the inflated currency. George was not happy, but told Lund to accept the offer.[43] (Weedon's "Plantation over the River" cost him 1,484 pounds in paper currency in 1779. His profits in the same period in pork and corn were 350 pounds and 1,200 pounds.)[44] Mary's sales were not enough to float her for very long. Struggling with new taxes, Mary tried to squeak by. Late in 1778, she wrote to Lund to ask if he would send her 40 pounds to buy corn. She said they had not made more at the Quarter than would serve the plantation: "Thear is terrible doings thear. . . . Charls never goes over. I shall be Ruined. Corn at five pound a barrel. . . . I never lived soe pore in my life butt if I can gitt Corn I am contented."[45] Mother and son both feared ruin.[46] Mary, in straits, apparently comforted herself by remembering Hervey's distinction between "delicacies" and "necessaries."

Mary had depended vainly on Charles to manage the work at Little Falls. He had been nominated county escheator in July, a position George Eskridge had once used to great advantage. He was also involved in a number of local disputes that year about the place for the new courthouse and who would profit from the new ferry that needed to be run.[47] At the same time, he seems to have been completing work on his mansion, Happy Retreat, in Berkeley County, to which he would move in 1780. In 1788, George wrote that he thought Charles naturally indolent and that he spent his time drinking. Both might already have been true during the Revolution.[48] In those years, Charles ran up substantial debts at Weedon's Tavern.[49] Fielding Lewis had been increasingly unwell from the early spring and over the summer and could not help Mary at the Quarter.[50] It would turn out later that in the absence of any oversight but that of an old, straw-hatted woman, her overseer was cheating her, but it took her years and repeated complaints—which annoyed George tremendously—to be believed.

She asked Lund to send her cash by some "safe hand." She wrote, "I hear pore Mrs. [Martha] Washington is gone [to be with George.] God bles you & spear your health as pore George will be Ruined I am dear Lund your friend & kinswoman Mary Washington." Lund sent her forty pounds by Colonel Bassett, Martha's brother-in-law. He was to give the money to Fielding or Charles if he didn't find Mary.[51] Corn, which had cost ten shillings a barrel, now cost six pounds.[52]

The assembly decided to encourage the cultivation of tobacco, which they could now sell to the French. Fredericksburg provided 20 percent of the tobacco shipped in French vessels at the end of the summer of 1779. Because cash was becoming ruinously inflated, tobacco now could also function as money, as it once had. George Weedon was using wheat to pay for "New Bed Ticks."[53] The assembly tried to recruit Fielding for tobacco agent in the area, but he refused because of his poor health. He planned to go to Berkeley Springs soon to recuperate. He noted what Mary observed as well, that flour prices had gone to the sky because the distillers were buying up all the grain so millers couldn't complete.[54]

George reclaimed Silla from Mary in April 1779, after Silla had spent almost a year away from her husband. George told Lund to send her back "in order to gratify Jack."[55] In her stead, he told Lund to send one of his mother's own "fellows down—the greatest rogue of the two." George had rented Mary's slaves for six years and had two men at Mount Vernon, one of whom he exchanged for Silla. In sending his mother the more "rogue" of the two slaves he was renting from her, George was punishing her for her callousness.

Over the summer of 1779, Fielding, Betty, and their daughter, Betty, went to Berkeley Springs. On their return, they stopped at Mount Vernon to see Martha, whom Betty found "hearty" and looking very well. While there, Betty received a note from George with a miniature of himself that Charles Peale had painted. Peale had put it into a little box that he had made.[56] "And Could I of found you there it would of Compleat'd My Happiness, O when will that Day Come that we shall meet again?—I trust in the Lord soon," wrote Betty.[57] (Betty offered to pay, but Washington paid the five guineas in addition to twenty more for a portrait of himself that his friend Lafayette had requested.)[58] On Betty's return to Fredericksburg, Mary would have enjoyed the likeness of her son and shared Betty's longing for George, whom they had not seen since 1775.

The British, after years of inconclusive fighting in the North, decided that their chances were better in the South, where there were large numbers of disaffected slaves, in addition to a white settler population with more Tories than lived in the North. In the abysmally cold winter of 1779–1780, they turned south, taking Savannah in November.[59] Those Virginia troops with the Continental army marched from Philadelphia through Fredericksburg, arriving there on February 8. General William Woodford wrote to Washington that everyone was well, except Fielding, whose health was poor. Mary joined the town and the Virginia troops in celebrating her son's birthday with what had become an annual ball on February 11.[60]

Many Virginia soldiers came to the end of their enlistment time as the British soldiers turned south. Recruiters, hoping to get them to reenlist, offered a furlough through March 1780 with service beginning again on April 1. Few took the bait. The worried assembly reinstituted the draft, calling on all men to serve. Men with a little property pushed back, demanding shorter terms and to serve only near their homes, insisting on their right as patriarchs to provide for their wives and children.[61] Taxpayers grew angry that the taxes already levied had not been enough to create a standing army of the needy. The assembly, seeing that the draft was failing, passed a new recruiting law that equalized taxes so that all militia members (taxpayers) would contribute to any bounties paid, according to their taxable property. The militias themselves were permitted to raise money on top of state money to recruit soldiers so that they—militia members—could be exempted. The rich protested because the heaviest taxes would fall on them.

In May 1780, in Charleston, South Carolina, Washington's general Benjamin Lincoln accepted British terms of surrender for that city, and the Virginia troops in the Continental army became prisoners of war. The British, under the fearsome lieutenant colonel Banastre Tarleton, massacred many of the Virginia soldiers after Lincoln's surrender.[62]

In Fredericksburg in the spring of 1780, inflation was so bad that barter supplanted money. The price of sugar had gone from two shillings a pound in 1776 to over twenty in 1779. Rum flew from one pound a gallon to over eight. Salt, which had cost eight to ten pounds a pound, was now at twenty-five pounds a pound. Fielding was supposed to collect the levies in kind, but he was too ill. Trying to recoup some of his financial losses, he had his son John buy thirty thousand acres of land beyond the Proclamation Line and was interested in twenty thousand more. As he wrote to George, "Never was so fine a country sold for so trifling a sum."[63]

In the spring of 1780, and despite his bad health, Fielding put together a company with other merchants including James Hunter to outfit and sail ships to the West Indies for needed supplies. When this was completed, he went alone, earlier than usual, to Berkeley County for his seasonal rest, where he would be with his son Fielding and near Samuel and Charles Washington. Over the summer, the assembly impressed larger and larger amounts of food and supplies, but relatively little from the Lewises and Mary. Mary gave up twenty-five pounds of pork; the Lewis family twenty.[64] When Fielding returned in August, workers at the gun factory, sensing the state's desperate need for labor, petitioned for higher wages. The assembly granted the raise, without the money to pay for it. Fielding began selling property to pay for these and other expenses. The assembly owed him seven thousand pounds by now. He was housebound in the winter of 1780–1781. He resigned from the gun business, and at the end of the year the assembly voted him and Charles Dick ten thousand pounds of tobacco.[65]

A small British fleet arrived in the Chesapeake in October 1780 raiding the coast from Norfolk north. That fall, the assembly considered a proposal to give more prosperous Virginians who would fight "a Healthy sound negro" aged ten to thirty, or sixty pounds in gold and three hundred acres when the war was over.[66] James Madison instead thought the state should arm free blacks, as a proposal coherent with the ideals of the Revolution. This assembly never discussed his proposal.

In December 1780, Benedict Arnold, formerly of the Continental army, now in charge of the British assault on Virginia, sailed up the James River and marched unopposed to Richmond, then the state's capital. He successfully threw the then governor Thomas Jefferson's administration (1779–1781) into disarray. Mary and the Lewises feared a full-on attack on Fredericksburg in the winter of 1781, but the fear diminished when the British remained in Richmond. Nevertheless, with its ironworks and gun manufacturing, Fredericksburg was a logical spot for an attack. George Weedon replaced Fielding in trying to protect the Rappahannock, Fredericksburg, and Hunter's ironworks. Weedon had trouble knowing where to deploy the few troops he had, not being able to anticipate the British moves. The workers in the gun factory had disappeared—some because they were no longer exempt from military service. Weedon reported that local volunteers, both men and women, were making bullets and gun belts.[67] Fielding and Charles Dick both tried to get funds to continue operations and pay debts, but Jefferson and the assembly failed to deliver. Fielding wrote to the state treasurer that he was so in debt to the cause that he could no longer pay his own creditors. "Can it be expected that the State can be well served when its best friends are used in the manner I have been treated?"[68]

The British advance created physical chaos and also displayed most nakedly the conflicts among Virginians about what the war was worth and who should risk life and livelihood for it. In Richmond, the militia barely resisted. Many of the wealthy moved their slaves and valuables out of the way of trouble. Militia officers told their troops that if they had families, they should do the best they could to protect them.[69]

In the confusion and relentless anxiety of the late winter and early spring of 1781, Mary fell ill. Fielding wrote to George that she was improving in April, but Fielding was not. In the middle of these frightening circumstances, Fielding and Betty's daughter, Betty, had decided to marry Charles Carter. They married on the anniversary of Betty and Fielding's marriage, May 7, 1781. The bride wore a dress of embroidered muslin, to whose stitchery her grandmother no doubt contributed her expertise.[70]

Fielding described the fear Virginians were living with. "No person who lives on the banks of the Potomac can have any certainty of not being taken out of his bed before morning . . . our distress is truly alarming, taxes high, no price for corn, wheat, flour, or tobacco equal to the depreciation of our money."[71]

Cornwallis moved his troops north from North Carolina, in pursuit of Lafayette, then at Richmond, boasting prematurely, "The boy cannot escape me."[72] Lafayette, who feared Cornwallis would attack Fredericksburg, instructed Weedon to evacuate Washington's family.

By the time Mary recovered from her illness, George Weedon recommended the arduous journey for the extended family of nearly a hundred miles over the mountains and across the Shenandoah River to Frederick County. Mary found the trip overwhelmingly difficult and the lodgings with so many fleeing family and dependents in Fielding's house suffocating. In the end, Cornwallis did not attack Fredericksburg, although he raided and disrupted the colony.

Meanwhile, Washington had long planned a rendezvous with the French fleet, returning from the West Indies, to concentrate the Whig forces. When ordered to send several thousand troops north, Cornwallis chose Yorktown as his embarkation point. The British found themselves caught between Washington's land forces and the French fleet. Or, as George Weedon wrote poetically, "We have got him handsomly in a pudding bag."[73]

Lord Cornwallis surrendered on October 17, 1781. By the time of the confrontation between Washington and Cornwallis that fall, of about fifty thousand (theoretical) Virginia militiamen, only about three thousand mustered at Yorktown, compared with five thousand Continental army and seventy-eight hundred Frenchmen.

The Americans took almost seven thousand prisoners. Many of them were marched through Fredericksburg and on west close to the Lewis home in Frederick County. Mary and Betty and Lewis could have seen the sight. The Virginia government had essentially disintegrated; Jefferson's term was expired, and there was no successor. Jefferson had to run from Monticello to avoid capture by the British.[74]

17.

MARY'S WAR ENDS

||||||||||||||||||||||||||||||||||||||||||||||||||||||||||||||||||||||||||||||||||||||||||||||||||||||||||||||||||||||||||||||||||||||||||||

HEN MARY AND THE SEVERAL LEWISES, who included Betty, probably the newlyweds, Betty and Charles, and the two boys, Robert and Howell, as well as slaves to serve the family, reached Frederick County, they stayed with Fielding Lewis Jr. and possibly Samuel Washington. Charles lived not far away, in what is now West Virginia. Samuel, like Fielding, was extremely ill. After the refugees arrived in the west, George went through Fredericksburg on his way to Yorktown. Betty and Mary were both painfully disappointed not to see him.[1] In October, in the Alleghenies, the dying Fielding wrote his will. Within a space of three weeks, both Samuel Washington and his brother-in-law Fielding Lewis died.

Betty later recalled in a letter to George that "with the confinement and uneasiness of mind, it caused me to get in such a state of ill health that I expected to follow them."[2] The distress and fear that these deaths and Betty's near death caused Mary can only be judged by the frightened letter she wrote to George once she was back in Fredericksburg in March 1782. By then, Betty's health was somewhat restored, although she would continue to suffer with worsening respiratory problems for the rest of her life. George stopped in Fredericksburg on March 13 to see his mother, but missed her. She wrote to thank him.

> My dear Georg,
>
> I was truly unsy [uneasy]. My Not being at [home?] when you went throu fredricksburg it was an [] thing for me now I am afraid I Never shall have that pleasure again. I am so very unwell & this trip over the Mountins has almost killd me I got the 20 five ginnes you was soe kind to send me [&] am greatl[y?] obliged to you for it I was greatly [short?]
>
> [Break in letter]
>
> ever be driven up this way again by [] will goe in some little hous of my one if it is [] twelve foot Squar Benjamin Hardistey has four hindred akers of Land of your out [?] by George Le [] if you will let me goe thear if I should be obliged [to] Come over the Mountains agin I shall be very Much able[ged?] pray give my kind love to Mrs. Washington & am My Dear George your
>
> Loveing & affectionat Mother,
>
> Mary Washington
>
> Mr. Neius [?] desired me to Mention his son to you he works in the Treasure office of Congres
>
> mw[3]

Written and struck out after "love" is "I would have wrote to her but my reason has jis left me."[4]

To some of George's biographers this sad letter demonstrated that Mary had lost her mind and/or had made an unnecessary trip. Douglas Southall Freeman wrote, "There was no reason why she should leave Fredericksburg."[5] But her exile, her discomfort in a several-day-long, hundred-mile jolting carriage ride over primitive dirt roads and ferrying across the Shenandoah River, the ongoing war, and Mary's ruptured dependence particularly on the Lewises leave little about her letter that doesn't make sense. She worried that she might have to be transplanted again. In March 1782, this was not an idle worry. She was shaken at the prospect of never seeing her son again—a heartbreaking concern that her devotional reading gave her a way to prepare for but that still terrified her.

In the west, she had been crammed into Fielding junior's house. Betty, too, spoke of "confinement" as one cause of her health breakdown. The frightened, sickly, and grieving family had to live on top of one another for several months. Fighting and local rebellions continued in the west of Virginia, and privateers continued to patrol the Chesapeake. Prisoners forced into captivity in Winchester, not too far away, were restive and unruly.[6] Lord Dunmore, meanwhile, was in New York advocating raising an army of black men to invade from the southwest. There was a rumor about four thousand British troops landing in Charleston and the need for Virginia militia. It was impossible to feel safe or to know what to believe.

George, the day after Mary wrote this letter, and after sending his mother money, wrote to Benjamin Harrison, who had succeeded the nearly impeached Thomas Jefferson and his successor, the planter and signer of the Declaration of Independence Thomas Nelson, as governor of Virginia. Harrison had informed his friend George that discussion had arisen in the assembly of a proposed pension for Mary, because she was a widow, seemingly without support, and unable to pay her taxes.

Under Thomas Jefferson, in December 1781, the state agreed to pay pensioners in specie because the currency was so depreciated.[7] But Harrison, who repeated over and over in his official letters that the treasury had "not a shilling," could assume that George Washington was doing better than the State of Virginia.

Harrison apprised Washington of the pension idea as a friend who knew he would find it embarrassing. Washington most certainly did. He composed for Harrison what would be his standard and oft-repeated exculpatory history of his relationship with his mother.

True it is, I am but little acquainted with her *present* situation, or distresses, if she is under any. As true it is, a year or two before I left Virginia (to make her latter days comfortable, & free from care) I did, at her request but at my own expence, purchase a commodious house, Garden & Lotts (of her own choosing) in Fredericksburg, that she might be near my Sister Lewis, her only daughter—and did moreover agree to take her Land & Negroes at a certain yearly Rent, to be fixed by Colo. Lewis & others (of her own nomination,) which has been an annual expence to me ever since, as the Estate never raised one half the Rent I was to pay—Before I left Virginia, I answered all her calls for money; and since that period, have directed my Steward to do the same. Whence her distresses can arise therefore, I know not, never having received any complaint of his inattention or neglect on that head; tho' his inability to pay my own taxes, is such I know, as to oblige me to sell negroes for this purpose—The taxes being the most unequal (I am told) in the world—some persons paying for things of equal value, four times, nay ten times, the rate that others do. But putting these things aside, which I could not avoid mentioning, in exculpation of a presumptive want of duty on my part; confident I am that she has not a child that would not divide the last sixpence to relieve her from *real* distress. This she has been repeatedly assured of by me: and all of us, I am certain, would feel much hurt, at having our mother a pensioner, while we had the means of supporting her; but in fact she has an ample income of her own.

I lament exceedingly that your letter, which conveyed the first hint of this matter, did not come to my hands sooner; but I request, in pointed terms if the matter is now in agitation in your assembly, that all proceedings on it may be stopped—or in case of a decision in her favor, that it may be done away, & repealed at my request.

George's "if she is under any" distress and his emphasis on "real" told Harrison that she was not actually in want, and that if there was any need, she had imagined it, an interpretation he found useful. He was not exactly suggesting that she was unsound in her mind. At the time of her death, he wrote to Betty that age had not compromised her faculties. He implied that she had unrealistic wishes.

Mary's wartime fears and losses, the long years of instability, wild inflation, and unpredictability were invisible to George. Of course, he had pressing national and international concerns and had tried to do what he could for his mother. Still, when she entered his mind, he could not help seeing her through his concern for his own reputation, rather than as a frightened old woman living as best she knew how through hard times. She, too, saw through her own lens. Her age intensified this experience of loss— or reexperience, because she had been through the successive breakdown of crucial, dependent relationships as a child. That, added to the physical disabilities of old age, her illness before the trek, her exhaustion afterward, and the ongoing wartime chaos swirling around her, plunged her into unrelenting, debilitating anxiety. An old woman, she had talked frequently and unhappily to acquaintances about her want. She had lost Samuel, had not seen George in five years, had lost Fielding, and had almost lost Betty, after seven increasingly hard years of war. She had been feeling desperate for a long time. Her desires might have been unreal, as George suggested, because what she desired was some security and peace from her constant fears, not luxuries.

Historians have blamed Mary for the loose talk that led to the discussion of the petition, and some have even said that she herself made the petition, though it did not actually materialize. But discussion about the petition might have had as much to do with George as it did with Mary. Adam Stephen, an acquaintance and military companion and competitor of George's for decades, represented Berkeley County, adjacent to Frederick, in the Virginia General Assembly in 1780–1781, the year before Harrison's letter. He was extremely well connected and could easily have encouraged such a discussion because he would have been privy to the local gossip when the Washingtons and Lewises arrived in the neighborhood just after his term ended.[8]

Stephen had served with Washington at Fort Necessity and in Braddock's campaign. He became Washington's political competitor for the House of Burgesses in 1761. Washington, the incumbent, heard from a supporter that Stephen was promising to "diffuse gold and opulency through Frederick." Washington and his correspondent expressed contempt for Stephen. George wrote to the county sheriff who oversaw elections, suggesting, illegally, that the votes for him be voiced first to show him as the favorite. The sheriff did as George asked, and Washington won handily, 505 to 293. In 1764, Washington was part of a committee that docked Stephen's pay for derelictions in billing for military spending. Washington long thought Stephen inflated deeds to his superiors and accused him of such an incident when Stephen was his brigadier general.[9]

Stephen incurred Washington's rage when he sent a group of soldiers across the Delaware to scout the position of the British just before the Battle of Trenton. His exploration provoked gunfire. "You, Sir," Washington yelled at Stephen, "may have ruined all my plans by having put them on their guard."

After the Battle of Germantown, Stephen was accused of "unofficer-like behavior" in the retreat and "of having been frequently intoxicated since in the service to the prejudice of good order and military discipline." Stephen was convicted and sentenced to be cashiered from the army. George approved the court-martial on November 20, 1777. Stephen defended himself, saying that he was "the object of hatred of a person of high rank for no other reason but for delivering my sentiments on . . . this campaign with that candor which an old soldier of experience who has the interest of America at heart."[10] Despite his dismissal, Stephen continued on good terms with Virginia's elite, corresponding with Thomas Jefferson and Richard Henry Lee. His friend and neighbor General Horatio Gates, who was removed from command in 1780, also had strong reasons to dislike George. Stephen lived in the neighborhood of Fielding Lewis and Samuel and Charles Washington. Samuel had long been a friend of Gates's. If Stephen and/or Gates wished to embarrass Washington, local gossip gave them the opportunity.[11] Whether Stephen helped circulate this idea or someone else did, it seems to have been motivated by bad will, because pensioning off the ancient mother of the very wealthy and most celebrated leader of the Revolution would make George look like a scoundrel of the first order.

The incident agitated feelings George already nurtured about his mother's disregard for appearances and what he thought were her imaginary needs. He blamed her for unseemly behavior, rather than being able to understand her compulsion to talk about her woes. His fierce focus on how things looked could obscure his vision of how things actually were. As Lund had reported over and over, George's own plantations were rendering nothing. He faced returning to a mountain of debts, like those of his siblings. He refused to believe that there could be any truth to her complaints because he believed that his intentions—and those of his siblings— were good. But Samuel and Fielding had died, Charles had not helped her, nor apparently had John Augustine, and Betty was sick and destitute. Unable to drop his own defense, he decided Mary's poverty had to be imaginary or exaggerated. His advice to her would come from Matthew Hale and would consist of learning that in "whatsoever estate [she was] therewith to be content."[12]

18

"YOU MUST ONE DAY FADE"[1]

Bring up your children "in the Nurture and Admonition of the Lord:
Their unblameable and useful Conduct will be the Staff of
your Age, and a Balm for declining Nature."

—JAMES HERVEY, *MEDITATIONS AMONG THE TOMBS*

*M*ARY AND BETTY RETURNED from their miserable sojourn in the west to a Fredericksburg that was as impoverished as they both were. Betty tried repeatedly to reach George and was hurt by his silence:

I am at a loss how to account for your long silence . . . my dear brother, was there not a half hour you could spare a few lines to an only sister who was labouring under so much affliction.

My poor dear Mr. Lewis and my brother both lay ill at the same time and it was the Lord's will to take them to Himself, in three weeks, one after another And with the confinement and uneasiness of mind, it caused me to get in such an ill state of health that I expected to follow them. It happened at a time when everything contributed to my uneasiness . . . (Your being in Fredericksburg the only chance we had of seeing you from the commencement of the war), that my spirits were quite gone.

I thank God I am recovering my health fast, and please myself with thoughts of seeing you once more with us.[2]

It seems that only one of Betty's four letters reached her brother. He was, at the time, grieving for his stepson, Jacky, who had died from a fever he caught while visiting Yorktown just after the British surrender. The young man's death, combined with Martha's deep grief, affected him strongly.[3]

||||||||||||||

MARY RESUMED her persistent but feeble oversight of her land at Little Falls. George reported to John Augustine that she had discovered *"Knavery"* on the part of the overseer. "She says she can get nothing from him. . . . *The whole profit of the Plantation according to her Acct. is applied to his own use,"* while George was paying eighty to a hundred pounds in rent. George was in Newburgh, dealing with a potential revolt by riled-up, unpaid soldiers. He was exasperated by Mary's request, felt he had no reason to have to be invited back into the arrangement he had set up, he said, for the convenience of his mother. He seems to have given little credence to her account.

Writing to his favorite brother, George unburdened himself of his frustrations. "It is too much while I am suffering in every other way (and hardly able to keep my own estate from sale) to be saddled with all the expence of hers and not to be able to receive the smallest return from it." Given Virginia's ruined economy, it is surprising that he allowed himself to be disappointed over the fact that he got no return from Mary's estate. In any case, he thought John Augustine the best person to look into the matter.

George also passed on to John Augustine the story he had heard from Benjamin Harrison about the discussion of a pension for Mary. He had been aggrieved about the stain on his reputation as a good son ever since, saying, "Since then I have heard nothing of *that* matter; I have heard from very good authority that she is upon all occasions, and in all Companies complaining of the hardness of the times, of her wants and distresses, and if not in direct ways at least by strong innuendoes inviting favors which not only makes her appear in an unfavorable point of view but *those* who are connected with her. That she can have no *real* wants that may not be supplied I am sure of; imaginary wants are indefinite and oftentimes insatiable, because they are boundless and always changing." He went on to ask John Augustine to "enquire into her real wants and see what is necessary to make her comfortable. If the Rent is insufficient to do this, while I have anything I will part with it to make her so: and wish you to take measures on my behalf accordingly; at the same time I wish you to represent to her in delicate terms the impropriety of her complaints and acceptance of favors even where they are voluntarily offered, from any but relations. It will not do to touch upon this subject in a letter to her, and therefore I have avoided it."[4]

Betty was not George's "good authority" for these tales. She had been quite out of touch with George. She was in financial straits herself and was the person who had long looked out for Mary, to the extent she could. His source, I believe, was either Burgess Ball, married to Charles's daughter, Fanny, or his nephew George Augustine Washington, who was with George's military family and transcribed some of his letters. George Augustine, the son of Charles, was the only family member who, other than Betty, would have seen Mary on some if not "all" occasions. Very likely, Mary complained repeatedly. Old people repeat themselves. It deeply embarrassed George at a distance and might have embarrassed Charles's children in person. Mary had already complained to George that Charles was not looking out for her interests on her piece of land near Ferry Farm. Complaining in front of Charles or his offspring might have helped her unburden herself of *her* frustrations—a once independent woman running a plantation, now dependent on a family that was running a war. In that unwelcome process, they had turned her life into an endless crisis.

George had trouble grasping the cost to Virginia of the long years of uncertainty, the economic chaos, and the struggles among rich, middling, and poor over who would shoulder the burden of the conflict. After Cornwallis's surrender, George pressed Virginia for more recruits, not knowing what the British would do. The many prisoners in the west of the state would need, he wrote, a "strict hand." When Benjamin Harrison complained that there was no money in the treasury, George said he thought the victory at Yorktown would have given the state a chance to recover.[5] Despite his own losses and reports from Lund and others, he was still unrealistic about conditions back home.

George was taken aback that Fielding had died "very much indebted." Fielding had been a very wealthy man, but wartime inflation, the embargo prohibiting his usual export revenue, the state's inability to pay him for large sums of money he had spent in the Whig cause, and the cost of maintaining his expensive plantations near Fredericksburg and in the west left him and his widow without the wherewithal to pay their creditors.[6]

When John Augustine was in Berkeley sorting through the financial wreckage that Samuel had left behind, George wrote of his "extreme pain. . . . In Gods name how did my Brothr. Saml. contrive to get himself so enormously in debt? Was it by purchases? By misfortunes? Or shear indolence and inattention to the business."[7]

When facing his own wartime losses head-on, George wrote Lund, whom he both trusted and cared for, a stinging letter, part rebuke but also part lament as he began to grasp what the war had meant. John Augustine from on-site had alerted him that he had suffered *"greatly"* in rent collection, a task for Lund. Lund would have tried to get the rents from Samuel, who had collected them, but Samuel was elusive. Furthermore, Lund did not command the authority over Samuel that George did. George grieved, "I shall be more hurt, than at anything else, to think that an Estate, which I have drawn nothing from, for eight years, and which always enabled me to make any purchase I had in view, should not have been able for the last five years to pay the manager; And that, worse than going home to empty coffers, and expensive living, I shall be encumbered with debt."[8]

John Augustine did uncover years of knavery by Mary's overseer. (George's biographers do not mention this part of the story.) When George had sorted it out, he admitted in June 1783 that the Quarter "has been under the most wretched management, equally burthensome to me and teazing to her."[9] He does not mention the adequacy of his rent. Perhaps he adjusted it.

According to her grandson Rob Lewis, Mary continued to visit her land daily, although she had turned over her accounts to Fielding at some point because her eyesight was poor. Presumably, Betty continued that work. Mary had spotted "knavery," and John Augustine had found another overseer, but the land and slaves were still hers, and she felt a responsibility to herself and to the property to keep watch.

Mary resumed gardening and reading and sometimes re-created the meditative state she achieved in thinking about God's ways and his will, reciting well-known passages from Matthew Hale and reading her family Bible to the grandchildren. She continued to visit her beloved large flat rocks, surrounded by trees, where, according to her step-grandson and others, "she communed with her Creator in humiliation and prayer." One grandson, probably Rob or Lawrence Lewis, remembered her teaching lessons about natural history, finding illustrations in their surroundings. She would tie the natural world around them to the Bible story of creation, the Flood, and what followed when the waters receded. Much later, one grandchild spoke for the others when he said, "There was a spell over them as they looked into their grandmother's uplifted face, with its sweet expression of perfect peace." They would walk home very quietly.[10] Lawrence

Lewis recalled an afternoon when "we all sheltered under the Rocks from a heavy rain accompany [*sic*] by Thunder & lightning, the high hills in front clothed with . . . timber concealed its approach . . . we were compelled to [search?] their protection."[11] Subsequent events and family propaganda of course influence memories long after the remembered moments themselves. Still, the *feeling* of a remembered event is often what carries through over the years. Like Lawrence of Chotank so many years earlier, her grandchildren remembered sweetness but also something remarkable in Mary's ability to command their wide-eyed attention and respect. She inhabited her faith—a faith that seems to have been strongly tinged with nature worship—which fortified her with a special strength and power evident to others. George, too, of course, commanded awe and respect, but historians have always found that perfectly natural. Mary was a woman and without education; only a few young people recorded her power.

Many years after her death, at a commemoration of what was to be a monument to her on her favorite spot, Andrew Jackson laid the cornerstone of a foundation in 1833. In his speech, he might have been citing the Lewis children, now grown, with this: "It is said by those who knew her intimately that she acquired a wonderful mastery over those around her."[12]

With Betty back at Kenmore, Mary and she resumed their lives as neighbors and helpers. A grandchild remembered her "nervous energy" knitting and in other ways engaged in productive work. She welcomed guests to her home and gave to charities, despite her recurring financial straits. In June 1783, a neighbor, William Simmes, wrote to his family that he lived near both Betty Lewis and Mary. He described Betty Lewis as

a fine figure of an old lady as ever I have seen. But what is more, [George Washington's mother is an] older lady no doubt, but equally active and sprightly notwithstanding. She goes about the neighborhood to visit our quality on foot, with a cane in her hand & sometimes a Negro girl walking behind her to assist her in case of necessity.

She must be near eighty years old—& talks of George without the least pride or vanity. She will not keep any carriage, but a chair and two old family horses. . . . She lives in a little house of one story without the least affectation of magnificence. The front windows are always shut & barred—for she delights to live in a little back room or two where I have seen her sitting at work with a slave to attend her—such is her taste.[13]

The war had aged both Betty and her mother, depleting their strength and health.[14] On February 17, 1783, Mary's granddaughter Fanny Washington Ball, wife of Burgess Ball, gave birth to an infant girl she named Mary. Burgess Ball's first wife (who died in 1775) had been named Mary (Chichester) as well, so it was a split honorific. Her grandmother Mary became one of the infant's godmothers. The infant Mary died the following year of dysentery.[15]

On February 21, 1784, Mary finally saw George when he came to Fredericksburg to see the family and to participate in a local celebration for him. He stayed with Betty at Kenmore and visited Mary. According to George Washington Parke Custis, they talked of many things, but not of his military conquests. Assuming this was fact, George's biographers have criticized her for a want of interest in her son. But George could not bring her into his world of war and politics in an hour or two. Her praise of his military prowess would have been both ridiculous and presumptuous. She has been quoted as saying that George was always a good boy and she expected no less of him than to be a good man. Knowing her as he did, he would probably have appreciated such an accolade. He wished to be a good man in her eyes, and she could still wound him by finding him an undutiful son. There is no record of what they did talk about, but people, after a long separation, usually speak of the things they have in common. Probably they caught up on family and friends, health, and the ancient trivia of an earlier life. Without doubt, they both spoke of God's infinite mercy in keeping them both alive and giving her the chance to see him again.

Among the festivities was a visit by the mayor and his council praising Washington for his "long and meritorious services in the cause of liberty." George replied graciously about his happiness to be a private citizen once more and his gratitude to his soldiers and to the populace for their support. He added that his pleasure in their praises was increased by the respectability of the citizens and the "honourable mention which is made of my revered mother, by whose maternal hand, early deprived of a father, I was led to manhood." This was a public event, and George carefully weighed his words to reflect maximum credit on himself as a dutiful and vulnerable son and on his mother as the pious bearer of extraordinary responsibilities. It is, nevertheless, a real tribute and one that must have given both of them pleasure. This was followed by an enormous midday meal and, in the evening, a ball, which Mary attended.

Mary arrived on George's arm, in a black silk dress with a white kerchief and a white hat. At an early hour she left, citing her age. Her tall, aging son walked his tall, aged mother home to the white house with a garden that he had bought for her.[16]

Mary attended and encouraged Betty as she regained her health and struggled to hold on to her inheritance. Fielding had left her ten slaves, a brick warehouse on Sophia Street, livestock, furniture, and Kenmore, which sat on eleven hundred acres, to be shared with John, his son by his first wife, Catharine. He had left land and property in Fredericksburg to him, contingent on John's payment of certain debts. Fielding and John had discussed this arrangement, and Fielding had written a codicil to his will to that effect. The codicil instructed John to pay to his stepmother the same rent he had paid to his father (seventy-five bushels of corn). It provided that she would have unlimited rights to cut timber on the land they would share to be able to heat Kenmore and other buildings on the property.[17] John did not add the codicil to the will despite his apparent understanding with his father. It took Betty eighteen months and a payment to have the codicil legalized. Illness and conflict over property and money with John darkened her last years. She also had to pay for her son Fielding junior's impoverished grandchildren. By the end of the decade, Fielding junior was in debtors' prison.[18]

Betty managed to pay the taxes on her slaves and Kenmore and pay her bills, in part probably from renting out her slaves. After the war, there was money to be made renting slaves to stem tobacco, to care for the town streets, and to handle wagons with produce. Mary, too, with Betty's encouragement and example, might have raised money this way.[19]

In the fall of 1784, the expressive, courtly Marquis de Lafayette, whom George loved above all his officers, visited his friend and also made time to visit Mary. Rob Lewis walked him from Kenmore to her house, where he found her in the garden, raking leaves in a straw hat and a short black dress[20]—the equivalent of a housedress. She greeted him by saying that they could sit comfortably, and she could make him welcome "without the parade of changing my dress." He told her in his inimitably charming way how much he admired her son and what a glorious change he had helped bring to the country. According to tradition, he asked for her blessing, which she gave. Lafayette later wrote of his admiration for her simplicity and refusal to take on airs given the astonishing achievements of her son. He wrote to George that he had seen "the only Roman matron of my day," although, unlike the Roman matrons of legend, Mary had not been a bit happy to sacrifice George for the cause of independence. She wanted her son to survive and be what she raised him to be: a good patriarch. Lafayette was amazed that she was not surprised at—or unduly proud of—George's victories, courage, and vision. In that way, she was like George, who himself was not filled with pride for his achievements but seems to have felt immense relief and satisfaction at having discharged his duty as he saw it and at having emerged with a stainless reputation.

In correspondence with George, Lafayette repeatedly offered his special respects to Mary. George responded to one of these salutes, in the spring of 1786, saying, "My mother will receive the compliments you honor her with, as a flattering mark of your attention; and I shall have the great pleasure in delivering them myself."[21] Mary's ability to elicit glowing praise from Lafayette could only have raised George's esteem for his mother.

That fall, John Augustine visited George at Mount Vernon, for what would be the last time. His son William Augustine Washington had died in a dreadful, accidental shooting at school in April 1784, and his and his wife's health both suffered.[22] He died in January 1787.

In the late fall of 1786, Mary had written to John Augustine that she was borrowing a little corn—because there was "no corn in the corn house I have never lived soe poore on my Life was it not for Mrs. French and your sister Lewis I should be almost starvd butt I am Like an old almanac quit out of date."[23] Under John Augustine's supervision, Mary had managed, but whether from a bad harvest or a theft of corn, or because John Augustine had been unable for some months to watch over things at the Quarter, she found herself in difficulties again. Her sad, wry sense of herself as an out-of-date almanac, an old woman who dressed and behaved from another era, gives this plea a special poignancy.

After George visited Fredericksburg following John Augustine's death, Mary asked him for money. He sent her fifteen guineas, "which believe me is all the money I have." George blended his grief over John Augustine and his frustration at having his mother's responsibility back on his shoulders into an emotional letter. He laid out his grievances and his arguments block by block, defending himself as he often did, by explaining how generous he had been and wished to be, but for the constraints on him. He explained how expensively he had to live and how short his cash was. He went on about his willingness to pay her "what may really be due" but rehearsed at length his observations about her having everything she wanted from her plantation, "when I had not received one farthing from the place directly or indirectly . . . for more than twelve years if ever" and had paid her 260 "odd pounds out of my own Pocket." As he warmed up, he was claiming to have paid her 300 or 400 pounds out of his own pocket and yet was "viewed as a delinquent and considered perhaps by the world as an unjust and undutiful son." He suggested alternatives for her future, including turning over the place to her grandson Bushrod, John Augustine's son, who would rent it all from her, or letting the overseer rent the land and rent out her slaves. Alternatively, he advised her to rent her house and all but two of her slaves and to go live with one of her children. He and John Augustine had decided she should live with the latter, but "he alas is no more. . . . My house is at your service, and would press you most devoutly to accept it, but I am sure and candour requires me to say it will never answer your purposes . . . for in truth it may be compared to a well resorted tavern, as scarcely any strangers who are going from north to south, or from south to north do not spend a day or two at it—This would . . . oblige you to do one of three things, first to be always dressing to appear in company, second to come in a dishabille or third to be, as it were, a prisoner in your own chamber. The first you'd not like, indeed for a person at your time of life it would be too fatiguing. The second I should not like because those who resort here are . . . strangers and people of the first distinction, the third . . . would not be pleasing to either of us—nor indeed could you be retired in any room in my house; for what with the sitting up of Company; the noise and bustle of servants—and many other things you would not be able to enjoy that calmness and serenity of mind, which in my opinion you ought now to prefer to every other consideration in life." He suggested that she live with one of his siblings, but Charles now lived across the mountains, and Mary bore him a grudge, so George knew he was telling her to go live with Betty.

In fact, Betty would ask Mary from time to time to come live with her, worried that her elderly mother was not able to manage on her own. Mary held out. She had marked with work and responsibilities her path through life. When faced with grief, fear, or loneliness, she could always find comfort in taking care of things, making something useful, mending something broken. She never agreed to move in with Betty.

George added that "the charge of a family" (by which he meant slaves and any other dependents) "without anybody to assist you—the charge of an estate the profit of which depend on wind weather and a good Overseer—an honest man—and a thousand other circumstances, cannot be right or proper at your advanced age . . . by the mode I have pointed out, you may reduce your income to a certainty, be eased of all trouble—and if you are so disposed, be perfectly happy—for happiness depends more on the internal frame of a persons mind—than on the externals of the world. Of the last if you will pursue the plan here recommended I can assure you can want nothing that is essential—the other depends wholly upon your self, for the riches of the Indies cannot purchase it."

He concluded with a little sermon on her time of life. An old person should want peace and quiet, not hustle and bustle, so she could think those thoughts that were appropriate to her age. The mind was thought to improve in old age, because it was less subject to the agitation of passions. And retirement and solitude, philosophers wrote, were believed to benefit the mental activity of the elderly as they rehearsed their memories and found unfamiliar, enhanced meanings in familiar recollections. Deborah Norris Logan (1761–1839), a Quaker writer, disagreed with the traditional wisdom and thought a life of activity was best suited to older women.[24] Mary would have concurred. George wrapped up with his customary advice on carrying one's happiness within one. Controlling one's own disposition was the most important protection against unhappiness.

One of George's reasons for discounting the possibility that Mary might reside at Mount Vernon was her preference for "dishabille" over dressing up. Thomas Jefferson, soon to be George's secretary of state, had written his daughter Martha a letter in 1783 registering disgust for women who appeared "under the privileges of dishabille loose and negligent of their dress in the morning. A lady who has been seen as a sloven or a slut in the morning will never efface the impression she has made. . . . Nothing is so disgusting to our sex as a want of cleanliness and delicacy in yours."[25] Jefferson ran together the meanings of "dishabille," or wearing the more informal and comfortable clothing of the early eighteenth century, and being dirty and slutty. They were not the same, but in elite circles they signified both a class difference and, by the inevitable association, a difference in cleanliness and in presentability.

George elided "dishabille" and dirt less explicitly than Jefferson, but historians have easily inferred their equivalency. Mary has often and falsely been accused of having been unclean and slatternly. Despite Lafayette's admiration for her simplicity and lack of ostentation, George found her an embarrassment.

In her son's eyes, Mary had received his cherished noble French friend in something perilously close to her nightgown. George and Martha led Virginians in sharpening class distinctions. As Mary said, she was out-of-date.

George's letter closely resembles others he had written and would write on the topic of Mary's requests and his assessment of them. It also resembles a letter he wrote defending himself against criticism for a money-saving project he tried on his slaves in May 1793.

George wrote to his manager that it was "not his wish . . . that my Negros should have an oz. of meal more, nor less than is sufficient to feed them plentifully. . . . Formerly, every Working Negro used to receive a heaping and squeezed peck at top of unsifted Meal . . . with which I presume they were satisfied, inasmuch as I never heard any complaint. . . . Since the meal has been given to them sifted and a struck peck only [level] of it, there has been eternal complaints; which I have assumed arose as much from the want of husks to feed their fouls, as from any other cause 'till Davy [an enslaved overseer for many years at Mount Vernon] assured me that what his people received was not sufficient, and that to his certain knowledge several of them would be without a mouthful for a day, and (if they did not eke it out) sometimes two days. . . . Like complaints" at other plantations, these "altogether hurt my feelings too much to suffer this matter to go without a remedy. . . . I am no more disposed to squander than to stint . . . surely the . . . true and just quantity may be ascertained; which is all they have a right to ask, or I will allow them."[26]

Just as George suspected the motives of his slaves who said they had not enough to eat, so he suspected his mother when she said the same thing. In both cases, he hated accusations that injured his feelings, but reserved to himself the right to judge the quantity of meal and money to justly satisfy another's hunger and need.

Mary resisted the idea of moving to Bushrod's. She grieved for John Augustine, a dearly beloved son. He had looked out for her when she was in trouble at the end of the war despite living at a greater distance than Charles. She had raised him at Ferry Farm and had stayed at Mount Vernon with him and his wife, Hannah, all those years ago when George was away fighting. They had named their first, short-lived daughter after her. He had been affectionate and a comfort to her.

Usually cancer makes slow progress in the old. Mary might not have been aware of the gravity of her own illness for some time. But by April 1787, she was so sick that the family sent George at Mount Vernon an urgent message that made him decide to come to Fredericksburg, to see both his mother and Betty, who was also suffering from one of her more and more frequent respiratory crises. By the time George got there, they had both rallied a bit. His sister was no longer in danger, but his mother's "extreme low state . . . left little hope of her recovery, as she was exceedingly reduced and much debilitated by age and disorder."[27]

About a year later, feeling it was time, Mary initiated the ritual she had witnessed often in her life, will making. James Mercer and Joseph Walker drew hers up for her.[28] In June 1788, Mary saw her son at about the same time she made her will. He came with Martha to visit Mary. George Washington Parke Custis described their meeting, but neither of the protagonists left a record. Mary, frail and unwell, perhaps offered her son and daughter-in-law tea, which she could now drink again, from one of her handsome services. They said the goodbyes that they had often said, Mary typically believing it was the last time she would ever see her son. This time she was right. George left expecting, correctly, never to see his mother again.

Breast cancer was not an uncommon disease. George Mason had written to George years before, in perhaps more detail than George wished, about his mother-in-law's experience with the disease and her need to undergo a mastectomy, which seems to have given her another five years of life.[29] Betty called in Dr. Mortimer, who had tended the family for decades. She also consulted by letter Dr. Elisha Hall, a cousin of the renowned Dr. Benjamin Rush. Mary's condition and her years did not warrant the trauma of surgery without anesthetic. Doctors could offer little beyond opium and camphor, supporting the system with wine and bark (quinine, which was used for malaria).

On May 13, 1789, Rob Lewis, Mary's dear grandson, left to accompany Martha Washington to New York, to join George. He drove off in Mary's phaeton, which she been happy to let him use with the provision that he return it to Betty, to whom she had left it in her will.[30] He left the two women in Fredericksburg "after," in his words, "I had experienced the most disagreeable sensations imaginable with the reflections of parting with an Aged Mother and Grandmother—besides other numerous relatives and acquaintances, *who all appeared equally affected at our separation*—when our hands touched, perhaps, for the last time and our tongues refus'd to perform their office in bidding farewell. Heaven I am assured witnessed and approved the purity and ardour of our affections." Lewis's flowery account of wordless goodbyes to his failing grandmother and fragile mother has the ring of truth, unlike Custis's even more flowery improvisations of Mary and George's farewell.

Rob brought his uncle news that Mary was quite unwell and unlikely to recover. At the same time, Betty and Mary had themselves been distressed by the news of George's frighteningly poor health that late spring and early summer. He had pneumonia and an infected tumor on his thigh that was extremely painful. The fever abated only when the tumor was removed. He recovered slowly.[31] Toward the end of July, Betty wrote to George about Mary's deterioration and the pain she was suffering. "God only knows how it will end. I dread the consequences, she is sensible of it and perfectly resigned—wishes for nothing more than to keep it easy. She wishes to hear from you, she will not believe you are well until she has it from your hand. The doctors think if they could get some hemlock, it would be of service to her breast." They couldn't. Betty, kind soul that she was, promised her convalescing brother a large pot of "very fine [honey] in the comb."[32] Any letter George might have written does not survive, but it is hard to imagine that he would have withheld the comfort of his recovery from his dying mother.

Betty apparently feared her mother's death more than Mary did. Betty and Mary had cared for each other most of their lives and were rarely apart. But Mary was enfeebled, exhausted, and without independence or initiative. She had no responsibilities left, and her fear for George's health had dissipated. Beginning her life shadowed by the deaths of her parents, she had studied the Christian path to death for more than six decades. She accepted and perhaps even longed for her dissolution in the strong hope of forgiveness, salvation, and entry into a better world.

In August 1789, Mary stopped speaking for fifteen days, and during her last five days she slept or was in a coma.[33] On Mary's death, August 25, her family paid the town crier, Joseph Berry, to toll the bell for her at St. George's Church. He would have rung it two times because a woman had died and then once for every year of her age.

When Mary died, Betty suffered a collapse from exhaustion, grief, and her own weakened constitution. Rather than write to George about Mary's death, she had Burgess Ball do it—she, as Burgess put it, "being in much trouble." When Ball's news arrived, Rob wrote of his worry for his mother, "knowing how attentive she always was during the indisposition of the Old Lady."[34]

Women made shrouds or winding-sheets from muslin or linen. Betty was probably too ill, so the job might have gone to Betty Carter or to an enslaved woman. Perhaps Betty took on another woman's task, washing and laying out her mother, but in her weakened state she would have needed help.[35] It was hot, and in any case decomposition was rapid, so Mary's interment was quick. A local furniture maker built her coffin, charging eight pounds, six shillings, and four pence.[36] Businesses were reportedly all closed on the sweltering day of Mary's funeral. Because Mary was a member of a prominent family, the town crier tolled the St. George's bell on the day of her funeral as he had on the day of her death. The Reverend Thomas Thornton, a kinsman and Mary's minister, officiated.[37]

When George received Ball's letter, he, Rob, and the Revolutionary comrades Baron von Steuben and Brigadier General Arthur St. Clair were enjoying a "mirthful" visit. George went to a room by himself and stayed alone for a while.

George sent Betty condolences that were pompous and patriarchal, instructing Betty how to feel. They reflected his sense of the momentousness of his mother's death and his inability to find comfortable language in which to write about it. "Awful, and affecting as the death of a Parent is, there is consolation in knowing that Heaven has spared ours to an age, beyond which few attain, and favored her with the full enjoyment of her mental faculties, and as much bodily strength as usually falls to the lot of four score. Under these considerations and a hope that she is translated to a happier place, it is the duty of her relatives to yield due submission to the decrees of the Creator." He continued that after getting the news, he would not normally have taken the things his mother left him, but they "are meant and ought to be considered and received as mementoes of parental affection in the last solemn act of life . . . in this point of view I set a value on them much beyond their intrinsic worth."[38]

Those things said, he repeated his familiar defensive litany, a detailed description of how much money she had had from him and how he never thought it anything but his filial obligation to supply her with everything she asked for, despite never having received a "copper" from her farms. "She has had a great deal of money from me at times, as can be made appear by my books, and the accounts of Mr L. Washington during my absence—and over and above this has not only had all that was ever made from the Plantation but got her provisions and every thing else she thought proper from thence. In short to the best of my recollection I have never in my life received a copper from the estate—and have paid many hundred pounds (first and last) to her in cash—However I want no retribution—I conceived it to be a duty whenever she asked for money, and I had it, to furnish her notwithstanding she got all the crops or the amount of them, and took every thing she wanted from the plantation for the support of her family, horses &ca besides."

It was the story he had constructed for Benjamin Harrison and perfected in letters to John Augustine and Mary herself. He wanted Betty to know it. There is literal truth in it, but it is a partial story, leaving out his father's ungenerous treatment of Mary in his will (even for a society miserly toward widows), not counting income that George did sometimes receive from his reorganization and rental of Ferry Farm, the diminishing value of the money that Lund gave her during the Revolution, and his relentless skepticism about her understanding of her own needs. It also obscures what he himself said to Lund: that he had, before the war, an estate that would permit him to buy anything he "had in view." He was an immensely wealthy man, too wealthy, one might think, to begrudge his elderly mother some money here and there. But it was his story, and it comforted him to repeat it to his sister. Most historians and biographers have, by and large, taken it as the truth, and it has limited subsequent accounts of her to the subject of how he had to deal with this supposedly troublesome, insatiable old woman.

George's secretary and biographer, David Humphreys, lost both his parents in 1787. George wrote in commiseration that because they had both been old, David had to have been prepared for the "shock; Tho' there is something painful in bidding adieu to those we love or revere, when we know it is a final one, Reason, religion & Philosophy may soften the anguish, but time alone can irradicate it." George, like his correspondent, was prepared for the "shock" of his elderly mother's death. He would call on time as well as his deep reserves of "Reason, religion & Philosophy" to abate the "anguish." Of the two verbs he offered David, "revere" probably came closer to his core feeling about Mary than "love."[39]

Mary opened her will by asserting her good health and sound mind. She invoked "the uncertainty of this life," as well she might at about seventy-nine years old. She had lived a remarkably long time for the period, outliving two of her grown children, the others dying at much younger ages than Mary had attained. Only 5 percent of the population in colonial America lived beyond sixty.[40]

Unlike her late husband, Augustine, she recommended her "soul in the hands of [her] Creator, hoping for a remission of all [her] sins through the merits and mediation of Jesus Christ." With the religious formula observed, not perfunctorily in Mary's case, she bequeathed six slaves with apparently reckless disregard for them and their ties—separating her cook Old Bet and young Bet (and her "increase"), who were without doubt mother and daughter. She gave the Negro boy "George," who was probably Old Bet and Stephen's other child, to his namesake, her firstborn son, separating him from his mother. Old Bet instead went to Mary's grandson Corbin Washington (John Augustine and Hannah's son). Her daughter, "Little Bet," went to Mary's granddaughter Betty. Lydia went to Lawrence Lewis, Betty and Fielding's son (who married Martha's granddaughter Nelly Custis). Mary left Fielding junior the enslaved Frederick and an array of silver spoons, a blue-and-white tea service, and household furnishings.

She did not dispose of Patty, because it seems likely that Patty was the child Augustine gave to Betty in his will; that is, Patty already belonged to Betty. Whether Mary discussed her plans for her slaves is unknown. What little we know of Silla's unwilling months of service to Mary suggests that Mary did not discuss such matters with slaves. George had come to yield to the preferences of his slaves not to be sold away. It is not at all clear that Mary allowed those kinds of conversations even to take place.

Mary left "little Bet and her future increase" to her granddaughter Betty Lewis Carter, who had been close to both her mother and Mary. (Betty and her husband, Charles, married just before the family exile to the mountains, had to leave his father's house unexpectedly and moved into one of Betty's properties. After Mary's death, they lived in her house for a while.)[41] She left her granddaughter Betty furniture, household goods, her red-and-white tea service, teaspoons, and other useful items more or less equivalent to those left to Fielding junior. Mary gave Betty her phaeton and her bay horse. To Corbin, she gave her riding chair and two black horses. She left her lined shag cloak ("purple" in the will, "red" when ordered from London) to her recently widowed daughter-in-law, Hannah Bushrod Washington. And, recalling her mother's careful division of clothes, she invited Betty to select two or three favorites before her grandchildren Betty, Fanny Ball (the daughter of Burgess Ball and Frances Washington, Charles and Mildred's daughter), and Mildred Washington divvied them up among themselves. Those who selected and wore Mary's clothes were believed to "animate" them, and "the clothes seem to reciprocate, recalling the shape of the absent body and accommodating its current inhabitant in the remembered form."[42]

Mary left George the most meaningful and "best" of her possessions. She left him the land her father had willed her as a tiny child, the only thing left from that time of her life. Eighteenth-century thinkers saw a direct link between objects and memory. "Particular rooms of things contained traces of original experiences, triggering an endless train of related impressions."[43] Mary left George furnishings from her "best bedroom": her "best bed" and curtains and her "best" dressing glass, and her blue-and-white quilt. She insisted, poignantly, on only the best for George, and her bequests were strikingly intimate, replete with, perhaps, her "best" memories. She left him her marriage bed, possibly the bed George was first nursed in, and a coverlet she probably quilted and certainly slept under. She wanted him to know that whatever she had done for him, it had been her best. She left her son Charles a slave named Tom.

The family was precise in divvying up those people and items that Mary had and had not mentioned in her will. Burgess Ball wrote that the "negroes" were "divided" after Betty learned that she was not to share in them because her father's will, which determined their distribution, excluded her. How she received that news, given her debts, is not recorded.

Ball and George were pleased that no families had to be separated. George sold her white Fredericksburg house for a hundred pounds more than he had paid for it.[44]

The remains of Mary's agriculture enterprise included a modest array of tools, hoes for the slaves, two flax wheels, three plows, axes, two grindstones, a crosscut saw, and a pair of hand irons. She left twenty-odd cows and heifers, a few sheep and oxen, a boar, four sows and numerous piglets, and four hogs ("not choice"). The Quarter had produced nineteen bushels of wheat, four and a half bushels of oats, one of flaxseeds, half a bushel of corn, and four hundred pounds of hay. On hand were three yards of linen and two yards of "cloth." The total of these and other household items like sugar boxes, tea canisters, counterpanes, curtains, and tables came to seventy-six pounds and some change as her grandson Bushrod recorded on October 29, 1798. Among the buyers were Isaac Newton, whom Mary had thought was encroaching on her brother Joseph's land; her granddaughter Betty's husband, Charles Carter; Burgess Ball; and Lewis Willis, a contemporary and school friend of George's. These sales more than paid off her few debts. Materially, she ended life in some ways as she had begun it, except that no overseer left her farm with a cart piled high with her produce.[45]

Mary's views of slavery did not alter during her life, at least if her will is evidence. Born and raised in the fierce years of large importations of Africans, Mary owned slaves from the time she was a small child. Being a slave owner shaped her consciousness and was a constant piece of her identity in the years when her family members were dying around her and forcing her to rethink herself after relationships evaporated. Her mother had left her a woman and her "increase," providing Mary with the imaginary yet psychologically powerful security of someone else's future. Mary did the same thing.

Her views on family obligations and the responsibilities of kin to take care of each other changed little as well. Forced early to a brittle self-reliance, she remained actively productive and independent as long as her health would allow. When her independence failed to provide for her and her "family," she asked that her blood family help her out. Over their lifetimes, she and George struggled over the terms of this bargain but not its basic justice.

After Mary's death, and in grateful, perhaps guilty, memory of her, George took under his wing Elizabeth Haynie and her daughter, Sally (also called Sarah and Sallie), the daughter and granddaughter of his mother's half sister Elizabeth. He gave them a cabin, or "tenement," in the west, rent-free, and some help in "putting the place in order," for their lifetimes.[46] Rob Lewis described Elizabeth as "genteel" and nearly blind, and Sally as a "beautiful girl of 16 or 17 helping to support her mother by hard work."[47] Washington instructed Lewis that he must not let Mrs. Haynie "suffer, as she has thrown herself upon me; your advances [of money] will be allowed always," and for the daughter "make the latter a present, in my name, of a handsome but not costly gown."[48] George carried on his careful, measured help to Mary's closest surviving relatives. He wanted Rob Lewis to understand that his heart and purse were open to these indigent maternal kin, up to a certain point.

EPILOGUE:
AN UNEASY AFTERLIFE

*I*N 1826, GEORGE WASHINGTON PARKE CUSTIS appealed for money to build a monument to Mary. He succeeded in getting some local donors and a wealthy New Yorker to contribute. On May 7, 1833, officials, including President Andrew Jackson and future justice Roger B. Taney, presided over the laying of the cornerstone. All Fredericksburg turned out: the Masons, teachers and students, and three local military companies, despite Mary's distaste for the armed services.

Not known for his feminism, but closely in touch with the antebellum zeitgeist as it related to mothers, Andrew Jackson said, "[George] approached her with the same reverence she had taught him to exhibit in early youth. This course of maternal discipline no doubt restrained the natural ardour of his temperament, and conferred upon him that power of self-command, which was one of the most remarkable traits of his character. . . . Affection less regulated by discretion might have changed the character of the son, and with it the destinies of the nation. We have reason to be proud of the virtue and intelligence of our females."[1] The president, surprisingly, came closer to describing Mary and George's relationship than many scholars have.

George Washington Parke Custis's wealthy New Yorker appointed a contractor to erect the monument, but the former left for China, and the contractor died. The Fredericksburg monument remained unfinished. Meanwhile, the nascent Mount Vernon Ladies' Association had managed to acquire Mount Vernon and was beginning the long work of establishing the country's first and most significant house museum.[2] In December 1862, the Union general Ambrose Burnside failed to proceed with his troops to Richmond according to his battle plan. The fighting that Mary hated spilled over her uncompleted monument lying on its side in her once peaceful spot for prayer and meditation.

In 1878, Captain George Washington Ball, a descendant of Burgess Ball and Fanny Washington, helped found the Mary Ball Washington Association, hoping to restart the enthusiasm for a monument for Mary. Before much money could be collected in those poor years, a real estate firm in 1889 advertised that the land on which Mary was buried was for sale. George Shepherd, who owned the land, evidently did not know either that Mary was buried there or that it was illegal to sell a grave in Virginia, or both. In either case, public outrage encouraged him to withdraw the land from sale, but the realtors sued him. Shepherd won the suit (although the realtors' lawyer reportedly threw a bottle of ink on the suit of Shepherd's lawyer).

Two associations gathered to repair the near disaster to Mary's grave site and do her honor, at long last. One was based in Fredericksburg, the other national in membership. Like many other late-nineteenth-century southern women's associations, they celebrated the Lost Cause vision of the harmonious antebellum South and its brave soldiers as a way to reconcile the white people of both sections. Two association members, the writers and energetic rehabilitators of the South, Marion Harland (the pen name of Mary Hawes Terhune) and Sara Agnes Pryor (the wife of Roger Atkinson Pryor), wrote laudatory biographies of Mary Washington to help raise money and awareness for the monument and contribute to the larger task of reconciliation. The scarcity of established facts of Mary's life made her eminently useful for their dual purposes.[3]

Marion Harland (1830–1922), born Mary Hawes, a Virginian who spent most of her life in New Jersey with her Presbyterian minister husband, Edward Payson Terhune, wrote prodigious numbers of novels and housekeeping guides. She looked back lovingly on antebellum Virginia and idealized it in her books. Her Virginia included "negroes no better than grown up children" whose cares Mary bore while assuming "the responsibilities of their physical, moral, and spiritual condition."[4] Off by a century, she had Mary growing cotton, not tobacco. In her lush prose, she painted an empathic mother and a devoted and honorable boy. Harland wrote, "The mother-heart must often have reckoned [that she had] a Pyrrhian victory over the dearest wishes of the gallant boy whose filial obedience under the crucial test enhanced her appreciation of his noble nature."

Sara Pryor (1830–1912) was born in Virginia and married to Roger Pryor, a Virginian and fire-eating secessionist. The couple and their children moved north after the war. He became a lawyer and later a judge devoted to the Lost Cause; she became a writer, interested in historic preservation, and a member of the Daughters of the American Revolution as well as the Lost Cause organization the United Daughters of the Confederacy. Sara Pryor's paean to Mary was equally a paean to antebellum Virginia. She wrote that there was "reason to believe that [Mary's] house servants were treated with all the affectionate consideration they deserved." Many slave-owning Virginians in the period, she argued, were abolitionists who freed their slaves after the war and gave them land. She observed that "the negro was docile, affectionate, and quick to learn, at least these were the characteristics of those employed in households."[5] As to Mary, her strength derived partly from "the priceless gift of a long happy girlhood— that sweet fountain of pure waters, the memory of which has cheered so many women throughout a long and difficult life."[6] Both authors deflected criticism circulating about Mary's parsimony, alleged sour temper, and "ungraceful . . . dress." Mary might have had trouble recognizing herself, her childhood, and her Virginia in these portraits.

Although the associations agreed on their larger goals, the Fredericksburg one did not want to hand over the land George Shepherd had given them and lose control to the national group. Fredericksburg men persuaded them to do it, however, on the grounds that the national association, unlike the local women, could bring in helpful money to Fredericksburg. Mrs. Vivian Fleming, president of the local association, wrote with dismay that Marion Harland "went over to the nationals, horse, foot, and dragoons."[7] The local association unwillingly agreed to cede the land, and the national association had a monument built. It did not conform to the wishes of the local association but was in any case completed and dedicated by President Grover Cleveland in 1894.

The orator for the day was the Virginia senator John Daniel, a promoter of the Lost Cause and a Democratic politician who campaigned on the slogan "I am a Democrat because I am white and I am a Virginian." He told the gathering, "It was fitting indeed that your pious hands should rear the first monument on earth erected by women to a woman." His eulogy of Mary bore considerably less resemblance to her than Andrew Jackson's had. He praised her as "the good angel of the hearthstone—the special providence of tender hearts and helpless hands, content to bear her burden in the sequestered vale of life. . . . This memorial might indeed be due to her because of who she was, but it is far more due because of what she was. It is . . . as the type of her sex, her people and her race that she deserves this tribute."[8]

For many decades after that, interested citizens of Fredericksburg watched unhappily as weeds obscured Mary's monument. Title to the land had somehow been misplaced between the two organizations, and concerned members of the local association could not rescue the grounds from neglect without retrieving ownership. Eventually, they were able to raise some money and establish title to the monument and grounds. The staff of Kenmore Plantation, Betty and Fielding's mansion (which became a National Historic Landmark in 1970), took over the maintenance of Mary's park and memorial. It is now under the direction of the George Washington Foundation. Since the 1970s, a number of local historians and archaeologists, including but not limited to the late Paula Felder, Carolyn Jett, David Muraca, Laura Galke, and Michelle Hamilton, have found out more about Mary: her ancestry, the objects she owned and their origins and uses, her court appearances, and details of her life at home. They have created the foundations of another overdue monument to Mary: reliable information on her life.

NOTES

IIIIIIIIIIIIIIIIIIIIIIIIIIIIIIIIIIII

MARY BALL WASHINGTON: LIKE MOTHER, LIKE SON

1. Except Dorothy Twohig. "The Making of George Washington," in Warren R. Hofstra, ed., *George Washington and the Virginia Backcountry* (Madison, Wis.: Madison House, 1998).

2. Thavolia Glymph, *Out of the House of Bondage: The Transformation of the Plantation Household* (New York: Cambridge University Press, 2008), 64.

3. Peter Henriques, unpublished MS, chap. 3. Shared by the author.

4. Glymph, *Out of the House of Bondage,* 47.

1. A CHILD IN THE CHESAPEAKE

1. Four historian-genealogists (Paula Felder, Elizabeth Combs Peirce, George H. S. King, and John Copley) have all contributed to the strong hypothesis that Mary Ball was originally Mary Bennett, who was indentured at eighteen years old to Abraham Wild, a London merchant and trafficker in indentures. She traveled to Maryland, leaving London in August 1684. In February 1689, Bennett married the ship captain William Johnson in Christ Church Parish in Middlesex County, Virginia. Johnson purchased fifty acres to grow tobacco but did poorly and was imprisoned for debt in 1696. After that, he disappears from the records. As late as 1708, the sheriff of Middlesex County tried to retrieve debts from Mary Johnson, who was living there. As yet, the records affirming the identity of Mary Bennett with Mary Johnson Ball have not been recovered. Paula Felder, "The World of Mary Washington," *Fredericksburg (Va.) Free Lance-Star*, Fredericksburg.com.

2. David Hackett Fischer, *Albion's Seed: Four British Folkways in America* (New York: Oxford University Press, 1989), 226–31; "Elizabeth Sprig's Letter," in *American Women Writers to 1800*, ed. Sharon Harris (New York: Oxford University Press, 1996), 50.

3. Lancaster Order Books, 1696–1702 and 1703–1713, Tithing lists, in December of each year. For fourteen slaves, Lancaster Court Records, bk. 3, Oct. 9, 1695, 163.

4. Lancaster Order Books, 1703–1713.

5. Lancaster Order Books, 1696–1702.

6. Warren M. Billings, ed., *The Old Dominion in the Seventeenth Century: A Documentary History of Virginia, 1606–1700* (Chapel Hill: University of North Carolina Press, 2007), 96–99.

7. Lancaster Wills, Joseph Ball, Inventory, July 1713.

8. A. G. Roeber, "Authority, Law, and Custom: The Rituals of Court Day in Tidewater Virginia, 1720 to 1750," *William and Mary Quarterly*, 3rd ser., 37, no. 1 (Jan. 1980): 32–36; Carolyn Jett, *Lancaster County, Virginia: Where the River Meets the Bay* (Lancaster, Va.: Mary Ball Washington Museum and Library, 2003), 75; Rhys Isaac, *The Transformation of Virginia, 1740–1790* (Chapel Hill: University of North Carolina Press, 1982), 88–94; Lancaster Order Books, 1696–1712, 1713–1721, Lancaster Order Book, 1696–1702, Dec. 1701; Margaret Lester Hill, *Ball Families of Virginia's Northern Neck: An Outline* (Lancaster, Va.: Mary Ball Washington Museum and Library, 1990); Paula Felder, *Fielding Lewis and the Washington Family: A Chronicle of 18th Century Fredericksburg* (Fredericksburg, Va.: American History Company, 1998), 10–11; Nina Tracy Mann, *Millenbeck: An Archaeological Excavation of a Colonial Mansion* (Lancaster, Va.: Mary Ball Washington Museum and Library, 1976), 7; Christine Adams Jones, *Queenstown, Early Port Town of Lancaster County, Virginia, 1692* (Lancaster, Va.: Mary Ball Washington Museum and Library, 1980), 2.

9. Allan Kulikoff, "The Colonial Chesapeake: Seedbed of Antebellum Southern Culture?," *Journal of Southern History* 45, no. 4 (1979): 521.

10. John C. Coombs, "Beyond the 'Origins Debate': Rethinking the Rise of Virginia Slavery," in *Early Modern Virginia: Reconsidering the Old Dominion*, ed. Douglas Bradburn and John C. Coombs (Charlottesville: University of Virginia Press, 2011); William Pettigrew, "Transatlantic Politics and the Africanization of Virginia's Labor Force, 1688–1712," in Bradburn and Coombs, *Early Modern Virginia*. Thanks to Mary V. Thompson for this citation.

11. Anthony Parent Jr., *Foul Means: The Formation of a Slave Society in Virginia, 1660–1740* (Chapel Hill: University of North Carolina Press, 2003), 1, 23, 37; James Horn, "Adapting to a New World: A Comparative Study of Local Society in England and Maryland, 1650–1700," in *Colonial Chesapeake Society*, ed. Lois Green Carr, Philip D. Morgan, and Jean B. Russo (Chapel Hill: University of North Carolina Press, 1988), 149–57; Joan Gundersen, "The Anglican Ministry in Virginia, 1723–1776: A Study in Social Class" (Ph.D. diss., Notre Dame, 1972).

12. John K. Nelson, *A Blessed Company: Parishes, Parsons, and Parishioners in Anglican Virginia, 1690–1776* (Chapel Hill: University of North Carolina Press, 2001), 4.

13. Darrett B. Rutman and Anita H. Rutman, *A Place in Time: Middlesex County, Virginia, 1650–1750* (New York: Norton, 1984), 143; Nelson, *Blessed Company*, 4; Edward L. Bond, *Spreading the Gospel in Colonial Virginia: Sermons and Devotional Writings* (Lanham, Md: Lexington Books, 2004), 1; John C. Van Horne, ed., *Religious Philanthropy and Colonial Slavery: The American Correspondence of the Associates of Dr. Bray, 1717–1777* (Chicago: University of Illinois Press, 1985), 90.

14. Gundersen, "Anglican Ministry in Virginia," 4.

15. Michael Anesko, "So Discreet a Zeal: Slavery and the Anglican Church in Virginia, 1680–1730," *Virginia Magazine of History and Biography* 93, no. 3 (July 1958): 247–78; Horne, *Religious Philanthropy and Colonial Slavery*, 29, 32; see also Susan Dwyer Amussen, *Caribbean Exchanges: Slavery and the Transformation of English Society, 1640–1700* (Chapel Hill: University of North Carolina Press, 2007), 114–16.

16. Bond, *Spreading the Gospel*, 17–18.

17. Dell Upton, *Holy Things and Profane: Anglican Parish Churches in Colonial Virginia* (New Haven, Conn.: Yale University Press, 1997), 178–81; Fischer, *Albion's Seed*, 339.

18. Upton, *Holy Things and Profane*, 182–83.

19. Linda L. Sturtz, *Within Her Power: Propertied Women in Colonial Virginia* (New York: Routledge, 2002), 5.

20. Cynthia Kierner, *Beyond the Household: Women's Place in the Early South, 1700–1835* (Ithaca, N.Y.: Cornell University Press, 1998), 36–68; Joseph Ball deed, to Rawleigh Chinn, Feb. 12, 1703, Ball Papers, Library of Virginia, Richmond; Sturtz, *Within Her Power*, 3, 29.

21. Tamara Thornton, *Handwriting in America: A Cultural History* (New Haven, Conn.: Yale University Press, 1996), 4–33; Kenneth Lockridge, *Literacy in Colonial New*

England: An Enquiry into the Social Context of Literacy in the Early Modern West (New York: Norton, 1974).

22. Lancaster Wills and Inventories, Joseph Ball, June 5, 1711, 88.

23. Lancaster County Deeds, etc., no. 9, 1701–1715, 163, 245–46.

24. Lancaster County Deeds, 271–73.

25. Jett, *Lancaster County, Virginia*, 79; Felder, *Fielding Lewis and the Washington Family*, 11; Lancaster County Deeds, 247.

26. Horace Hayden, *Virginia Genealogies* (Wilkes-Barre, Pa.: E. B. Yordy, 1891), 64.

27. Kathleen Brown, *Good Wives, Nasty Wenches, and Anxious Patriarchs: Gender, Race, and Power in Colonial Virginia* (Chapel Hill: University of North Carolina Press, 1996), 286.

28. Lancaster Court Records, bk. 3, Nov. 19, 1695, 176, 178.

29. Brown, *Good Wives, Nasty Wenches, and Anxious Patriarchs*, 288–89; Parent, *Foul Means*, 215–16; Jett, *Lancaster County, Virginia*, 64; Sturtz, *Within Her Power*, 29; Lancaster Order Book, 1696–1702, Sept. 1702; Order Book, 1703–1713, April 1712.

30. Lancaster Records Book, 1703–1713, Dec. 1712, 294–99.

31. For an excellent account of the development of this ruling, see Brown, *Good Wives, Nasty Wenches, and Anxious Patriarchs*, 107–36.

32. Lorena Walsh, "'Till Death Do Us Part': Marriage and Family in Seventeenth-Century Maryland," in *The Chesapeake in the Seventeenth Century: Essays on Anglo-American Society*, ed. Thad Tate and David L. Ammerman (Chapel Hill: University of North Carolina Press, 1979), 136–37; Darrett B. Rutman and Anita H. Rutman, "'Now-Wives and Sons-in-Law': Parental Death in a Seventeenth-Century Virginia County," in Tate and Ammerman, *Chesapeake in the Seventeenth Century*, 161–62.

33. *Oxford English Dictionary*.

34. Jennifer Morgan, *Laboring Women: Reproduction and Gender in New World Slavery* (Philadelphia: University of Pennsylvania Press, 2004), 81.

35. Joseph Ball deed to Rawleigh Chinn, Feb. 12, 1703, Ball Family Papers, Library of Virginia.

36. Northumberland County, Va., Court Order Book, pt. 2 (1706–1713), 44, 63, 77, 93, 103, 108, 126.

37. The two meticulous scholars who have studied the question are Jett, *Lancaster County, Virginia*, 59, and Felder, *Fielding Lewis and the Washington Family*, 11–12.

38. Carolyn Jett, "Where Was Mary Ball Washington Born?," *Northern Neck of Virginia Historical Magazine* 51, no. 1 (Dec. 2001): 6062–71; Lancaster Order Books, 1702–1713, for example.

39. Clifford Dowdey, *The Virginia Dynasties: The Emergence of "King" Carter and the Golden Age* (Boston: Little, Brown, 1969), 98.

40. Felder, *Fielding Lewis and the Washington Family*, 10–12; Rutman and Rutman, *Place in Time*, 65–69.

41. Jett, "Where Was Mary Ball Washington Born?," 6068–69.

42. Lorena Walsh, "Urban Amenities and Rural Sufficiency: Living Standards and Consumer Behavior in the Colonial Chesapeake, 1643–1777," *Journal of Economic History* 43, no. 1 (March 1983): 109–17; Keith Thomas, *The Ends of Life: Roads to Fulfillment in Early Modern England* (New York: Oxford University Press, 2009), 118.

43. Conversation with Laura Galke, analyst of small findings at Ferry Farm, Fredericksburg, Va., Oct. 11, 2017.

44. Lancaster Wills and Inventories, Joseph Ball, June 5, 1711, 88; Ann Smart Martin, *Buying into the World of Goods: Early Consumers in Backcountry Virginia* (Baltimore: Johns Hopkins University Press, 2008), 54, 75, 80–81, 184.

45. Martin, *Buying into the World of Goods*, 116; Lois Green Carr and Lorena Walsh, "Economic Diversification and Labor Organization in the Chesapeake, 1650–1820," in *Work and Labor in Early America*, ed. Stephen Innes (Chapel Hill: University of North Carolina Press, 1988), 145–47.

46. Inventory of Joseph Ball, Mary Ball Washington Museum, courtesy of Carolyn Jett.

47. Kevin Sweeney, "High-Style Vernacular: Lifestyles of the Colonial Elite," in *Of Consuming Interests: The Style of Life in the Eighteenth Century*, ed. Cary Carson, Ronald Hoffman, and Peter J. Albert (Charlottesville: University Press of Virginia, 1994), 4.

48. Mary Beth Norton, *Founding Mothers and Fathers: Gendered Power and the Forming of American Society* (New York: Knopf, 1996), 222–24; Rutman and Rutman, *Place in Time*, 179; Jean Towler and Joan Bramall, *Midwives in History and Society* (London: Croom Helm, 1986), 64–98.

49. Nelson, *Blessed Company*, 217; Patrick Henry Butler III, "Knowing the Uncertainties of This Life: Death and Society in Colonial Tidewater Virginia" (Ph.D. diss., Johns Hopkins University, 1998), 46–47; Lauren F. Winner, *A Cheerful and Comfortable Faith: Anglican Religious Practice in the Elite Households of Eighteenth-Century Virginia* (New Haven, Conn.: Yale University Press, 2010), 45; see also Bond, *Spreading the Gospel in Colonial Virginia*, 1, 12–13.

50. Karin Calvert, *Children in the House: The Material Culture of Early Childhood, 1600–1900* (Boston: Northeastern University Press, 1992), 67, 20–27, 35–37; Joseph E. Ilick, "Anglo-American Child-Rearing," in *The History of Childhood*, ed. Lloyd de Mause (New York: Harper Torchbooks, 1974), 307.

51. On nursing and its controversies, see Martha Saxton, *Being Good: Women's Moral Values in Early America* (New York: Hill and Wang, 2003), 271, 370n7; Merril D. Smith, *Women's Roles in Seventeenth-Century America* (Westport, Conn.: Greenwood Press, 2008), 15.

52. Calvert, *Children in the House*, 48–52; Thomas, *Ends of Life*, 89, 93; Saxton, *Being Good*, 100–103.

53. Northumberland (1706–1713), 201; Douglas Southall Freeman, *George Washington: A Biography* (New York: Scribner's, 1948), 1:532; Ida J. Lee, *Abstracts of Lancaster County Wills, 1653–1800* (Richmond: Dietz Press, 1959), 7; Charles Hamrick and Virginia Hamrick, *Northumberland County, Virginia, Court Order Book*, pt. 2 (Athens, Ga.: New Papyrus, 2004), 248, 275, 371, 350, 363; Joseph Ball II's Will, Lancaster Wills no. 10, 1709–1727.

54. See chapter 4 for the story of Easter Ball Chinn.

55. Lucinda M. Becker, *Death and the Early Modern Englishwoman* (Hampshire, U.K.: Ashgate, 2003), 29–33; Joseph Ball's Will, Lancaster Wills, no. 10, 1709–1729.

56. Churchman, *Colonial Churches*, quoted in Winner, *Cheerful and Comfortable Faith*, 99.

57. Joseph Ball Jr. Letterbook, Library of Congress.

58. See Thomas Lacquer, *The Work of the Dead: A Cultural History of Mortal Remains* (Princeton, N.J.: Princeton University Press, 2015), 125–27.

59. John McManners, *Death and the Enlightenment* (New York: Oxford University Press, 1981), 234; Nelson, *Blessed Company*, 227–29; Butler, "Knowing the Uncertainties," 135, 142, 155; Winner, *Cheerful and Comfortable Faith*, 153.

60. Hamrick and Hamrick, *Northumberland County, Virginia, Court Order Book*, pt. 2, Aug. 15, 1711, 371.

61. See Jan Lewis, *The Pursuit of Happiness: Family Values in Jefferson's Virginia* (New York: Cambridge University Press, 1983), 70–76; Nelson, *Blessed Company*, 225–26; Butler, "Knowing the Uncertainties"; Bond, *Spreading the Gospel*, 85–87.

62. On the capacity of contemporary children for understanding death and its attendant anxiety, see Erna Furman, *A Child's Parent Dies: Studies in Childhood Bereavement* (New Haven, Conn.: Yale University Press, 1974), 50–51, 96–97; on the early eighteenth-century attitude toward death, see Daniel Blake Smith, *Inside the Great House: Planter Family Life in Eighteenth Century Chesapeake Society* (Ithaca, N.Y.: Cornell University Press, 1980), 260–70; on the debate about the shift from a focus on death to a focus on the bereaved, see Lawrence Stone, "Death and Its History," *New York Review of Books*, Oct. 12, 1978; Philippe Aries, *Western Attitudes Toward Death from the Middle Ages to the Present* (Baltimore: Johns Hopkins University Press, 1974), 58–60.

2. A GENERATION OF ORPHANS

1. Allan Kulikoff, *Tobacco and Slaves: The Development of Southern Cultures in the Chesapeake, 1680–1800* (Chapel Hill: University of North Carolina Press, 1986), 169–72; Rutman and Rutman, *Place in Time*, 114–20. They use the more conventional definition of "orphan" as the loss of both parents, but the colony could and did intervene at the death of a father.

2. Smith, *Inside the Great House*, 21–22; Charles Taylor, *Sources of the Self: The Making*

of Modern Identity (Cambridge, Mass.: Harvard University Press, 1989), 258, 291; Michael Mascuch, *Origins of the Individualist Self: Autobiography and Self-Identity in England, 1591–1791* (Cambridge, U.K.: Polity Press, 1997), 18–21. Clearly, the emergence of individualism is a lengthy and complex process and varies a great deal by region and according to gender. Historians of the family no longer see the world as either authoritarian and extended or affective and nuclear. Instead, both formations coexisted, and "family" might well mean different things to the same person. Naomi Tadmor, *Family and Friends in Eighteenth-Century England: Household, Kinship, and Patronage* (New York: Cambridge University Press, 2001), 9–11.

3. McManners, *Death and the Enlightenment,* 66, 448.

4. See G. J. Barker-Benfield, *The Culture of Sensibility: Sex and Society in Eighteenth-Century Britain* (Chicago: University of Chicago Press, 1992); Lawrence Stone, *The Family, Sex, and Marriage in England, 1500–1800* (New York: Harper Torchbooks, 1979).

5. Smith, *Inside the Great House,* 22; Dror Wahrman, *The Making of the Modern Self: Identity and Culture in Eighteenth-Century England* (New Haven, Conn.: Yale University Press, 2004), 280–83; Kierner, *Beyond the Household,* 36–42; Brown, *Good Wives, Nasty Wenches, and Anxious Patriarchs,* 247–318.

6. For an example of the birth of the child focusing the attention of an emotionally porous mother, see Lydia Maria Child, *The Mother's Book* (Boston, 1833). For an example of the latter-day version of the same thing, see Erna Furman, "Mothers, Toddlers, and Care," in *The Course of Life,* ed. Stanley I. Greenspan and George H. Pollock (Madison, Conn.: International Universities Press, 1989), 2:61–82; Wahrman, *Making of the Modern Self,* 282–83.

7. See Jan Lewis, "Domestic Tranquillity and the Management of Emotion Among the Gentry of Pre-Revolutionary Virginia," *William and Mary Quarterly,* 3rd ser., 39, no. 1 (Jan. 1982): 135–49.

8. Carole Shammas, *A History of Household Government in America* (Charlottesville: University of Virginia Press, 2002), 24–36; Kulikoff, "Colonial Chesapeake," 534.

9. Freeman, *George Washington,* 1:43.

10. Felder, *Fielding Lewis and the Washington Family,* 12.

11. Lancaster County Wills, no. 10, 1709–1727, June 5, 1711.

12. Jean Butenhoff Lee, "Land and Labor: Parental Bequest Practices in Charles County, Maryland, 1732–1783," in Carr, Morgan, and Russo, *Colonial Chesapeake Society,* 308, 311–14, 328, 331–32, 340; Brown, *Good Wives, Nasty Wenches, and Anxious Patriarchs,* 288.

13. Joseph Ball's Inventory, courtesy of Carolyn Jett, Mary Ball Washington Museum and Library, Lancaster, Va.; Ira Berlin, *Generations of Captivity: A History of African-American Slaves* (Cambridge, Mass.: Harvard University Press, 2003), 61.

14. Philip D. Morgan, *Slave Counterpoint: Black Culture in the Eighteenth-Century Chesa-peake and Low Country* (Chapel Hill: University of North Carolina Press, 1998), 198, 380; Sturtz, *Within Her Power*, 3.

15. Jett, *Lancaster County, Virginia*, 77; Daniel Blake Smith, "Mortality and Family in the Colonial Chesapeake," *Journal of Interdisciplinary History* 8, no. 3 (Winter 1978): 403–27; Rutman and Rutman, *Place in Time*, 179–80; Darrett B. Rutman and Anita H. Rutman, "Of Agues and Fevers: Malaria in the Early Chesapeake," *William and Mary Quarterly*, 3rd ser., 33, no. 1 (Jan. 1976): 31–60.

16. Kulikoff, *Tobacco and Slaves*, 169–73.

17. Ibid., 256, 342, 343; on tithing and tobacco work, see Brown, *Good Wives, Nasty Wenches, and Anxious Patriarchs*, 107–36; on servitude, see David Galenson, *White Servitude in Colonial America: An Economic Analysis* (New York: Cambridge University Press, 1981); T. H. Breen, "Looking Out for Number One: Conflicting Cultural Values in Early Seventeenth-Century Virginia," *South Atlantic Quarterly* 37 (1979): 341–60; Parent, *Foul Means*, 36–39.

18. See, for example, Tatiana Van Riemsdijk, "His Slaves or Hers? Customary Claims, a Planter Marriage, and a Community Verdict in Lancaster County, 1793," *Virginia Magazine of History and Biography* 113, no. 1 (Dec. 2005): 46–79; Parent, *Foul Means*, 107–34; Brown, *Good Wives, Nasty Wenches, and Anxious Patriarchs*, 107–36.

19. Morgan, *Laboring Women*, 111.

20. Kirsten Fischer, *Suspect Relations: Sex, Race, and Resistance in Colonial North Carolina* (Ithaca, N.Y.: Cornell University Press, 2002), 5–7.

21. Lancaster County Records, 1703–1713, Dec. 1711.

22. He had ten in 1710, nine in 1709. Lancaster Records, 1703–1713, Jan. 1708/1709; Dec. 1710.

23. However, in the rice-growing low country of Georgia, Fanny Kemble wrote of seeing slave mothers swaddle their infants. Maria Jenkins Schwartz, *Born in Bondage: Growing Up Enslaved in the Antebellum South* (Cambridge, Mass.: Harvard University Press, 2000), 43, 55, 61.

24. Joseph Ball, Inventory; Joseph Ball Jr. Letterbook, Feb. 1743, Library of Congress.

25. Parent, *Foul Means*, 226; William Hugh Grove Diary, April 1732, Colonial Williamsburg Foundation, microfilm; Morgan, *Slave Counterpoint*, 132.

26. Ball Letterbook, Feb. 1743.

27. Anesko, "So Discreet a Zeal," 247–78; Van Horne, *Religious Philanthropy and Colonial Slavery*, 29, 32; Brown, *Good Wives, Nasty Wenches, and Anxious Patriarchs*, 108, 131, 135–36, 223–25.

28. Susan Westbury, "Slaves of Colonial Virginia: Where They Came From," *William and Mary Quarterly*, 3rd ser., 42, no. 2 (April 1985): 236.

29. Mary V. Thompson, "'They Appear to Live Comfortable Together': Private Lives of the Mount Vernon Slaves," in *Slavery at the Home of George Washington*, ed. Philip J. Schwarz (Mount Vernon, Va.: Mount Vernon Ladies' Association, 2001), 99.

30. Parent, *Foul Means*, 86–89; Allan Kulikoff, "The Origins of Afro-American Society in Tidewater Maryland and Virginia, 1700 to 1790," *William and Mary Quarterly*, 3rd ser., 35, no. 2 (April 1978): 255.

31. Morgan, *Laboring Women*, 69–143.

32. Lancaster County Records, 1703–1713, Dec. 1713, 298.

33. Joseph Ball Jr. Letterbook, Feb. 5 and 19, 1754, Library of Congress; David Dabydeen, *Hogarth's Blacks: Images of Blacks in Eighteenth Century English Art* (Athens: University of Georgia Press, 1987), 21–28.

34. Thomas Jefferson, *Notes on the State of Virginia*, in *The Life and Selected Writings of Thomas Jefferson*, ed. Adrienne Koch and William Peden (New York: Random House, 1944), 278.

35. Ibid., 279; Joseph Ball, Inventory; Berlin, *Generations of Captivity*, 2–3, 61; Marion Tinling and Louis Wright, eds., *The Secret Diary of William Byrd of Westover, 1709–1712* (Richmond, Va.: Dietz Press, 1941), 199.

3. BRUISING THE SMALL SPIRIT

1. Matthew Hale, *Contemplations Moral and Divine* (London: William Goodbid, 1676), 195.

2. Also given as Hews or Hewes.

3. This according to the 1751 map made by Peter Jefferson, Thomas's father. The Jefferson-Fry map of 1750 placed Cherry Point on the Chesapeake Bay at the southern lip of the Rappahannock River.

4. Northumberland Order Book, pt. 2, 44, 62, 63, 77, 84, 93, 103, 108, 126, 127, 157, 179, 298; Rutman and Rutman, *Place in Time*, 144–46; Lancaster Order Book, 1703–1713, Dec. 1712.

5. Rutman and Rutman, *Place in Time*, 152.

6. Carr and Walsh, "Economic Diversification and Labor Organization in the Chesapeake," 158–60; Lancaster Court Records, 1713–1722, Nov. 14, 1716, *James Ball and Rawleigh Chinn v. Heale*.

7. Brown, *Good Wives, Nasty Wenches, and Anxious Patriarchs*, 197–98.

8. Lancaster Order Book, 1703–1712, Dec. 1712, 1713–1721, July 8, 1713, Aug. 1713.

9. Coverture meant that once married, a woman had no legal identity separate from her husband. He owned her property and anything she earned, had rights to her sexually and to her labor, and was legal guardian of their children.

10. Sturtz, *Within Her Power*, 20–21.

11. Charlotte Richardson Swift, "Elizabeth Johnson," *Bulletin of the Northumberland County Historical Society* 19 (1982): 49; in other court records, one Ellen or Eleanor Garvey appears as the sometime servant of Richard Hughes, and local planters were competing with one another to put her into their service. Cranford and Garvey might have been the same woman. Garvey "absented" herself from Hughes, who, when she was apprehended, was paid five hundred pounds of tobacco of her resale price of twenty-five hundred pounds of tobacco, "which was the most anyone would give for her as was lawfull." Lancaster County Order Book, 1713–1721, Nov. 14, 1716.

12. Brown, *Good Wives, Nasty Wenches, and Anxious Patriarchs*, 197–98; Lancaster County Records, 1703–1713, May 14, 1712.

13. Joseph Ball's will.

14. Lancaster Order Book, 1703–1712, Dec. 1712; Lancaster Order Book, 1713–1721, Aug. 1713, Nov. 1713, Jan. 1714, March–April 1714, June 1714, Dec. 1712.

15. There was a legal dispute with a Joseph Ball later, but I believe it was the other Joseph Ball who lived in Lancaster County, not Mary Hughes's stepson-in-law (Northumberland Record Book, 1713–1719, 108); in this I differ with Felder, "World of Mary Washington"; Swift, "Elizabeth Johnson," 51.

16. Charles Willard Hoskins Warner, "George Eskridge of Westmoreland: His Age and Political Career," *Northern Neck of Virginia Historical Magazine* (1966): 1457.

17. *Journals of the House of Burgesses of Virginia*, 5:205.

18. Berlin, *Generations of Captivity*, 55–56; Rutman and Rutman, *Place in Time*, 173–74; Marion Tinling, ed., *The Correspondence of the Three William Byrds of Westover, Virginia, 1684–1776* (Charlottesville: University Press of Virginia, 1977), 2:488.

19. Kulikoff, "Origins of Afro-American Society in Tidewater Maryland and Virginia," 230, 245; Westbury, "Slaves of Colonial Virginia," 233.

20. Thomas D. Morris, *Southern Slavery and the Law, 1619–1860* (Chapel Hill: University of North Carolina Press, 1996), 231–33; Rutman and Rutman, *Place in Time*, 173–74.

21. Roeber, "Authority, Law, and Custom," 50.

22. See Morgan, *Slave Counterpoint*, 414–15, for the fear and hatred planters had of poor whites and blacks mixing; Northumberland Order Book, pt. 2, 447–50, 454–57, 461, 463.

23. Brown, *Good Wives, Nasty Wenches, and Anxious Patriarchs*, 290.

24. Ibid., 474.

25. Lancaster Court Order Book, 1713–1721, Nov. 1716.

26. Swift, "Elizabeth Johnson," 49.

27. Rutman and Rutman, "'Now-Wives and Sons-in-Law,'" 166.

28. Kenneth A. Lockridge, *The Diary and Life of William Byrd II of Virginia, 1674–1744* (New York: Norton, 1987), 55–58; Vivian Fox and Martin Quitt, *Loving, Parenting, and Dying* (New York: Psychohistory Press, 1980), 284–86; Nelson, *Blessed Company*, 225–27.

29. Rutman and Rutman, "'Now-Wives and Sons-in-Law,'" 168–69.

30. Richard Allestree, *The Whole Duty of Mourning*, quoted in Winner, *Cheerful and Comfortable Faith*, 151.

31. Bertram Wyatt-Brown, *Southern Honor: Ethics and Behavior in the Old South* (New York: Oxford University Press, 1982), 129–38.

32. Lancaster Court Order Book, 1714–1724, Oct. 1723.

33. Northumberland Record Book, 1718–1726, 38, 46, 53–54, 58, 60, 91, 105, 108.

34. There is disagreement between Timothy Breen's account (seeds in December or January) and that of Thomas Jefferson, who says the seeds went in in April. Thomas Jefferson, *The Papers of Thomas Jefferson*, ed. Julian Boyd (Princeton, N.J.: Princeton University Press, 1953), 7:209–12.

35. Carr and Walsh, "Economic Diversification and Labor Organization in the Chesapeake," 150–51; T. H. Breen, *Tobacco Culture: The Mentality of the Great Tidewater Planters on the Eve of the Revolution* (Princeton, N.J.: Princeton University Press, 1985), 47–51.

36. Breen, *Tobacco Culture*, 53–55; Jefferson, *Papers of Thomas Jefferson*, 7:109–12.

37. Sharon Kettering, "The Historical Development of Political Clientelism," *Journal of Interdisciplinary History* 18, no. 3 (Winter 1988): 425.

38. Thornton, *Handwriting in America*, 7.

39. See Saxton, *Being Good*, 107–13, for a description of the kind of education that prepared girls to perform in this way; Thornton, *Handwriting in America*, 8.

40. Thornton, *Handwriting in America*, 35–41.

41. Smith, *Inside the Great House*, 65–81; Saxton, *Being Good*, 114–21.

42. Sturtz, *Within Her Power*, 89–110.

43. Wyatt-Brown, *Southern Honor*, 232–33.

44. Motley Booker and James F. Lewis, "Cox's Old Place Now Yeocomico View Farm in Cherry Point," *Bulletin of the Northumberland County Historical Society* 21 (Dec. 1984): 45.

45. Swift, "Elizabeth Johnson," 52; Walsh, "'Till Death Do Us Part,'" 131.

46. Swift, "Elizabeth Johnson," 52.

47. Northumberland Record Book, 1718–1726, 177.

48. For this conclusion, see Northumberland County, Va., Order Book, 1719–1729, 42. "John Johnson deceased did by his last will and testament constitute his Mother Mary Hughes executor, dec'd before him."

49. See chapter 4 for more on Mary's riding.

50. Morgan, *Laboring Women*, 86–95.

51. Swift, "Elizabeth Johnson," 51.

52. Freeman, *George Washington*, 1:44–45; Felder, *Fielding Lewis and the Washington Family*, 12–14.

53. Smith, "Mortality and Family in the Colonial Chesapeake," 421.

54. Rutman and Rutman, "'Now-Wives and Sons-in-Law,'" 168.

55. Colin Murray Parkes, *Bereavement: Studies of Grief in Adult Life* (Madison, Conn.: International Universities Press, 1987), 141, 153; Felder, *Fielding Lewis and the Washington Family*, 14.

56. Lois Green Carr and Lorena Walsh, "Changing Lifestyles and Consumer Behavior in the Colonial Chesapeake," in Carson, Hoffman, and Albert, *Of Consuming Interests*, 129; Sweeney, "High-Style Vernacular," 2–3.

57. Rutman and Rutman, "'Now-Wives and Sons-in-Law,'" 162.

58. Ball Letterbook, [May?] 1745.

59. Lancaster Order Book, 1721–1729, Jan. 1722/1723, Oct. 9, 1723.

60. For example, see note 4 in chapter 18 below.

61. Furman, *Child's Parent Dies*, 96–97.

62. Freeman, *George Washington*, 1:45n176.

63. Ella Bassett Washington, "The Mother and Birthplace of Washington," *Century Magazine* 43 (April 1892): 838.

4. MARY, HER KIN, AND HER BOOKS

1. W. W. Abbot, ed., *The Papers of George Washington*, Presidential Series (Charlottesville: University Press of Virginia, 1987), 9:130.

2. Fischer, *Albion's Seed*, 273–74.

3. Hayden, *Virginia Genealogies*, 77.

4. Bell to Gibson (response no. 46 to survey of colonial ministers), Bishop Edmund Gibson Papers, Lambeth Palace Library, London.

5. Gundersen, "Anglican Ministry in Virginia," 35.

6. Ibid., 5, 7, 22, 35; Nelson, *Blessed Company*, 122–27; Bond, *Spreading the Gospel*, 15, 24.

7. Dates for Joseph Ball's transatlantic crossings are confusing. Two sources include Hayden, *Virginia Genealogies*, and David E. Masnata Jr., *Colonel William Ball of Lancaster County, Virginia, and His Descendants* (New York, 1966), but both seem to have inaccuracies. I try to rely on court and church records to establish his presence in Virginia. A problem is the existence of another Joseph Ball as well as Major James Ball. E. Alfred Jones, *American Members of the Inns of Court* (London, 1924).

8. Hayden, *Virginia Genealogies*, 64.

9. Elizabeth Combs Peirce, "The Unhappy Life of Esther Ball, Half Sister of Mary Ball and Wife of Rawleigh Chinn, Gent.," *William and Mary Quarterly*, 2nd ser.,

18, no. 4 (Oct. 1938): 294–96; Southall, *George Washington*, 1:532–33; W. Preston Haynie, "Marital Discord, Separate Maintenance, and Divorce," *Bulletin of the Northumberland County Historical Society* 31 (1994): 75–84.

10. James Gordon, "Journal of Col. James Gordon," *William and Mary Quarterly* 11, no. 4 (April 1903): 217.

11. Brown, *Good Wives, Nasty Wenches, and Anxious Patriarchs*, 336–38; Susan Dwyer Amussen, "Punishment, Discipline, and Power: The Social Meaning of Violence in Early Modern England," *Journal of British Studies* 34, no. 1 (Jan. 1995): 1–34; Susan Dwyer Amussen, "'Being Stirred to Much Unquietness': Violence and Domestic Violence in Early Modern England," *Journal of Women's History* 6, no. 2 (Summer 1994): 70–89; Christine Daniels and Michael V. Kennedy, eds., *Over the Threshold: Intimate Violence in Early America* (New York: Routledge, 1999), 3–21; Thomas Buckley, *The Great Catastrophe of My Life: Divorce in the Old Dominion* (Chapel Hill: University of North Carolina Press, 2002), 7–8, 16, 17.

12. Daniels and Kennedy, *Over the Threshold*, 6, 8.

13. Brown, *Good Wives, Nasty Wenches, and Anxious Patriarchs*, 145–49.

14. Amussen, "Punishment, Discipline, and Power," 34.

15. Beverly Fleet, *Abstracts* (Baltimore: Genealogical Publishing Company, 1988), 411.

16. Gail Kern Paster, *The Body Embarrassed: Drama and Discipline of Shame in Early Modern England* (Ithaca, N.Y.: Cornell University Press, 1993), 183.

17. Ibid., 171, 172–95.

18. What writing there was, like the Puritan Anne Bradstreet's works, treated childbirth as miserable and shameful:

> *Conceived in sin and born with sorrow,*
> *Whose mean beginning blushing can't reveal,*
> *But night and darkness must with shame conceal.*
> *My mother's breeding sickness I will spare,*
> *Her nine months weary burden not declare.*
> *To shew her bearing pains, I should do wrong,*
> *To tell those pangs which can't be told by tongue.*

Anne Bradstreet, *The Works of Anne Bradstreet in Prose and Verse*, ed. John Harvard Ellis (Charlestown, Mass., 1867), 149–50; Saxton, *Being Good*, 78–79.

19. David Cressy, "Purification, Thanksgiving, and the Churching of Women in Post-Reformation England," *Past and Present*, no. 141 (Nov. 1993): 110.

20. Nelson, *Blessed Company*, 257–58.

21. Fleet, *Abstracts*, 411.

22. *Deed & Will Abstracts of Westmoreland County, Virginia, 1726–1729*, ed. Ruth Sparacio and Sam Sparacio (McLean, Va.: Ancient Press, 1994), 10; Swift, "Elizabeth Johnson," 52.

23. Felder, "World of Mary Washington," chap. 4; Samuel Bonam's will, in Sparacio and Sparacio, *Deed Will Abstracts of Westmoreland County, Virginia, 1726–1729*, 10; Holly G. Wright and F. Edward Wright, *Colonial Families of Northern Neck Virginia* (Lewes, Del.: Colonial Roots, 2005), 1:85.

24. Julia Cherry Spruill, *Women's Life and Work in the Southern Colonies* (1938; New York: Norton, 1972), 108–9.

25. Wm. J. Hinke, "Report of the Journey of Francis Louis Michel from Berne, Switzerland, to Virginia, October 2, 1701–December 1, 1702," *Virginia Magazine of History and Biography* 24, no. 1 (Jan. 1916): 36.

26. Devereux Jarratt, *The Life of the Reverend Devereux Jarratt, Rector of Bath Parish, Dinwiddie County, Virginia* (Baltimore: Warner and Hannah, 1806), 20, 26.

27. T. H. Breen, "Horses and Gentlemen: The Cultural Significance of Gambling Among the Gentry of Virginia," *William and Mary Quarterly*, 3rd ser., 34, no. 2 (April 1977): 249.

28. Fairfax Harrison, "The Equine FFVs," *Virginia Magazine of History and Biography* 35, no. 4 (1927): 332, 342, 336.

29. Alexander Mackay-Smith, Jean R. Druesedow, and Thomas Ryder, *Man and the Horse: An Illustrated History of Equestrian Apparel* (New York: Metropolitan Museum of Art and Simon & Schuster, 1984), 59–60.

30. Nancy L. Struna, "Sport and the Awareness of Leisure," in Carson, Hoffman, and Albert, *Of Consuming Interests*, 416.

31. Harrison, "Equine FFVs," 331.

32. Jane Carson, *Colonial Virginians at Play* (Williamsburg: Colonial Williamsburg, 1965, distributed by University Press of Virginia), 105–32; Billings, *Old Dominion in the Seventeenth Century*, 388; Hinke, "Report of the Journey of Francis Louis Michel," 36; Spruill, *Women's Life and Work*, 88–89.

33. Carson, *Colonial Virginians at Play*, 112–13.

34. Paul Longmore, *The Invention of George Washington* (Berkeley: University of California Press, 1988), 182.

35. Carson, *Colonial Virginians at Play*, 22–23.

36. Kevin Hayes, *A Colonial Woman's Bookshelf* (Knoxville: University of Tennessee Press, 1996), 28–57 on devotional reading for women and 58–79 on conduct books.

37. Kevin Hayes, *The Library of William Byrd of Westover* (Madison, Wis.: Madison House, 1997), 353; Louis B. Wright, ed., *The Letters of Robert Carter, 1720–1727: The Commercial Interests of a Virginia Gentleman* (San Marino, Calif.: Huntington Library, 1940).

38. John Scott, *The Christian Life, from Its Beginning, to Its Consummation in Glory* (London, 1757), 289.

39. See Saxton, *Being Good*, 107–13.

40. For a discussion of the implications of the reading experience that the novel offered, see Cathy Davidson, *Revolution and the Word: The Rise of the Novel in America* (New York: Oxford University Press, 1986).

41. Hayes, *Colonial Woman's Bookshelf*, 33.

42. Ibid., 47.

43. George Washington Parke Custis, *Recollections and Private Memoirs of Washington by His Adopted Son*, ed. Benson J. Lossing (New York: Derby and Jackson, 1860), 141.

44. Scott, *Christian Life*, 266, 269, 203–4.

45. Kevin R. Hardwick, "Mirrors for Their Sons: A History of Genteel Ethics in England and Virginia, 1500–1750" (Ph.D. diss., University of Maryland, College Park, 1997), 240–42.

46. Scott, *Christian Life*, 79.

47. Bond, *Spreading the Gospel*, 65.

48. Mary V. Thompson, *"In the Hands of a Good Providence": Religion in the Life of George Washington* (Charlottesville: University of Virginia Press, 2008), 21–22.

49. Almost all divines supported the stratified social system as it was, teaching the faithful to embrace it and make the best of it. Thomas, *Ends of Life*, 17–20.

50. Scott, *Christian Life*, 137.

51. Ibid., 166.

52. Ibid., 149.

53. Ibid., 236, 278.

54. Joseph Ball Letterbook, Feb. 18, 1743.

55. Keith Thomas notes that Max Weber was wrong in arguing that it was Puritans that gave the benediction to a life of business. Like Anglicans, they saw business as potentially one of many callings but not a substitute for charity, merely a way to fulfill one's obligations to God (*Ends of Life*, 142–44). Ira Berlin makes this important distinction in *Many Thousands Gone: The First Two Centuries of Slavery in North America* (Cambridge, Mass.: Harvard University Press, 1998).

56. Upton, *Holy Things and Profane*, xxi; Scott, *Christian Life*, 276.

5. MARY BALL, AUGUSTINE WASHINGTON, AND MATTHEW HALE

1. Augusta B. Fothergill, *Wills of Westmoreland County, Virginia, 1654–1800* (Baltimore: Genealogical Publishing Company, 1973), 19.

2. Ibid., 65.

3. Whitehaven Records, 66, 69, Cumbria Record Office and Local Studies Library, www.cumbria.gov.uk.archives.

4. Compare Freeman, *George Washington*, 1:33, Clifford Dowdey, *The Virginia Dynasties* (Boston: Little, Brown, 1969), 343, and Smith, *Inside the Great House*, 127, on majority.

5. Freeman, *George Washington*, 1:34–35.

6. Kettering, "Historical Development of Political Clientelism," 425; see also Thomas, *Ends of Life*, 187–214.

7. Freeman, *George Washington*, 1:41; Westmoreland Order Book, 1721–1731, 66.

8. Westmoreland Order Book, 1721–1731, 88.

9. Gertrude E. Gray, *Virginia Northern Neck Land Grants, 1694–1742* (Baltimore: Genealogical Publishing Company, 1987), 2:84.

10. Ibid., 98, 102; Westmoreland County Deeds and Wills, 1723–1738, bk. 8 (McLean, Va., 1994), 26, 45; *Deed & Will Abstracts of Westmoreland County, 1729–1732*, ed. Ruth Sparacio and Sam Sparacio (McLean, Va., 1995), 51, 79–80, 86.

11. *Journals of the House of Burgesses of Virginia, 1727–1734*, 6:52.

12. Warner, "George Eskridge of Westmoreland," 1462.

13. Wright and Wright, *Colonial Families of Northern Neck Virginia*, 1:16–17, 118.

14. *Journals of the House of Burgesses*, 6:10; Charles Sydnor, *American Revolutionaries in the Making* (New York: Free Press, 1965), 32.

15. *Journals of the House of Burgesses*, 6:10.

16. *Abstracts of Westmoreland Co.*, bk. 15, 38–39.

17. Westmoreland County Deeds and Wills, 1723–1738, 8.

18. See Kenneth Lockridge, *On the Sources of Patriarchal Rage* (New York: New York University Press, 1992), for the many challenges to patriarchy.

19. Earl Chapin May, *Principio to Wheeling, 1715–1945: A Pageant of Iron and Steel* (New York: Harper Brothers, 1945), 30–31.

20. Ibid., 40–43.

21. Freeman, *George Washington*, 1:41.

22. Ibid.

23. See Steven Mintz, *Huck's Raft: A History of American Childhood* (Cambridge, Mass.: Harvard University Press, 2004). Some scholars say eighteen was normal for native-born women, unlike servants like Mary's mother, who married later. Other scholars put the age at twenty in Maryland in the late seventeenth century; see Rutman and Rutman, "'Now-Wives and Sons-in-Law,'" 158. Another says the age difference was significant, with husbands usually ten years older than brides. Fischer, *Albion's Seed*, 284–85.

24. Washington, "Mother and Birthplace of Washington."

25. Saxton, *Being Good*, 29–35, 113–14; Roger Thompson, *Women in Stuart England and America: A Comparative Study* (Boston: Routledge and Kegan Paul, 1974), 117–31; Spruill, *Women's Life and Work*, 136–62.

26. Scott, *Christian Life*, 6, 369.

27. Nicole Eustace, *Passion Is the Gale: Emotion, Power, and the Making of the American Revolution* (Chapel Hill: University of North Carolina Press, 2008), 3–59;

Martha Tomhave Blauvelt, *The Work of the Heart: Young Women and Emotion, 1780–1830* (Charlottesville: University of Virginia Press, 2007), 86–87.

28. Walsh, "'Till Death Do Us Part,'" 129.

29. Robert K. Headley Jr., *Married Well and Often: Marriages of the Northern Neck of Virginia, 1649–1800* (Baltimore: Genealogical Publishing Company, 2003), 394.

30. Fischer, *Albion's Seed*, 284.

31. Felder, "World of Mary Washington."

32. Fischer, *Albion's Seed*, 282.

33. The Reverend Walter Jones was married to the daughter of the wealthy parishioner Thomas Newton. Eskridge's daughter Sarah was married to Newton's son, who was the brother of Jones's wife. These (dizzying) interrelations make the likelihood of Jones's officiating very high. Lucy Brown Beale, "The Early Clergy of Cople Parish and the Marriage of Augustine Washington and Mary Ball," *Northern Neck of Virginia Historical Magazine* 18, no. 1 (Dec. 1986): 1746.

34. Ibid., 100; Carson, *Colonial Virginians at Play*, 12–24.

35. Lawrence Washington, Will, June 20, 1752, mourning ring to his wife and "mother-in-law." "Stepmother" is the second meaning of mother-in-law in the seventeenth through nineteenth centuries, and Lawrence's wife's mother, Sarah Walker Fairfax, died in 1731, and her stepmother, Deborah Clark Fairfax, was also dead. Helen Bryan, *Martha Washington: First Lady of Liberty* (New York: Wiley and Sons, 2002), 103; *OED*; Mary Washington, Will, May 20, 1788.

36. Her mother left her two gold rings, a hoop and another with a stone in it. In Mary's will, she left her clothing to her granddaughters, leaving her daughter, Betty, the choice of up to three things first if she desired. She received one ring with a lock of his hair from the estate of Lawrence Washington, her stepson who predeceased her by decades, so it was not one of these, one of which seems to have been her mother's.

37. Taylor, *Sources of the Self*, 5.

38. Hale, *Contemplations Moral and Divine*, 16.

39. On the consumer revolution that affected the colonies, see Richard Bushman, *The Refinement of America: Persons, Houses, Cities* (New York: Knopf, 1992); T. H. Breen, *The Marketplace of Revolution* (New York: Oxford University Press, 2004).

40. Custis, *Recollections and Private Memoirs*, 137.

6. WIFE AND MOTHER

1. Seth Bruggeman, *Here, George Washington Was Born: Memory, Material Culture, and the Public History of a National Monument* (Athens: University of Georgia Press, 2008), 95–98. After Mary and Augustine moved out, the Pope's Creek house came into the hands of one and then another of George's brothers, and it burned

in 1778. George later referred to it as the ancient mansion seat, leading historians to assume it was imposing. On the basis of the (imperfect) memory of George
Washington Parke Custis, Martha Washington's grandson, the WPA built a two-
story wooden house with five dormer windows described as a replica of George's
birthplace in 1926–1930, on the foundation of an outbuilding that turns out to
have been about fifty feet north from where archaeologists now believe the house
actually sat. Archaeologists have since discovered a number of outbuildings including a still, and one of these was the foundation for the misplaced reconstructed
house. There are currently new plans for the construction of a home that will more
accurately represent George's birthplace.

2. Winner, *Cheerful and Comfortable Faith*, 135–39.
3. Keith Thomas, *Man and the Natural World: A History of the Modern Sensibility* (New
   York: Pantheon, 1983), 76, 147.
4. Quoted in Rutman and Rutman, "'Now-Wives and Sons-in-Law,'" 168.
5. Glymph, *Out of the House of Bondage*, 72–73.
6. Inventory of Ferry Farm at the time of Augustine's death in 1743, www.kenmore
   .org.
7. Catherine Scholten, *Childbearing in American Society, 1650–1850* (New York: New
   York University Press, 1985), 13; see Mintz, *Huck's Raft*, 42–43, for a chilling discussion of slave children's health and work vulnerabilities.
8. Joseph Ball Letterbook, Library of Congress.
9. Sarah Hand Meacham, "'They Will Be Adjudged by Their Drinke, What Kind
   of Housewives They Are': Gender, Technology, and Household Cidering in
   England and the Chesapeake, 1690 to 1760," in *Colonial Chesapeake: New Perspec-
   tives*, ed. Debra Meyers and Melanie Perreault (Lanham, Md.: Lexington Books,
   2006), 213, 219.
10. Ibid., 203–4.
11. Joseph Ball's Will, Lancaster Wills no. 10, 1709–1727.
12. Thanks to Mary V. Thompson for the charming word "perry."
13. Anthony Fletcher, *Gender, Sex, and Subordination in England, 1500–1800* (New
    Haven, Conn.: Yale University Press, 1995), 46.
14. Ibid., 46–57.
15. Elizabeth Garrett, *At Home: The American Family, 1750–1870* (New York: Harry N.
    Abrams, 1989), 230.
16. Kathleen Brown, *Foul Bodies: Cleanliness in Early America* (New Haven, Conn.: Yale
    University Press, 2008), 228–36, 142.
17. Scholten, *Childbearing in American Society*, 14.
18. Jan Lewis and Kenneth Lockridge, "Sally Has Been Sick," *Journal of Social
    History* 22, no. 1 (Oct. 1988): 5–19.
19. Scholten, *Childbearing in American Society*, 13.

20. Ibid., 11; Jon Kukla, *Mr. Jefferson's Women* (New York: Knopf, 2007).

21. Fischer, *Albion's Seed*, 305.

22. Ibid., 11.

23. Ibid., 22.

24. Spruill, *Women's Life and Work*, 50–51.

25. Scholten, *Childbearing in American Society*, 20.

26. Winner, *Cheerful and Comfortable Faith*, 133.

27. Brown, *Good Wives, Nasty Wenches, and Anxious Patriarchs*, 302–5.

28. Scholten, *Childbearing in American Society*, 26–27.

29. Spruill, *Women's Life and Work*, 50; Garrett, *At Home*, 229.

30. His original birthdate was given as February 11, 1731 or 1732, but with the slow changeover from the Julian to the Gregorian calendar, which shortened the year slightly to make dates conform better to the equinoxes and solstices, two dates were typically given (Old Style and New Style). The year began on different days depending on which calendar one used.

31. Fischer, *Albion's Seed*, 306–8.

32. Scholten, *Childbearing in American Society*, 27–28.

33. Nelson, *Blessed Company*, 258; Thomas Comber, *Short Discourses upon the Whole Common-Prayer* (London, 1684), 450–51.

34. Nelson, *Blessed Company*, 258; Comber, *Short Discourses upon the Whole Common-Prayer*, 450–51.

35. Cressy, "Purification, Thanksgiving, and the Churching of Women in Post-Reformation England," 144.

36. Comber, *Short Discourses upon the Whole Common-Prayer*, 450–51.

37. John Washington to Captain Whiting, July 12, 1744, Morristown, N.J.

38. I am most grateful to Laura Simo, associate curator at Mount Vernon, for showing me a fragment taken from the lining of the robe.

39. Seven months seems to have been common. The Reverend Robert Rose noted that he and his wife weaned their daughter at seven months on May 11, 1750. See Ralph Emmett Fall, ed., *The Diary of Robert Rose: A View of Virginia by a Scottish Colonial Parson, 1746–1751* (Falls Church, Va.: McClure Press, 1977), 66, 79.

40. Walter Jones to Bishop Edmund Gibson, 1733, no. 199–200, Gibson Papers.

41. Calvert, *Children in the House*, 42.

42. Jeanne Abrams, *Revolutionary Medicine: The Founding Fathers and Mothers in Sickness and in Health* (New York: New York University Press, 2013), 35.

43. Freeman, *George Washington*, 1:55–57.

44. Ibid., 53.

45. May, *Principio to Wheeling*, 15.

46. Ibid., 33–43.

47. Thomas, *Ends of Life*, 190.

48. Laurel Thatcher Ulrich's term for women doing their husband's business. *Good Wives: Image and Reality in the Lives of Women in Northern New England* (New York: Random House, 1982).

49. Freeman, *George Washington*, 1:57.

50. Ibid., 56.

51. Fletcher, *Gender, Sex, and Subordination in England*, 307, 310.

52. Ibid., 307.

53. Mason Locke Weems, *The Life of Washington* (Armonk, N.Y.: M. E. Sharpe, 1996), 45.

54. Jean B. Lee, "Mount Vernon Plantation: A Model for the Republic," in Schwarz, *Slavery at the Home of George Washington*, 20.

55. Saxton, *Being Good*, 102.

56. Thompson, "'They Appear to Live Comfortable Together,'" 87.

57. Mechal Sobel, *The World They Made Together: Black and White Values in Eighteenth-Century Virginia* (Princeton, N.J.: Princeton University Press, 1987), 86.

58. Freeman, *George Washington*, 1:59.

59. Lawrence Washington to Augustine, May 30, 1741, in *The Magazine of American History with Notes and Queries* (New York: A. S. Barnes, 1878), 2:435–37.

60. Burgess Ball Jr. to his father, Sept. 9, 1793, Ball Family Papers, Library of Virginia.

61. Fischer, *Albion's Seed*, 314–15.

62. Saxton, *Being Good*, 156–59.

63. Fletcher, *Gender, Sex, and Subordination in England*, 308.

64. Thompson, *"In the Hands of a Good Providence,"* 15–17.

65. Jane Taylor Duke, *Kenmore and the Lewises* (Garden City, N.Y.: Doubleday, 1949), 19–20.

66. Washington, "Mother and Birthplace of Washington," 837.

67. Custis, *Recollections and Private Memoirs*, 131; thanks to Laura Galke, analyst of small findings at Ferry Farm, for emphasizing this point in her talk on Mary Ball Washington, "The Mother of the Father of Our Country," on the Ferry Farm website: www.kenmore.org/ff_home.html; Peter Henriques, "'Honored Madam': George Washington's Complicated Relationship with His Mother, Mary Ball Washington," courtesy of the author.

68. James Gordon, "Journal of Col. James Gordon of Lancaster County, Va.," *William and Mary Quarterly* 11, no. 2 (Oct. 1902): 108, and *William and Mary Quarterly* 11, no. 3 (Jan. 1903): 204.

69. Thena S. Jones, "Reconstructing the Washington Farm and the Catlett Patent," May 1, 1993, unpublished paper, 1–2.

70. Freeman, *George Washington*, 1:57–59.

7. PEOPLE AND PROPERTY AT FERRY FARM

1. Based on the reconstruction and discussion of Ferry Farm under the supervision of its chief archaeologist, David Muraca. Visit Oct. 11, 2017.
2. Laura Galke, "The Mother of the Father of Our Country: Genteel Domestic Habits," *Northwest Historical Archaeology* 38 (2009): 29.
3. Six others sprang up in the eighteenth century. Oscar Darter, *Colonial Fredericksburg and Neighborhood in Perspective* (New York: Twayne, 1957), 21.
4. Because furniture specialists believe the chair could not have been made earlier than just before Augustine's death, it is unclear if he or someone else bought it. There is a note in George Washington's account with his mother for October 1773 for a "Chair of Mr. Todd" for forty pounds. Mary might have purchased it against money that would come to her from George's rental of her slaves and land after she moved into Fredericksburg in 1772. Mary Washington's account with George Washington, Gratz Collection, case 1, box 31, Historical Society of Pennsylvania, Philadelphia.
5. Carr and Walsh, "Changing Lifestyles and Consumer Behavior in the Colonial Chesapeake," 59–69.
6. Carol Borchert Cadou, *The George Washington Collection: Fine and Decorative Arts at Mount Vernon* (Manchester, Vt.: Hudson Hills Press, 2006), 266; Carr and Walsh, "Changing Lifestyles and Consumer Behavior in the Colonial Chesapeake," 103.
7. Dave Muraca, chief archaeologist at Ferry Farm.
8. Galke, "Mother of the Father of Our Country," 37.
9. David Muraca, chief archaeologist at Ferry Farm.
10. Laura Galke, "Wigs: Their History in British North America," courtesy of the author; Kierner, *Beyond the Household*, 22.
11. William Hugh Grove, "Virginia in 1732: The Travel Journal of William Hugh Grove," ed. Gregory Stiverson and Patrick Butler III, *Virginia Magazine of History and Biography* 84, no. 1 (Jan. 1977): 29.
12. Lorena Walsh, "The Chesapeake Slave Trade: Regional Patterns, African Origins, and Some Implications," *William and Mary Quarterly*, 3rd ser., 58, no. 1 (Jan. 2001): 145, 147, 149, 152–53.
13. Lorena Walsh, "Summing the Parts: Implications for Estimating Chesapeake Output and Income Subregionally," *William and Mary Quarterly*, 3rd ser., 56, no. 1 (Jan. 1999): 60.
14. "Inventory of Ferry Farm at the Time of Augustine's Death in 1743," www .kenmore.org/genealogy/washington/probate.html.
15. Laura Galke, analyst of small findings at Ferry Farm, letter, Dec. 4, 2017; Sobel, *World They Made Together*, 112–26; Morgan, *Slave Counterpoint*, 110.
16. Personal information from David Muraca, chief archaeologist at Ferry Farm; Morgan, *Slave Counterpoint*, 116.
17. Joseph Ball to Joseph Chinn, Ball Letterbook.

18. Some privileged slaves elsewhere did have locks, but it was rare. Morgan, *Slave Counterpoint*, 113–14.

19. Schwarz, *Slavery at the Home of George Washington*, 116; Walsh, "Chesapeake Slave Trade," 145, 147, 149, 152–53. As late as 1761, Colonel James Gordon wrote of a "Guineau man coming in with about 140 slaves" directly on the Rappahannock. Gordon, "Journal of Col. James Gordon," *William and Mary Quarterly* 11, no. 4 (April 1903), 220.

20. John Mbiti, *African Religions and Philosophy* (Garden City, N.Y.: Doubleday, 1970), 154.

21. Jerome Handler and JoAnn Jacoby, "Slave Names and Naming in Barbados, 1650–1830," *William and Mary Quarterly*, 3rd ser., 53, no. 4 (Oct. 1996): 693; Sobel, *World They Made Together*, 154–58.

22. David Muraca, chief archaeologist at Ferry Farm, personal information, July 31, 2008; Jerome Handler and Frederick Lange, *Plantation Slavery in Barbados: An Archaeological and Historical Investigation* (Cambridge, Mass.: Harvard University Press, 1978), 147, 149–50; Anne Elizabeth Yentsch, *A Chesapeake Family and Their Slaves: A Study in Historical Archaeology* (New York: Cambridge University Press, 1994), 194.

23. Akinwumi Ogundiran, "Of Small Things Remembered: Beads, Cowries, and Cultural Translations of the Atlantic Experience in Yorubaland," *International Journal of African Historical Studies* 35, no. 2–3 (2002): 455.

24. Muraca, personal information; Schwarz, *Slavery at the Home of George Washington*, 116.

25. Handler, *Plantation Slavery in Barbados*, 199–201.

26. Grove, "Travel Journal," *Virginia Magazine of History and Biography* 85, no. 1 (Jan. 1977): 31.

27. Lorena S. Walsh, "Slavery and Agriculture at Mount Vernon," in Schwarz, *Slavery at the Home of George Washington*, 71.

28. Donald Wax, "Preferences for Slaves in Colonial America," *Journal of Negro History* 58, no. 4 (Oct. 1973): 391–96.

29. Ibid., 397.

8. "AS SPARKS FLY UPWARD"

1. "Yet man is born unto trouble, as sparks fly upward" (Job 5:7).

2. Freeman, *George Washington*, 1:56–57; May, *Principio to Wheeling*, 42–44; G. McClaren Bryden, "The Bristol Iron Works in King George County," *Virginia Magazine of History and Biography* 42, no. 2 (April 1934): 102.

3. Catherine La Courreye Blecki and Karin Wulf, eds., *Milcah Martha Moore's Book: A Commonplace Book from Revolutionary America* (University Park, Pa.: Pennsylvania State University Press, 1997), 136–37.

4. Freeman, *George Washington*, 1:61.

5. Weems, *Life of Washington*, 45–47.

6. De Butte to Bishop Edmund Gibson, no. 54, Gibson Papers.

7. Anne Bradstreet, "Some Verses upon the Burning of Our House, July 10, 1666," in *The Literatures of America, 1500–1800*, ed. Myra Jehlen and Michael Warner (New York: Routledge, 1997), 559.

8. Thomas, *Ends of Life*, 73–74.

9. Freeman, *George Washington*, 1:65–67; David Humphreys, *David Humphreys' "Life of General Washington," with George Washington's "Remarks,"* ed. Rosemarie Zagarri (Athens: University of Georgia Press, 1991), 8.

10. Lawrence to Augustine Washington, May 30, 1741, in *Magazine of American History*, 2:435–37.

11. Ibid.

12. James D. Alsop, "Royal Navy Morbidity in Early Eighteenth-Century Virginia," in Meyers and Perreault, *Colonial Chesapeake*, 141.

13. For the Washington-Lewis connections, see Felder, *Fielding Lewis and the Washington Family*, 47.

14. John Lewis to Lawrence Washington, June 28, 1742, Morristown National Historical Park, Morristown, N.J.

15. Yates to Augustine Washington, Oct. 9, 1741, Morristown, N.J.

16. Sarah Pearsall, *Atlantic Families: Lives and Letters in the Later Eighteenth Century* (New York: Oxford University Press, 2008), 37, 43, 13.

17. Brown, *Foul Bodies*, 120, makes this point.

18. Swift, "Elizabeth Johnson," 54.

19. Kevin Hayes, *George Washington: A Life in Books* (New York: Oxford University Press, 2017), 1.

20. Swift, "Elizabeth Johnson," 50, 53; Booker and Lewis, "Cox's Old Place Now Yeocomico View Farm in Cherry Point," 43, 45–46.

21. Freeman (*George Washington*, 7:390, 589) says Elizabeth Straughan (who had married four times) was a "pensioner" of Mary Ball Washington's; for a good discussion of the strength and importance of sibling relations in this period, see C. Dallett Hemphill, *Siblings: Brothers and Sisters in American History* (New York: Oxford University Press, 2013), 32–48.

22. Swift, "Elizabeth Johnson," 58.

9. THE WIDOW WASHINGTON

1. Freeman, *George Washington*, 1:27–33; Deed and Will Abstracts, Westmoreland County, 1738–1744, 23–26; Moncure Conway, *Barons of the Potomack and the Rappahannock* (New York: Grolier Club, 1892), 104.

2. www.kenmore.org/genealogy/washington/augustine_will.html.

3. Freeman, *George Washington*, 1:72n156.

4. *Papers of George Washington*, Colonial Series, 1:7n2; Upton, *Holy Things and Profane*, 202.

5. Butler, "Knowing the Uncertainties," 136.

6. John Harrower, *The Journal of John Harrower, an Indentured Servant in the Colony of Virginia, 1773–1776* (Williamsburg, Va.: Colonial Williamsburg, 1963), 87.

7. Butler, "Knowing the Uncertainties," 155–56, 163.

8. Freeman, *George Washington*, 1:39; *Papers of George Washington*, Colonial Series, 1:7n2; Augustine Washington's will, www.kenmore.org/genealogy/Washington /augustine_will.html.

9. *Papers of George Washington*, Colonial Series, 1:7, 173.

10. Kulikoff, *Tobacco and Slaves*, 140–41.

11. Gordon, "Diary of Col. James Gordon," *William and Mary Quarterly* 11, no. 4 (April 1903): 220, 233.

12. "It is my will and desire that my said four sons Estates may be kept in my wife's hands until they respectively attain the age of twenty one years, in case my said wife continues so long unmarried but in case she Should happen to marry before that time I desire it may be in the power of my Executors to oblige her husband from time to time as they shall think proper to give security for the performance of this my last will in paying and delivering my said four sons their Estates respectively as they come of age, or on failure to give such security to take my said sons and their estates out of the custody and tuition of my said wife and her husband." Augustine Washington, Will, www.kenmore.org/genealogy/washington /probate.html.

13. Carson, *At Play*, 73–83.

14. Kulikoff, *Tobacco and Slaves*, 225, 219.

15. Ibid., 218.

16. This was particularly true in the late eighteenth century. Thomas Jefferson at least was happy in his marriage. The marriage of Frances Randolph Tucker and St. George Tucker seems to have been mutually loving, as does the marriage of Thomas and Elizabeth Jones earlier in the century. See Smith, *Inside the Great House*, 155–56; Kukla, *Mr. Jefferson's Women*. Keith Thomas argues that the ideal of companionate marriage had arrived in the seventeenth century but was by no means universal even by the eighteenth; see *Ends of Life*, 214–20.

17. Hemphill, *Siblings*, 47–48.

10. SINGLE MOTHER

1. Freeman, *George Washington*, 1:76.

2. Ibid., 187–89, 78.

3. Kierner, *Beyond the Household*, 40–41.

4. Paula Felder, *Forgotten Companions: The First Settlers of Spotsylvania County and Fredericksburg Town* (Fredericksburg, Va.: Historic Publications of Fredericksburg, 1982), 113; Byrd Charles Willis and Richard Henry Willis, *A Sketch of the Willis Family of Virginia, and of Their Kindred in Other States* (Richmond, Va.: Whittet & Shepperson, 1901), 27. Some scholars, including Peter Henriques, doubt that George Washington ever studied with Maury. I am inclined to credit the Willis recollection but think George spent more of his school time in Westmoreland County.

5. Jack D. Warren, "The Childhood of George Washington," *Northern Neck of Virginia Historical Magazine* 49, no. 1 (Dec. 1999): 5802–5.

6. Hardwick, "Mirrors for Their Sons," 1; Bushman, *Refinement of America*, 31–33; *Papers of George Washington*, Colonial Series, 1:1; *Papers of George Washington*, Confederate Series, 3:149.

7. *Papers of George Washington*, Presidential Series, 2:386.

8. Freeman, *George Washington*, 1:73–77.

9. William Guthrie Sayen, "George Washington's 'Unmannerly' Behavior: The Clash Between Civility and Honor," *Virginia Magazine of History and Biography* 107, no. 1 (Winter 1999): 8–9. The text was published in England in 1671 by Antoine de Courtin and derived from a Jesuit manual published in Rouen in 1618. The *Rules* that Washington wrote down in 1745 are many fewer and less elaborate than those of the original, and some have speculated that the Reverend Maury might have dictated an English condensation of them to his students, although other scholars have argued that George encountered the *Rules* elsewhere. Virgil Heltzel, "The Rules of Civility (1671) and Its French Sources," *Modern Language Notes* 43, no. 1 (Jan. 1928): 18; see *Papers of George Washington*, Colonial Series, 1:4n6; Warren, "Childhood of George Washington," 5802–3.

10. *George Washington's Rules of Civility and Decent Behaviour in Company and Conversation* (Boston: Applewood, 1988). Richard Norton Smith has written about the importance of Washington's adherence to these precepts and sees his ability to defer to others and to command himself as foundational to his ability to create and govern a republic. See his *Patriarch: George Washington and the New American Nation* (New York: Houghton Mifflin, 1993).

11. Warren, "Childhood of George Washington," 5805; Felder, *Fielding Lewis and the Washington Family*, 38.

12. David Muraca and Laura Galke, archaeologists at Ferry Farm, Oct. 11, 2017; see also Laura Galke, "The Mother of the Father of Our Country."

13. Humphreys, *"Life of General Washington,"* 7.

14. Smith, *Inside the Great House*, 85; Wyatt-Brown, *Southern Honor*, 154–55; Philip Vickers Fithian, *Journal and Letters, 1767–1774*, ed. John Roger Williams (Princeton, N.J.: University Library, 1900), 245; Saxton, *Being Good*, 161–64.

15. Saxton, *Being Good*, 116.

16. *Papers of George Washington*, Colonial Series, 8:226–27; Marie Jenkins Schwartz, *Ties That Bound: Founding First Ladies and Slaves* (Chicago: University of Chicago Press, 2017), 64; *Papers of George Washington*, Colonial Series, 9:209–16.

17. Humphreys, *"Life of General Washington,"* 6.

18. George Washington's Earliest Account Book, L. L. Smith Collection, Morristown National Historical Park, N.J.

19. Karin Calvert, "The Function of Fashion in Eighteenth-Century America," in Carson, Hoffman, and Albert, *Of Consuming Interests*, 272–74.

20. Laura Galke, analyst of small findings at Ferry Farm, Oct. 11, 2017.

21. George Washington's Earliest Account Book, Morristown.

22. Emory G. Evans, *A "Topping People": The Rise and Decline of Virginia's Old Political Elite, 1680–1790* (Charlottesville: University of Virginia Press, 2009), 161–62; George Washington, Account Book, 7. Many thanks for this information to Laura Galke, analyst of small findings at Ferry Farm.

23. Felder, *Fielding Lewis and the Washington Family*, 38.

24. *The Papers of George Washington: Digital Edition*, ed. Theodore Crackel (Charlottesville: University Press of Virginia, 2008), Revolutionary War Series, vol. 21 (Sept. 21, 1779).

25. Eliza Haywood, *The Female Spectator* (reprinted from the Bodleian Library, Gale Ecco Reprints, 1744), bk. 1, 23.

26. Hayes, *George Washington*, 11–12; Kristin M. Girten, "Unsexed Souls: Natural Philosophy as Transformation in Elizabeth Haywood's *Female Spectator*," *Eighteenth-Century Studies* 43, no. 1 (Fall 2009): 65–66.

27. Martin, *Buying into the World of Goods*, 173.

28. David S. Shields, *Civil Tongues: Polite Letters in British America* (Chapel Hill: University of North Carolina Press, 1997), 104–20.

29. Marla Miller, *The Needle's Eye: Women and Work in the Age of Revolution* (Amherst: University of Massachusetts Press, 2006), 108.

30. Donald Jackson and Dorothy Twohig, eds., *The Diaries of George Washington* (Charlottesville: University Press of Virginia, 1976), 1:238.

31. Shields, *Civil Tongues*, 116.

32. Galke, "Mary Ball Washington," 37–40.

33. Miller, *Needle's Eye*, 69, 101–3, 112, 193.

34. *Papers of George Washington*, Presidential Series, 11:201–2, 590–91; ibid., 12:60–61.

35. Felder, *Fielding Lewis and the Washington Family*, 68; Saxton, *Being Good*, 103.

36. N.A.M. Rodger, *The Wooden World: An Anatomy of the Georgian Navy* (New York: Norton, 1986), 125, 24, 68.

37. Edward Neill, John Washington, and Robert Orme, "The Ancestry and Earlier

Life of George Washington," *Pennsylvania Magazine of History and Biography* 16, no. 3 (Oct. 1892): 270–71.

38. Galke, "Mother of the Father of Our Country"; Roland Pietech, "Ships' Boys and Youth Culture in Eighteenth-Century Britain," *Northern Mariner* 14, no. 4 (Oct. 2004): 11–24.

39. Paula Felder, "Fredericksburg's Origins and a History of Its Neighborhoods," Mid-century Fredericksburg, 1745–1755.

40. Neill, Washington, and Orme, "Ancestry and Earlier Life," 271; Conway, *Barons of the Potomack and the Rappahannock*, 238.

41. Thomas, *Ends of Life*, 192.

42. Freeman, *George Washington*, 1:194–95; Warren, "Childhood of George Washington," 5806–8.

43. Ball Letterbook, Library of Congress.

44. First Generation, www.yatesandmore.com/Blain/d1180.htm.

45. Humphreys, *"Life of General Washington,"* 8.

46. Neill, Washington, and Orme, "Ancestry and Earlier Life," 272.

47. Freeman, *George Washington*, 1:193.

48. Samuel Eliot Morison, *The Young Man Washington* (Cambridge, Mass.: Harvard University Press, 1932).

49. *Papers of George Washington*, Colonial Series, 1:37–38n.

50. Warren, "Childhood of George Washington," 5809.

51. Carol Stearns, *Anger: The Struggle for Emotional Control* (Chicago: University of Chicago Press, 1986), 57; Mintz, *Huck's Raft*, 17.

52. Custis, *Recollections and Private Memoirs*, 132.

53. Hayden, *Virginia Genealogies*, 80.

54. James Kirke Paulding, *Letters from the South* (New York: Harper Brothers, 1835), 205. My thanks to Professor Rhys Isaac for alerting me to this source. Paulding (1778–1860) was secretary of the navy under Martin Van Buren and a prolific author. He was friend and brother-in-law of Washington Irving, author of a five-volume biography of Washington. Paulding wrote that an intimate friend of the Washington family, "a gentleman of Alexandria, of high character," recorded this testimony from Jeremy or "Jeremy Prophet" at Mrs. Washington's. "The gentleman who took the testimony went several times to Mt. Vernon and acted as 'amanuensis; without reference to any other authority than himself in his own words.' Jeremy was formerly a servant of John Washington's whom he shared with George, and who claimed to have gone with him on Braddock's expedition. According to his amanuensis, he was a man of 'high reputation in the family.' The amanuensis wrote of Jeremy that he is 'as fine a specimen of an old-fashioned servant as you ever met with, an oracle among blacks, and with the family, a sort

of relic of their ancestors that they seem proud to cherish and make comfortable. . . .' By the time the amanuensis interviewed Jeremy, Washington, of course, was a god and his respect and affection for the general were in a sense required, but also enhanced his own reputation. Nevertheless his portrait of Mary Washington as obsessed with George's safety, careful of her horses, and willing to move heaven and earth to accommodate him were not part of the Mount Vernon script." Paulding, *Letters from the South*, 196.

55. Joseph Ball to Mary Ball Washington, May 19, 1747, in Ball Letterbook.
56. Patricia Cline Cohen, *A Calculating People: The Spread of Numeracy in Early America* (New York: Routledge, 1999), 77, 81–85, 105; Felder, *Forgotten Companions*, 111.
57. Freeman, *George Washington*, 1:183, 234; *Papers of George Washington*, Colonial Series, 1:9. For a description of his preparation for this office and planter's life, see ibid., 1–4; for his early surveying, see ibid., 8–19.
58. Thompson, *"In the Hands of a Good Providence,"* 24; perhaps he meant Isaiah. There is no book of Israel. Thanks to Peter Henriques, Dec. 5, 2017.
59. *Papers of George Washington*, Colonial Series, 1:38.
60. Hale, *Contemplations Moral and Divine*, 1:28, 38, 72, 76, 101–2; ibid., 2:125, 135; ibid., 3:6.

11. MARY'S STEWARDSHIP: SCRAPING BY

1. *Papers of George Washington*, Colonial Series, 1:5.
2. These crops are listed in the Account of Mary Ball Washington's estate, Oct. 29, 1789, Mount Vernon.
3. Joseph Ball to Joseph Chinn, May 16, 1745, in Joseph Ball Letterbook, Library of Congress.
4. Joseph Ball to Joseph Chinn, June 27, 1749, in Ball Letterbook.
5. Custis, *Recollections and Private Memoirs*, 139–40.
6. Washington, *Diaries*, 1:xxxvi.
7. Douglas Southall Freeman wrote, "In her dealings with servants, she was strict. They must follow a definite round of work. Her bidding must be their law." His use of the word "servants" signals his deference to slavery, and his preference for deferential women is evident throughout. *George Washington*, 1:193.
8. Frederick Douglass repeats a related maxim in his *Narrative*: "It is better that a dozen slaves suffer under the lash than that an overseer should be convicted in the presence of slaves, of being at fault." *Narrative of the Life of Frederick Douglass, an American Slave* (Boston: Elegant Ebooks, 1845), 18.
9. Kierner, *Beyond the Household*, 26–27.
10. Rhys Isaac, *Landon Carter's Uneasy Kingdom: Revolution and Rebellion on a Virginia Plantation* (New York: Oxford University Press, 2004), 63–64.
11. Yentsch, *Chesapeake Family and Their Slaves*, 173.

12. Washington, *Diaries*, 1:311, 314.
13. Carr and Walsh, "Economic Diversification and Labor Organization in the Chesapeake," 163, 167.
14. Breen, *Tobacco Culture*, 127.
15. Orders and Judgments (1751–1759) King George County Court, King George County, Virginia Clerk's Office, P221. My thanks to Laura Galke for this citation; on the laws and their results, see Kulikoff, *Tobacco and Slaves*, 107–17. Mary Washington to Joseph Ball, July 2, 1760, Emmet Collection, New York Public Library.
16. Lewis Cecil Gray and Esther Katherine Thompson, *History of Agriculture in the Southern United States to 1860* (New York: Peter Smith, 1941), 1:179–82.
17. Brown, *Foul Bodies*, 28. Laurel Thatcher Ulrich's description of flax treatment in New England is excellent: *The Age of Homespun: Objects and Stories in the Creation of an American Myth* (New York: Knopf, 2001), 282–86; thanks to Julie Miller, historian at the Library of Congress, for this.
18. Paulding, *Letters from the South*, 200.
19. Lorena Walsh, "Slave Life, Slave Society, and Tobacco Production in the Tidewater Chesapeake, 1620–1820," in *Cultivation and Culture: Labor and the Shaping of Slave Life in the Americas*, ed. Ira Berlin and Philip Morgan (Charlottesville: University Press of Virginia, 1994), 180.
20. Isaac, *Landon Carter's Uneasy Kingdom*, 69.
21. Edward Baptist, *The Half Has Never Been Told: Slavery and the Making of American Capitalism* (New York: Basic Books, 2014), writes powerfully about the speedup on cotton plantations over the nineteenth century; eighteenth-century planters were capitalists as well.
22. Ball to Chinn, March 19, 1745, in Ball Letterbook.
23. *Papers of George Washington*, Colonial Series, 1:6.
24. *Papers of George Washington*, Confederation Series, 6:423.
25. Westmoreland Order Books, June 4, 1750.
26. Joseph Ball to Joseph Chinn, Feb. 18, 1743, in Ball Letterbook.
27. Kulikoff, *Tobacco and Slaves*, 99–103; Washington, *Diaries*, 1:226; Berlin, *Many Thousands Gone*, 134–35.
28. Joseph Ball to Aaron, Aug. 31, 1754, in Ball Letterbook.
29. Morgan, *Slave Counterpoint*, 95, 81.
30. Kulikoff, *Tobacco and Slaves*, 334–35; Morgan, *Slave Counterpoint*, 84–85.
31. Morgan, *Slave Counterpoint*, 87–89.
32. Ibid., 94.
33. Kulikoff, *Tobacco and Slaves*, 340–43.
34. Brown, *Good Wives, Nasty Wenches, and Anxious Patriarchs*, 358–59.
35. Joseph Ball to Mary Washington, May 1747, in Ball Letterbook.

36. *Papers of George Washington*, Colonial Series, 1:5–8.

37. Felder, *Fielding Lewis and the Washington Family*, 87. There were *two* Dr. Spencers in the neighborhood at the time, Archibald and Edward. It is unclear which visited Mary.

38. Kierner, *Beyond the Household*, 13.

39. Terri Premo, *Winter Friends: Women Growing Old in the New Republic* (Urbana, Ill.: University of Illinois Press, 1990), 25, 29, 105.

40. *Papers of George Washington*, Colonial Series, 1:38; Abrams, *Revolutionary Medicine*, 35–36.

12. MID-CENTURY: A WEDDING, A MURDER, A FAMILY DEATH

1. Freeman, *George Washington*, 1:222–23.

2. Felder, *Forgotten Companions*, 107.

3. Joseph Ball Letterbook, Feb. 18, 1743.

4. Account Book of Dr. Hugh Mercer, Folio 055, Mrs. Washington, 1771–1772, Fredericksburg; Mary Washington's Accounts, Mount Vernon Library; Joseph Ball Letterbook, Feb. 18, 1743.

5. Mary Washington's Accounts, Mount Vernon Library.

6. *Papers of George Washington*, Colonial Series, 7:173.

7. Ibid., 1:39.

8. Brown, *Foul Bodies*, 30–31.

9. *Papers of George Washington*, Colonial Series, 1:7n.

10. Ibid., 39n.

11. Pronounced "Bu-ee" or "wu-ee," Bohea was originally one of the finest kinds of Chinese black tea (*OED*). For more, see www.teamuse.com/article_03101.html.

12. Felder, *Fielding Lewis and the Washington Family*, 68.

13. David Muraca (May 18, 2009) writes of the types of tea ware unearthed: "Jackfield" (stoneware), Astbury (stoneware), Whieldon clouded ware (a very early creamware), and Astbury type (lead-glazed red earthenware made to look like Astbury stoneware). There was also "Imari porcelain which is Chinese porcelain that imitates Japanese porcelain."

14. Felder, *Fielding Lewis and the Washington Family*, 73.

15. Ibid., 46–56.

16. Freeman, *George Washington*, 1:139, 240; Felder, *Fielding Lewis and the Washington Family*, 69; Duke, *Kenmore and the Lewises*, 24–25.

17. Felder, *Fielding Lewis and the Washington Family*, 73.

18. Henry Wiencek, *Mansions of the Virginia Gentry* (Birmingham, Ala.: Oxmoor House, 1988), 97.

19. Felder, *Fielding Lewis and the Washington Family*, 60, 70; King George County Order Book, 1735–1751, no. 2.

20. King George County Order Book, 1735–1751, pt. 2, King George County Wills, King George County, Va., bk. 1, 670; Philip Levy, *Where the Cherry Tree Grew* (New York: St. Martin's Press, 2013), 71.

21. Gordon, "Journal of Col. James Gordon," *William and Mary Quarterly* 11, no. 4 (April 1903): 224; 12, no. 1 (July 1903), 3.

22. Brown, *Good Wives, Nasty Wenches, and Anxious Patriarchs*, 290.

23. *Papers of George Washington*, Colonial Series, 7:173–74n.

24. Abrams, *Revolutionary Medicine*, 38.

25. *George Washington's Barbados Diary, 1751–52* (Charlottesville: University of Virginia Press, 2018), 93, 113.

26. Washington, *Diaries*, 1:30–31.

27. "Miscellaneous Papers of Mary Ball Washington," 1751–1752, Bill from Dr. Sutherland, Mount Vernon; it is a little unclear reading the bill for whom the purging medicines were intended, but they are under "for Mr. Geo. Washington."

28. Freeman, *George Washington*, 1:246–47.

29. Felder, *Fielding Lewis and the Washington Family*, 106.

30. Ibid., 103.

31. Will of Lawrence Washington, Emmet Collection.

32. Lawrence Washington, "Will," Mount Vernon.

33. The second meaning in the seventeenth and eighteenth century for "mother-in-law" is "stepmother," *OED*; Bryan, *Martha Washington*, 103.

34. Winner, *Cheerful and Comfortable Faith*, 162–65.

35. *Papers of George Washington*, Colonial Series, 1:232.

36. Ibid., 231.

37. Ibid., 232–34.

38. Hale, *Contemplations Moral and Divine*, 3:152.

13. MARY AND GEORGE'S SEVEN YEARS' WAR

1. Hayes, *Colonial Woman's Bookshelf*, 53–54n78; Martin, *Buying into the World of Goods*, 85.

2. Hayes, *Colonial Woman's Bookshelf*, 53–54.

3. Hervey, *Meditations Among the Tombs*, 1:vii.

4. James Hervey, *Meditations and Contemplations* (London, 1746) 1:45.

5. Washington, *Diaries*, 1:226.

6. Freeman, *George Washington*, 1:186; Kulikoff, *Tobacco and Slaves*, 145; Fred Anderson, *Crucible of War: The Seven Years' War and the Fate of Empire in British North America, 1754–1766* (New York: Knopf, 2000), 20–22.

7. Anderson, *Crucible of War*, 20–22.

8. "Extracts," 3:32–34, Chalmers Collection, New York Public Library; Anderson, *Crucible of War*, 36; *Papers of George Washington*, Colonial Series, 1:59.

9. Anderson, *Crucible of War*, 36.

10. Freeman, *George Washington*, 1:268–69; Abbot, *Papers*, 1:53.

11. Freeman, *George Washington* 1:272–73.

12. Anderson, *Crucible of War*, 46, 57; Anderson spells his name as "Tanaghrisson." Washington spelled it "Tanacharison."

13. "Extracts," 3:38.

14. *Papers of George Washington*, Colonial Series, 1:56–58.

15. Washington, *Diaries*, 1:174–210.

16. Anderson, *Crucible of War*, 50–60.

17. *Papers of George Washington*, Colonial Series, 1:118.

18. Parent, *Foul Means*, 21–22; Wilcomb E. Washburn, *The Governor and the Rebel: The History of Bacon's Rebellion in Virginia* (New York: W. W. Norton, 1957), 21–24.

19. Anderson, *Crucible of War*, 61; *Papers of George Washington*, Colonial Series, 5:292.

20. Felder, *Fielding Lewis and the Washington Family*, 84.

21. *Papers of George Washington*, Colonial Series, 1:152–53.

22. Ibid., 157–73.

23. Ibid., 208, 224n1; Anderson, *Crucible of War*, 61.

24. *Papers of George Washington*, Colonial Series, 1:226.

25. Ibid., 228–29.

26. Ibid., 246.

27. *Papers of George Washington*, Presidential Series, 3:301.

28. Ibid., 38, 49.

29. Abrams, *Revolutionary Medicine*, 35–39.

30. Hale, *Contemplations Moral and Divine*, 108, 119, 6, 11, 280–81, 297.

31. *Papers of George Washington*, Colonial Series, 1:269, 305, 336–37.

32. For a good discussion of this valued state, see Pearsall, *Atlantic Families*.

33. For a detailed analysis of how men from the two cultures rubbed each other the wrong way throughout the war, see Fred Anderson, *A People's Army: Massachusetts Soldiers and Society in the Seven Years' War* (Chapel Hill: University of North Carolina Press, 1984).

34. *Papers of George Washington*, Colonial Series, 1:268, 266–67, 278.

35. Ibid., 289–90.

36. Paulding, *Letters from the South*, 194–95. Historians have said there is no evidence of Jeremy's presence at George Washington's side at the Battle of Fort Duquesne; however, there is no certainty that anyone, including George, would have recorded his presence. A problem with Jeremy's description of the battle is that he put John Washington there as well, but he was not present. Possibly Jeremy heard the stories of the battle, rather than witnessing it, or he remembered John Augustine's presence incorrectly.

37. *Papers of George Washington*, Colonial Series, 1:255n304.

38. Ibid., 312–15.

39. Margaretta Lovell, "Painters and Their Customers: Aspects of Art and Money in Eighteenth-Century America," in Carson, Hoffman, and Albert, *Of Consuming Interests*, 287–88; *Philadelphia: Three Centuries of American Art* (Philadelphia Museum of Art, 1976), 48.

40. *Papers of George Washington*, Colonial Series, 2:113n.

41. Lovell, "Painters and Their Customers," 287–88; *Philadelphia: Three Centuries of American Art*, 48.

42. *Papers of George Washington*, Colonial Series, 1:335n, 336–43.

43. Ibid., 336–37.

44. Ibid., 2:15.

45. *Papers of George Washington*, Colonial Series, 5:56–57.

46. Ibid., 42.

47. *Papers of George Washington*, Revolutionary War Series 1:3; Felder, *Fielding Lewis and the Washington Family*, 118; Don Higginbotham, ed., "Washington and the Colonial Military Tradition," in *George Washington Reconsidered* (Charlottesville: University Press of Virginia, 2001), 42–49; Freeman, *George Washington*, 2:107.

48. See Thomas, *Ends of Life*, 157–58, on the division of opinions over honorable behavior; *Papers of George Washington*, Revolutionary War Series, 1:3–4.

49. Paulding, *Letters from the South*, 198. Jeremy's account (see below) of George's preparations for his wedding correspond to other evidence, according to a scholar at Colonial Williamsburg. This anecdote seems of a piece with the wedding story in its portrait of Mary's well-known anxiety over her son. I find it credible, but others may disagree.

50. Paulding, *Letters from the South*, 197.

51. Ibid., 198.

52. *Papers of George Washington*, Colonial Series, 4:108; Washington, *Diaries*, 1:278–9; *Papers of George Washington*, Confederation Series, 1:262, 491. www.geni.com/people /John-Washington/6000000007408934870.

53. Freeman, *George Washington*, 2:266.

54. Ibid., 269.

55. Felder, *Fielding Lewis and the Washington Family*, 116, 133; *Papers of George Washington*, Colonial Series, 4:430; Washington, *Diaries*, 1:251.

56. 1769 Account with Mrs. Mary Washington with Thomason and Cox, "german oznabrigs 103 Ells, 3 pounds, 12 shillings and 11 pence."

57. Freeman, *George Washington*, 1:275.

58. *Papers of George Washington*, 5:82–83 and *n87*.

59. Ibid., 92.

60. Ibid., 88, 105.

61. Ibid., 102.
62. Ibid., 95. He was in close touch with his friend and doctor James Craik. Ibid., 96n1, 102.
63. Ibid., 103.
64. For a brief and thoughtful account, see Don Higginbotham, "George Washington and Three Women," in Tamara Harvey and Greg O'Brien, eds., *George Washington's South* (Gainesville, Fla.: University Press of Florida, 2004), 127–32.
65. Henry Wiencek, *An Imperfect God: George Washington, His Slaves, and the Creation of America* (New York: Farrar, Straus and Giroux, 2003), 68, 87.
66. Humphreys, *"Life of General Washington,"* xliii.
67. Gordon, "Journal of Col. James Gordon," *William and Mary Quarterly* 1, no. 2 (Oct. 1902): 110.
68. Mary Washington to Joseph Ball, quoted in Horace Edward Hayden, "Mary Washington," *Magazine of American History* 30, no. 1–2 (July–Aug. 1893): 81a.
69. Paulding, *Letters from the South*, 200–203. The historian Cathy Hellier at Colonial Williamsburg observed that the details of this story are corroborated by account books, documenting the places they stayed. There was a "strong probability" that he was with Washington at Mount Vernon at the time of his wedding. He was good with horses. He did repeat other people's stories if he wasn't present, so the story is plausible, but a reader should be cautious.
70. Freeman, *George Washington*, 3:1.
71. Ibid., 451.

14. BETWEEN THE WARS: KIN, CONSUMPTION, CONFLICT

1. Felder, *Fielding Lewis and the Washington Family*, 73.
2. *Papers of George Washington*, Colonial Series, 6:420.
3. Ibid., 415.
4. Mary Ball Washington to Joseph Ball, July 21, 1760, Emmet Collection.
5. *Papers of George Washington*, Colonial Series, 7:6n9.
6. Ibid., 80.
7. Ibid., 71.
8. Taking two sample years, some visits included ibid., Mar. 6, Mar. 31, Apr. 20, May 6, May 10–16, 1760; Sept. 8, 1761; Jul. 20, 1762; Jan., Apr., May 27–28, Aug. 20–22, Aug. 28, Sept. 2–4, Nov. 21–Dec. 3, 1768; Mar. 6, Apr. 7, Apr. 13, Jul. 13–15, Oct. 15, Nov. 1, Nov. 26–27, Dec. 23–25, 1769. Duke, *Kenmore and the Lewises*, 54.
9. Washington, *Diaries*, 1:225–26; Hemphill, *Siblings*, 48–51.
10. *Papers of George Washington*, Colonial Series, 8:246–47.
11. Ibid., 7:3.
12. Washington, *Diaries*, 2:193, 204.

13. William A. Little's notes about Mary Ball Washington, Farrar Papers, Virginia Historical Society.

14. *Papers of George Washington*, Colonial Series, 8:193, 204, 236, 239; Wiencek, *Imperfect God*, 67.

15. Bushman, *Refinement of America*, 45.

16. James Kirke Paulding, *A Life of Washington* (New York: Harper Brothers, 1835), 1:22.

17. Kierner, *Beyond the Household*, 15–17.

18. Schwartz, *Ties That Bound*, 59.

19. *Papers of George Washington*, Colonial Series, 6:203.

20. Ibid., 8:301–2.

21. Ibid., 6:415, 474; ibid., 8:52.

22. Ibid., 8:455.

23. Ibid., 6:417.

24. Ibid., 474; ibid., 7:190, 276, 333, 372; ibid., 8:132, 262.

25. Longmore, *Invention of George Washington*, 70–71.

26. Ibid.

27. The same scenario played out after Jacky had died and Martha was raising and indulging his son, George Washington Parke Custis. *Papers*, Presidential Series, 8:52–53n2.

28. Wiencek, *Imperfect God*, 87.

29. Humphreys, *"Life of General Washington,"* 6.

30. Washington, *Diaries*, 2:63; *Papers of George Washington*, Colonial Series, 8:226–27.

31. *Papers of George Washington*, Revolutionary War Series, 2:174, 355–57.

32. "Two Fragments of Bills of Mary Ball Washington, 1751–52, 1765, 1769," Mount Vernon.

33. Duke, *Kenmore and the Lewises*, 55.

34. Washington, *Diaries*, 2:190; "Letterbook of William Lee," Nov. 7, 1770, Nov. 9, 1770, July 26, 1771, Virginia Historical Society.

35. *Papers of George Washington*, Colonial Series, 8:567; ibid., 9:170.

36. Robert A. Rutland, ed., *The Papers of George Mason, 1725–1792*, vol. 1, *1749–1778* (Chapel Hill: University of North Carolina Press, 1970), 98; see also Evans, *"Topping People,"* 168–72.

37. *Papers of George Washington*, Presidential Series, 1:126.

38. *Papers of George Washington*, Confederation Series, 5:33–37.

39. Washington, *Diaries*, 2:346.

40. *Papers of George Washington*, Retirement Series, 3:111.

41. *Papers of George Washington*, Presidential Series, 13:257–59.

42. *Papers of George Washington*, Retirement Series, 1:54, 202.

43. Mary Dandridge Spotswood Campbell to Lord Dunmore, n.d., Letters of Dec. 1792 (MSS 1Sp687b8), Nov. 29, 1794 (MSS Sp687b17), John Spotswood Family Papers, Virginia Historical Society; *Papers of George Washington*, Colonial Series, 8:310–11n.

44. Ruth Coder Fitzgerald, *A Different Story: A Black History of Fredericksburg, Stafford, and Spotsylvania, Virginia* (Unicorn, 1979), 2–11, 22.

45. Ibid., 27.

46. Dorothy V. McCormick Powell, "Colonial Churches in Spotsylvania County, Virginia," *William and Mary Quarterly* 11, no. 1 (Jan. 1931): 3.

47. Van Horne, *Religious Philanthropy and Colonial Slavery*, 6, 23–24.

48. Ibid., 237.

49. Ibid., 273–74, 281.

50. Ibid., 306.

51. Ibid., 254–56, 260–61.

52. Lee, "Mount Vernon Plantation," 32.

53. Hale, *Contemplations Moral and Divine*, 2:127.

54. Glymph, *Out of the House of Bondage*, 46–51.

55. Schwartz, *Ties That Bound*, 78, 83–89.

56. Washington, *Diaries*, 2:268–69, 271, 286.

57. Lee, "Mount Vernon Plantation," 32.

58. Washington, *Diaries*, 3:21, 34, 37, 41, 45–47, 51–53.

59. Ibid., 52–53n.

60. Ibid., 53; *Papers of George Washington*, Colonial Series, 8:521–22.

61. Washington, *Diaries*, 3:53n.

62. Ibid., 59.

63. Ibid., 69–70, 77, 82–83, 90–91, 102.

64. Ibid., 92n, 111–12, 226–27, 341, 395.

65. *Papers of George Washington*, Colonial Series, 10:167–68.

66. Ibid., 114–15, 120, 123–25, 127–28, 130–31, 135.

67. Washington, "Mother and Birthplace of Washington," 835.

68. Rebecca Bushnell, *Green Desire: Imagining Early Modern English Gardens* (Ithaca, N.Y.: Cornell University Press, 2003), 83, 113.

69. Mac Griswold, *Washington's Gardens at Mount Vernon: Landscape of the Inner Man* (Boston: Houghton Mifflin, 1999), 3, 35.

70. Hervey, *Meditations and Contemplations*, 1:vii.

71. Sarah Knott, *Sensibility and the American Revolution* (Chapel Hill: University of North Carolina Press, 2009), 57–58.

72. Erica Dunbar, *Never Caught: The Washingtons' Relentless Pursuit of the Runaway Slave, Ona Judge* (New York: Simon & Schuster, 2016), 9.

73. *Papers of George Washington*, Colonial Series, 10:67–68.

15. THE REVOLUTION: A FAMILY AFFAIR

1. Felder, *Fielding Lewis and the Washington Family*, 171–74.
2. Washington, "Mother and Birthplace of Washington," 835, 836.
3. These memories come from ibid., 836–37. Some Washington herself remembered; others she heard from older family members, especially Rob Lewis, Mary's grandson.
4. Felder, *Fielding Lewis and the Washington Family*, 144, 191.
5. Longmore, *Invention of George Washington*, 77–78.
6. Rutland, *Papers of George Mason*, 1:96.
7. *Papers of George Washington*, Colonial Series, 9:455; ibid., 10:40.
8. Charles Hamrick, ed., *A Bag of Nails: The Ledger of George Weedon's Tavern, Fredericksburg, Va., 1773–1791* (Athens, Ga.: New Papyrus, 2007), 90.
9. Felder, *Fielding Lewis and the Washington Family*, 194.
10. *Papers of George Washington*, Colonial Series, 10:39.
11. Washington, *Diaries*, 3:249.
12. Michelle L. Hamilton, *Mary Ball Washington: The Mother of George Washington* (Ruther Glen, Va.: MLH, 2017), 20–21.
13. Felder, *Fielding Lewis and the Washington Family*, 195–96.
14. Harrower, *Journal*, 73.
15. Washington, *Diaries*, 3:249.
16. *Papers of George Washington*, Colonial Series, 10:45, 49–52.
17. Ibid., 59–67, 91.
18. Ibid., 93, 96.
19. *Papers of George Washington*, Revolutionary War Series, 7:435.
20. Ibid., 10:170n, 43–44, 193, 230.
21. Woody Holton, *Forced Founders: Indians, Debtors, Slaves, and the Making of the American Revolution in Virginia* (Chapel Hill: University of North Carolina, 1999), 33–35, 144.
22. Woody Holton, "The Ohio Indians and the Coming of the American Revolution," *Journal of Southern History* 60, no. 3 (Aug. 1994): 453–78.
23. Felder, *Fielding Lewis and the Washington Family*, 145.
24. Ibid., 171.
25. The others were Richard Bland and Edmund Pendleton. Felder, *Fielding Lewis and the Washington Family*, 197.
26. Ibid., 186.
27. Ibid., 210.
28. *Papers of George Washington*, Colonial Series, 10:154. George articulated precisely Edmund Morgan's classic perception (*American Slavery, American Freedom*) that slave owners had the clearest conception of the dependence that they thought haunted them, because they exploited Africans every day.
29. Washington, *Diaries*, 3:267–68, 274–76.

30. Felder, *Fielding Lewis and the Washington Family*, 204, 208–9.

31. Michael McConnell, "Class War? Class Struggles During the American Revolution in Virginia," *William and Mary Quarterly*, 3rd ser., 63, no. 2 (April 2006): 314–15; Allan Kulikoff, "The American Revolution: Capitalism and the Formation of the Yeoman Classes," in *Beyond the American Revolution*, ed. Alfred E. Young (DeKalb: Northern Illinois University Press, 1993), 81.

32. Washington, *Diaries*, 3:308, 314–15, 316–17; *Papers of George Washington*, Colonial Series, 10:240.

33. *Papers of George Washington*, Colonial Series, 10:308.

34. Felder, *Fielding Lewis and the Washington Family*, 201–3; Sweeney, "High-Style Vernacular," 27–28.

35. *Papers of George Washington*, Revolutionary War Series, 1:3.

36. Personal information from Amanda C. Isaac, Mount Vernon, March 1, 2018.

37. Washington, "Mother and Birthplace of Washington," 838.

38. *Papers of George Washington*, Colonial Series, 10:240, 308, 353, 369.

39. Holton, *Forced Founders*, 144.

40. "Virginians Protest the Removal of the Powder," in *The Spirit of 'Seventy-Six*, ed. Henry Steele Commager and Richard B. Morris (New York: Bobs-Merrill, 1958), 111; Felder, *Fielding Lewis and the Washington Family*, 207–8.

41. Felder, *Fielding Lewis and the Washington Family*, 208.

42. *Papers of George Washington*, Revolutionary War Series, 1:325; ibid., 2:115–16, 174, 219.

43. Ibid., 2:371.

44. "Proclamation by John, Earl of Dunmore," in Commager and Steele, *Spirit of 'Seventy-Six*, 111.

45. Peter Wood, "'Liberty Is Sweet,'" in Young, *Beyond the American Revolution*, 160–61.

46. *Papers of George Washington*, Revolutionary War Series, 7:467, 477–80, 553. (I exempt Betty because of her education experiment, and she left no records about her thoughts, although she always behaved like a committed slave owner.)

47. *Papers of George Washington*, Revolutionary War Series, 2:6, 4, 479, 481*n11*.

48. Ibid., 72, 371.

49. Ibid., 78.

50. Ibid., 372–73.

51. Michael McDonnell and Woody Holton, "Patriot vs. Patriot: Social Conflict in Virginia and the Origins of the American Revolution," *William and Mary Quarterly*, 3rd ser., 34, no. 2 (Aug. 2000): 241.

52. Ibid., 241–45.

53. *Papers of George Washington*, Revolutionary War Series, 7:421–23; Larry Bowman, "The Scarcity of Salt in Virginia During the American Revolution," *Virginia Magazine of History and Biography* 77, no. 4 (Oct. 1969): 465, 471.

54. Commager and Morris, *Spirit of 'Seventy-Six*, 113–14.

55. Felder, *Fielding Lewis and the Washington Family*, 21.

56. *Papers of George Washington*, Revolutionary War Series, 3:418–19.

57. Ibid., 128.

58. Ibid., 231.

59. McDonnell, "Class War?," 316–18.

60. *Papers of George Washington*, Revolutionary War Series, 3:418–19.

61. McDonnell, "Class War?"; Harrower, *Journal*, 316; Felder, *Fielding Lewis and the Washington Family*, 223; Kulikoff, "American Revolution," 81–82.

62. *Papers of George Washington*, Revolutionary War Series, 5:396.

63. Ibid., 8:396, 393; McDonnell and Holton, "Patriot vs. Patriot," 238–40.

64. McDonnell and Holton, "Patriot vs. Patriot," 243–48; *Papers of George Washington*, Revolutionary War Series, 8:393.

65. McDonnell and Holton, "Patriot vs. Patriot," 250–59.

66. *Papers of George Washington*, Revolutionary War Series, 3:418–19.

67. Felder, *Fielding Lewis and the Washington Family*, 225–26.

68. Ibid., 234; Warren M. Billings, John E. Selby, and Thad W. Tate, *Colonial Virginia: A History* (White Plains, N.Y.: KTO Press, 1986), 351.

69. Harrower, *Journal*, 158.

70. *Papers of George Washington*, Revolutionary War Series, 3:570.

71. Felder, *Fielding Lewis and the Washington Family*, 221, 224 and note, 231.

72. G. Melvin Herndon, "A War-Inspired Industry: The Manufacture of Hemp in Virginia During the Revolution," *Virginia Magazine of History and Biography* 74, no. 3 (July 1966): 303–5.

73. Harrower, *Journal*, 121.

74. Cynthia Kierner, *Southern Women in the Revolution, 1776–1800: Personal and Political Narratives* (Columbia: University of South Carolina Press, 1998), 1.

75. Hale, *Contemplations Moral and Divine*, 2:128, 54–62, 67, 130; Thomas, *Ends of Life*, 14–20.

76. Harrower, *Journal*, 82, 96, 132, 144.

77. Hale, *Contemplations Moral and Divine*, 2:106.

78. Winner, *Cheerful and Comfortable Faith*, 94–95.

79. Washington, "Mother and Birthplace of Washington," 837.

16. THE ENDLESS REVOLUTION: WARTIME VIRTUE, WARTIME WOE

1. *Papers of George Washington*, Revolutionary War Series, 6:354.

2. Ibid., 371–74.

3. Ibid., 441.

4. Ibid., 486–88, 369–71.

5. Ibid., 7:291.

6. Felder, *Fielding Lewis and the Washington Family*, 235.

7. Ibid., 237–40.

8. Ibid., 240.

9. Ibid., 241.

10. *Papers of George Washington*, Revolutionary War Series, 8:641–43.

11. Ibid., 13:505–6.

12. Ibid., 9:399.

13. Ibid., 8:584.

14. Ibid., 9:586.

15. Ibid., 10:580.

16. Hamrick, *A Bag of Nails*, 86.

17. *Papers of George Washington*, Revolutionary War Series, 11:4; Ron Chernow, *Washington: A Life* (New York: Penguin, 2010), 297–98.

18. Felder, *Fielding Lewis and the Washington Family*, 236.

19. *Papers of George Washington*, Revolutionary War Series, 11:36; Duke, *Kenmore and the Lewises*, 126.

20. Ibid., 10:551–52; Chernow, *Washington*, 302–6.

21. *Papers of George Washington*, Revolutionary War Series, 11:551–52.

22. Ibid., 12:35.

23. Ibid., 667, 675, 683–87; ibid., 13:17.

24. Felder, *Fielding Lewis and the Washington Family*, 244.

25. Ibid., 241.

26. Ibid.

27. Ibid.; *Papers of George Washington*, Revolutionary War Series, 15:62, 400–401.

28. *Papers of George Washington*, Revolutionary War Series, 12:698.

29. Ibid., 14:60–61.

30. Ibid., 381–83.

31. Ibid., 292.

32. Ibid., 17:388–90.

33. John E. Selby, *The Revolution in Virginia, 1775–1783* (Williamsburg, Va.: Colonial Williamsburg Foundation, 1988), 230.

34. *Papers of George Washington*, Revolutionary War Series, 18:604.

35. Felder, *Fielding Lewis and the Washington Family*, 260.

36. McDonnell, "Class War?," 325.

37. Felder, *Fielding Lewis and the Washington Family*, 259.

38. *Papers of George Washington*, Revolutionary War Series, 15:286.

39. Felder, *Fielding Lewis and the Washington Family*, 260.

40. McDonnell, "Class War?," 322.

41. Selby, *Revolution in Virginia*, 5, 152–53.

42. *Papers of George Washington*, Revolutionary War Series, 16:316; Dorothy Twohig,

"'That Species of Property': Washington's Role in the Controversy over Slavery," in Higginbotham, *George Washington Reconsidered*, 114–40.

43. Felder, *Fielding Lewis and the Washington Family*, 256; Washington, *Diaries*, 3:249n.

44. Hamrick, *A Bag of Nails*, 170–73.

45. Letter from Mary Washington to Lund Washington. Original owned by the Historical Society of Pennsylvania.

46. Felder, *Fielding Lewis and the Washington Family*, 257; *Papers of George Washington*, Revolutionary War Series, 2:371.

47. Felder, *Fielding Lewis and the Washington Family*, 253.

48. *Papers of George Washington*, Presidential Series, 1:116–17.

49. Hamrick, *A Bag of Nails*, 90, 92, 175; Felder, *Fielding Lewis and the Washington Family*, 248.

50. *Papers of George Washington*, Revolutionary War Series, 16:435; Felder, *Fielding Lewis and the Washington Family*, 248; Selby, *Revolution in Virginia*, 181.

51. Selby, *Revolution in Virginia*, 181. Letter from Mary Washington to Lund Washington.

52. *Papers of George Washington*, Revolutionary War Series, 18:459.

53. Hamrick, *A Bag of Nails*, 176.

54. Felder, *Fielding Lewis and the Washington Family*, 248–49.

55. *Papers of George Washington*, Revolutionary War Series, 19:735.

56. Lillian B. Miller, ed., *The Selected Papers of Charles Wilson Peale and His Family* (New Haven, Conn.: Yale University Press, 1983), 1:315.

57. Betty Lewis to George Washington, Sept. 21, 1779, in *Papers of George Washington: Digital Edition*.

58. Miller, *Peale*, 1:326, 346, 352.

59. Selby, *Revolution in Virginia*, 245.

60. Felder, *Fielding Lewis and the Washington Family*, 269.

61. Stephanie McCurry, *Masters of Small Worlds: Yeoman Households, Gender Relations, and the Political Culture of the Antebellum Low Country in South Carolina* (New York: Oxford University Press, 1995), elucidates this argument.

62. Commager and Morris, *Spirit of 'Seventy-Six*, 1109; Selby, *Revolution in Virginia*, 213, 227.

63. Felder, *Fielding Lewis and the Washington Family*, 270–71.

64. Ibid., 275–76.

65. Ibid., 276–77.

66. McDonnell, "Class War?," 334–35.

67. Felder, *Fielding Lewis and the Washington Family*, 281–82.

68. Ibid., 283.

69. Selby, *Revolution in Virginia*, 223–24.

70. Duke, *Kenmore and the Lewises*, 142.

71. Felder, *Fielding Lewis and the Washington Family*, 286.
72. Commager and Morris, *Spirit of 'Seventy-Six*, 1207.
73. Ibid., 1218.
74. Felder, *Fielding Lewis and the Washington Family*, 288.

17. MARY'S WAR ENDS

1. Felder, *Fielding Lewis and the Washington Family*, 299.
2. Ibid., 301.
3. Mary Washington to George Washington, March 17, 1782, Mount Vernon.
4. Quoted in Freeman, *George Washington*, 5:410.
5. Ibid.
6. Selby, *Revolution in Virginia*, 311–14.
7. Boyd, *Papers of Thomas Jefferson*, 7:140.
8. Cynthia Leonard, *The General Assembly of Virginia* (Richmond, 1978).
9. Longmore, *Invention of George Washington*, 56–67.
10. Freeman, *George Washington*, 3:55–61, 120, 416; ibid., 4:313, 513, 536; Chernow, *Washington*, 128, 275.
11. Felder, *Fielding Lewis and the Washington Family*, 120; Selby, *Revolution in Virginia*, 128, 187; Commager and Morris, *Spirit of 'Seventy-Six*, 625.
12. Hale, *Contemplations Moral and Divine*, 123.

18. "YOU MUST ONE DAY FADE"

1. Hervey, *Meditations Among the Tombs*, 1:ii.
2. Felder, *Fielding Lewis and the Washington Family*, 301.
3. Marquis de Chastellux, *Travels in North America in the Years 1780, 1781, and 1782*, 2 vols., trans. Howard Rice Jr. (Chapel Hill: University of North Carolina Press, 1963), 1:30–31, 298–99. My thanks to Mary V. Thompson for pointing this out to me.
4. Fitzpatrick, *Writings of George Washington*, 23:433–38; ibid., 27:11.
5. Ibid., 23:384, 485.
6. Ibid., 5:23, 129.
7. Ibid., 436.
8. Ibid., 27:1.
9. Ibid., 11.
10. Custis, *Recollections and Private Memoirs*, 140–41; Washington, "Mother and Birthplace of Washington," 837.
11. Lawrence Lewis to J. C. Dunn, Oct. 30, 1830, Mount Vernon.
12. Susan Hetzel, *The Building of a Monument: A History of the Mary Washington Associations and Their Work* (Lancaster, Pa., 1903), 13.
13. Quoted in Hamilton, *Mary Ball Washington*, 31–32.

14. Washington, "Mother and Birthplace of Washington," 837.

15. Burgess Ball Bible, Virginia Historical Society.

16. Felder, *Fielding Lewis and the Washington Family*, 310. Thanks to Peter Henriques for the correction of "reverend" to "revered" in George's tribute to his mother; Custis, *Recollections and Private Memoirs*, 143.

17. Felder, *Fielding Lewis and the Washington Family*, 306.

18. Ibid., 299–301, 309, 312.

19. Fitzgerald, *Different Story of Fredericksburg, Stafford, and Spotsylvania, Virginia*, 19–20.

20. Accounts differ about the style and color of the dress; all emphasize its informality.

21. *Papers of George Washington*, Confederation Series, 4:40.

22. Ibid., 1:261.

23. Ibid., 4:33–37n for the identity of Mrs. French; Mount Vernon. The editors of the *Washington Papers* identify her as Anne Brayen Benger French of Fredericksburg. A member of the Strother family also married someone named French.

24. Susan Stabile, *Memory's Daughters: The Material Culture of Remembrance in Eighteenth-Century America* (Ithaca, N.Y.: Cornell University Press, 2004), 132–33, 176.

25. Quoted in Brown, *Foul Bodies*, 142.

26. *Papers of George Washington*, Presidential Series, 12:634–35; Lee, "Mount Vernon Plantation," 13–45.

27. Washington, *Diaries*, 5:143–44.

28. Virginia Carmichael, Pamphlet, 47, Mary Washington Branch Association for the Preservation of Virginia Antiquities, 1967, Mount Vernon.

29. *Papers of George Washington*, Colonial Series, 10:254.

30. *Papers of George Washington*, Presidential Series, 1:404.

31. Abrams, *Revolutionary Medicine*, 63–64.

32. *Papers of George Washington*, Presidential Series, 3:301.

33. Ibid., 536–37.

34. Rob Lewis, Letters and Diary, Diary, Sept. 1, 1789, Mount Vernon.

35. Stabile, *Memory's Daughters*, 179–202.

36. Hamilton, *Mary Ball Washington*, 52.

37. Washington, "Mother and Birthplace of Washington," 842. A notice to sell the "Grave of Mary, the Mother of General Washington" to be auctioned as well as the material for an unfinished monument is dated March 5, 1889, and signed by "Colbert and Kirtly, Real Estate Agent and Auctioneers." The story did not finish there; see epilogue.

38. *Papers of George Washington*, Presidential Series, 4:32.

39. *Papers of George Washington*, Confederation Series, 4:366.

40. Carole Haber, *Beyond Sixty-Five: The Dilemma of Old Age in America's Past* (New York: Cambridge University Press, 1983), 8.

41. Felder, *Fielding Lewis and the Washington Family*, 169–70.

42. Stabile, *Memory's Daughters*, 203.

43. Ibid., 30.

44. *Papers of George Washington*, Presidential Series, 4:122; ibid., 5:6, 102.

45. "Account of Mr. Jesse Hill for Mrs. Mary Ball Washington with Rappahannock Forge," 1786–1789, Mount Vernon; Account of the Sales of the Stocks of the Late Mrs. M. B. Washington, 1789, Mount Vernon; A Memorandum of Effects Not Mentioned in Mrs. Washington's Will, n.d., document no. 21056, Library of Virginia.

46. *Papers of George Washington*, Presidential Series, 7:119–20.

47. Ibid., 119–20n.

48. Ibid., 17:553.

EPILOGUE: AN UNEASY AFTERLIFE

1. Quoted in Hetzel, *Building of a Monument*.

2. Patricia West, *Domesticating History: The Political Origins of America's House Museums* (Washington, D.C.: Smithsonian Books, 1999), 3–13.

3. Mrs. Roger A. Pryor, *The Mother of Washington and Her Times* (New York: Macmillan, 1903), 180.

4. Marion Harland, *The Story of Mary Washington* (Boston: Houghton Mifflin, 1892), 65.

5. Pryor, *Mother of Washington and Her Times*, 158, 165.

6. Ibid., 69.

7. Mrs. Vivian Minor Fleming, "Brief Personal Sketch of the Mary Washington Monument Association, Fredericksburg, Va." (Fredericksburg, Va., 1955), 2.

8. Hetzel, *Building of a Monument*, 154–55; Fleming, "Brief Personal Sketch," 2.

ACKNOWLEDGMENTS

This book has been many years in the works, and I owe deep debts of gratitude to family, colleagues, and people I have never met who have been generous with their learning. I began this project when I was still teaching at Amherst College, and I wish to thank Deans Lisa Raskin, Greg Call, and Catherine Epstein and Presidents Tom Gerety, Tony Marx, and Biddy Martin for their important support. Friends and colleagues helped in countless ways: Amrita Basu, Michele Barale, Kristin Bumiller, Frank Couvares, Marla Miller, Karen Sanchez-Eppler, Martha Sandweiss, Kevin Sweeney, Susan Galassi, Wendy Gimbel, Susan Moldow, Judith Thurman, and Diana Wylie number among the friends who listened, counseled, and read.

The many institutions that preserve the papers and possessions of the Washington family provided immense assistance. Mount Vernon's staff could not have been more helpful. The historian Mary V. Thompson answered countless questions with extraordinary promptness and read the manuscript, giving wise advice. If I did not take all of it, it is my fault. Dawn Bonner, Laura Cimo, Amanda Isaac, and Joan Stahl also extended themselves, as did Lynn Price and Dorothy Twohig at the Washington Family Papers at the University of Virginia. The historian Julie Miller at the Library of Congress commented helpfully on the manuscript, as did the Washington scholar Peter Henriques. Rijk Morawe and Logan Melish helped me understand the George Washington Birthplace National Monument. Staff at the L. L. Smith Collection at Morristown National Historical Park in New Jersey were generous with time and help, as were the librarians at the Gratz Collection at the Historical Society of Pennsylvania.

The staff at the Mary Ball Washington Museum and Library in Lancaster County provided great assistance, and the local historian Carolyn H. Jett went out of her way to be helpful. The late Paula Felder, historian of Fredericksburg and the Washington and Lewis families, was an invaluable resource. Cathy Hellier at Colonial Williamsburg and Professor Rhys Isaac gave extremely useful advice. The archaeologists at Ferry Farm (the George Washington Foundation) went out of their way to support my work. I am most grateful to David Muraca and his staff. Laura Galke supplied me with fascinating analyses of artifacts from the site. Thanks, as well, to Jessica Burger for providing photographs of the discoveries and projects at Ferry Farm. I profited as well from the Emmet Collection at the New York Public Library and the collections at the Library of Virginia in Richmond.

The Cullman Center at the New York Public Library and the C. V. Starr Center for the Study of the American Experience gave me time and resources to work on the book. Jean Strouse, the director of the Cullman Center, and Deborah Baker, lodged in the office next to mine, made that year memorable. My great thanks to Michael Buckley, Amanda Ceruzzi, Adam Goodheart, and Patrick Nugent at the Starr Center for contributing to several months of productive work.

To my friend and agent, Georges Borchardt, thanks for the decades of support, patience, sound advice, and belief in this and other projects. Jon Galassi, my friend and publisher, cheered on the (slow) progress of the book, edited it expertly when the time came, and carried it beyond with the help of his most able assistants, Carolina Baizan and Logan Hill. My great thanks to all.

My late husband, Enrico Ferorelli, took several of the pictures for this book, and I wish he could see the work he supported for so long. My son's and daughter's—and their spouses'—support and encouragement have buoyed me. Thanks, Francesco and Frances, Josephine and Chris. And my daughter's editorial advice is top-notch.

This would not be complete without thanking my friend and teacher Eric Foner and acknowledging my uncle the late Alexander Saxton, who have written histories that have enriched our understanding of our past and our lives.

INDEX

|||||||||||||||||||||||||||||||||||

"GW" refers to George Washington; "MBW" refers to Mary Ball Washington.